evolving CERTAINTIES

The heavens declare the glory of God;
the skies proclaim the work of his hands.

Psalm 19:1

evolving CERTAINTIES

Resolving Conflict at the Intersection of Faith and Science

TERRY DEFOE

ISBN 978-1-7753486-0-3 Paperback

To Kathleen, my loving wife, for her patient forbearance with a husband who spent far too many hours ensconced in his study. To our daughter Michelle and son Joel and for patiently reading the material sent their way for comment and review. And to our boisterous Beagle Sadie, for all those missed opportunities to play fetch.

ENDORSEMENTS

Modern Christianity is at a crossroads. Some major denominations are in turmoil around social and political issues, and there is no question that the church is in crisis; the massive departure of large numbers of young people from the pews is one symptom of that crisis. There are many challenges facing the church, but one of the most powerful, and potentially dangerous is the challenge of modern science, especially when wielded as a weapon in the hands of a new and aggressive form of atheism. The claim that science has displaced faith, that logic and reason convict God of non-existence has achieved widespread acceptance among the youth of the Western world and has been almost totally incorporated into the academic world view. How can Christians counter this alarming trend? The first step is to understand the details of the various points of view of contemporary Christian thinkers about the relationship of science to Christianity.

Pastor Terry Defoe's book, Evolving Certainties is an excellent tool to gain the basic knowledge needed to understand where we are, and where we should be heading. Defoe covers every aspect of the various belief systems proposed by Christians to handle the mass of scientific information now flooding our culture. From Young Earth Creationism to Intelligent Design to Evolutionary Creationism, Defoe presents a thorough and beautifully written analysis of the logic, history, benefits and pitfalls of each of these very different ways handling science within the context of Christian faith. This book tackles difficult questions head on and is an example of intellectual honesty and courage that all Christians can emulate. The book delves into the thorny issues of hermeneutics for each of these belief systems, and presents all sides of the controversies surrounding each of them. Defoe has his own point of view, which he expresses with love and tolerance for all those who advocate the cause of Christ. This book will go a long way to educating the Christian public on what their fellow believers actually believe and why. Armed with this understanding, readers of Evolving Certainties will be able to make choices, and unite in common cause for the sake of faith in our common Savior.

Sy Garte, PH.D. (Biochemistry)

It's here at last! I'm extremely excited about this book! It is the most thorough compilation of Tweetable well-researched and documented science/faith quotes and resources that I have ever come across. If only for that reason it should be a must-have resource for anyone interested in science/faith questions. But this book is far more than that! It is also a gospel-affirming and God-honoring intellectually honest and insightful synthesis of all those resources on this topic. Accordingly, it should also be on the must-read list of anyone who is into the topic, no matter their personal science/faith view. Author, Terry Defoe, was a young-earth creationist and Lutheran pastor who spent the last two decades conscientiously studying science/faith issues and sifting through the gamut of science/faith views. During that time he very gradually came to hold an evolutionary creation view – essentially the same view I also came to hold that is also the view held by a growing number of leading evangelical theologians who espouse evolutionary creation. Note that, in changing his science/faith view in this way as a Lutheran pastor, Terry Defoe had almost everything to lose and almost nothing to gain – nothing except intellectual integrity and guarding of the credibility of our witness for the glorious Gospel. Accordingly, you can likely trust Terry Defoe more than you can a hundred paid university Bible scholars and theologians who have to toe-the-line on their school's theology or risk expulsion. You will enjoy this courageous author as he leads you through the history of this controversial topic and into his own personal journey to find the perspectives that make sense of it all.

Keith Furman, PH.D, (Molecular Genetics)

This is an incredibly bold project on two different levels for Terry Defoe to undertake: a pastor writing a book on science ... a Lutheran taking on evolution! However, Terry is exceptionally well-prepared and strategically-placed for this important task. Having been a pastor for the Lutheran Church – Canada for over thirty years, he is thoroughly familiar with Lutheran theology and the confessional Lutheran view on Holy Scripture, and fully aware of the sensitivity of this discussion. As an inveterate reader who, as part of his duties at a local congregation almost thirty years ago, met with students on the campuses of the University of British Columbia as well as Simon Fraser University, he got a taste for science while perusing the university bookstore shelves, and has since added that subject to his personal curriculum. That in turn led him to pursue a degree in Psychology, which complements his degree in Sociology (Simon Fraser University) and M. Div. degree (Lutheran Theological Seminary, Saskatoon, Saskatchewan).

Clearly then, he is equipped to write on this topic of evolution and Christian theology, and the immense friction being generated as recent scientific discoveries push up against long-held theological views. Having taken part in, and witnessed, numerous conversations pertaining to science and faith, he understands the diversity of emotional and intellectual responses that this can evoke. This is an important time in the history of the church to address this important issue. Church thinkers for centuries prior to Luther had never looked back upon Earth from a few kilometers up, let alone while essentially standing on the outskirts of our solar system, and so could only rely on Holy Scripture when they stood against Copernicus and the heliocentric model of the cosmos: eventually they accepted the overwhelming evidence that the Earth does indeed move, and sought ways to harmonize that with their theology. In the same way, those sixteenth century church leaders and all of their predecessors had never encountered fossil and genetic evidence of extensive biological change over time. But we have. We now have evidence that is written indelibly in stone, bone and genome. And it is therefore up to us to respond: to bring the Book of God's Word into conversation with the Book of God's Work. Terry has done an excellent job at carefully presenting that scientific evidence in the words of a non-expert, and proposing ways for a thoughtful believer to harmonize that factual evidence with their strongly held Christian belief. He has done this in part by quoting profusely from leading Christian and scientific thinkers throughout history, adding strength to his argument.

Luke Janssen, PH.D. Professor of Medicine, McMaster University
Author of Standing On The Shoulders Of Giants

Pastor Terry Defoe has given in this book, the precious product of a serious labor of love to the church. The current confusion about science, within evangelical Christianity in particular, is poisoning the church's mission and confusing its pastoral mandate. Defoe offers several mutually-supporting pathways to clarity: his personal story helpfully accompanies a detailed historical account of how Genesis 1 came to be read as a scientific text in the 20th century. The book also weaves into its text a theological interpretation of the Biblical creation narratives that retains an authoritative view of scripture and also an appreciation of science as God's gift and our route to knowledge of the material world. I recommend it strongly to any Christian, and especially those in pastoral and leadership responsibility within churches. It is my great hope that through the honest and faithful work of Defoe and others like him, I will meet with fewer and fewer young Christians with vocations as scientists who are being torn apart emotionally and spiritually by their churches' insisting that their science is a lie. It is time to correct this damaging misinterpretation of scripture - Defoe shows us that this can be done without compromise, and far from it, with a deeper appreciation of Biblical wisdom.

Tom McLeish, Ph.D., (Physics) University of York, UK.
Author of Faith and Wisdom in Science

"It is a disgraceful and dangerous thing for an infidel to hear a Christian, while presumably giving the meaning of Holy Scripture, talking nonsense....If they find a Christian mistaken in a field which they themselves know well, and hear him maintain his foolish opinions about the scriptures, how then are they going to believe those scriptures in matters concerning the resurrection of the dead, the hope of eternal life, and the kingdom of heaven?"

This quotation from St. Augustine encapsulates the problem the church faces if it rigidly holds onto scientifically-discredited theses, such as young earth creationism – it creates an obstacle to the favorable reception of the gospel by our youngest members, and by the unchurched. Therefore, there is an urgent need for Christian believers to have a discussion on these matters, and come to an understanding on how to accommodate current scientific understanding while maintaining a strong grace-based doctrine. The scientific method has fundamental constraints, and church and science can peacefully thrive together, provided there is the right dialogue and understanding. Terry Defoe's Evolving Certainties is an important step towards this goal. It begins with five chapters on the scientific method and the notable scientific discoveries in cosmology, geology and biology upon which our understanding is based. Six chapters on possible theological responses to these findings follow. Every chapter is filled with many contemporary quotations and numerous references for further reading. Those who are willing to give this work the time it deserves will be richly rewarded.

Garth Huber, PH.D. (Physics) University of Regina

Many Christians are troubled by apparent conflicts between their religious convictions and the steadily increasing knowledge of the natural world. As Pastor Defoe shows, this view is too narrow. Science and religion are not conflicting, but complementary. Science without religion has no moral compass or philosophical foundation. Religion without science has no grasp of the breadth and depth of God's power and compassion. Yet some on both sides insist that their knowledge is superior, and even that other knowledge has no value. Surely the appropriate attitude is humility, a quality lauded in the Bible (Philippians 2:3-4, 1 Peter 5:5-6), but in remarkably short supply on both sides. In a century of effort science has been unable to reconcile the towering achievements of general relativity and quantum electrodynamics, or discover anything about the dark matter and dark energy comprising 95 percent of the matter of the universe, let alone deal with the disturbing philosophical and epistemological implications. Christian theologians, on the other hand, have failed to deal with the implications of Goedel's theorem demonstrating that for any system of axioms (which includes systematic theology) there are meaningful questions whose truth or falsity cannot be decided."

Kenneth Currie, PH.D. (Geology)

The 16th century scientist and Christian philosopher Francis Bacon expressed that some books are to be tasted, others to be swallowed, and some few to be chewed and digested. Terry Defoe brings a scholarly yet personable voice to the topic of how to approach science as a Christian, and has produced a work which is worthy of the latter treatment. The challenge for anyone who engages this topic, either as a student or as a teacher, is how to assess the many positions that are taken on the topic of creation and evolution. It can seem overwhelming. In many cases, the voices which most stridently claim to affirm Biblical truth are seen to add more to the text than they draw from it, while casually glossing over swaths of clear scripture. Likewise, voices which claim to assert science's domination over scripture don't understand the methodology or purpose of science, and neither do they respect the authority of the Bible or what it teaches. In Evolving Certainties, Defoe takes a measured approach that returns us to a bit of wisdom from Francis Bacon: "God has, in fact, written two books, not just one. Of course, we are all familiar with the first book he wrote, namely scripture. But he has written a second book called creation."

Defoe recounts the work of numerous figures who have charted this way before us, navigating a clear path through the extremes to find a middle-ground course that is straight and true. In following this path we, the readers, find some surprising harmonies. And in doing so, we gain clarity on the essentials versus the non-essentials when we examine the various disagreements. We are not prompted to compromise any of the fundamentals of our Christian faith, nor are we encouraged to distort the laws of nature which God ordained. God's revealed truth does not change, but our understanding of it, with a little help, can become sharper, as it has many times through history.

Jude George, Principal, www.truecreation.org

To many of us conservative Christians, Lutheran and others, who accept the entire Bible as inspired by God, Terry Defoe's Evolving Certainties is a long awaited assistance in working through the issue of the relationship between Holy Scripture and evolution. This volume is the most well thought out, organized and documented study of this still crucial topic that I have encountered. In good, logical order each topic of relevance is addressed with clarity, followed by impressively copious footnotes. For a topic that has all too long brought an unneeded and, to many, scandalous division within the Christian Church, he deals with each issue and its proponents as much as possible as a neutral observer. Not an easy feat for something that can so easily lead to explosive emotional excesses.

Here is a resource that can help to move us, seriously and dispassionately, toward a resolution of our divisions, if not to a comprehensive agreement, at least to a better understanding of each others positions and to seeing that this is an issue that has unnecessarily divided us. May this then also help us to proclaim together to an ever more godless society what does unite us: that there is one Creator of all who graciously offers salvation to all in his Son Jesus. Some will find this a heavy read, so you might not want to take it to the beach on holidays, but you will find it worth its weight to have on your bookshelf as a ready resource.

Rev. Warren Steckelberg, Emeritus. Edmonton, Alberta

This is the book I've been waiting for. Written by an Evangelical Christian pastor whom I know and trust, the book allows me to affirm the Bible and faith as a natural partner to science and reason. The Bible informs me that God created everything (including science) and science is very slowly learning how God is doing it. I've been enjoying a life-journey of discovering the vastness of God by following scientific discovery. Terry Defoe assures me that I can be secure in my faith and enjoy the journey at the same time.

This is not a quick read. It's a thorough discussion of the questions many have been asking. Many of my friends and I have found that our children and grandchildren have given up finding a resolution to this unnecessary and hurtful conflict at the intersection of religion and science. My hope is that you and those who have already left the church may find renewed encouragement in what this book offers. This book has helped me to take the time to appreciate the relationship between the endless time that God took to create the universe and the eternity that God has given us to enjoy after our last breath. "Don't let your hearts be troubled," Jesus reminds us. It's fun to read John 14:2-3 again with "Evolving Certainty" in mind.

Dr. Les Stahlke, CEO, Governancematters Inc.

In Evolving Certainties, Pastor Defoe explores one of the most controversial topics facing the faithful in this day and age, evolution. As one who is both a believing Christian, and has chosen to dedicate his life and career to the study of science, I know firsthand that there is a great deal of conflict and misunderstanding between different schools of thought regarding the origins of life. Evolution can be a major challenge to the beliefs of the faithful. Upon first learning the theory many years ago, I myself had many doubts and questions. But with thorough research and an earnest attempt to understand, my faith was reconciled with science. It is my sincere wish that anyone wondering how to reconcile their faith with science read this book, as the answers to their questions lie within.

Pastor Defoe presents the issue of evolution, and the controversy surrounding it, from all angles. From science, to history, to philosophy, to theology, and more. He digs deep to cover all relevant information, never omitting anything important, while maintaining a clear and concise writing style. He explains the theory of evolution in a thorough and scientifically accurate manner. He succeeds in explaining advanced scientific concepts without any oversimplification, yet in such a way as to be accessible to those totally unfamiliar with the material. Even those who have an in depth knowledge of the subject will find a great deal to learn about the different schools of thought, what they think of one another, and why they believe what they believe.

Evolving Certainties has the potential to bridge together people from all beliefs, from atheists, to young earth creationists, and everyone else, to have a proper dialog with each other about life and its origins. Pastor Defoe makes a very strong case for the reality of evolution, and shows that there is no real conflict between the truths of science and faith in God. He stays true to the science, and faithful to the Lord, as he presents an informative and insightful look into the theory of evolution, and the many beliefs and viewpoints surrounding it.

Paul Ostlund, Physics Student, University of Regina

TABLE OF CONTENTS

Part two
Grappling with darwin's dangerous idea

Part three
An opportune time

TABLES & FIGURES

ACKNOWLEDGEMENTS

It may seem that writing a book is a solitary pursuit. That may be true at the beginning, but it is certainly not true as the manuscript takes on its final form. Evolving Certainties is written in the context of the evangelical Christian faith, informed by the best of current science. Sincere thanks go out to fellow Canadian, Darrel Falk, retired biology professor at Point Loma Nazarene University in San Diego, former president of the BioLogos Foundation. Dr. Falk was one of many individuals – scientists and laypeople alike – who read drafts of the manuscript and offered insightful comments. Dr. Falk's review led to a major update of my chapters on young earth creationism and intelligent design. Dr. Falk kindly agreed to write the Foreword.

Denis Lamoureux, influential advocate for a rapprochement between science and faith, provided valuable support from the early days of this project. Dr. Lamoreaux graciously provided the illustrations that appear in these pages. Molecular Geneticist Keith Furman of the American Scientific Affiliation has been a strong advocate for Evolving Certainties. Sy Garte also offered encouragement, and his thoughts on intelligent design creationism are included in chapter 10. Luke Janssen, professor of medicine at McMaster University, has been a tremendous support. Matthew Becker, professor at Valparaiso University provided helpful insights on science in a confessional Lutheran context. Tom Kaden of Leipzig, Germany, visiting sociologist at York University, interviewed me for a book he is writing on the topic of science and religion.

I very much appreciated comments and support I received from individuals in my own denomination, from Lutheran scientists as well as clergy, laypeople and students. Kenneth Currie, retired geologist, and Garth Huber, physics professor at the University of Regina in Saskatchewan, helped clarify some of the scientific concepts covered in these pages. Pastors Les Stahlke and Warren Steckelberg provided ongoing support. During the course of my research I networked with bloggers, laypeople working in scientific vocations, those involved in church administration, and many others.

Special thanks to the more than fifty individuals who reviewed various iterations of the manuscript. Special thanks to Kim Kreis, Paul Ostlund, Brian Wonnick, Gerald and Valeira Lawson and Jude George. My wife Kathleen and our children, Michelle and Joel, provided strong and abiding support. Michelle put her literary skills to work in proofreading the manuscript. And Lori Rietze connected me to Moses Rietze who designed the book cover and formatted the manuscript.

DISCLAIMER

The concepts, ideas, and arguments put forward in this book are not those of the Lutheran Church - Canada or of The Lutheran Church - Missouri Synod but are solely the responsibility of the author. This information is offered as a representative overview of current research at the intersection of faith and science and is intended to foster discussion of these important issues, especially among people of faith who are concerned about the impact of scientific discovery on religious faith.

FOREWORD

The Church is in crisis. Young people are leaving it in droves, perhaps like never before. The reasons are multi-faceted, but one component stands out in an especially poignant fashion: the seeming discord between the Church's dogmas and what appears to them to be scientific reality. It doesn't take a young person many sessions in a general education course in astronomy or geology to be confronted with a significant dichotomy from what they were told in Sunday School and what they now perceive as scientific reality; the universe is billions of years old. Similarly, as they learn about the vast array of hominin fossils changing over time to become more and more like their own bodies, they are left in a quandary: why, they reason, were they misled by those they trusted in their churches and Christian schools? As they study the basis of the famous adage, "nothing in biology makes sense except in the light of evolution," they think back to their days as children when they were told that it is evolution that makes no sense.

Now their professors seem to be showing them for the first time that it makes perfect sense and the scientists themselves, they come to see, are hardly the sinister perpetrators of evil they were expecting; instead they are kind, intelligent, sincere and most important of all—it seems—they are right. Suddenly faced with a different reality, they far too often dismiss the beliefs of their youth as childish, and in this age of "fake facts," they conclude that the Church which had so badly distorted one component of reality can't be trusted in what it has to say about the rest. Out with the bathwater go their supposedly unscientific beliefs in a resurrected Jesus, a God who answers prayer, and life everlasting. Prematurely and without careful consideration, they mistakenly start a new life independent of the God of their childhood.

Sadly, it is we in the older generations who have made it easy for them to distrust God's Word and to abandon God's Way. We are to blame. We have buried our heads in the sand, refusing to carefully consider the possibility that maybe we don't have things quite right after all. After years of standing over our children day after day telling them to do their homework, the fact is that we are the ones who have refused to do ours. If we have studied at all, we have focused on material that simply reinforces our own perspective refusing to put on the lenses that would enable us to carefully examine the views of others. We owe it to our young people – to the souls of our young people – to expand our own minds and to at least catch a glimpse of what they will see as they venture out away from the shelter of our loving arms.

With that in mind, this book is literally a godsend. It is a book about biology and the Christian faith by a pastor who has spent his entire career within a conservative denomination and remains thoroughly committed to all the biblical tenets of his evangelical faith. He has wrestled first hand with how to bring the two seemingly disparate realities into a harmonious whole and has spent much time with others as they shared their struggles as well. It is out of those struggles – his own and that of parishioners – that this book has emerged after a quarter century of doing the "homework." As a Christian biologist, I have greatly appreciated Pastor Defoe's work. His grasp of the scientific issues is truly amazing for someone who has had many other important pastoral responsibilities throughout this time.

From my perspective as a former leader of a key organization at the center of science/faith discussions, I have been equally appreciative at his understanding of the landscape of the different organizations and their perspectives. He has done his "homework" here as well. And finally, from my view as a longtime Sunday School teacher and layperson in an evangelical church, I have been moved by the love he expresses for his Church and the depth of his concern for its welfare. He loves his denominational community and seeks for it to remain relevant to its all-important calling of speaking into this 21st Century age, centered as it in the whirlwind of technological and scientific advances.

Pastor Defoe is thoroughly familiar with the writings of the leading scientific spokespersons. Within the secular sphere he has immersed himself in the writings of all the key figures from biologists Stephen Jay Gould to Richard Dawkins and philosophers Daniel Dennett to Michael Ruse. In the Christian sphere, he expounds beautifully on the work of Francis Collins, Karl Giberson, and John Polkinghorne. His knowledge of the work of the key players in the Intelligent Design movement runs deep and extends into the work of leading proponents of the young earth position as well. This book with its hundreds of references is any scholar's dream, but each concept is well-explained and never presented in a dry scholarly fashion.

For many years, those of us in leadership positions in the scientific discussions of the science/faith interface have longed for a pastor's perspective on this topic. The challenge has been that pastors have many vital and urgent responsibilities that prohibit them having the time to learn the science, while also caring for the day-to-day challenges of their parishioners. This book is the exception that we have hoped would one day emerge. Written with the heart and sensitivity of a pastor, it is a call to the Church to bring the two different aspects of God's reality into one united whole. The call this book makes is urgent, but it is nonetheless patiently and beautifully presented. It is my hope and expectation that in future years, church persons will look back at this book, with a sense of thankfulness – both to Pastor Defoe for his faithfulness and to our God for the majesty of his creation process.

Darrel r. Falk, Ph.D (Biology)
Author of Coming to Peace with Science
Past President of the BioLogos Foundation
Emeritus Professor of Biology, Point Loma Nazarene University

PREFACE

For more than twenty-five years, I have been interested in the relationship of science and faith. I have invested much time and effort balancing my professional life and my scientific interests. In more than three decades in the ministry, I have come to believe that faithfulness to one's theological heritage may mean a willingness to challenge that same heritage. My denomination is part of the North American Protestant evangelical culture. Over the years, our U.S. sister synod has maintained a long-standing relationship with, and provided significant support to, young earth creationism.

In the early years of my ministry, my understanding of scripture's creation narratives was inadequate. I knew that young earth creationism was an important part of my denomination's history and systematic theology, but I wasn't sure what I personally believed, or why. This seems to be the case for many church workers and laypeople as well. Comments about evolution by fellow Christians that I have heard over the years have convinced me that many professional church workers, as well as laypersons, do not possess even a basic understanding of evolutionary theory. I cannot recall evolution being on the agenda of any denominational meeting or conference I have attended. My denomination argues that there are significant theological reasons why evolution must be rejected. That makes it a "third-rail issue," potentially threatening to a church worker's reputation or career. This metaphor refers to the high-voltage third rail in some electric railway systems. Stepping on that third rail usually results in electrocution. Church workers know that should they depart from the party line, it is best to keep their views to themselves. Even though I have not attended a church conference where evolution was on the agenda, that's not necessarily the case everywhere in my church culture. A colleague mentioned a denominational conference where a representative from Answers in Genesis will be promoting young earth creationism to six hundred church workers. Unfortunately, these presentations tend to be one-sided affairs. Alternate points of view are either not mentioned, or are presented in an entirely negative light.

As a young pastor, I read some young earth creationist material, including a book defending so-called "flood geology" written by Alfred Rehwinkel.[1] I wanted to know what scientists, especially believing scientists, had to say on the subject. Two incidents sparked my interest. The first was a Canadian Broadcasting Corporation (CBC) science broadcast back in 1989. The topic was the Cambrian Explosion and the Burgess Shale, which, I was told, was the home of a large number of exceedingly rare and unusual soft-bodied fossils dated to approximately 540 million years ago. The second was a book written by paleontologist Stephen Jay Gould, titled Wonderful Life.[2] It, too, focused on the Burgess Shale. Gould's books opened a door to the world of science for me. In his many books and essays, he refused to dumb down the technical material he was discussing. Most important for me as a pastor was the fact that, although Gould was an atheist and an evolutionist, he was also a friend of faith.

My goal is to present Darwin's theory (and the various responses to it) as objectively as possible. I will leave it to the reader as to what their response ought to be. I look forward to the day when Christians can discuss issues such as these in a non-threatening way. I prefer dialogue over debate, irenics over polemics. I would hope that those who do not have the time or the inclination to read this book in its entirety will at least read the overview for each chapter. Many in the wider society, as well as many Christians, are unsure of what they ought to believe about creation. A record of my own struggles can be found in the marginal comments I have made over the years. A good deal of cognitive dissonance is evident. I struggled with the question of trust. How could I as a pastor in a young earth creationist denomination sing the Lord's song in this strange new land of science? This incredibly interesting intellectual journey challenged some of my most cherished assumptions – especially about the scripture and their interpretation.

Some Christians argue that should a believer begin an intense study of science and the theory of evolution, (typically described as "entering a rabbit hole," or something similar), there is a good chance they will become disoriented and may even lose their faith. This, of course, is the slippery slope argument. The idea that the study of science could actually strengthen faith is alien to this kind of thinking. I would suggest following the example of Ariadne in Greek mythology. Ariadne gave Theseus a ball of red thread which he unrolled as he made his way into the abyss so he could find his way out again. Christians embarking on this journey need a strong connection to their faith as they investigate these complicated, controversial, and, at the end of the day, critically important issues.

As a seminary student in the late 1970's and early 1980's, I was given an assignment in which I was to visit an inactive member of a local congregation. As the conversation progressed and a level of trust was established, that individual asked, "Must I believe in a literal six-day creation to be a Christian?" I said that was not necessary. I said that being a Christian had everything to do with having faith in Christ as Savior and Lord and that a proper understanding of the creation narratives was, and would remain, secondary. I am reminded of the words of Lutheran patriarch C.F.W. Walther who said, "The findings of science can neither give us the faith nor rob us of it."[3] For Walther, the purpose of the scripture is primarily spiritual, that is, to teach the way to heaven.

Evangelical Christians understand the importance of defending Biblical authority, of retaining the important concepts of inerrancy and inspiration. In a discussion of the theory of evolution, evangelicals expect their theologians to accurately interpret the scripture's creation accounts, that those theologians will, in more technical terms, establish and defend hermeneutical integrity. Christians of all stripes recognize that God wants his people be good stewards of all his gifts, including the gift of knowledge – secular as well as spiritual. Traditional Christianity stresses the importance of being open to the guidance of the Holy Spirit. Christians pray that God would grant them a teachable spirit and open their minds to the entirety of his truth. They know that a God–pleasing interpreter of scripture "...correctly handles the word of truth." (2 Timothy 2:15, NIV) Despite our differences in explaining creation, "... we all believe that people are created by God in his image, that sin is real and we are all subject to it, and that Christ's death was necessary to resolve the sin issue."[4]

It is important for Christian leaders to be scientifically literate – in the context of the scriptures and of faith in God. Christian leaders know that "... zeal not based on knowledge..." is harmful to the faith. (Romans 10:2, NIV) It is helpful for believers, and especially for young adults, to know what various Christian groups (and others) believe about science and the theory of evolution. Christians are aware of the importance of "...speaking the truth in love." (Ephesians 4:15, NIV) Lutheran Christians, in particular, are aware of Luther's advice (in his discussion of the commandment dealing with false witness) to, in his words, "put the best construction on things," and to "speak well of the neighbor."

Faithfulness to a particular theological heritage may require challenging that body of doctrine from time to time. Martin Luther knew this truth – and acted upon it – despite great danger to life and limb. At the end of the day, this journey has impressed upon me the critical importance of hermeneutics – an accurate interpretation of the Holy Scriptures. If, at the end of the day, our interpretation of the scriptures is more accurate, our doctrines have been appropriately reviewed, our respect for science has grown, and our personal faith has been enriched, then the excursion described in this book has been worthwhile.

PART ONE

A revolution like no other

From the sixteenth century onward, a scientific revolution took place, a revolution very different from any other the world had ever known. The scientific revolution challenged the way people thought about natural phenomena. It pulled back the curtain on that aspect of reality. Francis Bacon said that the untutored human mind is prone to all kinds of error. Scientific methodology fosters critical thinking that seeks to overcome these biases and the inclination to interpret information in a way that confirms views we already hold. The scientific revolution took humanity beyond simple common-sense explanations of natural phenomena. Scientific methodology revealed the counter-intuitive discoveries, for example, that the earth was incredibly ancient, that the earth travelled around the sun, that there was a hidden world of microscopic life in a drop of water, and that light emanating from stars revealed their chemical makeup. Science and its associated technologies revealed phenomena previously inaccessible to human senses. Scientific methodology keeps people from fooling themselves. As this world-changing revolution gained momentum, scientific methodology made important discoveries in the areas of cosmology, geology and biology.

1. INTRODUCTION

Overview

In evangelical Christian circles, the theory of evolution is near the top of the list of controversial topics. Evangelicals have a great deal of spiritual capital invested in the creation accounts. It is said that a correct understanding of creation validates the truth of the gospel. In addition, a right understanding of these accounts supports the doctrines of biblical inspiration and inerrancy and upholds the authority of God's Word. In the sixteenth century, Francis Bacon argued that God speaks through the Book of His Word and also through the Book of His Works. For evangelicals, the Bible is God's Word. The cosmos as well as the earth and its precious cargo of living things are his Works. Both Books reveal important truths about God, his will, and his ways. Rightly understood, these two Books do not contradict each other.

With Bacon, I propose that science, with its study of God's Works, assists Christians in understanding God's Word. Although the Bible often speaks of natural phenomena, it is not a science book. Science has revealed much about the natural realm that the ancients did not (and could not) know. The Bible's ancient science was the best science of the day. But, from today's perspective, that information is often inaccurate, incomplete, and sometimes downright misleading. The Bible's ancient science is a common-sense knowledge based on limited and often fallible human senses. The motivation of those who sought to explain natural phenomena in ancient times was correct. Through no fault of their own, they were lacking the proper tools which would have allowed them a fuller understanding.

In the sixteenth century, in the early days of the scientific revolution, most scientists were believers. Even today, a substantial minority of scientists (around 40 percent) fit into this category. Surprisingly, that number has remained stable for quite some time. Most mainline Christian denominations have a positive relationship with science. Many evangelicals and conservative Christians, however, find themselves at odds with science. For many evangelicals, the theory of evolution is an expression of an atheistic point of view. Anti-evolutionists almost always reject evolution for theological rather than for scientific reasons. Christian stewardship requires the wise management of all God's gifts. One of those gifts is the ability to accumulate knowledge. In the anti-evolutionist subculture, it is argued that the theory of evolution is man's word. Young earth creationism, on the other hand, is based on God's inerrant, infallible, and unchanging Word. Anti-evolutionists argue that there is nothing – nothing, that is, in God's Word – that would indicate evolution is true.

The "E-word"

In evangelical Christian circles, evolution is "the 'E' word," a word so controversial many avoid discussing it.[1] Since the publication of Darwin's On the Origin of Species[2] in 1859, no scientific theory has been more problematic for Christians than the theory of evolution.[3] A discussion of evolution often takes place in an emotionally-charged atmosphere.[4] Sometimes it seems that anti-evolutionists are more concerned with public relations than with facts and evidence.[5] A deep-seated antagonism of this sort brings to mind a poem by Matthew Arnold (1822-1888), Dover Beach (1867):

> *And we are here as on a darkling plain*
> *Swept with confused alarms of struggle and flight,*
> *Where ignorant armies clash by night.*[6]

Kenneth Miller of Brown University, Roman Catholic evolutionist, biology professor, and textbook writer, says "Whenever I show up on a radio talk show and the topic of evolution is announced, the switchboard lights up immediately."[7] Dennis Venema and Scot McKnight outline three common evangelical responses to scientific discovery. Christians can engage with science. They can ignore it. Or they can vilify it.[8] Many evangelicals choose the third option. Science denial, however, tends to erode the intellectual integrity of the church and has caused some individuals to leave the church altogether.[9] Much of science denial is caused by a failure to understand basic scientific methodology and principles. Pastor Gregory A. Boyd says,

I am deeply invested in presenting the gospel in an intellectually credible fashion to nonbelievers in our culture. For this reason, I think it is incredibly significant that, from Galileo's inquisition to the Scopes trial to the present evolution debates, whenever the church has assumed a rigid opposition to the consensus of the scientific community, it has eventually harmed the credibility of the church in the eyes of the broader culture.[10]

Many secular individuals associate all Christians with young earth creationism.[11] And many scientists are put off by the constant barrage of criticism they receive from anti-evolutionists. Science denial can have serious negative consequences.[12] Some issues, such as global warming and environmental degradation, demand immediate action. Science denial, especially among elected officials, typically leads to delay and obstruction. In scripture's creation accounts, humanity is given authority by God Himself to care for his creation.[13] Science denial is a denial of God's call to exercise non-destructive stewardship over his creation.

A Fundamental Doctrine

The topic of origins is very important for evangelicals.[14] Anti-evolutionists generally argue that their doctrine of creation validates the truth of the gospel and supports their belief in an error-free Bible.[15] They believe that Biblical inerrancy is under attack by those who assert that some of the Bible's statements about nature are inaccurate.[16] In the nineteenth century, Princeton seminary's Charles Hodge (1797-1878) claimed that Darwinism was atheistic because it accounted for design in nature without the need for divine intervention.[17] For some anti-evolutionists, the theory of evolution is nothing less than an alternate religion which threatens the very existence of traditional Christianity.[18] For anti-evolutionists, their God-given faith and salvation are far too important to be set aside in the name of science.[19] Biologist Theodosius Dobzhansky (1900-1975) observes that "... some people have emotional biases and preconceptions strong enough to make them reject even completely established scientific findings."[20]

Two Books

British scholar Francis Bacon (1561-1626) said that one cannot know too much about the Book of God's Works (the natural realm) or the Book of God's Words (Holy Scripture).[21] Bacon argued that these two books, properly understood, do not contradict one another.[22] Gary Fugle says, "We cannot argue that God created one reliable source of information in the Bible and created a second, conflicting, unreliable source in nature."[23] An educated person needs to be familiar with both books.[24] Moses Maimonides (1135-1204), medieval Jewish philosopher and astronomer, and prominent in the history of Islamic science, said that the scriptures are true. But if they disagree with the results of scientific study, it's time to review one's interpretation of those same scriptures.[25] Church father Augustine of Hippo (354-430 A.D.) declared that all truth is God's truth.[26]

Early editions of Darwin's On the Origin of Species quoted Francis Bacon with approval, encouraging readers to carefully consult these two God-given sources of information before coming to a conclusion about evolutionary theory.[27] Contemporary British physicist Brian Cox says that faith and science do not have to be in opposition. He quotes Belgian priest and professor of physics Georges LeMaitre (1894-1966) who said, "There are two paths to truth and I have decided to follow both of them."[28] Science and faith are two pillars holding up the building of truth.[29]

Nineteenth century essayist, lecturer and poet, Ralph Waldo Emerson (1803-1882) indicated that when faith shuns science God is dishonored.[30] Paleontologist Simon Conway Morris describes two very different kinds of people, people he characterizes as homo scientificus and homo religiosus.[31] In other words, some individuals are interested in science from an early age, while others gravitate to a life-long interest in faith. Familiarity with both is the best option. Many early scientists were people of faith, both Christian and Islamic. The Islamic culture of the early Middle Ages had an important influence on the history of science that is often overlooked or forgotten today.[32]

Johannes Kepler (1571-1630), Lutheran astronomer, mathematician, and key figure in the seventeenth century scientific revolution is an example of an early scientist who was also a person of faith. Significantly, Kepler said that science helped him understand the ways of God.[32] For Kepler, much of his motivation to do science was motivated by his faith. Contemporary Old Testament scholar John Walton compares the relationship of science and religion to a layer cake. Scientific investigation is interested in the lower layer of the cake. The top layer represents the work of God and spiritual concerns.[33] Although believing scientists often get the feeling that their work is not valued by the church, science is a truly a worthy Christian vocation. Inscribed above the door of the Cavendish laboratory at Cambridge University are words from the 111th Psalm: "Great are the works of the Lord, studied by all who delight in them."[34] (ESV)

The gift of curiosity

Science is motivated by a deep and abiding desire to understand nature. Scientific discoveries have greatly expanded human capabilities and enriched human life.[35] Christians believe that the ability to comprehend is a gift from God. It is a gift to be used for the good of humanity and the glory of God.[36] God is surely pleased when His people discover new truths about His creation. This curiosity and ability to comprehend is best exercised in a disciplined manner, however. Louis Pasteur, (1822–1895), French chemist and bacteriologist, once said "...fortune favors the prepared mind."[37] It is impossible, for example, to understand the internal combustion engine by standing on a street corner watching cars whiz by.[38] Science has revealed much that Biblical writers could not have known. Ancient people did not know, for example, ... that the stars were suns; they did not know that the earth was spherical and moving through space; they did not know that the sun was much further away than the moon, or even further than the birds flying in the air.[39]

The ancients had never seen the earth from an airplane. They were unaware of fossils. They had no clue about genetics. They had likely never thought of the possibility of one species evolving into another.[40] At that time, "... the physiology of nearly all the bodily systems were (sic.) largely misunderstood." It was commonly believed that cognitive and emotional processes originated in the gut.[41] King David, for example, living around 1000 B.C., could only see five other planets and 6000 stars. He was unaware of galaxies. He had no knowledge of the Milky Way.[42] This common-sense knowledge carried through to Luther's day. At that time, individuals believed that intelligence, emotions, and personality came from the liver and the intestines.[43] We tend to underestimate just how much the human race has learned in the last few hundred years, information that was not available to the ancients.[44]

Scripture's authors were people of their own time and place, thoroughly steeped in Jewish history, Jewish culture and Jewish thinking. Luke Janssen writes:

> *[They]... believed that the earth was flat and the sun revolved around the earth. They believed in the existence of Leviathan, which they took to be either a great sea monster or a fire-breathing dragon. They held that dietary laws and circumcision were of paramount importance, that animal sacrifices needed to be offered at various times, and that people and things were often susceptible to becoming religiously unclean ... and sometimes needed to undergo elaborate purification rites... These are all legitimate pre-modern Jewish beliefs and values most of us don't hold anymore.*[45]

Ancient science was a common-sense knowledge based on what limited human senses could detect. It was, indeed, the best knowledge of the day but, in most cases, it does not correspond to modern scientific information. Does a rabbit chew the cud? (Leviticus 11:6) Is a mustard seed the smallest seed?[46]

(Mark 4:31) Jesus' comments about the mustard seed were intended to teach a spiritual lesson about the power of God's word to change the human heart, not a lesson in botany.[47] Does an insect walk on all fours? (Leviticus 11:20) According to the ancient understanding of human reproduction, resident inside male seed were tiny infants, which simply needed the proper environment to spring up and grow, a concept called preformism.[48] If there was a problem with conception, it was the woman's fault.[49] It was said that the Lord had closed her womb. (eg., 1 Samuel 1:5) Scientist and Christian believer Andrew Briggs says, "What we scientists are doing is studying how God makes the world work; there is an added pleasure in studying the world if you know the Creator."[50]

Scientists who are people of faith may legitimately consider their work to be a form of worship. In addition to the wise stewardship of accumulated knowledge, believers are called upon to be good stewards of the gift of time. Life is short. Each of us has a limited time to discover God's truths. Stephen Jay Gould (1941-2002), paleontologist, tireless advocate of evolution, (and, ironically, friend of faith) died of cancer in 2002 at 60 years of age. He said, prophetically, in 1989, "The Lord gives us so little time for a career, forty years if we start early as graduate students and remain in good health, fifty if fortune smiles."[51]

Noble and ignoble

Baptist theologian Bernard Ramm (1916-1992) outlined two very different approaches to the science / religion debate. One he called noble and the other ignoble. According to Ramm, the noble approach is irenic, marked by a collegial relationship in which those with differing views deal with each other respectfully. The ignoble approach, on the other hand, is polemical, attacking and demeaning opponents.[52] Ramm argues that the inflexibility of what he calls the hyper-orthodox has done great damage to the relationship of science and religion. As professionals, both scientists and theologians rightfully defend their interests from inappropriate outside interference. But this doesn't rule out common courtesy and respect. Evolutionary creationist Francis Collins is a former physician, now world-class scientist. Collins once spoke at a national gathering of Christian physicians. When his pro-evolutionary views became clear, some of those physicians walked out.[53]

There is no place for hubris on either side of this debate.[54] Bernard Ramm laments the fact that the determined enemies of science have "buried the noble tradition."[55] And, as we will see in chapter 6, some scientists, particularly the so-called "new atheists," have returned the favor. Surprisingly, considering his atheism, Stephen Jay Gould was, as I say, a friend of the Christian faith. In his writings, Gould laments Biblical illiteracy in society, parallel to what he sees as a widespread scientific illiteracy in the church. Without an adequate knowledge of both, says Gould, one cannot claim to be truly educated. Gould was not pleased that when he quoted either the Bible or Shakespeare in his university classes, most students were unable to recognize the source.[56] And, more seriously, scientific illiteracy provides fertile ground for error. Many evangelical Christians, outside of a brief contact in school, have never been exposed to real science. Charles Darwin (1809-1882) once said:

> *Ignorance more frequently begets confidence than does knowledge; it is those who know little, and not those who know much, who so positively assert that this or that problem will never be solved by science.*[57]

Brother Guy J. Consolmagno, S.J., research astronomer and director of the Vatican Observatory in Rome, once remarked that many creationists have only a grade-school knowledge of science. And many scientists, on the other hand, have only a grade-school knowledge of faith.[58] Many Christians are not adequately prepared to evaluate scientific claims and counter-claims.[59] And many scientists, on the other hand, are lacking basic knowledge about religion.

The warfare model

The so-called warfare model of the relationship between science and religion can be traced back to two books written in the late nineteenth century. The first was written by John W. Draper (1811-1882), titled History of the Conflict Between Religion and Science, published in 1874.[60] Draper's book went through fifty printings in fifty years. The second was written by Andrew Dickson White (1832-1918), founder of Cornell University. It was titled A History of the Warfare of Science with Theology in Christendom.[61] White's book was published in 1896. Draper says:

> *The history of science is not a mere record of isolated discoveries; it is a narrative of the conflict of two contending powers, the expansive force of the human intellect on one side, and the compressing arising from traditional faith and human interests on the other... Faith is in its nature unchangeable, stationary; Science is in its nature progressive; and eventually a divergence between them, impossible to conceal, must take place.*[62]

With reference to Draper's book, contemporary historian J.B. Russell says:

> *The History of the Conflict is of immense importance, because it was the first instance that an influential figure had explicitly declared that science and religion were at war, and it succeeded as few books ever do. It fixed in the educated mind the idea that "science" stood for freedom and progress against the superstition and repression of "religion." Its viewpoint became the conventional wisdom.*[63]

John Draper directed his criticism primarily at the Catholic Church. He agreed that science could coexist with more liberal forms of Christianity.[64] White, for his part, claimed that he was not critical of religion in general, but only its hardline, fundamentalist expressions. White's ultimate goal was the discovery of truth for truth's sake, not, to use his term, "stretched" to fit religion.[65] White claimed that the triumph of science in its warfare with fundamentalist religion would benefit true religion as much as science. White especially objected to religion's attempts to interfere with science, a process which, he said,

> *... has resulted in the direst evils, both to religion and to science and ... on the other hand, all untrammeled scientific investigation, no matter how dangerous to religion some of its stages may have seemed for the time to be, has invariably resulted in the highest good, both of religion and of science.*[66]

Not surprisingly, both Draper and White developed their warfare model in the context of the battle over evolution. No single issue, since the days of Galileo, has so seriously challenged the traditional Christian understanding of human origins, as has the theory of evolution.[67] Unfortunately, the warfare model remains an everyday reality, not for all Christians, but primarily for those in the young earth and intelligent design camps. Young earth proponent Albert Mohler, for example, president of the Southern Baptist Seminary, describes the current conflict as a head-on collision between evolutionists and creationists.[68]

Young earth creationists respond negatively to science because they believe they are being attacked by it. In some cases that is true, but the majority of those attacks, as we will see in chapter 6, come from the so-called new atheists, a small but vocal minority in the scientific community, and a group that does not represent scientists as a whole. As we will see, the creationist rejection of science is based on a faulty interpretation of scriptures' creation accounts, compounded by a faulty understanding of the limitations of science.[69] Christians are in the business of pursuing truth and, as such, ought to be able to handle all expressions of it, including scientific truth, even if it makes them uncomfortable.[70]

In one of several books he has written on the subject of evolution and faith, atheist historian and philosopher of science (and another friend of faith) Michael Ruse asks, "Can a Christian be an Evolutionist?" He answers in the affirmative.[71] Science can assist Christians in determining God's actual method of creation. Properly understood, science is an encouragement, not a hindrance, to faith.[72] When Christians consider the cosmos through the "lens of faith," they see "... amazing evidence of God's power, love of beauty, patience, and ultimate desire for life."[73] The Christian faith is greatly enriched by a close relationship with the natural sciences.[74] Scientist John T. Houghton: "It is very important to me that the two strands of my life, as a scientist and as a Christian, are brought together side-by-side and, so far as it is possible, intertwined."[75]

If conflicts arise between science and religion, it is because our understanding of one or the other, or both, is faulty.[76] Astronomer Jennifer Wiseman says:

> *Contrary to the "science vs. religion" motif routinely promoted in popular media, I have found that most scientists I work with are humble, curious, and whether they are religious believers or not, quite respectful and interested in the beliefs of their friends and colleagues.*[77]

Three problems

Scientific discoveries have brought significant challenges for the Christian church. These discoveries have raised at least three separate but related problems – important questions that must be answered, while, as much as possible, maintaining a traditional understanding of the scripture's creation accounts.

1) The time problem. How old is the earth and the cosmos?
2) The species problem. Do species evolve?
3) The mechanism problem. How was creation accomplished?

A journey of discovery

Once, on a long drive to a church-workers conference, conversation in the vehicle turned to the topic of science and the theory of evolution. It did not take long to realize that the driver of the van was a fellow pastor who took a strong anti-evolution stance. His argument against evolution was not theological or doctrinal, which I would have expected, but he did raise several arguments against evolution, the kind that are commonly found in young earth creationist literature. It soon became clear that he had been exposed to information supporting only one side of the argument. He did not know that all of his claims had been refuted. Not long after, that same pastor publicly criticized evolution in one of his sermons. I am a pastor. I write as an interested layperson. Coming to terms with science generally, and evolution in particular, has consumed a significant portion of my adult life. I compare this intellectual journey to traveling to a foreign country. This journey has the potential to fundamentally alter one's worldview. My goal is to inform, not persuade. I am well aware that accepting the risk of being wrong is the price of publishing one's ideas.[78] I am of the opinion that much more can be accomplished through respectful dialogue than could ever be accomplished through negative attacks, polemics, and criticism.

I agree with Thomas Henry Huxley (1825-1895) who encouraged individuals to hold their ideas up to the light of truth in order to see what they are made of.[79] Many contemporary Christians are not sure how to sing the Lord's song (Psalm 137:4) in the strange new land of science. No one should discard a critically important part of their belief system until they are fully convinced that such a change is necessary, and is, in fact, beneficial.[80] For those with the courage to travel this road, there will be periods of confusion in which old and new ideas stand side-by-side in unresolved tension.[81] In the pages that follow, it is my goal to show why it is possible to leave young earth creationism for biblical reasons! Alfred North Whitehead captures the essence of the science / religion debate with these words:

> *When we consider what religion is for mankind and what science is, it is no exaggeration to say that the future course of history depends upon the decision of this generation as to the relations between them.*[82]

2. THE SCIENTIFIC REVOLUTION

Overview

Science is the closest humanity has come to a universal language and culture. Scientific methodology, the scientific rulebook, determines how science is to be carried out. Scientific methodology transcends cultural barriers. In the sixteenth century, in the early days of the scientific revolution, most scientists were people of faith. Their faith did not stand in the way of their science. Galileo's telescope was a technology that enabled the investigator to move beyond the limitations of the natural senses. Since then, a long succession of scientific technologies, combined with human ingenuity, have resolved many mysteries. As the scientific revolution gained momentum, the Bible's common-sense explanations of the natural realm were increasingly questioned.

Both science and theology seek truth. The scientific method guides scientific investigation and, at the same time, places boundaries on what science can and cannot do. Scientific methodology is an organized form of skepticism designed to eliminate confirmation bias. In the early days of the scientific revolution, scientists began to realize the need to distance themselves from the supernatural because supernatural phenomena cannot be falsified or replicated. Because of the limits to scientific investigation, and because the supernatural is out of bounds, science must be agnostic to the existence of God, to miracles, and other metaphysical ideas. Science can neither prove nor disprove the existence of God since it is presently unable to assemble any data directly relevant to the question. Science therefore cannot legitimately make pronouncements about basic Christian teachings like the virgin birth or the resurrection of Christ from the dead.

Some scientists, however, ignore these methodological restrictions and argue that science alone can determine truth. Rather than practicing neutrality when it comes to religion, a small percentage of scientists proclaim the absolute superiority of science – what has come to be called scientism. This attitude is characteristic of the new atheists and has led many non-scientists to believe that science is inherently antagonistic towards religion. The New Atheism is, in reality, a secular fundamentalism, not all that different, in its hardline attitudes and inflexibility, from anti-evolutionism.

Science defined

Science is a systematic quest for understanding. The term "scientist" was coined by nineteenth-century Anglican cleric and scientist William Whewell (1794-1866). The words "science" and "scientists" have Latin origins, drawn from the word which means "I Know."[1] "Science" soon came to be associated with a particular methodology – a method for pursuing knowledge as well as that knowledge itself. Science gathers and organizes information in the form of testable explanations and predictions. As early as the thirteenth century, the Christian church was the patron of universities, which would have supported the early scientific investigations taking place there.[2] In the middle ages, science and religion were inseparable. Scientists (then known as 'natural philosophers') and theologians were often the same individuals.[3] Science was nurtured in the Judeo-Christian West, supported by a doctrine of creation in which the world was understood to be orderly and intelligible.[4] Nature behaves consistently not capriciously. The same rules apply in London or New York. According to the Judeo-Christian understanding of creation, God is both the supreme lawgiver and cosmic planner.[5]

The scientific method can be traced back to individuals like Francis Bacon (1561-1626).[6] By the sixteenth century (around Luther's time) the scientific revolution was fully underway. By the seventeenth century, it had swept through Western Europe, setting the stage for discoveries in areas as diverse as geology, cosmology and biology.[7] Many early scientists, including Nicolaus Copernicus (1473-1543), Johannes Kepler (1571-1630), Galileo Galilei (1564-1642) and Isaac Newton (1643-1727) were religious believers.[8] According to physicist Stephen Hawking (1942-2018), Galileo was responsible for the birth of modern science.[9] The early phase of the scientific revolution coincided with the introduction of new technologies including the telescope and the microscope.[10] Galileo's telescope, for instance, revealed that which could not have been known by limited human senses alone.[11] The Industrial Revolution (~ 1760-1840) gave science a huge boost, providing the tools and technology required for disciplined investigation.[12] Science needs technology to progress, as much as technology needs science.[13] The genius of the scientific method lies in its power to expand the limits of human perception. Science has discovered, as one example of many, that the human eye can perceive only a small fraction of electromagnetic energy.[14] Thus, science has opened previously inaccessible windows of observation to natural phenomena. Science allows us to penetrate mysteries that used to be invisible to us.[15]

Science and religion both seek truth but have very different ways of apprehending it.[16] In science, truth is approached in a series of successive approximations. Empirical knowledge is contingent, subject to revision as data accumulates. Scientists are called upon to express their ignorance to each other. It is always possible – even expected – that a scientific theory will be overturned.[17] Scientific conclusions are written in pencil, as it were, with the anticipation that they will be updated as new data are found.[18] In religion, on the other hand, truth is apprehended primarily through authoritative documents and inspired prophets. Here's the bottom line: anti-evolutionists demand a level of certainty science cannot provide.[19] All measurements in science have the possibility of error, and this must be acknowledged and preferably estimated. Science seeks to investigate the true cause – the vera causa – of natural phenomena. Science takes things apart to see how they work. Religion, on the other hand, puts things together to see what they mean in the context of God's activity in individual human lives and in the cosmos as a whole.[20]

Roman Catholic and Neo-Orthodox theologians distinguish primary from secondary causation with God being the primary cause.[21] Science is methodologically limited to the study of secondary causes.[22] The difference between primary and secondary causation has been compared to the difference between a carpenter and the carpenter's hammer.[23] Secondary causation is evident in Genesis 1:24, for example, where God says, "Let the earth bring forth living creatures."[24] (ESV) A secondary cause is a usual natural cause.[25]

Scientific methodology

Scientific methodology is intentionally designed to filter out errors in human perception.[26] Science is a method of disciplined thinking.[27] According to Oxford physics professor Ard Louis, scientific methodology is "... a network of error-correcting mechanisms to prevent us from fooling ourselves."[28] Adam Rutherford says:

> *We humans are awful at perceiving objective reality. We come with inbuilt preconceptions and prejudices. We're dreadful at logic, and see patterns in things that are not there, and skip over trends that are. We attribute cause and agency to chance and coincidence, and blame the innocent as the root of all manner of evil. Our senses and psychology perceive the world in very*

particular ways that are comically easy to fool. But the great strength of science is that it recognizes the human fallibility that cripples our view of the universe. The scientific method attempts to remove these weaknesses.[29]

Francis Bacon claimed that the untutored human mind is "an enchanted glass, full of superstition."[30] Scientific methodology puts critical thinking to work with the goal of overcoming these inherent human limitations.[31] Scientific methodology is designed to identify and eliminate confirmation bias, that all-too-human tendency to interpret information in such a way as to confirm strongly held beliefs. Psychologist Jonathan Haidt notes that, on our own, we human beings do not do well at avoiding this kind of erroneous thinking.[32] Scientific methodology does us the favor. Scientists are obligated to reject an incorrect theory even when they desperately want it to be true.[33] An individual's likes and dislikes, their hopes and fears, are not to enter into what they do or say as a scientist.[34] Scientific methodology requires that predictions (hypotheses) must be capable of being falsified.[35]

Canadian geologist Kenneth Currie clarifies a common misunderstanding regarding scientific methodology:

In the early days of the scientific revolution, it was believed that science verified statements by induction, that is, by piling up confirming examples. Scottish philosopher David Hume (1711-1776) said that induction is not sufficient. Consider the statement, "All crows are black." It may be true that all the crows we have seen so far are black, and the crows seen after the statement was made were also black. However, a blue crow may be lurking just around the corner. To see it would disprove the statement. One might say, therefore, that scientific research is a search for blue crows.[36]

Kitty Ferguson compares hypothesis testing to a toy boat. "Set it on the water and test it," she says. "If it sinks, build a different boat."[37] When scientists make errors, they have an audience. Their findings are subject to peer review.[38] Fraud is rare in science, because when it is discovered, it is fatal to a career.[39] Science is constantly modifying, refining, and adapting its findings. Scientific knowledge is not validated by appeals to authority, but rather by appeals to evidence.[40] Scientists, along with Doubting Thomas (a Bible character whom many scientists would consider their patron saint) are trained to say, "Show me the evidence."[41] Ronald Reagan (1911-2004) is famous for the advice, "Trust, but verify."[42] Science is not a smorgasbord where individuals get to choose a favorite idea or two and reject the rest. (Neither is systematic theology for that matter). Scientific methodology requires that scientists admit their errors and revise their theories accordingly. Religion, on the other hand, with its unchanging creeds and confessional subscription, finds the correction of errors a much more difficult process.

Critical thinking skills are a must-have for contemporary Christians. Christian leaders are called upon to assist individuals in loving the Lord with all their mind, as well as with all their heart and soul. (Matthew 22:37) In Romans chapter 12, verse 2, the apostle Paul encourages Christian people to "...be transformed by the renewing of your mind." (Romans 12:2, NIV) The church must give its members theological permission to study the evolution issue. Unfortunately, some Christian leaders convey the distinct impression that critical thinking is a dangerous thing, that it is corrosive to a solid biblical faith. Some would say that Christians should simply listen to their pastors and be done with it.[43] Christians are often led to believe that these two accounts – faith and science – cannot both be true.[44]

The supernatural

Many early scientists, including such luminaries as Galileo and Newton (1643-1727), were aware that as they carried out their investigations they were studying God's will, as they encountered it both in the scriptures and in the natural realm.[45] Science, however, slowly and at times with difficulty, began to disengage itself from religion and the supernatural.[46] Early scientists were willing to put God into gaps in their understanding.[47] But by Newton's time, a transition from religious to scientific thinking was underway. Astronomers discovered, for instance, that adjustments to planetary orbits, which Newton had originally attributed to God, were best explained by interplanetary gravity.[48] It became a regular occurrence that when a valid scientific explanation was discovered, divine intervention was set aside.[49] Pierre-Simon LaPlace (1749–1827), influential French scholar, considered by many to be one of the greatest scientists of all time, once presented Napoleon with a copy of his work. Napoleon had been told beforehand that LaPlace's book contained no mention of the name of God, so Napoleon, who loved to ask embarrassing questions, said, "M. LaPlace, they tell me you have written this large book on the system of the universe, and have never even mentioned its Creator." LaPlace answered, "I had no need of that hypothesis."[50] LaPlace, it turns out, was simply advocating one of the basic ground-rules of science, that the supernatural be excluded.

It is easy to misunderstand the point LaPlace was making, assuming it was intended as an attack on religious faith. Luke Janssen asks us to imagine an individual receiving a phone call from a grandparent asking for help installing an office suite on their new computer. After the process is complete, they ask, "But where does God come into the process?" The response would be something like: "Grandma, you don't need God in order to install this software." Your statement, like that made by LaPlace, does not, and was never intended to, dismiss the existence of God. It simply indicates, says Janssen

> *"... that it is not necessary to invoke divine intervention in order to get the computer to work... you just follow the instructions. In the same way, Laplace was just telling Napoleon that you don't need divine intervention to describe the earth revolving around the sun... it can be explained by scientific equations like the ones in his book. Now of course we would agree that God was the one who created those equations and physical laws that make the solar system work, just like God would be the one who created those equations and laws which make the computer work with the new software."*[51]

An estimated 90 percent of all scientists in history are living today. Moving beyond biblical literalism made science what it is today.[52] Scientific methodology requires that scientists go about their business as if nature is all there is.[53] Scientist and theologian Alister McGrath says, "When I do science, I don't invoke God to explain things."[54] Science owes much of its success to the fact that it has been able to break free from the supernatural. Excluding the supernatural, however, is a conversation-stopper for many evangelical Christians. Physicist Garth Huber says:

> *The only reason why Alister McGrath does not invoke God to explain things is that such a supernatural explanation lacks any predictive power with regard to what God might decide to do next. Natural explanations can make predictions of what happens next. The best way to have science accept the supernatural is to invent a type of device which can measure it. The problem appears to be the sporadic and unpredictable nature of apparently supernatural events.*[55]

In 1983, in a discussion of scientific methodology, Wheaton College philosopher Paul DeVries coined the term "methodological naturalism."[56] For all intents and purposes, methodological naturalism is synonymous with scientific methodology as it is commonly practiced. Philosopher Robert T. Pennock uses this terminology when he emphasizes that the scientific method limits its investigations to natural phenomena, and is purposely agnostic to the existence or non-existence of the supernatural. Christians, however, have traditionally believed that God is involved in creation, right down to the plight of the sparrow (Matthew 10:29-31). It cannot be overemphasized that, for people of faith, divine intervention is not negated under methodological naturalism.[57] Scientific methodology only rules out the possibility that God's intervention is testable in any way.[58] According to the tenets of accepted scientific methodology, an individual may be a methodological naturalist (i.e., a scientist) and a metaphysical supernaturalist (a believer) at the same time without contradiction.[59]

For Christians, shifting from a theological to a scientific paradigm and back again without grinding the ideological gears is a critically important task, one that many employ on a daily basis. Science journalist Gordy Slack says:

> *I suspect the methodological naturalism / philosophical naturalism distinction appeals so powerfully to science-minded theists not because it describes an actual dividing line in the world but because it works as a kind of clutch to be pushed in when shifting between the two competing worldviews that so many of us hold simultaneously, despite the awkwardness of their relationship. Not that we think, "Okay, I am shifting from the materialist paradigm to the theist paradigm," when we stop working and start praying. We just clutch and shift one hundred times a day, as naturally as we do while driving. Except we are not shifting up or down between gears, but over between worldviews. We are mightily reluctant to give up either view of the world, and we are willing to make some dubious philosophical moves to make it impossible not to.*[60]

Methodological naturalism is not so much a philosophy as a method. It can be thought of as nothing more than the scientific method itself.[61] According to the tenets of methodological naturalism, invoking the supernatural is a science-stopper. Given this reality, it is not difficult to see why methodological naturalism, because of its agnosticism toward the supernatural, is rejected by both young earth and intelligent design creationists.[62] Methodological naturalism is put to use every day by scientist and non-scientist alike when a problem must be solved or a question answered. And most of the time it is completely noncontroversial.[63]

Limits of science

In a book titled The Limits of Science,[64] published in 1984, British biologist (and atheist) Peter Medawar (1915-1987) says there are some questions that science cannot and will never be able to answer, such as the purpose of life or the existence of God.[65] Science, says Medawar, must remain noncommittal when it comes to such things.[66] The majority of scientists recognize these limits.[67] But those who subscribe to what has come to be called philosophical naturalism, including the previously mentioned new atheists, deny the metaphysical and argue that science is the only legitimate method of ascertaining truth, a point of view known as scientism.

The ground rules of science require it be limited to the search for natural causes to explain natural phenomena.[68] Because science is limited in this way, believing scientists are free to practice their faith without interference.[69] Unfortunately, many anti-evolutionists conflate philosophical naturalism (which rejects the supernatural altogether) with methodological naturalism (which maintains neutrality toward religion),[70] arguing that all of science has an anti-religious bias.[71] Science, with its self-imposed limits, has been compared to a fisherman's net that cannot catch small fish because the holes in the net are too large.[72] As far as Christians are concerned, those "small fish" are elements of religious belief which swim right through the scientific nets. The bottom line is this: using science in general, or the theory of evolution in particular, to argue for or against the existence of God is simply inappropriate.[73] Christians should not allow themselves to be distracted by this non-issue.

Anti-evolutionists also claim that science rejects teleology.[74] Teleology explains things in terms of in terms of their purpose or goal. Anti-evolutionists unfairly criticize science for refusing to state whether the cosmos or living things have meaning or purpose[75] or whether there is a direction or goal to evolution.[76] Teleology is scientifically undetectable. It is a matter of faith, best left to religion.[77] Scientists must leave open the possibility of God's intervention in the natural world in such a way as to fly under the scientific radar.[78] Ironically, Darwin's 1859 publication On the Origin of Species incorporated the same teleological language employed by the theologians of the day.[79] It is important to emphasize that evolution may very well have a direction and be guided by the hand of God, as Christians have always believed, but this is not, and cannot be, a scientific concern.[80] Science cannot determine whether teleology, as one theistic evolutionist suggests, is "... programmed into the very fabric of creation."[81]

So when celebrity scientists like Steven Weinberg publicly complain that the universe is pointless, they have stepped outside the legitimate boundaries of science. When scientists make such statements, they are no longer doing science, but have entered the realm of philosophy.[82] Emphasizing the legitimate boundaries of science provides believing scientists with sufficient space for the exercise of both their science and their faith. Science must remain neutral toward religion. Science, therefore, is godless like plumbing is godless. Or medicine. Or farming.[83] Most people cannot live by science alone and should not have to.[84] The genius of science, and its great success, is due in large part to these self-imposed limits.[85] Many questions of great interest and importance to humanity are outside the bounds of science.[86] Professor Brian Cox asserts: "Meaning is something that scientists alone are not qualified to extract from the world. This is where art and music and philosophy and theology live, and not only have a role to play but are an essential part of our discussion."[87]

It must be emphasized that scientific methodology, properly understood, is friendly to faith. According to Stephen Jay Gould, it "... leaves religion's cosmic comfort intact."[88] Anti-evolutionists must understand that the limits of science allow Christians in science to go about their business without taking anything away from their faith.[89] Rather than erecting a barrier between science and religion, as anti-evolutionists do, scientific methodology provides legitimate grounds for an abiding truce.[90] God's involvement in creation, whatever that involvement may be, need not be diminished in any way under standard scientific methodology.[91] One way to illustrate the difference between a scientific and non-scientific orientation is by asking a simple question, "Why is the kettle boiling?" The standard scientific answer, perfectly valid in its own context, would refer to variables such as temperature and atmospheric pressure. An equally valid, but non-scientific, response would be, "Why is the kettle boiling? Because I want a cup of tea."[92]

Alister McGrath points out that scientific truth is characterized by the precision and the certainty of its predictions. But science achieves these admirable qualities at the cost of working at the level of secondary causation, leaving many decisive questions untouched. For the Spanish philosopher José Ortega y Gasset (1883-1955), the great intellectual virtue of science is that it knows its limits. It only answers questions that it knows it can answer on the basis of the evidence. But as human beings, we often want to go further. We want answers to the deeper questions that we cannot avoid asking. We develop multiple maps of reality which allow us to develop a "big picture" of life, part of which is disclosed by the natural sciences, and part by religion.[93]

Scientism

Today's new atheists (see chapter 6) are philosophical naturalists who fail to acknowledge the methodological limitations of science, in essence making science the new religion that nineteenth-century atheists like T.H. Huxley (1825-1895) had hoped for.[94] This viewpoint, called scientism, is essentially a monopolizing of knowledge.[95] Neither science nor religion can provide a total account of reality. Both lose their way when they try to be what they are not.[96] The scientism of the new atheists oversteps the disciplinary boundaries of science.[97] And scientism has a long history. Henri de Saint-Simon (1760-1825), for instance, once claimed that "... scientists are superior to all other men."[98] For the philosophical naturalist, science trumps religion. For the anti-evolutionist, on the other hand, the opposite is true – religion trumps science. Philosophical naturalism is an expression of an unfortunate scientific variant of fundamentalist thinking,[99] adopting a one-dimensional view of reality.[100] To Christians, scientism looks suspiciously like idolatry.[101] The bottom line is this: there will always be room for both science and faith.[102] Biologist and former Roman Catholic priest Francisco Ayala has said, "I don't believe for a minute that science tells us all that is worth saying about the world."[103]

3. THE COSMOLOGICAL REVOLUTION

Overview

In Part Three, we consider scientific discoveries in cosmology, geology, and evolutionary biology. We also compare what science has discovered with statements about nature found in the scriptures. We begin with cosmology. Biblical cosmology, as would be expected, is not scientific in the modern sense. It is phenomenological, that is, a common-sense description of cosmological realities as they appear to the naive observer without the benefit of science and its technologies. The descriptions of nature found in the scriptures reflect the limited understanding of ancient iron-age Semites. Many evangelicals are troubled by the claim that Israel's cosmology appears to have been influenced by its neighbors, including Egypt and Babylon.

In ancient scriptural cosmology, it was believed that the cosmos was unchanging. Stars were fixed and eternal. The earth was a flat circle of dry land with the chaotic surrounding waters pushed back by God, not a sphere floating in space. The sky (the 'firmament') was a metal plate God could walk on. The firmament had windows, which when opened allowed the waters above to flow down to the earth below. Astronomical bodies were fixed to the firmament, occasionally dislodging and falling to earth. As far as the ancient Israelites were concerned, these common-sense descriptions were not metaphorical. They were reality. Anti-evolutionists generally overlook (or ignore) this fact, inappropriately reading modern scientific notions back into ancient documents.

In the scriptures, critical theological truths are often embedded in pre-scientific statements – and are inaccurate by today's standards. These inaccuracies, however, are a reflection of the knowledge of the time period in which they were recorded and do not affect doctrinal or theological truths. In the middle ages, Nicolaus Copernicus was a thorn in the side of the theologians. His heliocentric hypothesis, which claimed that the earth circled the sun, was problematic because it did not match the accepted Bible interpretation of the day – the teaching that the earth was fixed and immovable. The Church, including some long-term holdouts, eventually came to terms with Copernicus. That cannot be said for Darwin and the modern-day expression of his theory (see chapter 5).

Scriptural cosmology

Scriptural cosmology is a common-sense description of what the ancients observed in the heavens. It is phenomenological; in other words, it describes how things appear to a naive observer standing on the earth, rather than the way modern science with its telescopes and other technologies would describe them.[1] Biblical authors described what the eye could see, not knowing otherwise.[2] Israel understood the cosmos in much the same way anyone in the ancient world would have.[3] We would most likely have had the same ideas had we lived at that time.[4] Israel's cosmology was similar to, and most likely influenced by, the cosmologies of Egypt, Babylon and other ancient near eastern nations.[5] Contrary to these other nations, however, Israel's cosmology taught that the stars and astronomical bodies were not autonomous divinities, but under God's control.[6]

In Job 42, verse 3, Job admits that he lacks knowledge about many things (both material and spiritual) when he says, "Surely I spoke of things I did not understand, things too wonderful for me to know." (NIV) In the New Testament, in 1 Corinthians 13:12-14, the Apostle Paul expresses a similar thought when he says: "For now we see only a reflection as in a mirror…" (NIV) Ancient Hebrew cosmology persisted into New Testament times and beyond. The apostle Paul spoke of an individual caught up to "the third heaven." (2 Corinthians 12:2) The first heavenly layer was in front of the firmament, where the birds as well as the heavenly bodies were found. The second layer housed the "waters above." (Genesis 1:7) And the third layer was the abode of God. It was this last layer that the Apostle Paul was referring to.[7]

A misunderstood and often unacknowledged biblical phenomenology is at the root of much of the current conflict between science and Christian anti-evolutionists. Old Testament professor John Walton of Wheaton College says, "There is not a single instance in the Old Testament of God giving scientific information that transcended the understanding of the ancient Israelite audience."[8] The mathematics and measuring systems found in the Bible, for example, are clearly pre-scientific.[9] The Genesis author does not seem to be aware of the limitations of his own knowledge; in other words, he does not know that he does not know.[10]

A basic Old Testament cosmological principle is found in 1 Chronicles 16:30: "The world is firmly established; it cannot be moved." (NIV) A literal interpretation of this passage (and others like it) persisted into the sixteenth century and led theologians, including Martin Luther (1483-1546), to reject the heliocentric theory proposed by Copernicus (1473-1543) in 1514. The ancients believed that the cosmos was unchanging.[11] When Genesis speaks of the "earth," we moderns assume that means a planet floating in space, but to the ancient Hebrews "earth" simply meant "land under sky." To the ancients, the earth was a flat circle of dry land surrounded by waters pushed back to clear the space.[12]

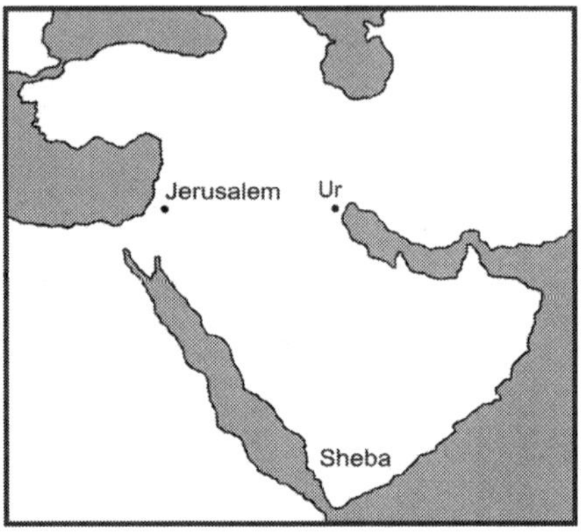

Figure 3.1 – Circumferential Sea. *People of the ancient near east believed that they were surrounded by water. This map shows the reason for that belief. The Israelites believed that God constantly held those threatening, chaotic waters at bay. Should he release them, destruction would surely follow.* Credit: Denis O. Lamoureux, I Love Jesus and I Accept Evolution, Kindle edition. Location 1420. Used with permission.

As we noted in chapter 2, modern science has revealed much that was previously hidden from limited human senses.[13] Young earth creationism, which asserts that the cosmos, along with the earth and its living organisms, were directly created by God less than 10,000 years ago, would be an entirely logical conclusion if all we knew about the natural world is what was known at the time the creation accounts were written.[14] The Oxford dictionary defines a "phenomenon" as "...the object of a person's perception; what the senses or the mind notice."[15] The genius of science lies in the fact that it frees us from the limitations of our physical senses, and, in the process, greatly expands our perception. The call to recognize the ancient science in the scriptures is not unique to our day. In the eighteenth century, John Wesley (1703-1791) said, "Scripture describes things by their outward sensible appearances..."[16] Ancient biblical writers, therefore, were not wrong, not deliberately misleading their audience about natural phenomena; they were simply people of their own time and culture.[17] As we have already seen, this limited scientific knowledge extended to many areas of life. For example, according to the understanding of ancient scriptural botany, seeds were passive; plant development was dictated by the soil.[18] Before the advent of modern genetics, common-sense suggested that the experience of a pregnant animal would affect its progeny's characteristics. So, in Genesis 30:37-43, Jacob tricks Laban by placing striped and speckled poles before the stronger breeding sheep and cattle so they would be striped and speckled, and he would receive them under the terms of his agreement with Laban (chapter 12).[19] The writer of Leviticus thought bats were birds.[20]

Suffice it to say, spiritual truths endure but the majority of ancient statements about natural phenomena are well past their best-before date. In the fourth century A.D., church father Augustine of Hippo (354-430) warned believers not to try to turn biblical texts into precise scientific statements.[21] Evolutionary creationist Denis Lamoureux says,

> *The earth "looks" flat, "seems" to be surrounded by water, and "feels" stationary; the sky gives the "impression" of being a blue body of water overhead; and the sun "appears" to cross the dome of the sky, rising and setting every day. However, to ancient peoples like the biblical authors and their readers, these are descriptions of the actual structure and operation of the universe.*[22]

Scott Buchanan lists several expressions of the Bible's ancient phenomenology, views, incidentally, that were not restricted to bronze-age Semites, but were also found among Israel's neighbors.[23]

- Water under the earth. (Psalm 136)
- The earth set on foundations or pillars. (Psalm 104)
- Waters above the firmament. (Psalm 148)
- The firmament is a sheet of metal, pounded thin. (Job 37:18)
- Heaven supported by foundations or pillars. (1 Samuel 2:8; Job 37:18)

The Hebrew word translated "firmament" or "expanse" is raqia, which suggests a metal plate, pounded out flat.[24] Old testament authors believed that the heavenly firmament was solid enough to support God's footsteps. Job 22:14 in the New English Bible says, "He walks to and fro on the dome of heaven."[25] The

ESV translation says "...he walks on the vault of heaven." And in Job, chapter 37, verse 18 we find this question: "Can you join God in spreading out the skies, hard as a mirror of cast bronze?" (NIV) Isaiah 40:22: "God sits enthroned above the circle of the earth, and its people are like grasshoppers. He stretches out the heavens like a canopy, and spreads them out like a tent to live in." (NIV)

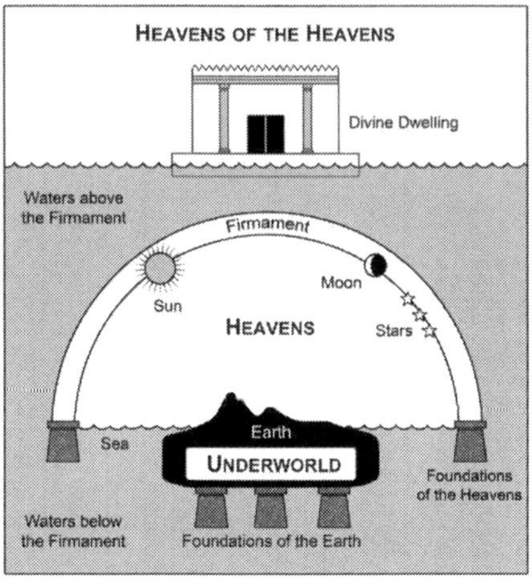

Figure 3.2 – Ancient Cosmology. *The ancients believed that the cosmos was constructed with a firmament above the earth. The firmament had windows, which, when opened, would allow the waters from above to flow down on the earth. The heavenly bodies were fastened to the firmament, and could be dislodged and fall to the earth. The earth rested on pillars, with water below the earth. God's heavenly dwelling was located above the firmament. This ancient cosmology still existed in Luther's day (16th century).* Credit: Denis O. Lamoureux, Evolutionary Creation. p. 108. Used with permission.

The ancient Israelites believed that God set the stars into the dome, exactly where they appear to the naïve observer.[26] The sun and the moon were also attached to that solid firmament.[27] To the ancients, the stars were quite small, sometimes dislodging from the firmament and falling to earth.[28] This idea is carried forward into the New Testament, in the book of Revelation, chapter 6, verse 13, (NIV) where the apostle John says "... and the stars in the sky fell to earth, as figs drop from a fig tree when shaken by a strong wind."[29] John Walton says: "The primary role (or function) of the firmament was to create the space in which people live. A second and more significant function was to serve as a mechanism by which precipitation was controlled – the means by which weather operated."[30] The ancient Hebrews believed that the firmament supported a body of water over the earth. For the ancients, those chaotic cosmic waters above the firmament were an ongoing danger, but the firmament restrained them.[31] Appearing on the second day of creation, the firmament separated the "waters above" from the "waters below" (Genesis 1:6-8).[32] In the Genesis flood account, in chapters 6 through 9, God opens the windows of the firmament and allows the waters above the firmament to pour down onto the earth, causing the destruction of the flood.[33] Significantly, the builders of the Tower of Babel (Genesis 11:1-9) believed their tower could reach the firmament.[34] By Luther's time, some scholars (called "philosophers" in those days) questioned the idea of a firmament. Luther was an accomplished Hebrew scholar, having translated the entire Old Testament from Hebrew into German. Luther took a firm stand against these individuals, defending what, to him, was the plain, literal meaning of the text:

> *Scripture says that the moon, the sun, and the stars were placed in the firmament of the heaven, below and above which heaven are the waters... It is likely that the stars are fastened to the firmament like globes of fire, to shed light at night... We Christians must be different from the philosophers in the way we think about the causes of things. And if some are beyond our comprehension like those before us concerning the waters above the heavens, we must believe them rather than wickedly deny them or presumptuously interpret them in conformity with our understanding.*[35]

Figure 3.3 – ***Luther's cosmology***. *This image reveals Luther's geocentric cosmology. Note the similarity to the cosmological understanding of ancient Israel in Figure 3.2. Again, we see the firmament above the earth, with the heavenly bodies affixed. There is water above the firmament. God's dwelling is above that. Note also the position of the sun, which in Luther's understanding circles the earth.* Credit: Denis O. Lamoureux. Evolutionary Creation, p. 122. Redrawn by Andrea Dmytrash. Used with permission.

It is evident from these examples that the inspired truths of the scriptures were originally conveyed to its readers in the cultural context of the author's time period, not our own.[36] The Bible, therefore, does not lie about natural phenomena. It simply accommodates the best knowledge of the day.[37] The Bible's ancient science should not be considered "wrong" or "false" as much as it offers a perspective from a different vantage point.[38] It is important to emphasize that the scriptures' pre-scientific statements about nature are not the ground of a believer's faith. That honor resides with the scriptures' God-given spiritual truths. More than a century ago, George Frederick Wright (1838-1921), geologist and professor at Oberlin Theological Seminary in Ohio, warned Christians that "... the utterances of the Bible are not infallible except as pertaining to things necessary to be known and observed for salvation."[39] Spiritual truths are timeless. Truths about the natural realm are not.

Tycho brahe

A well-known example of scriptural cosmology is found in Psalm 19, verses 1 and 2, where the Psalmist speaks of the heavens declaring the glory of God and extols the outcome of His creative efforts. These verses were used to support the natural theology so popular in nineteenth century Britain (see chapter 10). Greek philosopher Aristotle (384-322 B.C.) held views about the cosmos similar to those found in the Old Testament. Aristotle speculated that the universe is finite in size and that it exists eternally unchanged. He proposed that the heavenly bodies are perfect and that the heavens themselves are made of an imperishable ether. The motion of the heavenly bodies, Aristotle claimed, is eternal and perfect. Solid crystalline spheres provide structure to the universe and carry the planets around the earth. Aristotle's paradigm survived until the sixteenth century, when Tycho Brahe's (1546-1601) detailed observations of comets moving through the solar system replaced the Greek philosopher's pre-scientific speculations.[40] Brahe, in addition, was the first astronomer to imagine the planets hanging unsupported in empty space.[41]

A great commotion took place in 1054 A.D. when a so-called "new star" appeared in the heavens. That astronomical object was later determined to be a supernova. Significantly, that new heavenly body did not fit the astronomical paradigm of the day.[42] We should not be surprised to discover that because this appearance was an anomaly, it was given astrological significance. A similar portent occurred five centuries later, in 1572 (also, it turns out, a supernova). That sighting also challenged the dominant astronomical paradigm. After that, in 1577, a bright comet appeared in the heavens.[43] For Tycho Brahe, that comet was a theological puzzle which had a scientific solution.[44]

Nicolaus copernicus

Like the majority of sixteenth century scientists, Polish priest Nicolaus Copernicus was a deeply religious man.[45] Somewhere around 1514, he proposed a radical new theory called heliocentrism, claiming that the sun did not orbit the earth, but that the opposite was true. Many individuals are unaware of the fact that Copernicus did not invent heliocentrism. The concept had been advocated early on by a few ancient scholars, including Aristarchus. Copernicus knew his counterintuitive theory would cause a crisis in the church.[46] Physicist Stephen Hawking says, "At first, perhaps for fear of being branded a heretic, his model was circulated anonymously."[47] After initially accepting the Copernican theory, the Roman Catholic Church turned against him because his proposal had been taken up by the heretic Giordano Bruno (1548-1600).[48] Nearly a century passed before Copernicus and his radical theory were taken seriously.[49] Two prominent individuals who supported Copernicus were astronomers Johannes Kepler (1571-1630) and Galileo Galilei (1564-1642). In a letter to Kepler, written in May 1597, Galileo stated his enthusiasm for the Copernican model.[50] Supporting evidence for the theory came in 1609 by means of Galileo's own telescope.[51]

Martin Luther was a contemporary of Copernicus. Luther explained his philosophy of Biblical interpretation by saying: "We (i.e., the theologians) must be different from the philosophers (i.e., the scientists) regarding the causes of things."[52] Armed with common-sense interpretations of the Old Testament references that describe an earth that does not move, Luther felt he had sufficient evidence to dismiss Copernicus.[53] He said: "People gave ear to an upstart astrologer who strove to show that the earth revolves, not the heavens or the firmament, the sun and the moon. This fool wishes to reverse the entire science of astronomy; but sacred scripture tells us (Joshua 10:13) that Joshua commanded the sun to stand still, and not the earth.[54] Philip Melanchthon (1497-1560), Luther's close theological collaborator and friend, wrote in 1549:

> *The eyes are witnesses that the heavens revolve in the space of twenty-four hours. But certain men, either from the love of novelty, or to make a display of ingenuity, have concluded that the earth moves; and they maintain that neither the eighth sphere [the celestial sphere] nor the sun revolves. Now, it is a want of honesty and decency to assert such notions publicly, and the example is pernicious. It is the part of a good mind to accept the truth as revealed by God and to acquiesce in it.*[55]

John Calvin (1509-1564), for his part, said: "Who will venture to place the authority of Copernicus above that of the Holy Spirit?"[56] Critics of Copernicus argued that if the earth is spinning, people ought to feel it moving. And if the earth is spinning, a strong wind would blow.[57] In addition, heliocentrism was criticized by the theologians of the day because it contradicted their long-standing geocentric interpretation of scripture. Martin Luther, as we have seen, was among the theologians who defended the traditional interpretation. Many of these individuals continued to defended their position despite mounting scientific evidence to the contrary. Amazingly, Lutheran systematician Francis Pieper (1852-1931), highly respected among confessional Lutherans, in his three-volume Christian Dogmatics[58] (completed in 1924) continued to oppose Copernican theory well into the twentieth century. The parallels to today's conflict over evolution are compelling.[59]

Luther defended a pre-scientific cosmology because he believed that, in so doing, he was defending Biblical authority. Luther's hermeneutic lives on in today's anti-evolutionary movement.[60] Unlike Galileo, Luther steadfastly refused to allow science to influence his theology in any way.[61] Many modern-day Lutherans do the same. It would be interesting to know what Luther would do if he lived in our day and was exposed to the findings of modern science. Many Christians are unaware of the fact that the sixteenth-century Catholic Church was willing to discuss the radically new cosmological model proposed by Nicolaus Copernicus.[62] Cardinal Robert Bellarmine (1542-1621) indicated that the church would be willing to accept heliocentricity if proof could be given, with the proviso that "... one would then have to proceed with great care in explaining the scripture that appear contrary, and say rather that we do not understand them, rather than that which is demonstrated is false."[63]

The Catholic church argued that it would not overturn a long-held tradition unless convincing evidence was presented. Galileo was invited to write a book which would dispassionately lay out the various arguments, pro and con. But that's not what he did. Those reading his presentation quickly realized which position he preferred. An important aspect of Galileo's undoing was the fact that the character in his book defending the geocentric model was called "simplicio" – "fool" in Italian. The Pope, as expected, was not pleased. Galileo was sentenced to house arrest in his own villa. He was never threatened with execution and spent the next nine years, until his death, studying astronomy.[64] Galileo, it seems, was a victim of bad luck and bad judgment. He displayed what Stephen Jay Gould calls "...a fatal impetuosity."[65] Gould describes Galileo as a "...frightfully undiplomatic hothead who brought unnecessary trouble upon his own head."[66] In 1992, three hundred and fifty years after Galileo's death, Pope John Paul II (1920-2005) admitted that errors had been made by the theological advisers in the persecution of Galileo.[67]

Johannes kepler

Like Galileo and Newton, Johannes Kepler (1571-1630) was an ardently religious man, a Lutheran.[68] Kepler saw God's handiwork and purposes everywhere.[69] Kepler worked out the planetary laws. He argued that, using tools science provided, investigators could learn more about how God's will was manifested in the cosmos.[70] Kepler deviated from the orthodox Lutheran teaching of his time which claimed that the planets were guided by angels.[71] At that time, theologians began to realize that scientific discoveries sometimes challenge long-standing biblical interpretations.[72] Augustine, Kepler, and Galileo all advocated the acknowledgement of scientific advances by the church. Edward Davis says:

> *Kepler used the Augustinian principle of accommodation to justify the figurative interpretation of biblical references to the motion of the sun. The*

Bible, he noted, speaks in a very human way about ordinary matters in a manner that can be understood, using ordinary speech to convey loftier theological truths. Thus the literal sense of texts making reference to nature should not be mistaken for accurate scientific statements.[73]

Modern cosmology

Many Christians do not know that the Big Bang theory was proposed by Fr. Georges LeMaitre (1894-1966), a Roman Catholic Jesuit priest and leading scientist in Belgium.[74] According to the theory, the universe expanded from a high density state approximately 13.8 billion years ago. In 1951, LeMaitre's theory was officially pronounced to be in accordance with the Bible by the Roman Catholic Church.[75] Discoveries made by the modern disciplines of astronomy and cosmology have important implications for the understanding of human origins. Stars, for example, have a lifecycle; they evolve through time. The stellar lifecycle is an example of God's continuous creation, his creatio continua.[76] Stars are born in vast clouds of dust drawn together by gravity. And, after billions of years, they die in a massive explosion called a supernova, which, significantly, distributes far out into space the heavy elements essential for life.[77]

It is important for Christians to understand that the fundamental building blocks of all material things, including our own bodies, were forged eons ago in the furnaces of exploding stars. So the very atoms in our bodies today can be traced all the way back to an ancient supernova.[78] We are literally and truly made of stardust.[79] Genesis 3:19 says, appropriately, "...for dust you are and to dust you will return." (NIV) Here again, scientific discoveries have revealed what the ancients could not have known – in this case, that God took his time creating humanity and that the very elements in our bodies originated billions of years ago. The time span from the Big Bang to the point at which the earth is habitable for life was approximately 10 billion years.[80] An increasing number of Christians believe that God has continuously supervised an evolutionary process, a point of view called theistic evolution or evolutionary creation (see chapter 8). The New Testament book of Hebrews, for example (chapter 1, verse 3), says that God "... sustains all things by his powerful word."[81] (NRSV) The Apostle Paul adds "... all things were created through him and for him, [and] ... in him all things hold together." (Colossians 1:16-17, NIV)

Because of the typically enormous periods of time it takes light to reach the earth from deep space, today's telescopes provide us with a window deep into the past. The heavens are, in a very real sense, an immense time machine. An important piece of evidence supporting the great age of the earth comes from the great distances of galaxies.[82] By determining the currrent speeds and distances to galaxies, along with a calculation of the rate at which the universe is expanding, scientists have determined that the universe is approximately 13.8 billion years old. And the earth is approximately 4.3 billion years old. To help viewers wrap their minds around the significance of 4.3 billion years, the producers of a Nova TV Special called Australia: First Four Billion Years used the analogy of a car trip. They pointed out that if an automobile was to travel at a rate of one million years per minute, 4.3 billion years would be the equivalent of 74 hours of traveling time, or just over three full days![83] And remember, that is at the rate of 1 million years going by each minute. It is significant that an important consilience is evident here. Both geology and astrophysics provide similar ages for the universe.[84]

4. THE GEOLOGICAL REVOLUTION

Overview

By the early nineteenth century, the process of identifying and dating fossils in sedimentary rocks was well underway. An early debate in geology pitted uniformitarianism against catastrophism. Uniformitarianism claimed that slow, incremental changes, over very long periods of time, shaped the earth's geological features. Catastrophism, on the other hand, suggested that short-term, violent events were responsible. Today's anti-evolutionists carry the catastrophist banner, particularly with their doctrine of flood geology which argues that the earth's geological features, including fossils, reflect the impact of the global flood event recorded in the book of Genesis (see chapter 9).

Many nineteenth-century British geologists were Anglican clergy. They wondered whether the creation accounts in the book of Genesis could be reconciled with geological discoveries. It soon became evident that geology was going to challenge long-standing Christian interpretations of the Genesis creation accounts. By 1820, evidence for a very old earth was accumulating. Some Christians responded, as today's anti-evolutionists do, with an outright denial of the scientific evidence. Others, however, revisited the Old Testament creation accounts seeking the extra time an ancient earth demanded. As a result, various iterations of old-earth creationism, such as the gap and day-age theories, (see chapter 7) were formulated.

Charles Darwin was first and foremost a geologist. His five-year journey on the British surveying ship, HMS Beagle, provided an opportunity to study the effects of geographical isolation on various species. These insights later formed the basis of his evolutionary theory. Darwin understood that an ancient earth would provide evolution the time it needed. Around the turn of the twentieth century, additional evidence for deep time and an ancient earth came by means of radiometric dating.

Background

The science of geology matured in the nineteenth century.[1] In the 1820's, when Charles Darwin (1809-1882) was a youth, many scientists at Oxford and Cambridge were Anglican clergy. They had the financial means that allowed them to undertake their scientific investigations.[2] Ciaran Toal, writing for the British newspaper The Guardian says:

> *Early nineteenth-century science was dominated by clergymen-scientists; men dedicated to their scientific work but still mindful of their faith. Geologist William Buckland (1784-1856), mathematician Baden Powell (1857-1941), and polymath William Whewell (1794-1866) found little conflict in their roles as clergymen and men of science. The young Charles Darwin even considered taking holy orders – had the HMS Beagle not provided such an alluring distraction. And although the situation had changed by the late nineteenth century, this can't be simply explained by an erosion of religious faith among practicing scientists.*[3]

At the beginning of the nineteenth century, Christian geologists were already seeking to reconcile their science with the Genesis creation accounts.[4] Individuals who read their Bibles literalistically feared that geological discoveries would prove Genesis false.[5] The same basic fear motivates today's anti-evolutionists. British geologist and cartographer William Smith (1769-1839) produced the first geological map of England. He identified strata in sedimentary rocks across Britain by linking them to the fossil species they contained, a process called stratigraphy.[6] Smith discovered that fossils could be used to identify the same strata in different locations. He took samples and mapped the positions of the strata, noted their vertical extent, and drew cross-sections and tables of his observations. Smith collected fossils taken from the strata he examined. He proposed the principle of faunal succession, the idea that sedimentary rock strata contain fossilized flora and fauna, and these fossils succeed each other vertically in a specific, reliable order which can be identified over wide horizontal distances. Now, when geologists find identical fossils in strata in different parts of the world, they know those strata were laid down at the same time.[7] In general, older rocks contain fewer fossils, and rocks below the Cambrian period contain few fossils of any kind. Significantly, virtually all fossil forms that have ever lived are now extinct.

Charles lyell

Sir Charles Lyell (1797-1875), considered by many to be the foremost geologist of his day, is best known for his Principles of Geology, published in three volumes from 1830 to 1833. Lyell was an advocate of James Hutton's (1726-1797) uniformitarianism. Slow incremental changes such as erosion, it was argued, were the main source of the earth's geological features. Uniformitarianism asserts that the present is the key to the past; all things continue as they have from an indefinite past. By extending the time available for evolution and illustrating the power of small changes over long periods of time, Lyell's uniformitarianism helped make the case for Darwin's theory.[8] Catastrophism, however, was the reigning paradigm in Lyell's day. It proposed that the earth had been shaped by sudden, short-lived, violent events, possibly worldwide in scope. Nineteenth-century French scientist Georges Cuvier (1769-1832) promoted catastrophism, arguing that the geological epochs ended with natural catastrophes such as great floods and the rapid formation of major mountain chains. Plants and animals subject to such conditions were replaced abruptly by new forms. The current scientific consensus makes room for both uniformitarianism and catastrophism, pointing out that there were indeed catastrophic events in the earth's geologic past, but these were extreme examples of long-term natural processes. Uniformitarianism is now a key principle of modern geology and virtually all fields of science.[9]

Deep time

Given the persuasive geological evidence supporting an ancient earth, some nineteenth century Christian theologians looked for evidence of deep time in the Genesis creation accounts.[10] Church father Augustine of Hippo (354-430 A.D.) had long before set a precedent for an old-earth view, pointing out that the sun was not created until the fourth day.[11] Benjamin Silliman (1779-1864) was one of the individuals who sought to reconcile Genesis and geology.[12] Silliman was a Christian who, in an address delivered before the Association of American Geologists, spoke in favor of an old earth.[13] Some Victorian-era Christians acknowledged the findings of geology by proposing the gap or day-age theories (see chapter 7).[14] Many contemporary Christians are surprised to discover that William Jennings Bryan (1860-1925), of Scopes trial fame, was an advocate of an old-earth view.[15] Old-earth creationism remains popular among conservative Protestants today.[16]

Biogeography

The science of geology was well established before Darwin's day. The geological timescale, for example, had been instituted in the early nineteenth century by scientists, many of whom were creationists.[17] Many geological findings, it later turned out, had a direct bearing on the theory of evolution. Darwin himself was a geologist and his observation of South American fossils and other insights gained during his five-year voyage on HMS Beagle helped convince him of evolution.[18] Darwin was especially fascinated by the geographical distribution of living organisms and was very interested in the effect of geographical isolation (biogeography) on speciation.[19] Darwin discovered that isolated islands are natural laboratories where the effects of geographical isolation on evolution and speciation are clearly evident.[20] Organisms living in isolated regions evolve in unique ways, in response to unique environmental challenges.[21] Examples of the effect of geographical isolation on evolution can be found in areas as diverse as New Zealand, South America, Australia, Madagascar, Hawaii, and the Galapagos islands.

In 1837, in a stop-off in the Galapagos, Darwin wondered if bird species from the nearest landmass (which, in this case was South America, almost 1000 km to the east) had become isolated on the Galapagos islands, and had evolved there, adapting over a long period of time to the islands' unique environment.[22] Biogeography provides some of the strongest evidence supporting Darwin's theory.[23] An interesting example has recently been reported in Australia. An expedition to a remote area in the northern part of the country discovered three new and unique vertebrate species that had been isolated for millions of years. Discoveries included a bizarre-looking leaf-tail gecko, a gold-colored skink (a type of lizard), and a brown-spotted, yellow boulder-dwelling frog, none of these species ever seen before.[24]

Fossils

In the seventeenth century, scholars puzzled over fossils.[25] Long before, the Greek philosopher Aristotle (384-322 B.C.) had speculated that shifting sea levels preserved the remains of ancient shells and skeletons.[26] An early Christian explanation of fossils speculated that they were partially-formed creatures God had started to create from clay, but had left unfinished.[27] Some nineteenth-century creationists argued that fossils were put into the ground either to deceive believers or to test them.[28] The claim that fossils are Satanic deceptions, amazingly, is still being put forward by some anti-evolutionists today. As early as 1650, however, Robert Hook (1635-1703) correctly identified fossils as the remains of once-living creatures and plants.[29]

Paleontology is the scientific study of life-forms that existed prior to approximately 12,000 years ago. Paleontologists examine fossils in order to determine the evolution of organisms and their interactions with each other and with their environments. The scientific discipline of paleontology was established in the eighteenth century as a result of French scientist Georges Cuvier's (1769-1832) work on comparative anatomy, and developed rapidly in the nineteenth century.[30] Cuvier determined that the fossil record was progressive and concluded that humans must be a very recent arrival.[31] He suggested that life had a history different from the present, and that fossil fragments helped reveal that history.[32]

A date for creation

In 1650, Archbishop James Ussher (1581-1656), Anglican archbishop of Ireland, speculated, based on his interpretation of Biblical genealogies, that the date of creation was October 23rd, 4004 B.C.[33] Eight years earlier, in 1642, John Lightfoot (1602-1675) of Cambridge University, using a similar method, proposed a date of September 17th, 3928 B.C.[34] Many Bible scholars argues, however, argue that Biblical genealogies are not always exact, comprehensive lists of parent-child relationships. The unusual characteristics of ancient scriptural genealogies means that they should not be relied upon to provide an accurate basis for determining the age of the earth (see chapter 12). As we have seen, contrary to Ussher and Lightfoot, evidence gathered by early geologists suggested that the earth had a long history. Theologians of all persuasions have shown that counting the generations is not the best way to arrive at a date for Adam. Even eminent and learned scholars, it is clear, can seriously misinterpret the scriptures.

Conflict over the age of the earth began around 1750; geologists were close to a consensus by 1820.[35] Belief in an ancient earth came to be part of the scientific mainstream by the 1830's, twenty-five to thirty years before the publication of Darwin's On the Origin of Species.[36] It is important to keep in mind that, by the early twentieth century, many Protestant fundamentalists had accepted the idea of deep time and their theology accommodated that view by means of the day-age and gap theories (see chapter 7).[37] Although the majority of Christians in mainline denominations have long since made peace with geology, deep time remains problematic for many evangelicals, especially in the U.S. According to one study, 56 percent of U.S. evangelicals reject the concept of deep time compared to 36 percent of the general population.[38]

The apparent-age hypothesis

In 1857, Victorian writer, biologist and preacher The Rev. Philip Henry Gosse (1810-1888) formulated an hypothesis regarding the age of the earth. Two years before the publication of Darwin's Origin of Species, Rev. Gosse published An Attempt to Untie the Geological Knot.[39] There, he argued that if one assumed a creation ex nihilo, there would necessarily be traces of previous existence that had never actually occurred. Omphalos, by the way, is the Greek word for "navel." Gosse speculated that the first man, Adam, did not require a navel because he was never born; but he must have had one, as do all complete human beings, just as God must have created trees with growth rings even though those trees had been created in a mature state. Gosse argued that the fossil record might be evidence of life that never actually existed but which may have been instantly formed by God at the moment of creation.

The general response to Gosse's hypothesis was, as The Westminster Review put it, "too monstrous for belief." Even his friend, novelist Charles Kingsley (1819-1875), wrote that he had read "no other book which so staggered and puzzled" him and he could not believe that God had "written on the rocks one enormous and superfluous lie for all mankind."[40] Gosse's appearance-of-age thesis quickly fell out of favor, only to be reinvigorated by a new generation of anti-evolutionists (see chapter 9).[41] Gosse's speculations were a tacit admission of the validity of geology. Critics argued that for created things to show a deceptive appearance of age would violate God's clearly-stated character and purpose.[42] If Gosse was correct, the scientific evidence for evolution would reveal a fictional history of the universe,[43] making God a deceiver,[44] and in the process corrupting not just science but religion as well.[45] Francis Collins makes the point that, for believers, it strains credulity to have God provide rock-solid evidence for evolution and then expect them to reject it.[46] Theologian Peter Enns offers a thorough critique of the apparent-age hypothesis, arguing that it creates many more problems than it solves.[47]

Flood geology

Today's young earth creationists are modern-day catastrophists advocating what has come to be known as flood geology (see chapter 9).[48] Flood geology has its early roots, at least in part, in the work of the influential eighteenth-century German geologist Abraham Gottlob Werner (1749-1817).[49] It proposes that the earth's geological features, including spectacular sites like the Grand Canyon, are a direct result of the global effects of the Biblical flood. According to this view, fossils were formed subsequent to the great dying caused by the flood (see chapter 9). Belief in a worldwide flood was common from the sixteenth through the eighteenth centuries, but was challenged by geological discoveries in the nineteenth century.[50] British geologists Adam Sedgwick (1785-1873) and William Buckland (1784-1856), both conservative Christians, claimed that one flood could not have produced the deposits found.[51] A flood, for example, could not explain the presence of marine shells on mountains.[52] And many fossils, especially animal tracks, must be undisturbed if they are to be preserved properly, and therefore could not have been laid down in a flood.[53] In addition, many delicate fossils, like dinosaur eggs, would have been destroyed in raging floodwaters.[54] Geologist Kenneth Currie adds:

> *Flood geology also cannot account for thick deposits of limestone originating in calm waters. It cannot accommodate thick salt beds. In addition, flood geology does not give an explanation of strata formed under desert conditions. Flood geology simply cannot deal with the vast amount of physical evidence amassed by geologists in the past 200 years, except by denying the validity of the evidence.*[55]

Radiometric dating

Radiometric dating is the principal source of information about the absolute age of rocks and other geological features, including the age of the earth, and can be used to date a wide range of natural and man-made materials. Geologist Kenneth Currie offers a clarification:

Natural radioactivity provides a clock scientists can use to determine the age of rocks. The principle is that of the hourglass. The time since the glass was turned is measured by the amount of sand in the bottom of the glass. Radiometric dating is based on a comparison between the observed abundance of a naturally occurring radioactive isotope and its decay products, using known decay rates.[56]

Radiometric dating began with the discovery of radioactivity in the late 1800's.[57] By allowing the establishment of geological timescales, radiometric dating provides a significant source of information about the age of fossils and the rate of evolutionary change.[58] Radiometric dating transformed geology from an inexact, descriptive science into a rigorous, quantitative discipline.[59] Radiometric dating is a technical subject, challenging for non-scientists. A description of the process of radiometric dating was first published in 1907 by Bertram Boltwood (1870-1927). Nuclear fusion, discovered in the early 1900s, was found to be the source of the sun's energy. This, in turn, allowed for the calculation of the earth's true age.[60] There are forty different radiometric dating techniques.[61] Significantly, it has been found that extreme application of heat, cold, pressure (even explosion), or chemical reaction cause no change in radioactive decay rates.[62] Anti-evolutionists charge that this is a false assumption, but, in reality, radioactive decay rates have not been observed to vary since the rates were directly measurable, at least within limits of accuracy. This is despite experiments that attempt to change decay rates. Young earth creationists fail to acknowledge that radioactive decay rapid enough to permit a young earth would produce enough heat to melt the earth.

Carbon-14 dating

Radiometric dating is used to date materials that are millions or billions of years old. Carbon-14, another form of radiometric dating, is used to determine the age of biological materials less than 50,000 years old, such as bone, cloth, wood and plant fiber. When a living organism dies, it stops taking in new carbon. The ratio of carbon-12 to carbon-14 at the moment of death is the same as other living things, but, after death occurs, the carbon-14 decays and is not replaced. While the carbon-14 decays, the amount of carbon-12 remains the same. By examining the ratio of carbon-12 to carbon-14 in a sample and comparing it to the ratio in a living organism, it is possible to determine its age fairly precisely.[63]

Radiometric and carbon-14 dating are not the only dating methods available to scientists. Supplementary dating methods include the study of tree rings (dendrochronology) which provides an unbroken historical record going back more than 11,000 years.[64] In addition, varves are pairs of thin layers of clay and silt of contrasting color and texture that represent the deposit of a single year (summer and winter) in a lake. Such layers can be used to determine the chronology of glacial sediments. Collins and Giberson state that varves preserve a historical record as far back as 35,000 years.[65] But there are locations where varves go back almost 60,000 years. The Natural Historian website asks:

> *Do places on earth exist where annual records have been stored for tens of thousands of years and can be accessed today? Ice-cores and tree rings can preserve long records of yearly events but some of the best records come from layers of sediment underlying some lakes which, if formed under the right conditions, can be read like the annual rings of an oak tree. These alternating layers of sediments and sometimes organic material are called varves and by counting each varve sequentially a varve chronology can be con-*

structed. Varve chronologies are a window to the past and have been used to study past climate conditions, the periodicity of volcanic eruptions and as an independent test of radiocarbon (C-14) dating methods. One place were varves have been studied for decades is below a deep lake in Japan: Lake Suigetsu. Here a varve chronology stretching back well over 50,000 years has been established.[66]

Ice cores are another dating method. In Greenland, for example, ice cores go back 123,000 years. In addition to providing information about dates, ice cores also offer clues to the earth's ancient atmosphere and climate. Not long ago, the oldest Antarctic ice core was approximately 800,000 years old.[67] At that time, scientists speculated that new cores could conceivably stretch the climate record back 1.5 million years. In August of 2017, an article was posted on the American Association for the Advancement of Science (AAAS) website with the following headline: "Record-shattering 2.7 million-year-old ice core reveals start of ice-ages." The news article states that scientists have been able to determine the level of greenhouse gases in the sample, the only sample of that time period they have access to.

Traditionally, scientists drill ice cores in places where ice layers accumulate year after year, undisturbed by glacial flows. But because heat from the bedrock below can melt the deepest, oldest ice, that approach has not yielded ice older than 800,000 years. Using this traditional approach, scientists estimate that the oldest ice they can find would be in the range of 1.5 million years. A new technique, however, has discovered ice 2.7 million years old. There is evidence that Antarctica has hosted at least some ice for the last 30 million years. Scientists are hopeful that their next attempt could find ice that is as much as 5 million years old.[68]

Plate tectonics and continental drift

In 1915, German climatologist and geophysicist Alfred Wegener (1880-1930), published an expanded version of his 1912 book, The Origin of Continents and Oceans. Wegener was one of the first scientists to propose the theory of continental drift and plate tectonics. He argued that a supercontinent he called Pangaea had existed in the past, but, beginning 200 million years ago, had broken up, and the pieces had "drifted" to their present positions. As support for his theory, Wegener cited the fit of South America and Africa, ancient climate similarities, fossil evidence, and similarity of rock structures. Wegener's proposal remained controversial until the 1960's.[69] It was accepted when there was evidence of the mechanism that made it happen.[70] Plate tectonics and continental drift provide an important example of the consilience of inductions, which happens when evidence from different scientific disciplines come together with the same result.[71] In this case, three different types of evidence – radiometric dating, astrophysics, and continental drift – independently corroborate the age of the earth.[72] In 1840, philosopher of science William Whewell (1794-1866) coined the word consilience to refer to a "jumping together" of results from separate sources.[73] Controversial scientific discoveries such as the age of the earth, the theory of evolution, and plate tectonics, are best affirmed when entirely independent sources of data combine to achieve the same result.[74] Consilience is the strongest support a scientific hypothesis can receive.[75]

5. THE BIOLOGICAL REVOLUTION

Overview

Charles Darwin (1809-1882) was born into an upper middle-class family, the son of a physician. After a short, unsuccessful stint studying medicine at his father's insistence, he turned to theology, but did not complete his degree. Darwin was then mentored by several outstanding British scientists, including botanist John Henslow (1796-1861), historian William Whewell (1794-1866), and anatomist Sir Richard Owen (1804-1892). Young Charles eventually turned his attention to geology, which became a life-long passion. A five-year (1831-1836) voyage on HMS Beagle, a Royal Navy surveying ship, was a transformative experience. Despite struggles with seasickness and having to deal with an authoritarian sea captain, Robert Fitzroy (1805-1865), Darwin's time on the Beagle admirably prepared him for a scientific vocation.

Charles Darwin had been previously exposed to evolutionary ideas by his grandfather, Erasmus (1731-1802), and by popular publications of the day which discussed what was then called the "transmutation of species." A major shift in Darwin's thinking occurred when he read a book by The Rev. Thomas Malthus (1766-1834) that discussed rapid population growth competing for a limited food supply. Darwin was an introvert who had a few close friends. After the Beagle journey, his health was poor. Because his wife Emma (1808-1896) was a member of the wealthy Wedgewood family, the Darwins enjoyed financial independence, which afforded Charles the time he needed to devote to his studies. Daily walks around his property, on a path he called the Sandwalk, allowed him to organize his thoughts. In 1844, he began to reveal his theory to his closest friends, a theory he had kept to himself for twenty years. He correctly anticipated that his views, especially his assertions about human origins, would cause a great deal of controversy and he wanted to be prepared to deal with objections that would be raised.

Darwin's relationship with the Christian faith was complicated. His faith was strongest, and most traditional, when he was a young adult. It began to fade during his voyage on The Beagle and was severely challenged when his ten-year-old daughter, Annie Elizabeth (1841-1851), second child and eldest daughter in the family, died of tuberculosis in 1851. Darwin's wife, Emma (1808-1896), was a person of strong faith and told her husband that she was concerned about the status of his salvation. As the years passed, Darwin's faith faded. He was buried with full honors in Westminster Abbey in 1882.

Charles darwin

Charles Darwin was born February 12th, 1809, the same day as Abraham Lincoln. In 1825, when he was 16 years old, his father, Dr. Robert Darwin, (1766-1848) sent young Charles off to the University of Edinburgh to study medicine. Ill-suited for a medical career, Charles dropped out two years later. During that time, Dr. Darwin criticized his son for being a layabout: "You care for nothing but shooting, dogs, and rat catching. You are a disgrace to yourself and to your family."[1] From 1828 to 1831, Darwin studied theology at Cambridge, before turning his energies to his lifetime passion, the pursuit of scientific knowledge.[2] As a student, Darwin was fortunate to be mentored by several outstanding scientists. At Cambridge, for example, he was encouraged by botany professor, John Henslow (1796-1861).[3] It was Henslow, a British Royal Navy surveyor, who persuaded Darwin to study geology.[4]

Henslow recommended the 22-year-old Darwin for a position as ship's naturalist on HMS Beagle, a surveying ship.[5] At that time, Darwin was also acquainted with Dr. William Whewell (1794-1866), Master of Trinity College, Cambridge.[6] At this point in his life, Darwin was a conventional British catastrophist strongly influenced by Adam Sedgewick (1785–1873), one of the founders of modern geology.[7] Geologist Charles Lyell (1797-1875) introduced Darwin to uniformitarianism.[8] Darwin came to adopt Lyell's point of view and was later to say, "I always feel that my books came half out of Lyell's brains."[9] Darwin was acquainted with anatomist Sir Richard Owen, (1804–1892) an outstanding naturalist with a remarkable gift for interpreting fossils. Sir Richard examined the specimens Darwin brought back to England on The Beagle.[10]

The Beagle voyage was a critical component of Darwin's intellectual growth and maturity. Originally planned as a two-year surveying trip, the journey stretched to five years. Darwin's meticulous observations became the foundation of his theory.[11] In his autobiography, Darwin observed, "My mind seems to have become a kind of machine for grinding out general laws."[12] During the voyage, Darwin struggled with sea sickness and endured a continuing clash of personalities with the captain, Robert Fitzroy.[13] Fitzroy was a strict disciplinarian, and an ardent Tory. Darwin, on the other hand, was a Whig (a liberal), constantly stifled in his opinions by Fitzroy. Fitzroy has been described as "... a hard-working and competitive aristocrat with a short fuse and a melancholy heart."[14] During his time on The Beagle, Darwin possessed a traditional Christian faith, but that faith slowly faded to agnosticism.[15] The twenty-two-year-old had no scientific credentials when he embarked on the journey.[16] That journey, however, gave him the opportunity to hone his scientific skills. He returned to England with 5000 specimens and 2000 pages of notes.[17]

The historical context

It is important to be aware of the fact that evolutionary ideas were in the air during Darwin's lifetime and had been for some time. Darwin's grandfather, Erasmus, had himself speculated about evolution.[18] And then, in 1844, an anonymous book, Vestiges of the Natural History of Creation, written by Robert Chambers (1802-1871), caused a sensation.[19] Vestiges raised the possibility of evolution, then called the transmutation of species. It became an international bestseller, but its unorthodox ideas were criticized by clergy and scientists alike. Philosopher of science Michael Ruse has described Chambers' Vestiges as "... the Big Mac of popular science ... tasty, filling, accessible, but of dubious value to health!"[20] The book, however, despite its many faults, helped shift public opinion about evolution in a positive direction, which, according to Darwin, paved the way for his theory.

In July 1837, Darwin encountered an idea that would be critical for his theory. He had been reading Rev. Thomas Malthus' Essay on the Principle of Population, published in 1798.[21] Malthus was an ordained minister of the Church of England. He observed that, under optimal conditions, populations grow rapidly, at an exponential rate, through repeated multiplication. Food supplies, however, grow much more slowly, at an arithmetic rate, through repeated addition. Thus, populations can increase faster than the food required to support them. Darwin noted that this imbalance would inevitably lead to competition between offspring. Some would be better equipped to survive than others.

One fateful day in 1858, a letter arrived at the Darwin household from British naturalist and explorer Alfred Russell Wallace (1823-1913). The letter revealed that Wallace had independently discovered evolution by natural selection. When that letter arrived, Darwin had been working on The Origin for two years.[22] Wallace's letter, as might be expected, caused concern and dramatically sped up the writing of Darwin's book.[23] Darrel Falk makes the point that Darwin made Wallace a co-author in his first public presentation of the theory. Historians agree that Darwin appropriately acknowledged Wallace's contribution.[23]

Wallace, we are told, was a complex character. He was an outstanding scientist who formulated a theory virtually identical to that proposed by Darwin. Wallace travelled widely and put up with many hardships. Socially, Wallace was an outlier. He was a pacifist, a socialist, and an agrarian.[24] Michael Ruse notes that Wallace dabbled in spiritualism, supported feminist causes, and describes him as "a cranky contrarian."[25] Wallace, says Ruse, was "...attracted to outrageous positions, particularly if those positions were disliked by the respectable."[26] Wallace sought to introduce the supernatural into Darwin's theory,[27] arguing that an "overruling intelligence" had created the first humans from apes and had created them with enlightened minds.[28] Darwin rejected the idea.

Darwin's magnum opus, On the Origin of Species, was published in 1859, one year after he received Wallace's letter.[29] In it, Darwin compared the artificial selection performed by animal and plant breeders with the natural selection that takes place in the wild. Darwin challenged conventional thinking when he claimed that species evolved through time. Remarkably, he formulated his theory knowing virtually nothing about genetics and heredity. Darwin, of course, was a man of his time. No one knew about heredity when The Origin was published in 1859. But Darwin had the basics right and biological science was transformed. Darwin's theory took on new life in the 1930's when details about inheritance were discovered and incorporated into the theory.

The secret

Because of Emma's Wedgewood family connections, the Darwin clan was independently wealthy.[30] This wealth afforded Darwin the luxury of attending to his scientific interests with minimal distraction. After formulating his theory, he was a man with a secret.[31] He waited a full twenty years before publishing his thoughts,[32] knowing full well that his theory would cause a storm of controversy.[33] He publicly revealed his views when he could conceal them no longer.[34] Darwin wanted to be prepared to respond to the arguments he knew would be raised.[35] He was well aware that his theory, especially his views on human origins, would not sit well with many people of faith. The idea that humans are descended from "beasts" has always been the most troubling aspect of Darwin's theory for believers[36] and remains a major reason why his theory is rejected even today.[37] No other theory has had such a huge impact on the understanding of humanity's meaning and purpose.[38] Darwin's published views on human evolution would have to wait for The Descent of Man,[39] which was published in 1871, twelve years after The Origin.

The introvert

For more than forty years, Darwin suffered from various physical symptoms.[40] He was unable to attend his father's funeral due to ill health.[41] In addition to his frequent illnesses, Darwin was an introvert who was comfortable being alone with his thoughts.[42] In order to clarify his thinking, he took daily walks around his property on a path he called "The Sandwalk." Darwin has been described as "... a gentle soul, a genial and generous man..."[43] and "...a gentle revolutionary.'[44] During his lifetime, Darwin assembled a large correspondence, in the range of 15,000 pieces, much of which is now available online.[45] By the 1870s, he was an international celebrity.[46] Darwin spoke at meetings occasionally and entertained visitors from time to time. Darwin had a large family and made it a priority to be with them. He had the luxury of being able to live in a rural area and to do his work with minimal interruption. Despite his introverted nature, Darwin was still part of the social milieu of the scientific community and had a few trusted confidants. Among them was Joseph Hooker (1817–1911).[47] Hooker was a botanist and explorer, and director of the Royal Botanical Gardens for twenty years. He was awarded the highest honors of British science. Like Darwin, Hooker travelled widely on scientific expeditions.[48]

Hooker and Charles Lyell were the first to be told of Darwin's theory.[49] In 1844, Darwin confessed to Hooker that he believed species could change.[50] Darwin said that finally revealing his long-secret theory was "like confessing a murder."[51] Thomas Henry (T.H.) Huxley (1825–1895) was another trusted individual. Because of his dominating, aggressive personality, Huxley came to be known as "Darwin's bulldog."[52] Others have called Huxley Darwin's Apostle Paul because "... like the apostle Paul, Huxley went through a profound conversion experience. And like Paul, who carried on where Jesus left off, Huxley did the same for Darwin."[53] Huxley had the psychological toughness needed to deal with the conflict Darwin's theory would surely cause, a psychological toughness the gentle introvert Darwin lacked.[54]

Origins

The Origin of Species (1859) was, in Darwin's own words, one long argument.[55] In it, Darwin compared what he called natural selection with the artificial selection carried out by animal and plant breeders. In artificial selection, breeders manipulate natural variation within species in order to meet a desired end or goal.[56] Darwin argued that nature's work of evolution is parallel to what human breeders do, writ large, and occurring over vast periods of time.[57] Young earth creationists often conflate abiogenesis, the actual origin of life arising from non-living matter, with evolution, the development of living organisms through time. It is important to keep in mind that Darwin's goal was to explain the origin of species, that is, the ongoing development of living things, which he called "descent with modification," not the origin (or the meaning) of life.[58] The actual origin of life is "...what Darwin called in his travel journal 'that mystery of mysteries' – the first appearance of new beings on this earth."[59] Scientists have been unable to explain how it is possible for inanimate chemicals to arrange themselves in such a way as to produce a living cell.[60]

Given the lack of scientific knowledge about inheritance in his day, Darwin had no way of knowing what the underlying genetic mechanism of evolution might be. He was unaware of genetics and DNA. Molecular biology was in the future. Lacking an adequate theory of genetics and heredity,[61] Darwin struggled to understand how traits were inherited. He speculated that variations arose accidentally.[62] He proposed a theory called pangenesis which was based on the inheritance of tiny hereditary particles called gemmules.[63] These particles, he speculated, could be transmitted from parent to offspring. Darwin, it turns out, was wrong about the blending of traits.[64] In the early days of his theory, Darwin thought external conditions induced variation.[65] In addition to his lack of genetic knowledge, Darwin's understanding of the fossil record was fragmentary at best.[66] Natural selection remained controversial until the 1930's, when the underlying mechanisms of inheritance were discovered.[67] At that time, classical genetics and selection theory were combined into what came to be called the Evolutionary Synthesis,[68] a term suggested by Julian Huxley (1887-1975) in 1942.[69]

Darwin's faith

Darwin grew increasingly ambivalent toward religion as the years passed.[70] He was sincerely concerned that he would be reviled for undermining faith and religion.[71] Darwin was of the opinion, however, that his theory should not be a problem for Christians. He believed that God had brought the creation into existence and originated life itself. God was therefore the primary cause. Then evolution took over and was controlled by secondary (i.e., natural) causes.[72]

Darwin's On the Origin of Species went through six, increasingly revised, editions.[73] In The Origin, Darwin made several positive references to the Creator.[74] In some editions, Darwin was willing to say that life was "breathed into" organisms by the Creator.[75] But, by 1863, in a letter to Joseph Hooker, Darwin revealed his growing ambivalence toward religion, saying that he regretted using the term "Creator."[76] Darwin's religious beliefs had already begun to fade during The Beagle journey. He eventually came to believe that the Old Testament was "a manifestly false history."[77] Darwin's faith was tested when his father died in 1848. His faith was tested, even more severely, when his ten-year-old daughter, Annie, died of tuberculosis, three days after Easter in 1851, eight years before the publication of The Origin.[78] Reflecting on his faith, Darwin wrote,

> *I can indeed hardly see how anyone ought to wish Christianity to be true; for, if so, the plain language of the* [New Testament] *text seems to show that the men who do not believe, & this would include my Father, Brother & almost all my best friends, will be everlastingly punished. And this is a damnable doctrine.*[79]

Emma Darwin was so troubled by this passage in her husband's autobiography that she removed it from the first published edition. Darwin became increasingly agnostic in the last thirty years of his life. By 1871, when he was in his early sixties, his religious faith had faded to agnosticism.[80] "I deserve to be called a theist" he said.[81] He did maintain, however, that he was never an atheist in the sense of denying the existence of God.[82] Darwin's wife Emma retained a strong Christian faith. She expressed her concerns to her husband about the status of his Christian salvation.[83] Darwin said, "I was very unwilling to give up my beliefs; disbelief crept over me at a very slow rate, but was at last complete."[84]

Caricatures

In the one hundred plus years since Darwin's death, anti-evolutionists have created a series of false caricatures.[85] For example, some claim that he deliberately proposed his theory in order to rationalize disbelief.[86] Karl Giberson says, "Charles Darwin is not a villain, and these portraits of him are irresponsible and malicious caricatures distorting him beyond recognition. His detractors rewrite history and invent motives."[87] One critic made the bizarre claim that Darwin returned to the Christian faith shortly before his death and that, on his deathbed, he denied the truth of evolution. This story has been called "a grotesque gloss on real historical events."[88] It is linked to Christian evangelist Elizabeth Cotton (1842-1922), who called herself "Lady Hope." In August 1915, more than thirty years after Darwin's death, a Baptist newspaper, the Watchman-Examiner, published a story Lady Hope had told a few days earlier at a Bible conference in Northfield, Massachusetts. She said that she had visited Darwin on his deathbed and found him reading the Bible. When she mentioned the Genesis creation story, he was distressed and babbled a little about how "unformed ideas" of his youth had spread like "wildfire" and how some had "made a religion of them."[89]

Throughout his lifetime, Darwin remained sensitive to the religious anxieties caused by his theory.[90] He wondered whether he might be criticized for his views, which seemed to make God's intervention in the development of living organisms superfluous.[91] Darwin knew that some would consider his theory evil for its negative impact on Christianity. Darwin wrote: "What a book a Devil's chaplain might write on the clumsy, wasteful, blundering, low and horridly cruel works of nature."[92] Darwin, however, maintained his membership in the Church of England until his death.[93] When he died in 1882, he was buried in Westminster Abbey with full honors.[94] An anthem was composed especially for the funeral by Frederick Bridge, abbey organist, based on Proverbs 3:13: "Blessed is the man who finds wisdom, the man who gains understanding."[95] (NIV) In our day, when American evangelicals visit Westminster Abbey, many ask the tour guides whether it is true that Darwin is buried there.[96] These individuals are surprised by Darwin's presence in the Abbey because they associate Darwin with atheism.

Evolution by natural selection

As we begin an in-depth discussion of Darwin's theory of evolution by natural selection, it is critically important to realize that the vast majority of evolutionary change, spread out as it is over immense periods of time, is inaccessible to direct common-sense observation.[97] One lifetime, or even a series of lifetimes, therefore, is not enough to perceive evolutionary change. Since there is no observable change in one human lifetime, common-sense observation insists that species, for example, are static, unchanging. The same is true of the perception of geological change,[98] or change in the heavens, cosmological change. Science, with its methodology and its technology, and a lot of plain old hard work, has dramatically overturned the ancient common-sense understandings of geology, of cosmology, of biology, and of time itself. Science has repeatedly demonstrated that information long thought to be obviously true was in fact incorrect.

Genetic variation

Darwin hypothesized that evolution is driven by the requirement that organisms adapt to ever-changing environments.[99] The environment presents organisms with challenges that must be solved in order to ensure survival.[100] Stephen Jay Gould (1941-2002) says, "In conventional Darwinian theory, the organism proposes and the environment disposes."[101] Darwin understood that the environment is the source of selection, but, as we mentioned, he did not know the actual source of the variation.[102] It is significant that the fuller understanding of genetic variation that has been gained after Darwin's death has greatly strengthened, not weakened, the original theory.[103] Scientists now know that one of the ways evolution works is by modifying pre-existing genes to take on new roles required by changing environments.[104] In addition, the genetic shuffling which takes place through sexual reproduction bestows on certain organisms features that increase their likelihood of survival and reproduction in a particular environment.[105] These advantages are passed on to future generations. "Survival of the fittest" is not the best description of natural selection. A more accurate expression would be, "survival of the fit enough."[106]

Mutation

Without genetic variation, evolution would not occur.[107] In other words, if a species consisted of genetically identical individuals to start with, that species would not evolve.[108] Sexual reproduction, with its continuous shuffling of the genetic deck,[109] makes it possible for new genetic variations to be gathered together quickly in an organism.[110] Sexual reproduction generates a variety of possible solutions, and the environment selects those that work best for the problem at hand.[111] Thus, chance variations that may be passed on to succeeding generations, together with natural selection, drive evolutionary change, adapting species to changing environments.[112] Approximately one in a million genetic copies differs from the original; this is called the mutation rate.[113] Most mutations, genetic typos, if you will, are neutral, and most typos that are not neutral are, in fact, deleterious.[114] There are about 100 mutations per genome per generation in mammals, which means that children typically have about

100 differences from their parents, differences resulting from genetic copying errors.[115] The genetic code is the canvas; the painter is the environment.[116] Populations are constantly playing a game of catch-up with environmental change.[117] Evolution continually balances an external force, (environmental change), with an internal force (genetic mutation).[118] Environmental pressures such as predator-prey interactions, sometimes called "arms races," are particularly effective at producing an evolutionary escalation.[119]

A difference between a copy of a gene and the original is called a mutation.[120] Darwin did not know that genes are strings of letters from a four-letter alphabet.[121] Since the discovery of DNA in the early 1950's, scientists now understand how the genetic copying machine works.[122] Unraveling the precise reasons for mutation was a scientific triumph, a revelation that took place after Darwin's death and greatly strengthened his theory.[123] A mutation may be produced by an agent in the external environment, such as chemicals, radiation, or heat.[124] Creationists mistakenly believe that mutations always involve a loss of information, arguing that mutations are consistently negative and harmful.[125] Such is not the case, however. Mutations continually replenish the variability of the gene pool.[126] They provide the raw material, the variation, that is subsequently shaped by natural selection.[127] It is important to stress that mutations may be beneficial, neutral, or deleterious.[128] Since mutations can duplicate, rearrange, or change literally any gene, it follows that they can also produce any variation.[129] When a mistake in copying DNA occurs, there are no intermediate chemical forms. That change has a direct effect on the code of the gene.[130] Each mutation is a tiny experiment; a genetic search-engine if you will.[131]

Whether mutations are beneficial or not depends ultimately on the environment.[132] On rare occasions, a mutation will offer a selective advantage which may be spread to subsequent generations.[133] Richard Lenski, microbiologist at Michigan State University, is best known for a long-term evolution experiment. His project, which began back in 1988, has grown 12 populations of E. coli bacteria over 65,000 generations, keeping track of mutations which have occurred in those populations. Back in 2003, Lenski discovered that one strain of E. coli had evolved the ability to use citrate as an energy source, something never before seen in this type of bacteria. Lenski reiterates the scientific consensus that most mutations are harmful or at best neutral. He says, "Only the rare nugget in the mine is a beneficial mutation." Bacteria with a higher mutation rate are more likely to discover those beneficial mutations – those "rare nuggets," in Lenski's words – but, on the other hand, bacteria with a higher mutation rate are also more likely to produce harmful mutations. The benefit of a higher mutation rate, says Lenski, is an additional capacity for genetic exploration in response to environmental pressures. The genius of evolution is that it can generate this kind of diversity and consistently discover avenues of improvement.[134] Based on these principles, modern medicine is able to directly measure the rate of mutation of various microbes, and observe which of these mutations confer a survival advantage that is passed on. Evolution therefore is not something that happened some time ago in the historical record, but is observable today in species that reproduce quickly, like bacteria.

Contrary to claims made by anti-evolutionists, natural selection is a contingent, not a random or chance process.[135] For Darwin, "chance" means "contingency."[136] Contingent processes are dependent on certain other factors for their existence. Therefore, the exact path evolution takes cannot be predicted at the outset.[137] Contingency is pervasive in evolution, including the mutations and genetic recombinations we have been discussing.[138] In evolution, contingency is expressed in the form of mutation, as well as the shuffling of the genetic deck of cards that takes place through sexual reproduction.[139] Evolution is a tinkering process. It is opportunistic,[140] working with the genetic material it has at hand.[141] Evolution works with structures that already exist and seldom finds perfect solutions. It improvises and re-purposes. It finds new uses for old parts.[142]

Nature has to make do with what it has rather than with what it would like to have.[143] Evolution may take a structure that is functioning perfectly well in one capacity and shift it to another use. It often adds parts that "... expand, improve, and sometimes completely refashion living systems."[144] Thus, important evolutionary innovations often come from organs or systems that have been re-purposed.[145] Gene duplications are pre-adaptations, not necessarily useful at the time they occur, but waiting for an opportune time in the future, when they may be re-purposed for other functions.[146] Previously neutral features, called spandrels, may become part of a new evolutionary structure or feature at a later time.[147] Exaptation refers to the evolutionary re-use of machinery for new purposes. This functional shift is one of the secrets of natural selection's success.[148]

Convergent evolution

In evolutionary biology, convergence refers to unrelated organisms that superficially resemble each other because evolution has adapted them to similar lifestyles and similar environments.[149] Convergent evolution demonstrates the power of natural selection to craft optimal structures independently.[150] Convergent evolution often fashions equivalent solutions by entirely different routes.[151] There are only so many good ways of building things, given the starting constraints, and evolution consistently finds them.[152] The history of life has many examples of amazing similarity, evolved independently.[153] Replay the tape of life, says Simon Conway-Morris, and you will find remarkable similarities in the kinds of organisms that evolve.[154] Convergence often occurs in species that have been geographically isolated for millions of years. For example, the eye has developed independently in vastly different organisms at least seven times over the course of natural history.[155] Geographical isolation has produced multiple examples of similar creatures evolving separately, with biological form stumbling on the same solution.[156]

Speciation

Speciation is "...the evolutionary process by which new biological species arise."[157] A simple way to explain speciation is to say that "... environmental pressures confronting genetic mutation results in speciation."[158] Allopatric ("living in another place") speciation is the cornerstone of modern evolutionary biology.[159] It occurs when populations of the same species become isolated from each other to an extent that prevents or interferes with genetic interchange.[160] The term allopatric speciation was popularized by Ernst Mayr (1904-2005).[161] Sympatric ("living in the same place") speciation, on the other hand, is the process through which new species evolve from a single ancestral species while inhabiting the same geographic region.[162] Species have finite lifetimes.[163] Eighteenth-century French scientist Georges Buffon (1707-1788) gathered fossil evidence showing that certain species had in fact become extinct. This argument differed from the reigning paradigm of the day which held that species were unchanging.[164] According to Ernst Mayr, "Buffon brought the idea of evolution into the realm of science. More than anyone else, he was responsible for the acceptance of a long-time scale for the history of the earth."[165]

Extinction is the fate of species that fail to adapt quickly enough to unexpected and rapid environmental change.[166] Several global extinctions have shaped life on earth.[167] More than 98 percent of all species that have ever lived no longer exist.[168] Massive extinctions clear the deck for a fresh round of evolutionary change.[169] Rapid evolutionary change is possible when the environment changes radically or when extinction vacates ecological niches.[170] Success after a mass extinction may be due to features evolved for other reasons in earlier times.[171] It often takes five to ten million years for ecosystems to regain a semblance of normalcy after extinctions. After a major extinction event, the world's genetic information passes through an incredibly tight bottleneck.[172] Evolution works on what survives.[173]

Certain basic forms underlie the structure of all vertebrate animals.[174] Vertebrates have a unified architecture because they evolved from a common ancestor.[175] Modified forms in different organisms retain traces of their original.[176] "Arm of man, wing of bird, front leg of horse, flipper of whale," all show similarity due to common descent.[177] All vertebrate forelimbs are similar, because, as molecular biology has discovered, they are derived from the same embryonic germ layers.[178]

Fossils

A fossil is a remnant or trace of an organism from a past geologic age, such as a skeleton or leaf imprint, embedded and preserved in the earth's crust.[179] Fossils provide a rare window into the ancient world. A fossil is defined as

"...the remains of a once living organism, generally one that lived prior to the last glacial period (e.g. 10,000 years before present). They include skeletons, tracks, impressions, trails, borings and casts. Fossils are usually found in hard rock, but not always (e.g. amber)."[180]

Darwin was aware of fossil evidence, and he also knew that this evidence, although helpful, was severely limited. Much of the time, Darwin was on the defensive trying to explain why there were so many gaps in the fossil record.[181] In an attempt to illustrate his point, he used the metaphor of a book with many pages missing.[182] The majority of organisms that have lived on this earth have left no trace of their existence behind,[183] and when fossilization does occur, usually only hard parts are preserved.[184] This means that fossils constitute a distinctly biased sample of ancient life. In addition, the fossil record does not tell us how species change occurs.

Despite these caveats, however, and given the treasure trove of fossils that scientists now possess, the notion that they provide important information about past events in the history of life on our planet has been repeatedly reinforced.[185] Fortunately, the number and quality of fossils now available to researchers is vastly improved. Given the constraints limiting fossilization, paleontologists have still been able to describe an estimated 300,000 different types of fossil organisms.[186]

The requirements of fossilization normally preclude the preservation of the soft parts of an organism, but occasional rare exceptions do occur. For example, some extremely rare soft-bodied fossils have been found in China and at the Burgess Shale near the town of Field, in southeastern British Columbia, Canada.[187] The exquisite state of preservation of these organisms has provided researchers with valuable details about their structure. What cannot be determined, however, is information about reproduction or the transmission of genetic information.[188]

Intensive study of the Burgess Shale reveals that a wide variety of animals burst onto the evolutionary scene in an event known as the Cambrian Explosion, around 530 million years ago, (see chapter 9) In a geologically brief time span of as little as ten million years, marine animals evolved most of the basic body forms that we observe in modern groups. Among the organisms preserved in fossils from the Cambrian explosion are relatives of crustaceans and starfish, sponges, mollusks, worms, chordates, and algae.[189]

Anti-evolutionists argue that no transitional fossil forms exist. The creationist argument is countered by fossil evidence of the evolution of many species, with some of the best examples being whales as well as horses.[190] With regard to whale evolution, biologist Richard Dawkins says:

> *... the once rather scanty fossil record of whale evolution has been convincingly filled out, mostly by a new trove from Pakistan. The gradual disappearance of the hind limbs, the transformation of the front limbs from walking legs to swimming fins, and the flattening of the tail into flukes, are among the changes that emerged in elegant cascade.*[191]

Transitions from reptiles to mammals, and mammals to whales are clearly evident in the fossil record.[192] Since species are constantly evolving over long periods of time, much longer than a single human lifetime, there are no true missing links at any particular time in evolutionary history, only points on a continuum. Think of the color-choice circles in some word-processor programs. Each pixel on the circle is a point in its own right, but is also a point on a continuum, for example, from blue blending towards red.[193] The creationist argument that no transitional fossils exist is without merit, divorced from the evidence.[194] Many examples of transitional organisms (that is, transitional from one major animal group to another, in this case, from fish to amphibian) have been discovered. One of the most important is Tiktaalik Roseae. A University of Chicago website describes Tiktaalik this way:

Tiktaalik roseae, better known as the "fishapod," is a 375-million-year old fossil fish which was discovered in the Canadian Arctic in 2004. Its discovery sheds light on a pivotal point in the history of life on earth: when the very first fish ventured out onto land. Tiktaalik looks like a cross between the primitive fish it lived amongst and the first four-legged animals (a group called "tetrapods" from tetra-, meaning four, and -pod, meaning foot. Actually, all animals that descended from these pioneer amphibians, including us, can be called tetrapods). Tiktaalik lived about 12 million years before the first tetrapods (which are approximately 363 million years old). So, the existence of tetrapod features in a fish like Tiktaalik is significant because it marks the earliest appearance of these novel features in the fossil record.[195]

Richard Dawkins adds,

If you were to meet a real live Tiktaalik, snout to snout, you might start back as if threatened by a crocodile, for that is what its face resembled. A crocodile's head on a salamander's trunk, attached to a fish's rear end and tail. Unlike any fish, Tiktaalik had a neck. It could turn its head. In almost every particular, Tiktaalik is the perfect missing link, perfect, because it almost exactly splits the difference between fish and amphibian, and perfect because it is missing no longer.[196]

Preservation of soft anatomy

Paleogenomics is the process of recovering and sequencing the DNA of extinct organisms. Svante Paabo has developed techniques enabling researchers to extract, clone, and sequence long stretches of DNA from animals that have been dead for tens of thousands of years.[197] Paleogenomics made it possible to sequence the DNA of hominins as far back as 80,000 years.[198] The preservation of soft anatomy, such as organs, skin, feathers, and even individual cells, has been demonstrated from the rock record for decades, albeit an extremely rare occurrence. There are no established limits on how long organic molecules can survive in rocks, especially when encased in hard minerals, such as silica.[199]

Scientists have recently broken through another time barrier in their search for ancient proteins from fossilized teeth and bones, raising the possibility of using proteins to study extinct animals and humans that lived more than one million years ago. Until now, the oldest sequenced proteins came from a 700,000-year-old horse in Canada's Yukon territory. Geneticists recently reported that they had extracted proteins from 3.8-million-year-old ostrich egg shells in Laetoli, Tanzania, and from the 1.7-million-year-old tooth enamel of several extinct animals in Dmanisi, Georgia. The teeth came from extinct horses, rhinos, and deer. These studies show that such ancient proteins can survive.[200]

A few years ago, an amateur fossil hunter in England found a brown, pebble-sized lump on a beach. Scientists have now determined that the lump is the first-known fossilized brain tissue from a dinosaur. Scientists announced the discovery at a Society of Vertebrate Paleontology annual meeting in Utah. Finding fossilized soft tissue is very rare. Researchers believe that this brain tissue was preserved in a very special way shortly after the animal's death: "What we think happened is that this particular dinosaur died in or near a body of water, and its head ended up partially buried in the sediment at the bottom."[201] In 2015, scientist Lida Xing came across a beautiful and curious piece at an amber market in Myitkyina, Myanmar, likely destined to become a piece of jewelry. Trapped inside the yellow piece was a feather that others had overlooked as belonging to a plant. But Xing knew that it could be something more. And it was. It was a piece of 99 million-year-old history, a dinosaur feather."[202] The amber contained bones, soft tissue, and even feathers. While individual dinosaur-era feathers have been found in amber, and evidence for feathered dinosaurs is captured in fossil impressions, this is the first time that scientists were able to clearly associate well-preserved feathers with a dinosaur, and in turn gain a better understanding of the evolution and structure of dinosaur feathers.

Evo-devo

Modern molecular biology provides additional support for Darwin's theory. Molecular biology has uncovered compelling evidence that animals and plants have their evolutionary history written all over them.[203] All complex animal phyla, that is, groups that have a genetic relationship or common origin, have retained an extensive set of very ancient common genetic blueprints for building bodies called hox genes.[204] Hox genes are master planning genes.[205] They control the arrangement of the body plan during the formation and development of an embryo.[206] They sequentially order the manufacture of bodily parts.[207] They are "...an essential part of the blueprint and toolkit enabling the body plan to get built, turning genes on and off in the proper sequence."[208]

The most compelling evidence that living organisms share the same ancestor is that they share the same basic genetic code. The gene for an eye in a fruit fly will make an eye in a mouse.[209] An unexpected result of modern molecular studies of the genome, the complete set of genes or genetic material present in a cell or organism, was the discovery of the great age of many genes, including these hox genes.[210] At the present time, evidence from molecular genetics is currently being added to fossil evidence, powerfully supplementing evolutionary theory.[211] This new evidence is the result of work done in a relatively new area of study called evolutionary developmental biology.

Evo-devo combines developmental biology with evolutionary studies. Evolutionary biologists seek to understand how organisms evolve and change their shape and form. Developmental biologists, on the other hand, try to understand how alterations in gene expression and function lead to changes in body shape and pattern. In evo-devo, biologists use an individual organism's developmental gene expression patterns to explain how groups of organisms evolved.[212]

Simon Conway-Morris says: "Recent research into the developmental processes in animals has been little short of spectacular."[213] Evo-devo has discovered genetic mechanisms that can lead to rapid evolution. That is, small changes in certain ancient genes can result in dramatic morphological (relating to the form or structure of an organism) change.[214] In other words, a new body plan might involve a relatively modest molecular reorganization.[215] These ancient developmental genes can change everything at once, all over the body. Gary Fugle summarizes the general consensus among evolutionary biologists:

> *Recent studies in molecular developmental biology... show that there can actually be very substantial evolutionary modifications by reshuffling only existing genetic variability, particularly major effects from different combinations of developmental control genes. The addition of entirely new options through beneficial mutations is understood to be a fundamental mechanism for major transformations.*[216]

Sean Carroll has called these conserved genes and developmental mechanisms "the toolkit."[217] Interestingly, the Cambrian explosion occurred after much of the toolkit had already been assembled.[218] Hox genes emerged long before the Cambrian explosion, so something else must be involved in the great diversification of body plans evident at that time.[219] Scientists now realize that mutations in the Hox gene system almost always generate lethal conditions.[220] According to Gary Fugle, however, changes in hox genes are the ultimate source of much of the novelty in organisms. Natural selection then operates on this novelty.[221] Meyer quotes evolutionary biologist Sean Carroll as saying, "...some argue that the emergence of hox genes in Precambrian organisms may have triggered the Cambrian explosion by providing the raw materials for the diversification of body plans."[222]

Genomes

A genome is the complete set of genes or genetic material present in a cell or organism.[223] The human genome, for example, is made up of three billion base pairs. Nearly every cell in the body has a copy of the genome.[224] Scientists are now able to sequence an organism's genome in a short period of time.[225] Thanks to modern genetic discoveries, and to a substantial array of fossil evidence, scientists have come to understand that the story of human evolution is written into our genome, and they are quickly gaining proficiency in reading that story.[226]

Consilience

Evolutionary biology is built on a massive drawing together (consilience) of evidence from many disciplines.[227] Support for evolution comes from scientific disciplines as diverse as geology (sequential deposition), paleontology (fossils), cosmology (deep time), biology (comparative anatomy, DNA and genomics, developmental similarities, comparative biochemistry), and biogeography (convergent evolution).[228] As we have already mentioned, amazing fossil discoveries supporting the theory of evolution have occurred in the last fifty years.[229] It must be emphasized, however, that the fossil record, important as it is, is only one source of evidence supporting evolution. In recent years, critical additional information has come from developmental biology and from the study of DNA.[230] So now, even without fossils, scientists would know about common descent through DNA.[231] Incredibly, creationists pretend that the only evidence for evolution is fossil evidence; mysteriously, all other evidence is ignored.[232]

Punctuated equilibrium

In 1972, Stephen Jay Gould and Niles Eldredge proposed a non-gradualistic model of evolution called punctuated equilibria.[233] This model is based on the idea that the fossil record reveals that evolutionary history is composed of fits and starts. Punctuated equilibria challenges the idea that evolutionary change occurs gradually over very long periods of time. This perspective highlights the lack of transitional forms in the fossil record, as well as a phenomenon called stasis, where, for long periods of time, there is little or no change in a species. Basic body types often remain unchanged for tens or hundreds of millions of years.[234] Some scientists have humorously labelled punctuated equilibrium "evolution by jerks." Punctuated equilibria advocates have returned the favor by characterizing gradualistic evolution as "evolution by creeps."[235]

Luke Janssen says:

> *To explain why the fossil record looks like it skips and jumps: imagine watching a sunflower seed planted in your backyard garden beside a pond containing some frog's eggs. You know for a fact that the seed slowly unfurls itself into a seven-foot-tall plant, and that the amphibian eggs produce tadpoles that gradually morph into frogs. But now imagine that you only get snapshots of the seed and tadpoles whenever a lightning bolt strikes: a sudden flash and another frame is added to the movie. Sometimes you have to wait three weeks before the next set of pictures is taken, and at that time you get two dozen more frames. Then another two weeks before another dozen or three are taken. And so on until the end of summer. What are you left with? A series of snapshots that accurately captures the growth changes in the sunflower and frogs, but does so in fits and starts as you replay the movie. Just like the striking of the lightning bolts, fossilization is a sporadic event requiring very specific conditions.*[236]

Natural selection

A sometimes heated discussion has been taking place in evolutionary biology with regard to the status of natural selection – specifically, whether natural selection is in fact the main factor in evolution.[237] Charles Darwin believed that natural selection was the main driver of evolution, but not the only one.[238] Intelligent design proponent Michael Denton says that natural selection tunes the piano, but does not compose the melodies.[239] There is general agreement among biologists that natural selection by itself is insufficient to explain the development of new animal body plans.[240] It must be kept in mind, however, that these debates are not a denial of the theory. They simply raise legitimate questions about the details of the theory, not the theory itself.[241] Kevin Laland points out that all scientific theories, including evolution, must be open to new ideas and data. In the last few years, biological knowledge has grown rapidly. Advances in genetics, epigenetics and developmental biology have prompted scientists to reconsider the relationship between genes, organisms and the environment, with implications for the origins of diversity and the direction and speed of evolution. The latest findings are critical of Richard Dawkins' "selfish gene" argument. It now seems that organisms play active roles in their own development and that of their descendants, so that they impose direction on evolution.[242]

Physicist Garth Huber asserts:

> *It is extraordinarily likely that Darwin's theory of evolution will eventually be replaced by an even more comprehensive theory. In principle, there is controversy in all aspects of science. It is only by the continual probing of accepted theories and explanations that shortcomings are found which require new explanations. The existence of controversy in evolutionary biology only indicates that it is an active field of scientific inquiry. The controversies in this field over the years have provided additional support for evolution far beyond those originally envisaged by Darwin and not the opposite. It is certainly acceptable to poke holes in evolutionary theory and, in fact, that is welcomed within science. The replacing theory, however, must be superior in predictive power.*[243]

PART TWO

Grappling with Darwin's dangerous idea

In the mid-nineteenth century, Charles Darwin extended the scientific revolution into the biological realm. Darwin's theory of evolution by natural selection had a particularly significant impact on the Christian church and its scriptural accounts of creation. Evolutionary theory challenged the way individuals, both religious and secular, thought about the history of living things, including humans. Evolutionary theory led some to rejoice and caused tremendous anxiety for others. Atheists saw in Darwin's theory a powerful tool for attacking religious faith. Believers on the other hand quickly realized that Darwin's theory challenged some of their most basic doctrines. There were several different responses to Darwin's theory. Atheists happily removed God from a discussion of origins. Some Christians revisited the scriptures to see if there was any God-pleasing way to accommodate the scientific consensus regarding an ancient earth. Others came to the conclusion that God used evolution as his creative method. Still others rejected Darwin outright, arguing that the earth is young – as young as six thousand years – and that evolution contradicts their version of a plain reading of the word of God. And some argued that the universe bears abundant evidence of design and God's direct intervention in the creative process, claiming that evolution by natural selection is just not up to the task.

6. ATHEISTIC EVOLUTION

Overview

In eighteenth century France, a few philosophers argued that science ought to replace religion. And in nineteenth century England, no sooner had Charles Darwin's Origin of Species appeared than a few radical atheists seized what they took to be an opportunity to use evolution to attack, and eventually replace, the Christian faith. They were pleased to see that Darwin's theory could explain life's development without the need for divine intervention. Some sought to make evolution the basis of a new secular religion. These developments more than a century ago are precursors to the so-called warfare model we see in some parts of the Christian church today.

After The Origin was published, Thomas Henry Huxley congratulated Darwin for coming up with a theory that would assist in killing superstitious beliefs once and for all. Physicist John Tyndall argued that science is inherently superior to religion. And Herbert Spencer, like Huxley, wanted to make Darwin's theory the basis of a new religion. Spencer applied his "survival of the fittest" idea to human society, arguing that superior individuals naturally dominate the weak. Spencer's proposal, which came to be known as Social Darwinism, has caused problems for the theory of evolution ever since. Spencer's ideas, it should be pointed out, were never sanctioned by Darwin himself.

Those nineteenth century radical atheists have been replaced by a contemporary group with equally radical views. Often labeled the New Atheists, these individuals have succeeded in convincing many Christians, especially evangelicals, that the theory of evolution comes shrink-wrapped in atheism and, as such, is a real and continuing threat to traditional religious values. The New Atheism is a form of secular fundamentalism, not all that different from the Christian fundamentalism it abhors, and equally dogmatic.

Christianity's core beliefs, I have argued, are inaccessible to scientific investigation. But many in the general public, and many in the church as well, are unaware of that fact. In reality, there ought to be no conflict between science, properly defined, and religious faith. As I noted in chapter 2, scientific methodology as it is most commonly understood acknowledges that believers who have adopted an evolutionary perspective are free to practice their faith without interference. Young earth and intelligent design proponents continue to foster the conflict or warfare narrative, however, knowing that it is to their advantage to do so. Science ought to be able to assist Christians in developing a better understanding of God's method of creation. And religion can provide science with critically important ethical guidelines.

Divine intervention

An atheistic emphasis in evolution appeared soon after the publication of Darwin's Origin. Opponents of religion realized that Darwin's theory could be used to further their agenda. Those individuals were prepared to use evolutionary science as a weapon to attack religion, promoting what was, in their opinion, the superiority of reason over superstition.[1] One anxious Christian claimed that Darwin had come up with "... a theory which virtually annihilates religion and gives us a universe without God."[2] Militant atheists promoted the idea of an ongoing development of living organisms without the need for divine intervention. Natural selection, it was argued, was fully able, without God, to bring about an amazing diversity of life-forms. Any design in nature was said to be illusory.

Sociologist Susan Budd claims that many nineteenth-century British scientists, including Darwin himself, lost their faith, not because of scientific discoveries, but because of fundamental disagreements over Christian teachings.[3] Many individuals, Budd says, became apostate because of theodicy, the problem of the pervasive evil and suffering in the world contrasted to the Biblical teaching of God's goodness.[4] Not surprisingly, in the late nineteenth century, talk of conflict between science and religion increased in intensity (see chapter 1), a theme which lives on in large parts of the Christian church today.[5] The current generation of radical atheists, with their deliberately inflammatory rhetoric, have succeeded in mobilizing the creationist troops.[6] Intolerant and insensitive comments from the new atheists have provoked an equal and opposite reaction from anti-evolutionists.[7] When anti-evolutionists are attacked, like a hedgehog, they roll up into a ball and put out their spikes. The same, of course, is true of the new atheists. None of us is immune to over-reacting to a perceived threat.

Thomas henry huxley

For Thomas Henry Huxley (1825-1895), Darwin's theory provided a powerful argument against religion. Huxley praised Darwin for proposing "... the most effective new weapon for killing superstitious beliefs and clearing the field for rational materialism."[8] Huxley's grandson, Julian (1887-1975), followed in his grandfather's footsteps, advocating a religion without revelation based on evolutionary thinking.[9] In Julian Huxley's new faith, there would be no need or room for the supernatural.[10] British physicist John Tyndall (1820-1893) was another atheist who used science to promote secularization. Tyndall, too, proclaimed the superiority of science over religion.[11] In the late nineteenth century, most British physicists were religious and political conservatives. But Tyndall strongly supported Darwin's theory and worked tirelessly to disparage religion and praise science. Tyndall proposed a clear distinction between science (which he associated with knowledge and rationality) and religion (which he connected with faith and spirituality). As president of the British Association for the Advancement of Science, Tyndall gave a speech in 1874 in which he argued that religious sentiment should not be permitted to intrude into science.

Herbert spencer

Herbert Spencer (1820-1903) set out to create a new religion built on the foundation of evolutionary principles.[12] Spencer gained notoriety for his criticisms of traditional religion, and was frequently condemned by religious thinkers for allegedly advocating atheism and materialism. Unlike T. H. Huxley, however, whose agnosticism was of a more radical nature, Spencer insisted that his goal was never to use science to undermine religion, but only to find a way to reconcile the two. Spencer is best known for his Social Darwinism,[13] which emerged in the 1870's and was an attempt to draw a moral code for humanity out of the theory of evolution.[14] Spencer believed that "... groups or individuals dominate others by virtue of an inherent biological superiority."[15] Spencer argued that the "survival of the fittest," (a phrase he, not Darwin, coined) is nature's way and should also be the way individuals deal with others.[16] Spencer advocated cutthroat competitive practices in business and denigrated government efforts to help the poor.[17] According to historian and philosopher Michael Ruse, evolutionary theory was hijacked by Spencer's Social Darwinism.[18] Social Darwinism, never advocated by Darwin himself,[19] has been described as an "... odious misapplication of Darwinian thinking."[20] Spencer has been criticized for his "... appalling moral views."[21] Social Darwinism is a secular example of eisegesis, in this case, inappropriately reading nature's harsh realities into human behavior.[22] It is also an example of the naturalistic fallacy, confusing scientific description with moral and ethical prescription, transforming the descriptive "is" of evolutionary theory into the prescriptive "ought" of Social Darwinism.[23]

Eugenics

The goal of eugenics (from the Greek, "well-born") is to improve the genetic quality of the human race. Eugenics is a social philosophy that promotes higher rates of sexual reproduction among those believed to have desired traits (positive eugenics), or reduced rates of sexual reproduction and the sterilization of those believed to have less-desired or undesired traits (negative eugenics).[24] Both Social Darwinism and eugenics are guilty of reading into evolutionary theory concepts Darwin never intended. Biologists and historians agree that natural selection is a description of biological phenomena only, and was never intended as a moral guide for human society.[25]

Nineteenth century arguments promoting a new religion based on evolutionary thinking carry over into our day. Biologist E.O. Wilson, for example, considers the theory of evolution to be a new sacred narrative, a new and alternate mythology.[26] Wilson's goal, like that of Philip Kitcher,[27] is to substitute a kind of secular humanism, based on evolutionary thought, for traditional religion.[28] Wilson claims that religion can be explained from an evolutionary point of view. In his opinion, human behavior, including religion, is best explained by biological origins and genetics, a view that has come to be known as evolutionary psychology.[29] Wilson is willing to admit, however, that traditional religion does have beneficial societal effects.[30]

New atheists

Hyper-partisans reside at both extremes of today's science-religion debate. New Atheism is a social and political movement that began around the year 2000, stridently promoting atheism and secularism. It is advocated by a number of atheist academics who argue that "... religion should not simply be tolerated but should be countered, criticized, and exposed by rational argument wherever its influence arises."[31] The Four Horsemen of the New Atheism are Sam Harris, Richard Dawkins, Daniel Dennett, and the late Christopher Hitchens (1949-2011).[32] Secularization is their goal and science is their weapon of choice. Much of the anger these individuals direct at religion can be traced back to 9/11. Christian paleontologist Simon Conway Morris laments the new atheists' "... belligerence, contempt, loathing, derision, condescension, arrogance and sheer bad manners."[33] For the new atheists, evolution is a powerful philosophical sword that can be used to strike at the heart of Christian truth claims.[34] Scientism, as we noted in chapter 2, claims that science, not religion, is the ultimate arbiter of truth.[35] M.I.T. physicist Ian Hutchinson criticizes scientism's argument that "... science, modeled on the natural sciences, is the only source of real knowledge."[36] Philosopher Daniel Dennett, in his book Consciousness Explained,[37] says, "There is only one sort of stuff – the physical stuff of physics, chemistry and physiology."[38]

Commitment to the scientific method, as we have seen, does not require a corresponding commitment to scientific absolutism or atheism.[39] The scientism of the new atheists plays directly into the hands of creationists and provides them with a gift – a visible enemy to vilify. The hubris of scientism is a mirror image of the prideful self-confidence characteristic of anti-evolutionism.[40] Both sides are vulnerable to denigrating those with views very different from their own. Intelligent design advocate Stephen Meyer, for example, describes a troubling situation involving Dr. Richard Sternberg at the Smithsonian. In 2004, Sternberg, then editor of an academic journal, The Proceedings of the Biological Society of Washington, approved a pro-intelligent design article written by Meyer to be peer-reviewed and then published, a decision which caused great unrest among scientists. According to Meyer, false statements and claims were made against Sternberg. Sternberg's professional qualifications were questioned. This situation, to the degree that it is true, reflects poorly on the scientific community.[41]

The new atheists argue that religion, especially its fundamentalist expressions, is the source of some of the most serious problems around the world. They take an all-or-nothing approach, arguing that humanity would be better off without religion. Evolutionist and philosopher Michael Ruse has expressed his concern that new atheists like Dawkins and Dennett are making it difficult for mainstream advocates of evolution like himself to avoid being lumped together in the public mind with those few scientists who are radical enemies of religion.[42] Unfortunately, in any debate, the loudest voices are most likely to be heard, and strident new atheist voices tend to skew public opinion.[43] Research by sociologist Elaine Ecklund has shown that the new atheists are a much smaller group than most people believe. Ecklund's research shows that the new atheists comprise only about 5 percent of all scientists. They appear to be a much larger group because of the media coverage they garner.[44] Based on what the general public hears in the media, many believe that scientists not only lack faith, but are actively opposed to religion.[45] The unabashed scientism of the new atheists says to religious believers, in effect, "Render to Caesar the things that are Caesar's, and to God the things that Caesar says he can have."[46]

In his 1980 television series, Cosmos, Carl Sagan (1934-1996) famously said, "The cosmos is all there is or ever was or ever will be."[47] This statement caused angst in the scientific community, and with many unbelievers as well. Nobel laureate, biologist Francis Crick (1916-2004), expressed typical new atheist all-or-nothing-thinking when he says, "If some of the Bible is manifestly wrong, why should any of it be accepted?"[48] Richard Dawkins glowingly describes his conversion from religious belief to atheism as a "Road to Damascus" experience.[49] Dawkins claims that evolution has provided atheism with the firmest intellectual foundation it has ever had.[50] Dawkins agrees with fellow new atheist, philosopher Daniel Dennett, who argues that "religion doesn't just disable, it honors the disability."[51] Dawkins alienated Christians even further when he said that faith is a kind of mental illness, an excuse not to evaluate evidence.[52] When Dawkins was asked by science journalist Gordy Slack whether the existence of God was a question science could answer, he clearly betrayed his scientism by answering "Absolutely!"[53] Like many young earth creationists, Dawkins cannot bring himself to read the literature of his opponents.[54]

Alister McGrath accuses Dawkins of "... endless digressions, exaggerations and misunderstandings, of using shock and awe rhetoric."[55] Dawkins, one critic complains, contributes nothing but hard feelings to the discussion.[56] Daniel Dennett adds fuel to the fire by describing religion as a harmful parasite.[57] In his book Darwin's Dangerous Idea, (1995) Dennett compares evolutionary theory to a universal acid which "...eats through our most cherished assumptions."[58] Evolution's universal acid, says Dennett,[59] "... eats through just about every traditional concept, and leaves in its wake a revolutionized worldview, with most of the old landmarks still recognizable, but transformed in fundamental ways."[60] Gordy Slack characterizes the new atheists as "...hard-core, Harley-driving, helmet-free materialists."[61] Stephen Jay Gould describes such people as happy fools who live in a one-dimensional world. They think they know everything because they form their own entire universe.[62] At the end of the day, the New Atheism is an interesting amalgam of scientific fact and personal opinion.[63] The new atheists' philosophical and theological claims are often cloaked in scientific rhetoric.[64] Ironically, as scientists, they are very careful scholars; as polemicists they are not. Similar to the anti-evolutionists they revile, they are overconfident in their own version of reality.[65]

Science and atheism

Christians must not base their opinions only on the loudest voices in this debate.[66] Much like his young earth cousins, Phillip Johnson (1940-), the father of intelligent design creationism, labored valiantly to make evolution's extremists and hard-liners seem normative. And, like their intelligent design cousins, anti-evolutionists consistently link evolutionary theory with atheism, knowing full well that most Americans are uncomfortable with atheism.[67] Both groups, the anti-evolutionists and the new atheists, have set up a false dichotomy, arguing that one must choose either Christianity or evolution, but not both.[68] Significantly, a recent Rice University study revealed that a significant percentage of British scientists are critical of Richard Dawkins' brand of radical atheism. Those scientists claim that Dawkins misrepresents scientists, and gives the general public the wrong impression about what science is capable of and what constitutes the legitimate boundaries of scientific investigation. Researchers did not specifically ask scientists about Dawkins, but forty-eight of the scientists interviewed volunteered comments about Dawkins anyway and nearly 80 percent of that group expressed concern that he misrepresents science to the public. One biology professor said "Although there is a lot of truth behind what he says, he does it in a way that I think is deliberately designed to alienate religious people."[69]

The new atheists mistakenly assume that scientific concordism, the proposition that the Bible is error-free in both doctrine and science[70] is in fact the majority Christian position.[71] Both anti-evolutionists and new atheists share the warfare thesis – the belief that there is a deep and abiding conflict and distrust between science and religion. What we are seeing, according to Niles Eldredge, is "... no simple clash between science and religion but rather between two religions."[72] The dogmatizing theologian, says Bernard Ramm (1916-1992), has a blood brother in the dogmatic materialist.[73] Individuals at both extremes of this debate often employ inflammatory rhetoric and a selective manipulation of the facts.[74] Neither group holds a monopoly on tactlessness and paranoia.[75] A sizable minority of scientists are believers, many of whom are Christians. Joan Roughgarden, in her book Evolution & Christian Faith (2006) says, "A great many scientists... are active Christians and proud of being both a Christian and a scientist at the same time."[76]

Many believing scientists hesitate to share their faith[77] because it is such a volatile issue.[78] Christians must not let amateur theologians like Richard Dawkins do their theology for them.[79] Neither should amateur scientists, like the young earth creationists, presume to tell scientists how to do their work. Michael Ruse once sent emails to Daniel Dennett and Richard Dawkins making the point that these two men were unintentionally alienating Christians of goodwill, including those who advocate theistic evolution.[80] Ruse said, "We are in a fight and we need to make allies in the fight, not simply alienating everyone of goodwill."[81] Because Ruse has taken this middle-of-the-road position, recognizing concerns held by Christians and by the scientific community alike, he has been attacked by partisans on both sides of the debate.[82]

Like Richard Dawkins, Michael Ruse is an atheist. But, unlike Dawkins and the new atheists, Ruse refuses to pit science against religion because, in his opinion, they ask different sorts of questions. Ruse laments the unhealthy tenor that the science-religion debate has adopted, especially by some on the side of science. Ruse says there are some important questions outside the bounds of science such as 'Why is there something rather than nothing?' and 'Does life have a purpose?' If religion wants to answer questions like these, he says, science has no right to object.[83] For his part, Richard Dawkins claims that it is impossible to reconcile science and Christianity. Science, argues Dawkins, has an exclusive claim on truth. But science is not the real problem, according to Ruse. The real villain is a form of radical humanism that seeks to make science a new religion. Unfortunately, says Ruse, that brand of radical humanism "... does not exhibit the kind of openness to evidence and adaptability that we'd expect from a rational, non-religious mindset." Like religious fundamentalists, it "... encourages ... intolerance, hero-worship, moral certainty and the self-righteous condemnation of unbelievers."[84]

Sola scientia

Charles Darwin did not use his theory to promote atheism and never claimed that evolution implied the existence or nonexistence of God.[85] If I were to suggest a motto for the new atheists, it would be sola scientia – by science alone. Most people cannot, and choose not to, live by science alone. There are numerous important questions, as we have seen, that science cannot answer. Many anti-evolutionists mistakenly believe that science, by its very nature, is anathema to religion. Individuals who are comfortable in their dual role as scientists and people of faith, however, belie this view. For example, Clive Staples (C.S.) Lewis (1898-1963) began his academic career as an atheist. After his conversion, he became a prominent apologist for the Christian faith. Lewis said, "I believe in Christianity as I believe that the sun has risen, not only because I see it, but because, by it, I see everything else."[86] Lewis belonged to a group at Oxford with the motto: "Follow the argument where it leads." Lewis believed that non-materialistic evolution posed little threat to Christianity.[87]

7. OLD-EARTH CREATIONISM

Overview

This chapter defines, compares and contrasts the different kinds of responses the church has made in response to scientific evidence supporting an old earth.

Old-Earth Creationism has been popular among conservative Christians for more than one hundred years. It was considered a viable option well before young earth creationism, with its distinctive flood geology, captured the attention of evangelicals in the mid-twentieth century. Old-earth creationism comes in several different flavors. It is a conservative Christian response to the nineteenth-century geological consensus regarding the age of the earth. After Darwin's theory became well known, and increasingly accepted, some Christians revisited the Bible's creation accounts, looking for the extra time required to accommodate geological discoveries. Their goal was to maintain the traditional interpretation of these narratives while accommodating new geological realities. The process of adapting Christian theology to science remains highly controversial among evangelical Christians. Not surprisingly, young earth creationism rejects these efforts, considering them to be an affront to its understanding of biblical authority.

The Gap Theory proposes that the days of creation were literal 24-hour days, but that there was a time gap of unknown length between two separate creations, the first recorded in Genesis 1:1, and the second in Genesis 1:2-31. Some gap theory proponents claim that a race of humans existed before Adam, but was destroyed before God re-created the world in six days. As is true of the old-earth models described here (with the exception of evolutionary creation), gap creationism rejects the theory of evolution.

Day Age Creationism differs from the gap theory in its claim that the days of creation were very long periods of time – millions, perhaps even billions of years. Many early twentieth-century fundamentalists advocated a day-age position. Day-age proponents claim, in addition, that the Biblical flood was a local event. They, too, reject evolution, arguing that no new life forms have been created since the time of Genesis.

Progressive Creationism proposes that God created various life-forms gradually and sequentially over long periods of time. According to progressive creationists, divine creative activity occurred in clusters interspersed between times when no creation occurred. In this particular old-earth iteration, species appear all at once and fully formed. Like day-age creationism, progressive creationism maintains that Noah's flood was a local event.

Theistic Evolution, although it accepts the theory of evolution, is included here because it advocates an ancient earth. Theistic evolution is the majority position held by mainline Protestant denominations as well as by the Roman Catholic Church. Evolutionary Creation and theistic evolution are, for all intents and purposes, synonymous. Both regard scriptural creation accounts, accurately interpreted, to be entirely compatible with a modern scientific understanding of the evolutionary process.

Intelligent Design Creationism is also included here because many of its proponents accept the idea of an ancient earth. Many of the beliefs held by intelligent design advocates are similar to progressive creation. Like progressive creationists, intelligent design rejects evolution by natural selection and believes that God directly intervened at various points in history to create organisms of greater and greater complexity. All the non-evolutionary expressions of old-earth creationism mentioned here (evolutionary creation is the only evolutionary old-earth perspective in this context) advocate scientific concordism. And, as we will see in chapter 14, all of these positions – evolutionary as well as non-evolutionary – challenge traditional creation-related doctrines.

	DEEP TIME	RE-CREATION	SCIENTIFIC CONCORDISM	LIT. DAYS	ACCEPTS EVOLUTION	SALTATION	LOCAL FLOOD	ADVOCATES
GAP THEORY (~1656)	YES	YES	YES	YES	NO	YES	NO	1917 SCOFIELD REFERENCE BIBLE
DAY-AGE (~1884)	YES	NO	YES	NO	NO	YES	YES	HUGH ROSS
THEISTIC EVOLUTION (~1800)	YES	NO	NO	NO	YES	NO	YES	FRANCIS COLLINS
PROGRESSIVE CREATION (~1930)	YES	NO	YES	NO	NO	YES	YES	BERNARD RAMM
INTELLIGENT DESIGN (~1989)	YES	NO	YES	NO	NO	YES	YES	STEPHEN MEYER
YEC (~1960)	NO	NO	YES	YES	NO	YES	NO	HENRY MORRIS

Table 7.1 – Old-Earth Creationist Models vs. Young Earth Creationism

Old-earth creationism

Old-earth creationism has been popular among conservative, evangelical, and fundamentalist Christians for more than a century.[1] It appeared in the nineteenth century, well before its young earth cousin.[2] Christian fundamentalism and young earth creationism, it turns out, were largely separate entities until the 1920's.[3] The majority of late nineteenth century creationists, unlike those today, accepted a progressive fossil record, an old earth, and figurative language in Genesis.[4] Old-earth creationism is expressed in at least six different forms –

- The Gap Theory
- The Day-Age Theory
- Progressive Creationism
- Theistic Evolution (Evolutionary Creation)
- Intelligent Design

In the early nineteenth century, geologists arrived at a consensus about the age of the earth – a consensus that differed radically from the young-earth views held by many Christians. When Christian doctrines collide with empirical knowledge, some Christians revise their beliefs (a process called accommodation). Kenneth Miller: "The notion that religion must respect the finding of scientific reason is, in fact, a traditional Western view that has been expressed by many writers in the Abrahamic tradition, none more eloquently than St. Augustine."[5] Most mainline Christian denominations, on the basis of scientific discoveries, have chosen to do just that.[6] Already by 1900, accommodating church teachings to scientific findings was common practice for many Christians.[7] The gap and day-age theories provided proponents with the dual benefit of being able to defend biblical inerrancy while simultaneously acknowledging the claims of historical geology.[8] In today's highly polarized environment, most evangelicals are unaware of the fact that a substantial number of well-known Christians have held old-earth views.[9] A list of more recent advocates of old-earth creationism includes many names familiar to evangelicals.[10]

On April 18th, 1991, James Dobson's *Focus on the Family* radio broadcast discussed old-earth creationism with well-known advocate, Christian astrophysicist Hugh Ross, and young earth stalwart, Duane Gish (1921-2013). According to Dobson, that broadcast was one of the most listened-to in the history of Focus on the Family.[11] More than ten thousand requests for copies of the program were received. Forty or fifty very angry letters were also received from individuals who considered Ross's old-earth view to be heretical. One Christian radio station even threatened to take Dobson's program off the air.[12] As would be expected, Hugh Ross's old-earth position is strongly rejected in young earth creationist circles. Duane Gish once called Ross "... an apostate who has no heart for evangelism."[13] Gish also claimed that old-earth creationism is inherently atheistic, a commonly-held view among young earth creationists.[14] Hugh Ross has endured what he calls "... unimaginable and disheartening opposition" from offended creationists for his old-earth views, even though, as a progressive creationist, he rejects evolution. He has been called a "compromiser" and a "heretic."[15]

The gap theory

The gap theory upholds the traditional view that the days of creation are literal 24-hour days. Gap creationists, however, claim that important details about the past and about the age of the earth were left out of the Genesis account. They suggest that a gap of unknown duration occurred between a first creation, recorded in Genesis 1:1, and a second, recorded in Genesis 1:2-31. The gap theory, therefore, speculates that there was creation, followed by catastrophe, followed by re-creation.[16] In addition, some gap theory proponents speculate about the existence of a pre-Adamite race, a race of beings created before Adam, that was destroyed before Genesis 1:2 when God re-created the world in six days.[17] This pre-Adamite argument can be traced as far back as 1656, when Isaac de la Peyrere (1596-1676) published a book titled Men Before Adam.[18] A lawyer by training, and a Calvinist by upbringing, de la Peyrere argued that there must have been two creations – first, a creation of the Gentiles, and then of Adam, the father of the Jews. The existence of pre-Adamites, of course, conveniently explains Cain's wife after Abel's murder, which, in the Genesis account, involved the taking of a wife and the building of a city. de la Peyrere's account of human origins became the basis of nineteenth century theories claiming that the different races had been created separately, theories collectively known as polygenism.[19]

By adopting the gap theory, various scientific observations including the age of the earth, the age of the universe, dinosaurs, fossils, ice cores, ice ages, and geological formations are acknowledged, without contradicting a literalistic belief in Genesis. It is important to note that the gap theory differs from day-age creationism in that the day-age theory claims the "days" of creation were much longer than twenty-four hours. It also differs from young earth creationism, which, although it speaks of literal 24 hour days, does not argue for a gap in time. The gap theory conveniently allows both the Genesis creation account and geological science to be inerrant in matters of scientific fact.[20] This concept, known as scientific concordism, is very popular in evangelical Christian circles. It has been adopted by those who advocate anti-evolutionary old-earth positions, and is also a basic characteristic of young earth creationism. What these outwardly-disparate groups have in common is the view that the Bible has no out of-date statements about the natural realm.

We have already noted that early in the nineteenth century, geologists came to a consensus that the earth was far older than traditional interpretations of Genesis would allow. The gap theory, with its tacit acceptance of geology, is an example of a retroactive interpretation of the scriptures, in other words, reading modern knowledge back into ancient documents.[21] In nineteenth-century Britain, the gap theory was popularized by Thomas Chalmers (1780-1847), a natural theologian and theologically-trained geologist. Chalmers was a professor at the University of Edinburgh, and founded the Free Church of Scotland. He was the Dean of Westminster for eleven years.[22] Other early proponents included Oxford University geology professor William Buckland (1784-1856) who argued that God had created a progressive succession of species.[23] In the U.S., Amherst College geologist Edward Hitchcock (1793-1864) adopted Chalmers' gap theory and popularized it there.[24] Harry Rimmer (1890-1952) helped establish the gap theory as the dominant view of origins among pre-World War II fundamentalists.[25]

Buckland's proposal that God had created a progressive succession of species[26] is called saltation. In biology, saltation (from the Latin, saltus, "leap") is a sudden change from one generation to the next, that is large, or very large, in comparison with the usual variation of an organism. Saltation is the term used for non-gradual changes (especially single-step speciation) that are atypical of, or violate the gradualism assumed by modern evolutionary theory.[27] The gap theory rejects evolution by natural selection, as do all the old-earth views discussed here, with the exception of evolutionary creation.[28] The gap theory was popular among early twentieth-century Protestant fundamentalists.[29] It gained even greater prominence when a "second creative act" was mentioned in the reference notes for Genesis in the influential 1917 Scofield Reference Bible, a study Bible edited by Cyrus I. Scofield (1843-1921).[30] In 1954, Baptist theologian Bernard Ramm (1916-1992) said, "The gap theory has become the standard interpretation throughout hyper-orthodoxy."[31] Geologists, however, found no trace of the radical break in the geological record required by the gap theory's ruin-and-restoration scheme.[32]

As early as the 1830's, geologists Adam Sedgwick (1785-1873) and William Buckland (1784-1856) pointed out difficulties associated with a worldwide flood. A single global flood, in their opinion, could not have produced the deposits found. They therefore proposed that the biblical flood was a local event.[33] In our day, a local flood is rejected by gap creationism as well as young earth creationism. The other old-earth positions described in this chapter argue for a local, rather than a worldwide flood (see Table 7.1). Many generations of Christians have wondered whether the Genesis flood was truly global. And many Christians have wondered whether the flood, on its own, could account for the entirety of the earth's geologic record. The apostle Paul's letter to the church at Rome reminded Christians there that their faith was being proclaimed "...throughout the whole world." (Romans 1:8) Clearly Paul was referring to the world known to him and his readers at that time. Similarly, Noah's flood may have encompassed all of known humanity at the time without necessarily covering the entire planet.[34]

The day-age theory

Among biblical literalists, there are several views regarding origins. This is certainly evident in the various expressions of old-earth creationism described in this chapter. Day-age creationism, a second variation on the old-earth theme, claims that the six days of creation were not ordinary 24-hour days, but were much longer periods of time. Similar to other old-earth positions, day-age creationism seeks to understand the Genesis creation accounts in the context of an ancient earth, but that accommodation takes a slightly different form. By the early nineteenth century, many conservative Christians had come to equate the "days" of creation with the geologic ages.[35] For example, in 1833, Benjamin Silliman (1779-1864), American chemist and one of the first American professors of science, proposed six epochs, each corresponding to a biblical "day," but not twenty-four hours in duration.[36] Swiss-American geologist and geographer Arnold Guyot (1807-1884) also interpreted the "days" of Genesis 1 as epochs in cosmic history. In his book Creation (1884), Guyot criticized scientific concordism, (see chapter 9) saying that individuals should get rid of wrongful expectations of what the Bible can do for them with regard to science.[37]

The majority of contemporary day-age creationists consider themselves fundamentalists.[38] Many contemporary Christians are unaware that most of the authors of the early twentieth-century conservative Protestant manifesto, The Fundamentals, were day-age creationists.[39] William Jennings Bryan (1860-1925), as we have seen, adopted this point of view. Bryan was a fundamentalist but did not hold a young earth position.[40] He did share some beliefs with young earth proponents, however. He appealed to miracles to explain puzzling scientific phenomena and, although he believed in an old earth, he rejected Darwinian evolution.[41] A well-known contemporary day-age creationist is Christian astrophysicist Hugh Ross, founder of the Christian apologetic organization Reasons to Believe. Like other old-earth views (again, with the exception of evolutionary creation), day-age creationists reject evolution, claiming that God is no longer creating, and that no new life forms have been created since Adam and Eve. In the late nineteenth century, Arnold Guyot (1807-1884) believed that the "days" of Genesis 1 were epochs in history. But, at the same time, he rejected Darwin's theory of human evolution. Charles Hodge (1797-1878), also rejected evolution, while at the same time claiming that the days of Genesis were geological epochs.[42] Despite their acknowledgement of deep time, day-age creationists claim there simply has not been enough time for evolution to occur.[43] In addition, like their ideological cousins, the intelligent design creationists, day-age proponents believe that natural processes are insufficient to produce living organisms.[44]

Progressive creationism

Progressive creationism is another old-earth point of view that attempts to combine a literal Genesis account of creation with modern geology. A progressive creationist web site explains:

> *Progressive creationism accepts the findings of modern science with regard to deep time. The individual days of creation are interpreted to represent millions of years. This is called a day-age interpretation. Progressive creationists do not believe in evolution. They believe that God created each species a unique creation, not evolving from a previous species.*[45]

Progressive creationism claims that God created new life-forms gradually over hundreds of millions of years. This perspective can trace its roots as far back as St. Augustine (354-430 A.D.) who spoke of several acts of divine creation.[46] Progressive creationism claims that creation occurred in rapid bursts in which Biblical "kinds" (both flora and fauna) appeared in stages lasting millions of years. These bursts of creative activity were followed by periods of stasis in order to accommodate new arrivals. Progressive creationism believes that God created new types of organisms by direct divine intervention. Therefore, "... species do not gradually appear by the steady transformation of its ancestors; but they appear all at once and 'fully formed.'"[47]

Gap and day-age creationists, as well as progressive creationists, reject biological evolution. They argue that evolution is biologically untenable and not supported by the fossil record. They also reject descent from a universal common ancestor. Progressive creationism is a midway position between young earth creationism on the one hand (which is unacceptable to science), and biological evolution (which is unacceptable to most evangelical Christians).[48] It seems that progressive creationism has retained its popularity among evangelicals, especially educators. Denis Lamoureux notes that a recent survey revealed that 48 percent of biologists in American evangelical colleges are progressive creationists.[49]

In the nineteenth century, progressive creationism was advocated by Robert Chambers (1802-1871) in his Vestiges of the Natural History of Creation (1844).[50] Twentieth century Baptist theologian Bernard Ramm (1916-1992) was also a progressive creationist who was at least open to the theory of evolution.[51] Ramm interpreted the days of Genesis metaphorically claiming that "... creation was revealed pictorially in six days, not performed in six days."[52] Ramm claimed that God intervened periodically to create new "root-species" which then "radiated" out.[53] Ramm's progressive creationism, admittedly controversial in evangelical circles, was received positively by many evangelical scientists. No one had a greater impact on the American Scientific Affiliation in the mid-twentieth century than Ramm.[54] As a matter of fact, his views prompted a strong negative response from Henry Morris and John Whitcomb which became a major theme in their hugely influential young earth classic, The Genesis Flood (1961).[55] Many well-known evangelicals, however, including evangelist Billy Graham (1918-2018), adopted this point of view.[56]

Progressive creationism rejects the young earth argument that the earth is less than ten thousand years old, or that the creation "days" of Genesis 1 were literal twenty-four hour periods. Using the principle that "scripture interprets scripture," progressive creationist Alan Hayward (1923-2008) refers to the New Testament book of Hebrews, chapter 4, which discusses a continued seventh day of creation. Hugh Ross argues that the Hebrew word "yom" (day) can be translated several different ways. Ross contends that, at the end of each Genesis "day" (with the notable exception of the seventh "day") the phrase, "... and there was evening and there was morning..." marks an end-point to each event. He believes that the omission of that key phrase on the seventh day is in harmony with a literal translation of Hebrews 4 and its continuing seventh day.[57] Thus, because the New Testament book of Hebrews implies that the seventh day of creation is still in effect, and therefore spans far more than 24 hours, progressive creationists feel free to interpret the first six days of creation as extended periods of time.[58]

At the end of the eighteenth century, French anatomist Georges Cuvier (1769-1832), widely considered the father of old-earth creationism,[59] proposed a series of successive creations in the context of catastrophism.[60] Cuvier claimed that God had destroyed previously created forms through regional catastrophes, and afterwards re-populated those regions with new forms. Cuvier, however, never admitted to seeing progress in the fossil record.[61] Today's young earth creationists have adopted Cuvier's catastrophism and his views on successive creation. Progressive creationists, for their part, believe these same events occurred, but over a very long period of time. Cuvier argued that there are no intermediate forms in the fossil record, an idea which today's young earth creationists, progressive creationists, and intelligent design advocates have also adopted.[62] Nineteenth-century Scottish geologist and evangelical Christian Hugh Miller (1802-1856) made the case for several separate creation events brought about by divine interventions. Louis Agassiz, (1807-1873) Swiss-American naturalist at Harvard University, did the same.[63] According to Agassiz, adaptation of creatures to their environments testified to an intelligent plan. Agassiz also claimed that the different races of homo sapiens had been created separately.

The belief in a series of divine creation episodes, bringing about many new species, with long periods of time in between, was also proposed by nineteenth century Anglican geologist William Buckland (1784-1856). Buckland presented this idea to counter pre-Darwinian theories on the transmutation of species. Buckland's views regarding successive creations continue to be advocated by today's anti-evolutionists. The idea of a series of divine interventions, however, was criticized by John Dewey (1859-1952), American philosopher, as "... design on the installment plan."[64] This point of view is similar to intelligent design advocate Philip Johnson's claim that God causes the required mutations to arrive when they are needed.[65] Calvin College physics professor Howard Van Till characterizes this view as episodic creationism.[66]

Progressive creationists accept the geological column, which describes the successive appearance of plants and animals through time. They argue that the geological column reflects the order in which God sequentially created various kinds of organisms, beginning with simple, single-celled organisms and progressing through to complex multicellular organisms. Progressive creationists, however, do not accept the scientific consensus that these "kinds" evolved from each other, arguing that Biblical "kinds" are genetically limited, such that one "kind" cannot evolve into another.[67] Like their day-age cousins, progressive creationists argue that there has not been enough time for evolution to occur.[68] They maintain a strict separation between the geological record and the evolutionary hypothesis.[69] In addition, and again contrary to the views of young earth creationists, progressive creationists argue for a local, not a worldwide flood,[70] claiming that a universal flood presents imponderable difficulties, and is not supported by geology.[71] Progressive creationism, with its attempt to harmonize scripture and science, provides another example of scientific concordism.[72]

Evolutionary creation *(theistic evolution)*

Evolutionary creation, also known as theistic evolution, (see chapter 8) is included in this chapter because it accepts deep time. Evolutionary creation is a compromise position between young earth creationism on the one hand and atheistic evolution on the other. It accepts organic evolution, maintaining that evolution is a process initiated and supervised by God.[73] Although evolutionary creationists accept deep time, as do all of the old-earth positions described here, they differ in their belief that God created the world and living things through an evolutionary process.

Intelligent design creationism

Intelligent design creationism (see chapter 10) proposes that "... certain features of the universe and of living things are best explained by an intelligent cause, not an undirected process such as natural selection."[74] Intelligent design is included here because most (but not all) of its proponents accept deep time.[75] Intelligent design, however, differs from many of these other views in that many intelligent design proponents accept some (again, but not all) elements of evolutionary theory, specifically common ancestry. Philip Johnson, chief architect of intelligent design, has been described as an old-earth creationist.[76] Intelligent design seems to come closest to progressive creationism. For many intelligent design advocates, unlike proponents of the gap theory, the "days" of Genesis are to be understood metaphorically, not as literal twenty-four hour days.[77] And like progressive creationism, intelligent design claims that God intervenes in the creative process from time to time, creating increasingly complex organisms.[78]

Conclusion

Young earth creationist Duane Gish (1921-2013) explicitly stated that, in his opinion, all of creation is supernatural.[79] A scientist asks, "What does the evidence say?" A creationist, on the other hand, asks, "What does the Bible say?"[80] It is precisely at this juncture that a disconnect occurs.[81] The majority of old-earth creationists, like other anti-evolutionists, are scientific concordists, working valiantly to harmonize the Bible with science but, in order to do that, stretching the facts to make things fit. James Dobson argues that it does not follow that explaining the universe scientifically removes God from the process.[82] "You don't remove God from it simply by saying, 'How did he do it?' and trying to figure it out," he says.[83] Like other positions that accept deep time, the various examples of old-earth creationism discussed here raise several important theological issues which are discussed in chapter 12.

8. EVOLUTIONARY CREATION

Overview

Evolutionary Creation, also known as Theistic Evolution, brings God into the evolutionary process. For an evolutionary creationist, evolution is God's method of creation. Atheistic evolution, on the other hand, excludes God from the process. Both perspectives appeared after the publication of Darwin's Origin of Species. Theistic evolution, the original name for this perspective, was soon adopted by a number of Christians on both sides of the Atlantic. In the early twentieth century, as we have seen, American fundamentalists summarized their beliefs in a series of essays titled The Fundamentals. Surprisingly, some of those essays supported the concept of theistic evolution. Fundamentalism at that time was more concerned about theological liberalism and the higher critical method of biblical interpretation than it was in attacking Christians who had adopted the theory of evolution.

Evolutionary creation acknowledges validated scientific discoveries and allows them to inform its theological deliberations. It asserts that when biblical authors wrote about nature, they were limited to what was known at the time. As we have noted, much of that information, when viewed from a contemporary scientific perspective, is inaccurate and out of date. On the other hand, evolutionary creation recognizes that the limits imposed on science by its own methodological ground-rules allow Christians in scientific vocations to practice their faith without hindrance. It is cognizant of the fact that divine intervention in the evolutionary process is not a scientific concern. The same is true for teleology, that is, whether evolution has a goal or purpose.

Evolutionary creationists are fully aware that critically important theological issues are raised when scientific discoveries are applied to Christian theology (see chapter 12). But this is seen as an opportunity to revise and clarify earlier theological pronouncements that were made without scientific input. Evolutionary creation obviously challenges those who claim that the theory of evolution is inherently atheistic. A growing number of evangelical Protestants have adopted evolutionary creation. The Roman Catholic Church officially endorses this perspective as well.

It is important to point out that, at the end of the day, evolutionary creation is essentially synonymous with theistic evolution. The majority of individuals who hold this position are Christians. Evolutionary creationists seek to respect traditional Christian teachings while acknowledging the theory of evolution. For evolutionary creationists, science enables Christians to better understand the mechanisms God actually used to bring about biodiversity on earth. Because evolutionary creation is strongly motivated to uphold traditional Christian teachings and values, while recognizing the best of science, it tends to be more attractive to evangelicals than the more generic term theistic evolution. Groups currently discussing evolutionary creation include The American Scientific Affiliation and The BioLogos Foundation, begun by Francis Collins in 2007. The BioLogos website is a popular clearinghouse for evolutionary creation ideas, resources and discussion. The American Scientific Affiliation does not take an official position on any creation-related issue, and its members are advocates for a variety of views.

Background

Evolutionary creation (theistic evolution) is a positive, accommodationist, Christian response to Darwinian theory. It proposes that all life-forms developed through an evolutionary process. Theistic evolution has been known by that name since 1877. One of the first individuals to use the term was Canadian geologist John W. Dawson (1820-1899).[1] Theistic evolution maintains that the universe, the earth, and all living things are continuously evolving. It claims that God is as creative today as He was in the past.[2] In a very real sense, a continuing creation is woven into the very fabric of matter itself.[3] The entire cosmos and all living things are "...able to change and evolve at His will."[4] Sir Ghillean T. Prance, British botanist and ecologist, says, "The wonders of creation are just as great whether God created in a single step or used the gradual mechanism of evolution."[5]

The first written response to Darwin's Origin of Species came from Anglican cleric, the Rev. Charles Kingsley (1819-1875). Kingsley's review was so positive that Darwin quoted from it in his Second Edition. On November 18th, 1859, six days before the publication of the Origin, Kingsley thanked Darwin for an advance copy, commenting that it is "...just as noble a conception of Deity to believe that He created primal forms capable of self-development ... as to believe that He required a fresh act of intervention to supply the lacunas [gaps] which He Himself had made."[6] It was Kingsley who famously said "God can make all things make themselves."[7] Asa Gray (1810-1888), Professor of Natural History at Harvard, and one of America's leading botanists, was Darwin's strongest early supporter and most important advocate in the U.S.[8] Gray, however, was uncomfortable with the absence of divine intervention in evolution.[9] He suggested to Darwin that natural selection ought to be supplemented with guided variation.[10] Darwin did not agree.

George Frederick Wright (1838–1921), geologist and professor at Oberlin Theological Seminary in Ohio, collaborated with Gray in formulating theistic evolution.[11] In 1885, Congregational pastor and theistic evolution advocate Henry Ward Beecher (1813-1887) said that, in his opinion, "Design by wholesale is grander than design by retail."[12] In 1871, Princeton's James McCosh (1811-1894) adopted an evolutionary viewpoint in his book, Christianity and Positivism.[13] Henry Fairfield Osborn (1857-1935) was a dedicated theist and a skilled paleontologist who viewed evolution as the finest expression of God's will.[14] Significantly, Benjamin B. Warfield (1851-1921), who provided American fundamentalism with its doctrine of scriptural inspiration[15] also advocated theistic evolution. Warfield was an unusual individual – a fundamentalist and an advocate of evolution.[16] It is significant that "B.B. Warfield [manifested] ... the least enthusiastic form of theistic evolution, a grudging acceptance of scientific truth on the grounds that all truth rightly demands admittance to the Christian understanding of reality."[17] Still another well-known theistic evolution advocate was Charles Walcott (1850-1927) of Burgess Shale fame.[18]

Fundamentalism

Prior to the 1920's, only a few Protestant fundamentalists had adopted theistic evolution.[19] The Fundamentals, a series of ninety essays written between 1910 and 1915, outlined basic Christian doctrines from what could be characterized as a conservative or evangelical perspective. These essays emphasized the authority of a divinely inspired and inerrant biblical text, and disparaged the so-called higher critical method of biblical interpretation that had originated in Germany.[20] The Fundamentals criticized Darwinian evolution,[21] but surprisingly said little about six-day creationism. This lack of consensus regarding evolution shows that young earth creationism was not at the top of the fundamentalist agenda in the early twentieth century.[22] Surprisingly, The Fundamentals, Part IV, left open the possibility of theistic evolution.[23] As odd as it may seem to us today, two of the essays in this fundamentalist manifesto were submitted by James Orr (1844?-1913) and George Frederick Wright (1838-1921), scholars who advocated theistic evolution.[24] Contributors to The Fundamentals who accepted some form of evolutionary theory included well-known names like Benjamin Warfield, and Asa Gray.[25] Young earth luminary Henry Morris (1918-2006) had to admit that "... several of the fundamentalist booklets were actually written by men who were theistic evolutionists."[26]

Following the American Civil War (1861-1865), many evangelicals came to accept deep time and an ancient earth. They did not give up their belief in an inerrant Bible, however, but interpreted scripture in such a way as to make it consistent with modern science.[27] This was accomplished, as we saw in chapter 7, by means of the day-age and gap theories. It is important to realize that in the early decades of the twentieth century, few creationists, even among the fundamentalists, advocated flood geology (see chapter 9).[28] This is a not-so-subtle reminder that young earth creationism is a relatively recent phenomenon and that science and religion coexisted quite comfortably until about a century ago.[29] Early fundamentalism was certainly a great deal kinder and gentler with regard to the theory of evolution than is the current expression of young earth creationism.[30]

Accommodation

In these chapters, the word accommodation appears several times. In the context of our discussion of science and religion, accommodation has two basic meanings. First, it relates to communicating information about origins in a form that people living in the ancient world could understand. In that sense, then, we would say that the Holy Spirit accommodated the message to the understanding, limited as it was, of the people living at the time. The Holy Spirit did this for the sake of efficient communication. The second meaning of the word has to do with the way believers have responded to valid scientific discoveries since the scientific revolution. Some, fearing erosion of scriptural authority, resist what science says about origins. Others accommodate their theology so as to be more in line with what science has discovered. Old-earth creationism would be an example of an accommodationist approach. Evolutionary creation (theistic evolution) is another. Each of these approaches is willing to allow science to speak to their faith. It is important to keep these two meanings of accommodation separate. Both uses of the word have appeared in these pages.

By speaking to Israel in the context of an ancient understanding of science, God revealed that he had created the world, not how he created it.[31]

This primary understanding of accommodation can be traced back to the first Christian centuries and was not regarded as controversial at the time.[32] St. Augustine (354-430 A.D.), for example, said, "We do not read in the Gospel that the Lord said, 'I am sending you the Holy Spirit, that he may teach you about the course of the sun and the moon.' He wished to make people Christians not astronomers."[33] An early advocate of accommodation was Galileo Galilei (1564-1642), a prominent figure in the early days of the scientific revolution. In 1615, Galileo argued, in a letter to the Grand Duchess Christina[34] (1565-1637), that scripture's authors had accommodated their message to match the understanding of the ancients.[35]

Pressure to allow scientific discoveries to speak to theological issues intensified in the sixteenth century.[36] John Calvin (1509-1564) was another prominent theologian who argued that the Holy Spirit accommodated to the ancients, employing the best science of the day in the scriptural text.[37] As far back as 1534, Calvin held that scripture was never intended to provide infallible astronomical and medical information.[38] We have already noted that in response to the discoveries of Copernicus and Galileo, theologians grudgingly acknowledged that scientific findings may affect longstanding biblical doctrines.[39] They came to the conclusion that scriptural statements such as those found in Psalm 93:1 and Psalm 104:5, declaring that the earth cannot move, are poetic or metaphorical.[40] The Church's response to Copernicus, belated as it was, presents us with a model for an appropriate Christian response to science.

A great deal more is at stake with modern biological science, however, because of evolution's profound implications for human origins and its multifaceted challenge to orthodox Christian beliefs.[41] Accommodationists constitute the silent majority in contemporary Christianity, and are all but invisible both to the general public and to many evangelicals.[42] Influential evolutionist, Stephen Jay Gould has said, "A man may be both an evolutionist and a devout Christian."[43] Michael Ruse titled one of his many books, "Can a Christian be a Darwinian?" and answered his own question in the affirmative.[44] Alister McGrath, former scientist and atheist, now evangelical theologian, reminds Christians that the theologian's primary concern is Jesus Christ. Like Jesus the Messiah, the scriptures are both divine and human and convey God's gracious gift to humanity.[45] The Bible is not a reliable source of scientific information about the origin of the earth or the cosmos, or, for that matter, living organisms. It was never intended to be.[46]

Since the scientific revolution began, the church has encountered scientific discoveries which challenged traditional interpretations of the scriptural creation accounts. First were discoveries regarding astronomy and the cosmos, the counterintuitive notion that the earth orbits the sun, so-called "new stars" in the heavens and the sudden appearance of wandering comets. Then came geological discoveries related to the structure and age of the earth and the historicity of the Noahic flood. After that were discoveries in biology, including Darwin's theory of evolution by natural selection. In order to be good stewards of all truth, regardless of its source, Christians are duty-bound to acknowledge validated scientific truth and let those truths inform their theology. It is not the scientific community's responsibility to adapt its discoveries to any particular religious interpretive system.[47] An appropriate acknowledgement of scientific reality is not an expression of weakness or defeat for Christians, but of a healthy intellectual engagement which, at the end of the day, is a manifestation of true Christian stewardship and enhances scriptural authority as modern-day Christians learn to see the scriptures for what they actually are as opposed to what they want them to be.[48]

Astronomical discoveries, such as Copernican heliocentrism, initially rejected by the Church, were eventually accommodated by most Christians. The Lutheran Church - Missouri Synod, which officially rejected Copernicanism until the early decades of the twentieth century, is a notable exception (see chapter 9).[49] Other scientific discoveries, especially those related to biological evolution, the age of the earth, and human origins, remain contentious for many evangelicals. Mainline Christians have generally made peace with Darwin. In the news while this chapter was written was a headline declaring: "United Methodists Officially Accept Evolution."[50] In addition, the General Assembly of the Presbyterian Church (USA), held in June 2016, voted to adopt a proposed "Affirmation of Creation," affirming evolution as God's method of creation.[51]

Divine intervention

Evolutionary creation is interested in determining the nature and extent of God's intervention in the evolutionary process. In the nineteenth century, Louis Agassiz (1807-1873) compared the evolutionary process to the development of an embryo.[52] Contemporary evolutionary creationist Denis Lamoureux expands on this idea from Agassiz, comparing the evolution of living organisms to fetal development in the womb. Lamoureux says:

> *This first generation of evangelical evolutionists often compared the process*

of evolution to the mechanisms of embryology that fashion individuals in their mother's womb. These evolutionists argued that in both cases, humans were created by natural laws that were ordained and sustained by God.[53]

Lamoureux argues that as fetal development unfolds, new information appears which existed only as a potentiality in the fertilized egg.[54] This process, he says, is teleological, or, in Christian terminology, ordained by God.[55] God's creation of individual human beings and of all living organisms through the process of evolution is planned for a purpose. This point of view finds scriptural support in Psalm 139:13, which describes a miraculous knitting process in the womb, resulting in a body that is "fearfully and wonderfully made."[56] Significantly, when the evolutionary process is compared to embryological development in this way, the creator need not directly intervene once the process begins,[57] but oversees the process. Lamoureux illustrates various proposals regarding origins in this way –

Imagine that God's creative action in the origin of the world is like the stroke of a cue stick in a game of billiards. Divide and label the balls into three groups using the words heavens, earth, and living organisms, and let the 8-ball represent humanity. The Young Earth Creationist depicts the Creator making single shot after single shot, with no miscues, until all the balls are off the table. A Progressive Creationist sees the opening stroke that breaks the balls as the Big Bang. All of the balls labeled heavens and earth are sunk by this initial shot. Then God sinks those that signify living organisms and humans individually.[58] According to Evolutionary Creation, one shot sinks all the balls in sequence.[59]

Lamoureux says, "...the Creator loaded into the Big Bang the plan and capability for the cosmos and living organisms, including humans, to evolve over ten to fifteen billion years."[60] Evolutionary creation proposes that God does not micromanage his creation, and that evolution adheres to an overarching plan with occasional divine intervention in the evolutionary process. Each natural event, on its own, may seem random, but the overall pattern advances God's purpose.[61] According to biologist Kenneth Miller, evolution is best conceptualized as a continuing creation in which God's will is expressed in and through every living thing.[62] Alvin Plantinga speaks of front-loading, where God creates the conditions that issue in the right mutations arising at the right time.[63] This divine activity has been called orthogenesis, defined as "... an innate tendency to evolve in a unilinear fashion due to some internal or external driving force."[64] According to evolutionary creation, the driving force behind evolution and its manager, is God himself. Christian physicist Howard Van Till characterizes the entire universe as an expression of God's effective will.[65]

In Britain, George Campbell, Eighth Duke of Argyll (1823-1900) and St. George Jackson Mivart (1827-1900) separately explained evolution as the process by which God directs the laws of development so that species evolve over time to adapt to changed conditions.[66] Traditional Christianity asserts that nothing happens without God's knowledge. As we noted in chapter 3, Hebrews 1:3 states that God continually "... upholds all things by the word of his power" (NASB).[67] Without God's continuing supervision, but not necessarily His direct intervention, Christians believe the universe would immediately return to its original chaotic state.[68] The word 'providence' is derived from the Latin, providere, "to see ahead."[69] God's providential concern, according to the scripture, is for all of his creatures. (Matthew 6:28-30).[70] Christians generally believe that God is providentially active in all natural processes, and that all of creation declares the glory of God.[71] So, for Christians, if something happens "naturally," God is still in charge.[72]

In the eighteenth century, Alexander Pope (1688-1744) said, "All are parts of one stupendous whole, whose body nature is, and God the soul."[73] As far as science is concerned, any divine guidance in the creative process would be so subtle and subdued as to go completely unnoticed.[74] The Genesis creation accounts describe God as a purposeful Designer imposing order on chaos. In the scriptures generally, God is the Potter, the Architect.[75] Unlike the direct and occasional intervention advocated by intelligent design, evolutionary creationists argue that God conceptualized creation and evolution made it happen.[76] Evolutionary creation is best understood as "divinely planned evolution."[77]

In summary then, evolutionary creation advocates propose what is primarily a non-interventionist divine action position.[78] In the seventeenth century, Thomas Burnet (1635-1715) used a clock analogy, declaring that a superior clockmaker has a clock that works on its own rather than one that needs intervention every hour.[79] Evolutionary creation claims that God guides the evolutionary process and has an important relationship with creation, but, most of the time, creation unfolds on its own. This has been characterized as a theistically guided evolution which pictures God as a nurturing but not overbearing parent. This view is contrasted with deism, which asserts that life is left to develop by means of unguided chance plus natural selection and envisions God as a great engineer who, after the initial act of creation, abandons the world to its own devices. Even though advocates of evolutionary creation understand God's role in evolution as typically a "hands-off" process, the possibility of direct action by God, through miracles, remains a distinct possibility. In other words, evolutionary creation leaves open the possibility that God can, on occasion, stage an invasion.[80] Miracles are signs and wonders sent by God. They turn believers away from themselves and from their troubles, pointing instead to Jesus and his glory.[81]

The biologos foundation

Francis Collins is an internationally respected scientist, former atheist turned evangelical Christian, and current director of the U.S. National Institute of Health. Collins promotes the compatibility of Christianity and biological evolution in his influential book, The Language of God (2006).[82] Collins founded the BioLogos Foundation in 2007 (see chapter 8), an organization which promotes a positive relationship between science and religion and asserts that Christianity can be reconciled with evolution and science, especially through the promotion of evolutionary creation. In 2009, Pope Benedict XVI appointed Collins to the Pontifical Academy of Sciences. Individuals like Collins can have a powerful impact on anti-evolutionists. After hearing Collins, one individual said, "For the first time, I heard a Bible-believing Christian say that evolution is supported by science."[83]

BioLogos "... aims to contribute to the discussion on the relationship between science and religion and emphasizes a compatibility between science and Christian faith...."[84] The Biologos website says, "We believe that the diversity and inter-relation of all life on earth are best explained by the God-ordained process of evolution with common descent. Thus, evolution is not in opposition to God, but a means by which God providentially achieves his purposes. Therefore, we reject ideologies that claim that evolution is a purposeless process or that evolution replaces God."[85]

Evolutionary creation has been adopted by a growing number of evangelical educators.[86] A significant percentage of those responsible for passing along the evangelical Christian faith to the next generation believe that God uses evolution to do his creative work. A downside to this reality is that many evolutionary creationist educators at Christian colleges fear retribution from creationist administrators and supporters. Those concerns keep them from freely expressing their views. The acceptance of theistic evolution by Christian educators, however, is nothing new. A 1919 survey of Midwestern evangelical colleges found that, of the 53 institutions surveyed, 39 advocated theistic evolution, 10 gave ambiguous responses or none at all, and 4 were strictly creationist.[87]

Christian educators at evangelical institutions of higher learning must be circumspect with regard to sharing their views, however, because, in some denominations, individuals have had their employment terminated for espousing evolutionary views. Rachel Marie Stone says, "Unfortunately, evangelical culture encourages you to keep your eyes half closed, lest you see something that causes you to question orthodoxy."[88] Elaine Howard Ecklund has found that the vast majority of believing scientists, 94 percent, are theistic evolutionists.[89] She has found, in addition, that many scientists struggle to reconcile their scientific work with their faith. They resent being attacked, and profoundly misunderstood by young earth creationists, and from the other side of the fence, by the new atheists as well. As a result, many religious scientists practice a closeted faith, much like evangelical church workers and educators who advocate evolutionary creation practice a closeted adherence to scientific truths.[90]

The reconciliation model

The cover of the November 13, 2006 issue of Time Magazine featured Francis Collins and Richard Dawkins.[91] Titled "God vs. Science," the issue was subtitled "A Spirited Debate Between Atheist Biologist Richard Dawkins and Christian Geneticist Francis Collins." Like Christian apologist C.S. Lewis, (who, by the way, had an important positive influence on Collins), Collins is a former atheist.[92] Collins is an example of what Mikael Stenmark calls the reconciliation model. Stenmark says,

> *In my view, there is no conflict in being a rigorous scientist and a person who believes in a God who takes a personal interest in each one of us... I will argue that these perspectives not only can coexist within one person, but can do so in a fashion that enriches and enlightens the human experience.*[93]

Sociologist Elaine Howard Ecklund describes Collins as a boundary pioneer, which she defines as a scientist who has successfully reconciled religion and science.[94] Significantly, for evangelical Christians, Collins is "one of us," and is therefore an important voice in the debate.[95] Evolutionary creation rejects the warfare model, arguing that Biblical teachings about creation and scientific theories of evolution should complement and enrich, not contradict, each other. Like C.S. Lewis (1898-1963) and Francis Collins, Alister McGrath is also a former atheist. And like Collins, McGrath is also a scientist.[96] McGrath is now a respected theologian. In a book-length response to new atheist Richard Dawkins' The God Delusion (2006), McGrath says that the God that Dawkins doesn't believe in is a God he doesn't believe in either![97]

A list of advocates of theistic evolution, past and present, includes many recognizable names.[98] Michael Ruse adds information regarding the religious faith of some prominent names in the field.[99] Several research studies have indicated that theistic evolution is accepted by approximately one third of the U.S. population.[100] A 2009 survey indicated that almost half of the educators at evangelical seminaries are theistic evolutionists.[101] Eugenie Scott, former Executive Director of the National Center for Science Education, says, "... in one form or another, theistic evolutionism is the view of creation taught at the majority of mainline Protestant seminaries, and is the official position of the Roman Catholic Church."[102]

American scientific affiliation

The American Scientific Affiliation (ASA) was founded in the 1940's as an association of orthodox Christian scientists, under the auspices of the conservative Moody Bible Institute. Although the original leadership favored Biblical literalism, and the American Scientific Affiliation was intended to be anti-evolutionary, members generally rejected the flood geology (see chapter 9) proposed by George McCready Price (1870-1963), as well as Harry Rimmer (1890-1952) and his gap theory, moving increasingly toward theistic evolution,[103] with some members "stopping off" at progressive creationism, which had been popularized in the 1930's by Russell L. Mixter (1906-2007). Baptist theologian Bernard Ramm (1916-1992) was an associate of the inner circle of the ASA.[104] Membership currently includes about 1600 scientists.[105] In a 2011 mail survey of ASA scientists, 66 percent affirmed the statement that "Homo sapiens evolved through natural processes from ancestral forms in common with primates," and 90 percent agreed that the earth is some 4.6 billion years old.[106]

The roman catholic church

The Roman Catholic church, contrary to a common perception colored by the Galileo affair in the sixteenth century, has been deeply committed to science generally for many years, and has taken a very positive attitude toward evolutionary theory.[107] Kenneth Miller, American cell biologist, molecular biologist and Professor of Biology at Brown University, is co-author of a major introductory college and high school biology textbook published by Prentice Hall. Miller, himself a Roman Catholic, is known for his opposition to creationism, including intelligent design. His book Finding Darwin's God (1999) argues that acceptance of evolution is compatible with a belief in God; and Only a Theory (2008) explores intelligent design and the Kitzmiller vs. Dover Area School District case and its implications for science generally.[108]

In the late nineteenth century, American Catholic priest John Zaum praised evolution as "... the right creation."[109] Around the same time, Fr. Gregor Mendel, (1822-1884) Jesuit priest and science teacher, carried out his now-famous plant breeding experiments. Mendel's insights on dominant and recessive genes were foundational for the emerging science of genetics. In addition, the Big Bang theory was proposed by a Roman Catholic priest, Fr. Georges LeMaitre (1894-1966).[110] In 1936, Pope Pius XI (1857-1939) opened membership in the Pontifical Academy of Sciences to leading scientists worldwide, without discrimination.[111] And on the 12th of August 1950, in an encyclical titled Humani Generis, Pope Pius XII (1876-1958) stated that the Catholic church found no opposition between evolution and the doctrine of the faith about man and his vocation.[112] Also in 1950, Pope Pius XII declared that Catholics were free to believe in evolution but must accept the doctrine of an infused soul.[113] In 1951, Pius XII said that true science discovers God as though God were waiting behind each door opened by science.[114] In 1996, Pope John Paul II (1920-2005) caused quite a stir in the secular media when he said, "... evolution is more than a hypothesis..."[115] John Paul II also said that the Bible is not a scientific treatise, but states the correct relationship of humanity, God and the universe.[116] John Paul II said that evolutionary challenges to hermeneutics (scriptural interpretation) can assist Christians in determining the proper sense of scripture, so that unwarranted interpretations may be avoided.[117]

Over the span of approximately fifty years, therefore, from 1950 when Pope Pius XII opened the door to the acceptance of evolution, to 1996, when Pope John Paul II strongly affirmed the theory, the Roman Catholic church has been a leader in reconciling faith and science.[118] And then, on October 29th, 2014, Pope Francis made headlines around the world when he said that the theories of evolution and the Big Bang are real, and that God did not wave a "magic wand" to create the universe. Pope Francis also affirmed that current scientific theories concerning the origin of the universe and the development of life are compatible with Catholic doctrine. Speaking at the Pontifical Academy of Sciences, Francis urged Roman Catholics to embrace current scientific theories as "required" methods to understand existence. He said:

> *When we read about creation in Genesis, we run the risk of imagining God was a magician, with a magic wand, able to do everything. But that is not so.*

[God] created human beings and let them develop according to the internal laws that he gave to each one so they would reach their fulfillment.[119]

Atheism

In 1874, Charles Hodge (1797-1878) linked Darwinism with atheism. Anti-evolutionists have been doing the same ever since.[120] Evolutionary creation obviously challenges this assertion.[121] Young earth creationists adopt a typical fundamentalist all-or-nothing attitude, arguing that if Darwin is correct, God's purposeful action in the natural world is removed.[122] Because evolutionary creation is a middle-of-the-road position, it attracts criticism from new atheists on the one side and from young earth and intelligent design creationists on the other. Young earth advocates quote 1 Kings 18:21 which says, "How long will you waver between two opinions?" (NIV)[123] As far as they are concerned, evolutionary creation is heresy pure and simple, a complete capitulation to an ungodly philosophy.[124] Evolutionary creation, they believe, is theologically lethal because it denies the authority of the Holy Scriptures.[125] In conservative Christian circles, because traitors originate from within the group, they are considered worse than external enemies and are described using terms such as apostate, heretic, and heterodox.[126]

Evolutionary creation

According to evolutionary creationist Denis Lamoureux, "... the Creator planned and maintained evolutionary laws and processes in order to create the world and us..."[127] and "...God created life, including humans, through an ordained, sustained, and design-reflecting evolutionary process."[128] Evolutionary creation proposes a type of "intelligent design," arguing that design is evident in nature. But this "design" is not the result of God's direct and intentional intervention, but is inherent in an evolutionary process initiated by God in which he is providentially involved. Lamoureux:

... design is evident in the finely-tuned physical laws and initial conditions necessary for the evolution of the cosmos through the Big Bang, and design is also apparent in the biological processes necessary for life to evolve, including humans with their incredibly complex brains.[129]

Evolutionary creationists seek to balance a high view of scripture with the latest scientific discoveries. They believe that, by connecting faith and science in this way, the depth and richness of God's creative powers are fully revealed.

This partnership between faith and science has been compared to hearing two hands at the piano instead of just one.[130] Individuals are not required to choose God or evolutionary theory. Evolutionary creation encourages them to celebrate both,[131] claiming that God established the laws of nature and subsequently maintains them, including teleological evolution, characterized as "... a planned and purpose-driven natural process."[132]

Theologian John Haught proposes three dimensions of God's creative activity:

- creatio originalis (original creation),
- creatio continua (continuing creation)
- creatio nova (new creation).[133]

As we have seen, evolutionary creation advocates a divinely-supervised ongoing creation, a creatio continua.[134] Denis Lamoureux carefully explains the rationale behind the term "evolutionary creation."[135] Evolutionary creationists believe that God actively supervises his creation[136] through non-interventionist divine action.[137] Seventeenth-century chemist Robert Boyle (1627-1691) anticipated modern evolutionary creation when he said "...God's natural laws are so perfectly tuned and contrived so that history can unfold without any miraculous intervention on His part."[138] Charles Darwin took divine non-intervention to a logical conclusion, arguing that natural selection, without divine intervention, is solely responsible for evolutionary change. Christians believe, however, that the God of the Holy Scriptures is fully involved with, and not absent from, his creation. God, they believe, is concerned with all of his creation, including the sparrow, the animals, (Luke 12:6) and the lilies of the field (Matthew 6:28-30).[139] According to Augustine of Hippo (354-430 A.D.), "... God brought the creation into being in one act imbued with seed principles manifested over time."[140]

For Christians, teleology, the question of whether evolution has a plan or a purpose, is an important aspect of God's creative activity.[141] Of great interest to Christians is the scientific discovery that complex physical systems unfold in time almost as if they "know" where they are going.[142] So when believers trace the process of creation from the Big Bang to the origin of life, it certainly appears that life is not an accident, but has been planned by God.[143] Perhaps the best way to conceptualize this idea is to say that God has given creation a range of possibilities to explore and subsequently gives creation the freedom to explore them.[144] Francisco Ayala, evolutionary biologist and philosopher at the

University of California, Irvine, former Dominican priest, reflects a commonly-held view among evolutionary creationists when he says, "I would argue that evolutionary biology calls... for teleological explanations."[145] Roman Catholic theologian Ian G. Barbour proposes an evolving creation that takes place according to "...a detailed pre-existing blueprint in the mind of God."[146]

Miracles

Evolutionary creationists acknowledge miracles,[147] which are events outside natural laws. Statistically, they are extraordinarily improbable. Non-negotiable doctrines for evolutionary creationism include the virgin birth and Jesus' resurrection from the dead.[148] Philosopher and historian Michael Ruse claims that miracles are not against nature; contra naturam, but beyond our knowledge of nature, supra naturam, producing wonder. Therefore, he says, miracles are not trying to do the work of science. Christians should simply accept them on faith and leave it at that.[149] Sir Colin J. Humphreys points out that musical composers are not bound by their own rules.[150] From a Christian perspective, natural laws cannot limit God. Natural laws are human descriptions of God's activity in nature. Since God is the creator and sustainer of all physical laws, he has the freedom to suspend or override them. Miracles are simply cases where God has chosen to work outside known boundaries. Cambridge University paleontologist Simon Conway Morris says, "I am not surprised at those [New Testament miracles]... I am surprised that they are so few. What else would you expect when the Creator visits his creation?"[151]

For evolutionary creationists, as we have seen, God communicates his will through the scriptures (His Word) and also through nature (His Works).[152] In the spirit of Aristotle's Golden Mean, evolutionary creation chooses the middle path of accommodation. The Golden Mean encourages those on opposite sides of a debate to stop and listen to the still small voice of reason, seeking out good points on both sides of the issue.[153] Ian Hutchinson points out that many of history's greatest scientists viewed science and faith as compatible.[154] For evolutionary creationists the science-religion relationship is not a zero-sum game, with a winner and a loser, but a non-zero-sum game in which both win.[155] A growing academic literature challenges the assertion that science and faith must be at odds.[156] Significantly, research shows that only 25 percent of the American public believes scientists are hostile to religion (see Appendix).[157] The number of scientists who believe there is an inherent conflict between science and religion is only 15 percent.[158]

Intelligent design and evolutionary creation

Deborah Haarsma, president of the BioLogos Foundation since 2013, points out several issues on which evolutionary creation and intelligent design agree:

- The argument that the parameters of the cosmos are fine-tuned for life.
- In addition, both accept deep time and want to be faithful to the tenets of biblical Christianity.
- Both agree that evolution is not the work of meaningless blind processes but is designed by an intelligent creator with the purpose and intent of bringing about the life we see today.[159]

For Christians, the biblical story begins in Genesis as God takes the initiative, and then progresses through Israel's history and on into the New Testament church as it communicates the revelation of Jesus Christ to the world. For Christians of all stripes, God is directly involved in human history. Unlike atheistic evolution, evolutionary creationists believe that, as the evolutionary tree of life grew and branched, producing various species, God supervised and guided the entire process.[160] Evolutionary creationists are fully cognizant of the fact that these processes are not empirically detectable.[161] Scott McKnight makes the important point that "... just because science can explain a phenomenon does not mean that God's involvement is negated."[162]

Follow the evidence

A review of the literature reveals that a surprising number of evangelical Christians began their investigation of evolutionary theory as young earth creationists, but, after a thorough review of the evidence, came to adopt an evolutionary point of view.[163] Many evangelical Christians intuitively (and privately!) hold a position similar to evolutionary creation, and when they hear evolutionary creation explained in detail, adopt it. This perspective answers many questions these individuals have harbored for years.[164] Unfortunately, as we have already pointed out, in many Christian communities, pro-evolution positions like this are never presented as an acceptable option and, as a result, many believers are unaware of them.

Consider the following scenario. A pro-evolution pastor attends a meeting made up of clergy and laypeople. A fellow pastor lends him a book to read. A third pastor indicates a long-term interest in science and the theory of evolution without being able to come to any firm conclusions. He's looking for further clarification. Would the first pastor be able to suggest a book that would help him sort through the issues? The first pastor recommends Francis Collins' The Language of God. Two weeks later, he receives an email stating that the book was extremely helpful in enabling the colleague to understand how science and religion can relate in a positive way. That colleague is now comfortable in taking on a pro-evolution perspective. A chance encounter leads to the discovery of a common interest. And another individual joins the ranks of evolutionary creationists.

In young earth creationist denominations, outliers like the individuals just described must be circumspect about sharing their views. In these denominations, when individuals discover, often by chance, that they are kindred spirits in their pro-science, pro-evolutionary views, there is great rejoicing. But they hesitate to speak out publicly for fear of reprisal. Evangelical Christians generally have great respect for C.S. Lewis. Many do not know that Lewis held a position on evolution very similar to evolutionary creation. Lewis was not concerned about evolution per se, but with the scientism characteristic of the new atheists, a viewpoint which excludes any possibility of divine intervention in the process.[165]

Environmental stewardship

Adopting an evolutionary perspective has major potential implications for Christian stewardship. As we have seen, God calls His people to be good stewards of all his gifts, including the gifts of comprehension and knowledge, both theological and scientific. Rosalind Picard says, "God is the author of all intellectual tools, including our very ability to comprehend."[166] Adopting an evolutionary perspective has important implications for a Christian's stewardship of the earth and of all living things. In Genesis chapter 2, Adam and Eve are placed into the garden to tend and to serve. They are explicitly given dominion over creation, symbolizing humanity's obligation to care for it. [167] In order to be good stewards of creation, however, Christians must understand their place in it and their relationship to all other living things. Evolutionary creation declares that, because all organisms are related by common descent, human beings are biologically connected to all living things, and what they do profoundly affects all other creatures.[168] Humanity's place as the crown of God's creation carries with it a special responsibility to be good stewards of the environment. Each species has a long history and is irreplaceable.[169] Each species is intrinsically valuable. Human-caused extinctions result in the loss of billions of years of irreplaceable divine design work. Science can help humanity establish a right relationship with the environment. It is dangerous to give individuals dominion over something they do not properly understand.[170]

Evolutionary creation, with its respect for modern science, enables Christians to more accurately understand the scripture,[171] and promotes an enriched understanding of God, his works, and his ways, a position known as complementarity.[172] I contend that science has the very real potential to enrich the Christian faith, rendering it more scientifically relevant, and more appealing to scientifically-literate, spiritually-minded individuals, especially young people. Amazingly, after more than one hundred and fifty years, many Christians still reject Darwin and the theory of evolution.[173] All Christians should be able to agree that discovering truth - be it spiritual or scientific is their goal. God is certainly not threatened by humanity's efforts to understand his creation.[174]

A full experience of life

We have seen that the theory of evolution coexists with many religious faiths.[175] According to The Catechism of the Roman Catholic Church, both science and religion are needed for a full experience of life.[176] Section 283:

> *The question about the origins of the world and of man has been the object of many scientific studies which have splendidly enriched our knowledge of the age and dimensions of the cosmos, the development of life-forms and the appearance of man. These discoveries invite us to even greater admiration for the greatness of the Creator, prompting us to give him thanks for all his works and for the understanding and wisdom he gives to scholars and researchers.*[177]

Sections 337 and 338 add:

> *Scripture presents the work of the Creator symbolically as a succession of six days of divine 'work,' concluded by the 'rest' of the seventh day ....nothing exists that does not owe its existence to God the Creator. The world began when God's word drew it out of nothingness; all existent beings, all of nature, and all human history is rooted in this primordial event, the very genesis by which the world was constituted and time begun.*[178]

Every nook and cranny

It is my contention that scientific discoveries enable Christians to better understand how God actually governs the universe.[179] Ironically, and in contradiction to arguments made by young earth creationists, evolutionary creation restores God's influence to every nook and cranny of this vast universe.[180] A marginal comment I made in 1991 said, "If evolution is true in every aspect, you either have no need for God, or God has nothing to do!" Today, my certainties have evolved and I would say, "Actually, rather than having nothing to do, our amazing God oversees every aspect of the evolutionary process!" I want to emphasize that it would not be appropriate to adopt an evolutionary point of view without considerable thought, and, for Christians, much prayer. A great deal is unquestionably at stake here.[181] Those who travel this road often adopt different paradigms along the way.[182] In another marginal note, again from 1991, I asked, "Why not theistic evolution?" Why not, indeed!

The difference between young earth creationism and an evolutionary point of view has been compared to seeing God's creation in black and white rather than in color.[183] An 82-year-old farmer once said, "The more I learn about this amazing universe, the more amazing my God becomes."[184] Believers must not allow themselves to be caught up in the false dichotomy that insists Christians are limited to a choice between a literalistic interpretation of Genesis on the one hand, or godless evolution on the other.[185] Each of us, believer and unbeliever alike, should be able to agree that acquiring truth is our primary task.[186] Nineteenth century Congregational clergyman Edward Hitchcock (1793-1864) said "... the real question is, not whether these hypotheses accord with our religious views, but whether they are true."[187] It is the Christian's duty to discover the world God has made.[188]

9. YOUNG EARTH CREATIONISM

Overview

For more than a century, a close relationship has existed between the Seventh-Day Adventist Church and young earth creationism. In 1864, Adventist prophet Ellen G. White experienced a vision which she believed provided her with previously unknown details about Noah's flood. That vision became the basis for what was later to be called flood geology. White was convinced that her vision revealed how Noah's flood had literally changed the geology of the whole earth, carving out canyons and laying down fossils. White's ideas were later taken up by Canadian amateur geologist and fellow Adventist, George McCready Price.

It is noteworthy that young earth creationism was not well-known until the 1961 publication of The Genesis Flood, an attitude-changing book co-authored by Henry Morris and John Whitcomb. This book, written primarily for Christian laypeople, delivered McCready Price's flood geology to a much wider, mostly evangelical audience. The Genesis Flood strongly criticized the willingness of some Christians (Morris and Whitcomb were thinking of Bernard Ramm here) to accommodate their theology to scientific discovery. If there is one reason why young earth creationism grew so rapidly in popularity among U.S. evangelicals, it would have to be The Genesis Flood.

Young earth creationism came into its own in the 1960's. Previously, the day-age and gap theories were the preferred views, especially among Protestant fundamentalists. Much like the Seventh-Day Adventists, the Lutheran Church – Missouri Synod (LCMS) also had a significant impact on young earth creationism. The Missouri Synod has a lengthy track record opposing evolution. In the 1950's and 1960's, in the formative years of young earth creationism, the Missouri Synod provided expert leadership to the cause, including professors from its seminary in St. Louis.

Contrary to the geological consensus regarding deep time and an ancient earth, established by the 1830's, young earth creationists insist that the earth is between 6,000 and 10,000 years old. And, contrary to the findings of biological sciences and genomics, this perspective denies evolution and common descent. This rejection is based, not on scientific evidence, but on the presupposition that their interpretation of the Bible's creation narratives is beyond reproach. Young earth creationists are scientific concordists, a concept we have encountered several times already, believing that the ancient science in the scriptures is without error. Many young earth creationists believe that God created the earth and the universe with the appearance of age. This appearance-of-age thesis (see chapter 4), however, makes God a deceiver and is a not-so-subtle affirmation of the very geological facts it seeks to deny. Young earth creationists also believe that species (i.e., the Bible's kinds) are unchanging and do not evolve into new forms.

There are two living authors whose works have sold over half a billion copies. One is American novelist Danielle Steel. And the other is Christian pamphleteer Jack Chick. Now past 90 years of age, the reclusive Chick has reportedly sold a staggering 750 million copies of his illustrated tracts and comic books since 1960. His works have been translated into over 100 languages and are widely distributed by missionaries and other Christian workers. His anti-evolution pamphlet, titled Big Daddy, which first appeared in 1972, is reportedly the most widely distributed anti-evolution booklet in history. The complete tract is shown on the Chick Publications website. It portrays a scientific conspiracy against religion, to this day a prominent theme in anti-evolution literature.

Background

Very few of the Christian church fathers were six-day creationists in the pre-Reformation (up to the sixteenth century) period of church history. Martin Luther (1483-1546), however, was an important exception. Given his interpretive methodology, Luther could be considered the father of young earth creationism.[1] Martin Luther's literalisic hermeneutic has had a powerful influence on today's young earth creationists. In his Lectures on Genesis, Luther took issue with Augustine (354-430 A.D.),[2] contending that, "Moses spoke in the literal sense, not allegorically or figuratively, that the world with all its creatures was created within six days, as the words read. We know from Moses that the world was not in existence before six thousand years ago."[3]

As we have noted, Luther opposed the heliocentric theory put forward by his contemporary, Nicolaus Copernicus (1473-1543). Luther continued to advocate geocentrism (see chapter 3).[4] Luther accepted the Bible's common-sense phenomenological descriptions of nature and strongly criticized anyone who questioned them.[5] To this day, confessional Lutherans and many evangelicals follow his example.

Many Christians, evangelical or otherwise, are unaware of the direct connection between young earth creationism and nineteenth-century Seventh-day Adventism.[6] At that time, Adventists were led by the charismatic prophet Ellen G. White (1827-1915). White claimed to receive divine messages in visions. Adventists placed her pronouncements on par with the Bible.[7] Among Adventists, White's collected writings are called The Spirit of Prophecy.[8] Based on one of her visions, White erroneously predicted that Jesus Christ would return on October 22nd, 1844. White's dramatic vision regarding the Biblical flood became the foundation of what would later be called flood geology – the argument that the earth's geological features, including fossil deposits, were laid down by a global flood as described in Genesis chapters 6 through 8. White claimed that she was "... carried back to the creation and was shown that the first week... was just like every other week."[9] The Genesis flood, according to White, reshaped the earth's surface and the fossils laid down during and after the flood testify to its cataclysmic nature. Earth's history prior to the flood was obliterated, but the flood itself left clear evidence behind. This is her vision:

> *The entire surface of the earth was changed at the Flood. As the waters began to subside, the hills and mountains were surrounded by a vast turbid sea. Everywhere were strewn the dead bodies of men and beasts. The Lord would not permit these to remain to decompose and pollute the air, therefore He made of the earth a vast burial ground. A violent wind which was caused to blow for the purpose of drying up the waters, moved them with great force, in some instances even carrying away the tops of the mountains and heaping up trees, rocks, and earth above the bodies of the dead. At this time immense forests were buried. These have since been changed to coal, forming the extensive coal beds that now exist and yielding large quantities of oil.*[10]

After White's death, flood geology was reinvigorated and vigorously promoted by Canadian amateur geologist and fellow Seventh-Day Adventist George McCready Price (1870-1963). In 1891, McCready Price graduated from an Adventist school in Michigan. In 1896, he enrolled in a one-year teacher training course, with some elementary courses in the natural sciences.[11] Price was a self-taught geologist who considered it a virtue he had not attended university.[12] Over a thirty-year period, Price wrote more than two dozen books and hundreds of articles promoting flood geology, essentially a modern form of catastrophism.[13] It wasn't until the early 1920's, when evolution moved to the top of the fundamentalist agenda, that Price's reputation began to grow.[14] In 1923, he wrote his most influential book, The New Geology. In his published works, Price avoided mentioning Ellen White's vision about the flood and flood geology's connection to Adventism.[15] Price offered easy and simplistic answers to complex questions.

Price had no professional training in geology but was willing to single-handedly take on the entire discipline solely on the basis of events described in the Bible.[16] For Price, flood geology cleared up a host of geological problems.[17] Price drew attention, for example, to what he claimed were "upside down" strata covering at least fourteen square miles in the Canadian province of Alberta, just east of the Rockies, where "older" Cambrian fossiliferous rocks overlay "younger" Cretaceous rocks, which, in his opinion, disputed the sequential deposition of strata proposed by geologists.[18] Price never wavered from his conviction that the idea of successive geological ages, put forward by mainstream geology, represented the true source of the evolution problem.[19] As far as Price was concerned, true believers had only two choices. They could either reject God's inspired word or they could abandon the testimony of the geologists.[20]

For Price, and for the young earth creationism he promoted, science must always be subservient to theology, and should never be considered an equal partner in a quest for truth. Price's ideas were subsequently borrowed by John Whitcomb (1924-) and Henry Morris (1918-2006) and formed the main argument of The Genesis Flood (1961).[21] After 1960, motivated primarily by Price's flood geology, increasing numbers of evangelicals began to reject standard geological arguments for the age of the earth.[22] David MacMillan says: "The age of the earth wasn't a dividing issue in Christianity until Morris and Whitcomb plagiarized flood geology from the Seventh-day Adventists in the 1960's."[23] Before Price's flood geology, many Christian fundamentalists accepted the idea of deep time.[24] In 1982, the International Council on Biblical Inerrancy, a group comprised of conservative Christian scholars, stated in a majority decision that the days of Genesis need not be twenty-four hours long.[25]

The flood narrative

Over the years, the Genesis flood narrative has raised a host of questions. Robert A. Moore, for example, points out the obvious when he says that the account of the great flood and the voyage of the ark contains many incredible violations of the laws of nature. Supernaturalism would take care of that, but the geological evidence tells its own story. If all of creation is supernatural, of course, all bets are off, because anything is possible. But that is not what the evidence says. For young earth creationists, confronted by increasingly strong scientific evidence, the supernatural is a convenient fallback position. It all boils down to the age-old question of what God could do versus what he actually did.[26] Before Noah could even begin such a huge project, he would have needed knowledge of naval architecture, physics, calculus, mechanics, and structural analysis. There was no shipbuilding expertise in Israel during that time. There were no experienced craftsmen available. These sixty-eight verses of scripture, says Moore, when interpreted literally, are crammed with more miracles than any comparable piece of literature anywhere on earth.[27]

Henry Morris writes, "If we are to know anything about creation – when it was, what methods were used, what order of events occurred, or anything else – we must depend completely on divine revelation."[28] He adds,

> *... the main reason for insisting on the universal flood as a fact of history and as the primary vehicle for geological interpretation is that God's word plainly teaches it! No geologic difficulties, real or imagined, can be allowed to take precedence over the clear statements and necessary inference of scripture.*[29]

Notwithstanding Morris's protestations, post-flood questions abound. How, for instance, did the limited number of species assembled on the ark increase to the millions of species that populate the earth today?[30] And how did the lowly kangaroo make it all the way from Mount Ararat in Turkey to isolated Australia without leaving evidence of its presence along the way? Surprisingly, young earth creationist organizations like Answers in Genesis now propose that the rapid diversification of animals around the world after the flood was due to an extremely rapid form of evolution![31] It is proposed that all species living today evolved from single animal pairs released from Noah's ark after the flood.[32] So, by means of this extremely rapid evolution, the ten thousand pairs of land-dwelling animals estimated to have been preserved on the ark diversified to the more than six million species present on the earth today.[33] And young earth proponents claim all this happened in just a few thousand years. This speculation, however, is not supported scientifically.[34] Apparently, evolution is true, but only when it can be stretched a little so as to fit one's hermeneutic.

Bernard ramm

Bernard Ramm (1916-1992) was a respected Baptist theologian and apologist in the 1950's. The Christian View of Science and Scripture was published in 1954.[35] Ramm was strongly critical of George McCready Price's flood geology and the notion of a young earth. Ramm, incidentally, was influential in the American Scientific Affiliation's decision not to support Price's proposal that the Biblical flood was responsible for the broad sweep of the earth's geology and embedded fossils. In The Genesis Flood, Morris and Whitcomb strongly denounced Ramm's progressive creationism, with its acceptance of an ancient earth.[36] Many evangelicals in the 1950's and 1960's, including evangelist Billy Graham, did support Ramm, however. Billy Graham was a prominent advocate. He said, surprisingly,

> *I don't think that there is any conflict at all between science today and the scripture. I think we have misinterpreted the scripture many times and we've tried to make the scripture say things that they weren't meant to say, and I think we have made a mistake by thinking the Bible is a scientific book. The Bible is not a book of science. The Bible is a book of Redemption, and of course, I accept the creation story. I believe that God created man, and whether it came by an evolutionary process and at a certain point he took this person or being and made him a living soul or not, does not change the fact that God did create man... Whichever way God did it makes no difference as what man is and man's relationship to God.*[37]

The Genesis Flood is essentially two long arguments, the first explaining George McCready Price's flood geology, and the second a harsh critique of Bernard Ramm's accommodationism.[38] Historian Ronald Numbers points out that when Morris (1918-2006) read Ramm's The Christian View of Science & Scripture, he angrily lined the margins of the book with his private thoughts.[39] Henry Morris was a Southern Baptist with a PhD in hydraulics and civil engineering from the University of Minnesota, earned in 1950.[40] Co-author John Whitcomb (1924-) is an Old Testament scholar, with an honors degree in history from Princeton, and a doctorate from Grace Theological Seminary.[41] Numbers points out how flood geology was refurbished in The Genesis Flood.[42] Morris and Whitcomb deleted all but a few incidental references to Price and any mention of his Adventist connections.[43] They refused to be drawn into the scientific debate about evolution, arguing, "The real issue is not the correctness of the interpretation of various details of the geological data, but simply what God has revealed in his word."[44]

Henry Morris was, without a doubt, the most influential young earth creationist in the latter half of the twentieth century.[45] Most Christians today would be surprised to know that the evangelical Christian publisher, Moody Press, declined to publish The Genesis Flood when it had a chance, arguing that young earth creationism was not very popular and that most Christians had accepted a form of old-earth creationism called the gap-theory (see chapter 7).[46] It is worth noting that much of the science denial currently evident in the U.S. and elsewhere can be traced back to Price, as well as to Morris and Whitcomb. The young earth attacks on modern science have been harmful to the church, to its credibility, and to its outreach as well as to the cavalier attitude of many evangelicals regarding stewardship of the earth's precious life-forms and of the environment itself. How is it possible, asks Francis Collins, that the United States, the most advanced technological country in the world, is home to so much anti-scientific thinking?[47] Young earth creationists dismiss the claims of science with brusque denials rather than dealing with them in an open and objective manner.[48] Denial is defined by Paul Appelbaum, former head of the American Psychiatric Association, as the "... deliberate, often psychologically motivated, neglect of information that would be too upsetting or anxiety-provoking to allow into one's belief system."[49] Michael Milburn, professor of psychology at the University of Massachusetts, and coauthor of The Politics of Denial quotes Upton Sinclair who said, "...it is difficult to get a man to understand something, when his salary depends on his not understanding it."[50]

Anti-evolutionists often cite references from the scientific literature, but cherry-pick the material, often ignoring the context. Theologians would certainly cry foul if scientists did the same with theological literature.[51] Another common technique is called 'moving the goalposts' and involves responding to opponents by continuously demanding new sorts of evidence. Also commonly employed are conspiracy theories, which involve countering an opponent's statement of facts with an accusation that something is being maliciously covered up. This sort of denial enables individuals to maintain worldviews that make the most sense to them, whether they are supported by the facts or not. With the rapid growth of the internet and social media we have seen the impact of a 'filter bubble,' the growing practice of only acknowledging information that supports an individual's preconceived notions. Speaking of the proliferation of internet-related media, Shawn Otto says:

An example that helps put this practice into perspective is a device called the Volksempfanger, which was a radio the Nazis produced in the 1930's – "the people's radio." They filled it with propaganda and politically slanted news and patriotic music. And, if you think about it, that is a parallel to the political echo chamber that is created by politically-slanted cable television news today, and by the self-selected political echo chamber that people place themselves in via social media.[52]

In addition, in the name of balanced reporting journalists feel obligated to give attention to the 'other side' of an issue, when that other point of view has long been shown to be deficient. This practice may inadvertently lead individuals to believe that the other view is equally valid.

The Lutheran Church – Missouri Synod

The Lutheran Church - Missouri Synod (LCMS) is located on the conservative side of the Lutheran theological spectrum. Lutheran systematician Francis Pieper (1852-1931), highly respected among confessional Lutherans to this day, continued to oppose Copernican theory in his three-volume Christian Dogmatics (completed in 1924), well into the twentieth century. The parallels to today's conflict over evolution are compelling.[53] Fellow Lutherans ridiculed the Missouri Synod for claiming that the Bible taught Ptolemaic astronomy, which placed the earth at rest in the center of the solar system.[54] Most Lutheran laypeople would be surprised to know that their church had long denied this basic and well-established cosmological fact.[55] The reasons why Christian Dogmatics rejected Copernicus has little to do with the actual science involved, and a lot to do with long-standing theological beliefs. Pieper knew that acceptance of Copernican heliocentrism would immediately challenge the historicity of the account in the book of Joshua, in which it is said that the sun stood still for a day.[56] And that, in turn, would deny biblical inerrancy as it is traditionally defined.

The Missouri Synod has consistently opposed evolution, asserting, for example, in a 1932 doctrinal statement that "... God has created heaven and earth, in the manner and in the space of time recorded in the Holy Scripture, in six days3."[57] Most Christians today are unaware of the fact that the Missouri Synod was heavily involved in the formation of young earth creationist groups such as The Bible Science Association (1963) and The Creation Research Society, founded the same year.[58] Four of the original ten members of The Creation Research Society board of directors were from the Missouri Synod.[59] Strong support for young earth creationism came from professors in the synod including Theo Graebner, an instructor at the Concordia Theological Seminary in St. Louis. Synodical leaders were encouraged in their thinking by the views of Martin Luther, who, as we have seen, was himself a six-day creationist.[60] Alfred Rehwinkel (1887-1979) of the Missouri Synod was heavily influenced by George McCready Price's flood geology. Rehwinkel wrote The Flood: In the Light of the Bible, Geology, and Archaeology in 1951.[61] Rehwinkel praised Price as being the foremost defender of Genesis.[62] Walter E. Lammerts (1904-1996), another member of the synod, argued that evolution and a traditional interpretation of creation were fundamentally incompatible. Like Rehwinkel, Lammerts was a lifelong disciple of McCready Price.[63] Throughout the 1960's and into the early 1970's, scarcely a regular convention of the Missouri Synod occurred without some group or other introducing a resolution critical of evolution.[64] In 1959, on the centennial of Darwin's Origin of Species, the Missouri Synod published a collection of creationist essays titled Darwin, Evolution, and Creation.[65]

In most evangelical denominations, young earth creationism is the only game in town.[66] According to Denis Lamoureux, 87 percent of American evangelicals subscribe to this point of view.[67] Young earth creationism is, according to Michael Ruse, "... an idiosyncratic legacy of nineteenth century, American, evangelical Protestantism."[68] At its 2004 Convention, the Missouri Synod passed a pro-young earth resolution which clearly lays out its strong opposition to evolutionary theory.[69] Young earth creationism is currently promoted by organizations like Answers in Genesis, founded in 1994 by Ken Ham, and the ICR, the Institute for Creation Research, founded in 1970 by Dr. Henry Morris.

In the late twentieth century, no one has done more to popularize young earth creationism than Henry M. Morris and his colleagues at the Institute for Creation Research in San Diego.[70] In the 1960's and 1970's, the ICR and its flood geology rapidly reached across the spectrum of evangelical denominations.[71] In the twenty-year period from 1960 to 1980, adoption of young earth creationism surged ahead among evangelical Christians in the United States.[72] By 1980, nearly every American evangelical church and school had been influenced by flood geology.[73]

Beliefs

Young earth creationism, as its name implies, rejects evolution, and an ancient earth. It denies common descent, and is adamant that there has been no human evolution. It accepts microevolution, that is, evolutionary change within a species or small group of organisms, especially over a short period, but rejects macroevolution, change that occurs at or above the species level.[74] Young earth creationist literature betrays a clear and abiding contempt for mainstream science. For many years, creationists have burned bridges to the scientific world. As we have noted, anti-evolutionism is much more a theological than it is a scientific critique of evolutionary theory. Advocates believe that their proprietary literalistic interpretation of scripture's creation accounts mandates rejection of an old earth and of evolution. Given the high priority assigned to their beliefs as opposed to scientific evidence, it seems that no amount of evidence would be sufficient to change their minds.[75] Like Elijah in the Old Testament who believed he was the only one left serving the Lord, (1 Kings 19:10) today's young earth proponents believe they are the only ones left defending biblical authority. Old Testament scholar John Walton says that anti-evolutionists, mindful of the apostle Paul's advice about rightly handling the Word (2 Timothy 2:15), "... pride themselves on reading the Bible text literally and flash this as a badge of honor as they critique other views."[76] Duane T. Gish (1921-2013), creationist ambassador for many years, said the reason why he embraced strict creationism was because of his desire to read the Bible as "straightforwardly" as possible.[77]

Scientific concordism

Along with several other anti-evolutionary perspectives, young earth creationists promote scientific concordism, the idea, as Henry Morris explains it, that because the Bible is God-given, it could not possibly contain scientific mistakes or inaccuracies of any kind.[78] Morris claimed that should science and the Bible conflict, the problem cannot be with the Bible, but science has misinterpreted its data.[79] Since young earth creationists believe that the Bible is accurate in matters of science, this, in and of itself, is strong support, in their opinion, for its inspiration by the Holy Spirit and for its inerrancy.[80] If scientific concordism is incorrect, however, young earth creationists know that they would have to revise many of their most cherished doctrines (see chapter 12).

Warfare model

In previous chapters, we noted that a significant number of Christian groups cannot bear the consequences of Darwin's world.[81] The warfare model is, in a sense, the frame on the portrait of young earth creationism.[82] A prominent theme in young earth literature, consoling in its simplicity, is that of a massive scientific conspiracy directed primarily against Biblical authority, an understandable concern for those with a high view of scripture, including its inspiration and inerrancy.[83] In addition, many evangelicals associate science with a liberal worldview which seeks to overthrow traditional morality.[84] According to young earth creationist orthodoxy, creation is the work of an unchanging God, expressed in the context of His unchanging Word, interpreted in the context of an unchanging hermeneutic. Science, on the other hand, the argument goes, is an expression of man's ever-changing, and often contradictory, opinion. In the late 19th century, Charles H. Spurgeon (1834-1892) expressed strong anti-scientific sentiments, many of which are still heard today:

> *We are invited, brethren, most earnestly to go away from the old-fashioned belief of our forefathers because of the supposed discoveries of science. What is science? The method by which man tries to conceal his ignorance... Forsooth, you and I are to take our Bibles and shape and mold our belief according to the ever-shifting teachings of so-called scientific men. What folly is this?*[85]

In creationist literature there is a consistent (and ironic) effort to make scientists appear closed-minded.[86] Compromise is not an option. The new atheists, by their actions and by their words, present creationists with a valuable gift – an easily-identifiable enemy.[87] The driving force behind young earth creationism is fear, not fact.[88] In a culture war such as this, facts are secondary. Truth has value when it serves a purpose, not necessarily for its own sake.[89] This conflict is essentially a battle of two fundamentalisms – the religious dogmatist and the scientific idolater.[90] In many ways, what we have here is two monologues.[91] Scientific truths, however, are not decided by majority vote, but by rigorously-gathered data and solid evidence.[92] Quoting Colossians 2:8, (NIV) "Do not let your minds be captured by hollow and elusive speculations," creationists warn their constituency about the dangers of accepting evolution.[93] Young earth creationists, however, do not speak for all Christians, or even all evangelical Christians.[94] Anti-evolutionists exhibit the same "blinkered tenacity" characteristic of all fundamentalist thinking, be it religious, scientific, or political.[95] In the young earth subculture, everything is safe and comfortable. Everything is approved by others. Others are more than willing to do your thinking for you.[96]

Vapor canopy theory

An argument still heard in some young earth circles is the so-called vapor canopy theory. Historian Ronald Numbers outlines the version put forward by Henry Morris –

> *In sketching the history of life on earth between the creation and the flood, [Henry] Morris repeatedly alluded to 'a great vapor canopy' that enveloped the antediluvian earth. Formed on the second day of creation, when God divided the waters under the firmament from the waters above the firmament (Genesis 1:7), this canopy produced a 'greenhouse effect' that gave the entire world a relatively mild and uniform climate, protected antediluvians from the harmful effects of cosmic radiation and thus greatly extended their lives, and provided a vast reservoir of water that deluged the earth during the flood of Noah.*[97]

This speculation is no longer promoted by major creationist organizations. This withdrawal, however, is an exception to the rule. Creationists continue to propose a host of non-scientific speculations.[98]

Kinds

A core belief of young earth creationism is that evolution (in this case, microevolution) is only possible within created "kinds" of animals, not between kinds (macroevolution). This understanding of species is similar to that of the Greek philosopher Aristotle (384-322 B.C.) who proposed that each species (similar to the Biblical "kind") is set apart from every other by an immutable "essence," a view that has been called species essentialism.[99] The biblical argument of "... each according to its own kind" (cf. Genesis 1:21) is an ancient common-sense phenomenal observation about the apparent stability of species over time.[100] Baraminology is the name given to the creationist system that classifies animals into groups called "created kinds" or "baramin." Baraminology claims that kinds cannot interbreed, and have no evolutionary relationship to one another. The term was coined in 1990 by Kurt P. Wise, based on Frank Lewis Marsh's (1899-1992) 1941 use of the term "baramin" from the Hebrew words bara (create) and min (kind).[101]

The Answers in Genesis website says: "The Bible uses the term 'kind.' The Bible's first use of this word (Hebrew: min) is found in Genesis 1 when God creates plants and animals 'according to their kinds.' A plain reading of the text infers that plants and animals were created to reproduce within the boundaries of their kind."[102] Since creationists believe that species cannot evolve into other species, those species must either live on or become extinct. The number of species therefore cannot increase over time. Contradicting this is the fossil record which shows that new types of life have appeared regularly over the age of the earth, and old ones have disappeared.

Mutations

Young earth creationism argues that mutations have a consistently negative effect on organisms. The Answers in Genesis website says:

> *In the evolutionary model, mutations are hailed as a dominant mechanism for pond-scum-to-people evolution and provide 'proof' that the Bible's history about creation is wrong. But are we to trust the ideas of imperfect, fallible men about how we came into existence? If new genetic information – required to build eyes where there are none, for example – does not occur in nature, then evolution is stuck in the water. For evolutionists, the solution comes in the form of mutations. The problem is that the only beneficial mutations ever observed do not add new information to the genome.*[103]

Evolutionary biologists have repeatedly shown that certain mutations are critically important in evolution because they replenish the variability of the gene pool (see chapter 5).[104] In other words, beneficial mutations provide the critical raw material on which natural selection operates.[105]

The cambrian explosion

Between 540 and 510 million years ago, a huge increase in biological diversity occurred which has come to be called the Cambrian Explosion. That diversity resulted in the evolution of many groups of organisms that serve as the basic "templates" on which today's animals are based.[106] One of the challenges scientists face in explaining this event has to do with fossilization. Perhaps only 5 percent of the animals in the seas at that time were fossilized; a vast amount of information, therefore, has been lost.[107] Biologists are looking for an overall blueprint or set of assembly instructions that led to the explosion.[108] Dr. Tommy Michell, in an article found on the Answers in Genesis website, expresses a typical creationist argument:

> *How do these evolutionists know an event they call the 'explosion' was so*

important? Because they cannot explain the abrupt 'evolution' of diverse life forms all over the world at about the same time. And since they maintain these organisms were the evolutionary ancestors of all other animal life and ultimately even humans, they really need to explain how life popped into the fossil record so suddenly.[109]

Creation Ministries International suggests flood geology as the answer:

... the paradox vanishes when one removes the glasses of evolutionary presuppositions and sees the data in the light of biblical creation / flood. The entire set of unique body plans ever created is represented in all rocks bearing substantial numbers of animal fossils. The 'Cambrian' creatures, many of which are now extinct, are not 'primitive ancestors' to today's, but are complex creatures in their own right, with no trace of evolutionary ancestors.[110]

A scientific account of the Cambrian explosion is found on the PBS website.

Life flourished long before the "explosion." Then, between 570 and 530 million years ago, a burst of diversification occurred, with the appearance of the lineages of almost all animals living today. These changes occurred in a range of about thirty million years, and some stages took five to ten million years. The best record of the diversification is the Burgess Shale in British Columbia. Why did many fundamentally different body plans evolve so early and in such profusion? Some point to the increase in oxygen that began around 700 million years ago, providing fuel for movement and the evolution of more complex body structures. Others propose that an extinction of life just before the Cambrian opened up ecological roles, or "adaptive space," that the new forms exploited.[111]

External, ecological factors are the prime suspects in creating just the right conditions for the so-called explosion to occur.[112]

The young earth arguments we have just encountered reinforce the observation that the appeal of anti-evolutionism is primarily emotional and ideological, not scientific.[113] It's not surprising then to see that since their primary audience is comfortable with religious terminology, creationists deliberately use that kind of language in their discussion of evolution. Creationists claim, for instance, that evolution is a "secular religion" masquerading as science.[114]

Religious terms employed in their descriptions of evolution and evolutionists include words like: faith, secular religion, dogma, and priesthood.[115]

Debates

In the 1970s, Institute for Creation Research staff participated in more than one hundred debates.[116] Their strategy was to raise more arguments than their scientific opponents could deal with in the limited time available.[117] A favorite strategy, called the argument from incredulity, is commonly expressed as, "You haven't convinced me yet!"[118] Ironically, from a scientific point of view, vigorous debates about evolution have been occurring continuously for many years – in scientific meetings and publications. Young earth creationists, however, choose not to participate on this official level.[119] The very existence of a debate implies that there are two equal sides to an issue which has, in the present case, already been settled scientifically. By the mere fact of agreeing to a debate, the scientist grants a degree of legitimacy to the creationist. According to Michael Shermer, creationists are "...in it for the publicity. They know that the debate is really about religious belief, not scientific evidence and theory."[120]

Anti-evolutionists are not averse to using threats and intimidation. They will also play the doctrinal purity card if necessary, implying that, as true Christians, they are the only ones with the courage to stand up to atheistic scientists.[121] In the evangelical subculture, beliefs about evolution are often a sort of litmus test for determining the orthodoxy of a person's faith.[122] Because of the threat of sanctions, evangelical Christians who have adopted an evolutionary perspective often hesitate to speak freely.[123] Ironically, many believing scientists are also reluctant to go public with their faith, fearing a backlash from their scientific colleagues.[124] Believing scientists often find themselves under suspicion from both sides, from creationists on the one hand, and from unbelieving colleagues on the other.[125]

Only a theory

Anti-evolutionists claim that evolution is "only a theory."[126] However, in science, theory has a very different meaning than it does in everyday usage. In everyday use, a theory is no more than an educated guess or a hunch. In science, however, a theory is a well-substantiated, well-supported, well-documented explanation for observations. In science, a theory ties facts together, providing an explanation that fits the observations and that can be used to make predictions. In science, the ultimate goal of research is the explanation provided by a theory.

In science, a theory is as close to proven as anything in science can be.[127] Young earth advocates also insist that evolution is "a theory in crisis."[128] This claim is based on a 1985 book by Michael Denton titled Evolution: A Theory in Crisis.[129] Young earth biologist Todd Wood openly admits such is not the case.[130] Creationism's best-educated advocate, Kurt Wise, a PhD geologist who studied under Stephen Jay Gould at Harvard, admits that the scientific evidence is clearly stacked against creationism.[131]

Transitional fossils

Young earth creationists claim, in addition, that there are no transitional fossils. The creation.com website, for example, says:

> *Transitional fossils are the remains of those creatures which should be found 'in-between' one kind of creature and another kind. For example, evolutionists have long sought the 'missing link' between ape and human; some sort of half human – half ape intermediate form. None has ever been found, though many candidates have come and gone.*[132]

In reality, plenty of transitional fossils exist. Examples include horse and whale lineages.[133] An important example of a transitional fossil is tiktaalik roseae, described as "the perfect missing link between fish and amphibian" (see chapter 5).[134] Tiktaalik provides evidence that hind legs evolved from fins 375 million years ago.[135] Transitions from reptiles to mammals, and mammals to whales are quite common.[136] And a remarkable hominid-rich fossil record documents a gradual transition from Homo erectus through to Neanderthal.[137] A question young earth creationists often ask is: "If people are descended from monkeys, why are there still monkeys around?" That would be like asking "If many Americans and Australians are descended from Europeans, why are there still Europeans around?[138] Consider the following example of how difficult it can be to determine transitions from one state to another:

> *Philosophers like to talk about the heap problem. One grain of wheat is not a heap of wheat; two grains of wheat are not a heap; but a million grains of wheat are indeed a heap. At what point did the number of grains become sufficient to be considered a heap? Ten? One hundred? One thousand? Obviously, at no specific point, yet somewhere the heap became a heap. As we add grains of wheat, then, the collection of grains evolves into a heap. Precisely when it becomes a heap is both undefined and, in practice, unde-*

finable. Yet, when it contains enough grains, the heap is unambiguously a heap. In the same way, speciation is no more than small genetic changes – microevolution – accumulating over time until we may consider that a new species has evolved. Precisely when a new species evolves is indefinable, but that is a trivial fact and not an argument against speciation, as we can see by considering the heap problem.[139]

Misguided zeal

Misconceptions and misinformation keep many Christians from an honest evaluation of evolution. A favorite strategy of creationist leaders is to associate evolution with atheism.[140] Matthew Barrett of the Southern Baptist Theological Seminary says: "Science denies the miraculous and supernatural, so the entire biblical history of Jesus becomes suspicious and in need of demythologization."[141] Barrett makes the unwarranted claim that all scientists are philosophical naturalists who deny the supernatural. Scientific methodology, however, insists that scientists remain neutral to the metaphysical. Young earth advocates foster a conspiracy theory – that science is out to rid the world of religion.[142] From its earliest days, young earth creationism has portrayed Darwin's theory as the enemy of the true church,[143] the source of evils which, ironically, were common long before evolutionary theory was ever proposed.[144] Creationists claim that evolutionists seek to discredit the idea of a supernatural creator.[145]

A pervasive lack of scientific literacy means that creationist leaders generally offer simple answers to complicated questions.[146] Answers in Genesis founder Ken Ham, for instance, is a former high school teacher from Australia.[147] Young earth creationists generally avoid hands-on contact with genuine science.[148] And for those consuming the message, a lack of scientific knowledge on their part makes it difficult to recognize faulty arguments. Many anti-evolutionists have little idea what science actually says.[149] Young earth leaders typically give science a low priority. Many have had limited exposure to science and scientific methodology. And, since evolution is a highly controversial subject in conservative Christian circles anyway, most leaders fear departing from the party line. Creationist leaders, therefore, for several important reasons, are highly motivated to avoid (or summarily dismiss) the whole subject. I contend that these individuals are like those described by the Apostle Paul in his letter to the Romans, chapter 10, verse 2, where he says, For I can testify about them that they are zealous for God, but their zeal is not based on knowledge. (NIV) Creationist arguments are attractive to those "idling in intellectual neutral."[150]

Attempts to sow doubt and confusion,[151] are easier to accomplish when the audience lacks scientific literacy.[152]

Historical science

Young earth creationists have sometimes created their own vocabulary or redefined scientific terminology.[153] For example, creationists have invented a false distinction between operational and historical science. Whitcomb and Morris arbitrarily limit science to the study of "present and reproducible phenomena."[154] The Answers in Genesis website defines operational (i.e., experimental) science as that which "... deals with testing and verifying ideas in the present and leads to the production of useful products like computers, cars, and satellites."[155] The term operational science and the young earth creationist understanding of historical science are not valid scientific terminology. The distinction is entirely a creationist invention.[156] Historical science is, in fact, a legitimate term which refers to scientific disciplines where data is provided primarily from past events and for which there is usually no direct experimental data (see chapter 5). Historical sciences include cosmology, astronomy, astrophysics, geology, paleontology and archaeology. The term, however, is often misused by creationists to refer to science that "... interpret[s] evidence from the past and includes the models of evolution and special creation."[157] Historical science, then, is used to designate those sciences creationists have complaints about, such as evolution and abiogenesis, (the actual beginning of living organisms) and is, as they see it, the opposite of operational or experimental science.[158]

A commonly-heard creationist claim is that, in order to prove the truth of evolution, scientists would have had to be physically present to observe it.[159] "Were you there?" they ask. Henry Morris makes this point when he says, "No scientists were there to observe, and true science requires observation."[160] In response, cosmologists, for example, point out that, because of the great distances to objects in space, and because of the time it takes for light from those objects to travel to the earth, they are looking into the past with their telescopes so, in reality, they are there![161] Ironically, in cosmology, what astronomers cannot see is what is happening at great distances out in space right now. In geology and paleontology, past events leave evidence behind, such as fossils, which scientists study.[162] And, ironically, Christianity itself is based on events no one alive today has witnessed. So we weren't there for that either![163]

Evolutionary explanations are, by definition, primarily historical narratives. There are aspects, however, that can be tested in the present such as analyzing factors influencing speciation in certain populations as well as natural selection itself.[164] When it is acting as an historical science, (see chapter 9) evolutionary biology deals with events that happened when people were not there to witness them.[165] Many of the conclusions of science lie beyond the limited domain of direct observation.[166] As an historical science, evolutionary biology is called upon to explain unique and complex historical events that cannot be simulated in a laboratory.[167] Historical explanations are very challenging, but answers can be found through a combination of human mental processing power and a lot of hard work.[168] Evolution is the story of logic extended back in time.[169] Most often, historical processes leave only a few puzzle pieces behind for scientists to investigate. Assembling them into a coherent whole is a complex, long-term process.[170]

Intelligent inference

In their role as detectives, scientists look for clues. They analyze data. They formulate hypotheses.[171] A police detective would scoff at the notion that crimes can be solved only when they are witnessed directly.[172] All of science, in a real sense, is based on intelligent inference. [173] Scientists use inferential methods to test propositions in order to see if they are false.[174] And we must remember that even eyewitness accounts are subject to error.[175] Valid evidence is certainly not limited to what we can see.[176] The scientific method makes it possible to investigate the distant and the ancient.[177] Helium, for instance, was first discovered on the sun, 93,000,000 miles away.[178] The scientific method makes it possible to uncover leftover marks in the past.[179] Science often proceeds using the well-known and accepted process of inductive inference, weighing evidence and judging probability.

Abductive reasoning

Evolutionary biology and paleontology are both historical sciences. Much of what they investigate took place in the past. Historical sciences typically employ abductive reasoning. In abductive reasoning, inferences are made about past events based on present facts or claims. Investigators look for the simplest and most likely explanation for observations. Generally speaking, historical sciences work with incomplete or partial data.[180] Imagine a stretch of highway marked by prominent skidmarks. A police accident reconstruction team is called in to analyze what took place. They were not there when the accident occurred, but by abductive reasoning, they are able to put the events together and come to some important conclusions. Historical sciences do much the same.[181] It is important to emphasize, however, that this process does not, and cannot, provide the absolute proof creationists demand.[182] Christians must learn to live with a certain amount of ambiguity. Philosopher Daniel Dennett says, "...the power of the theory of natural selection is not the power to prove exactly how (pre-)history was, but only the power to prove how it could have been, given what we know about how things are."[183]

Pseudoscience

Young earth creationism is, as Michael Ruse describes it, "a marionette pulled by the strings of ideology."[184] J.B.S. Haldane (1892-1964) provides examples of pseudoscientific argument:

- The Bellman's Theorem: "What I tell you three times is true."
- Aunt Jobisca's Theorem: "It's a fact the whole world knows."[185]

Science historian Ronald Numbers describes flood geologist George McCready Price (1870-1963) as "... one of the twentieth century's most persistent scientific cranks, worthy of mention only in listings of pseudoscientific endeavor."[186] Commenting on the huge influence McCready Price had in fostering the rapid growth of young earth creationism, Stephen Richarz (1874-1934), German priest, missionary and geologist, said, "Mr. Price can deceive only those who are strangers in the science of geology."[187] Critics complained that Price's book, The New Geology (1923), contained nothing new nor any real geology.[188]

Stephen Jay Gould (1941-2002) characterizes pseudoscience as knowing the answer to a scientific problem before the investigation is done. Pseudoscience massages evidence to fit expectations. This is the opposite of what true science, or any honest intellectual inquiry for that matter, is all about.[189] Pseudoscience is motivated by an argumentum ad consequentiam: that is, something is true or false because of how much I like or dislike it.[190] Pseudoscience stifles motivation to pursue fruitful research, because the answers are already "known" before the investigation begins.[191] Legitimate scientific investigation is the result of exploratory thought, that is, an objective consideration of alternative points of view. Pseudoscience, on the other hand, is an example of confirmatory thought, defined as a one-sided attempt to rationalize a particular point of view.[192] The theory of evolution is able to make widespread predictions, from the nature of the fossil record to the changing nature of infectious agents in modern medicine, while anti-evolutionism is unable to make any predictions which can be empirically tested.

When an individual's worldview is threatened by disconfirming evidence, they are highly motivated not to see it.[193] This observation applies to all of us; young earth advocates are no different. When confronted with challenging scientific evidence, they will often simply repeat the party line.[194] Their portrayal of science is a caricature of the real thing.[195] From a Christian perspective, it could be said that creationists are guilty of breaking the scriptural standards regarding false witness and idolatry.[196] Over the years, they have made a few claims which can be falsified, such as the age of the earth, (and, as we have seen, the vapor canopy theory). There are others which have been shown to be incorrect such as the concept of flood geology, and the origins of the Grand Canyon.[197] Other refuted arguments include a predicted reduction of the earth's magnetic field over time, a predicted increase in ocean salt, and an increase in moon dust.[198] All of these arguments, and many more, have been found to be without merit. Mark Isaak has painstakingly assembled more than four hundred creationist claims, all of which have been debunked.[199]

Conclusion

At the time of the Scopes "Monkey Trial" in 1925, young earth creationism was a minority viewpoint, even among fundamentalists. It rapidly increased in popularity, as we have seen, mainly due to the surprising influence of George McCready Price and the publication of The Genesis Flood. In recent years, however, a growing number of evangelicals have adopted an evolutionary point of view.[200] Bruno Guiderdoni, an astronomer at the Paris Institute of Astrophysics, points out the error of mistaking the young earth branch of Christianity for the whole tree.[201] John Morris, son of young earth patriarch Henry Morris, has acknowledged that he never met a scientist, convinced by science alone, that creationism is correct.[202] Making an informed decision on matters as important as these requires careful information gathering. It requires a full deployment of critical thinking skills. As we have seen, many different positions on evolution are held by equally sincere Christians. Recent polling (see Appendix) indicates that, when pressed, individuals are not as sure about their views as earlier surveys may have suggested. For example, The National Study of Religion and Human Origins, a survey sponsored by the BioLogos Foundation, conducted by Calvin College sociologist Jonathan Hill, found that most people do not fit neatly into creationist or evolutionist camps.[203]

10. INTELLIGENT DESIGN CREATIONISM

Overview

Intelligent design creationism seeks to demonstrate God's existence based on the evidence of design in nature. In order to accomplish its goal, intelligent design has refurbished some nineteenth-century natural theology arguments, giving William Paley (1743-1805) and his venerable watchmaker analogy a new lease on life. The intelligent design movement has been given a boost by the strong version of the anthropic principle, which states that the presence of life and consciousness in the cosmos seems to be intentional, not fortuitous. All the dials, intelligent design proponents would argue, have been set at just the right position by a Divine Designer.

One of intelligent design's main arguments, irreducible complexity, was formulated by biologist Michael Behe. Behe argues that in an irreducibly complex biological system such as the bacterial flagellum, all subsystems must be present in order for that system to work properly. Remove one part, he says, and it fails. The implication for evolutionary theory, according to Behe, is that an irreducibly complex system could not have evolved in a step-wise fashion because it needs all of its parts in place to work properly. It must arise as a unit, and that is where a Designer comes in. Critics, however, argue that this is a "God-of-the-gaps" argument, placing God into a gap in scientific knowledge.

Like its young earth cousin, intelligent design creationism exists at a distance from the mainstream scientific community. The various groups gathered under intelligent design's big tent share a common goal, which is to discredit evolutionary theory. Intelligent design's mischaracterization of basic scientific methodology is designed to make science appear inherently atheistic. Like young earth creationism, intelligent design refuses to acknowledge the self-imposed limits of science. Despite its intention to support the Christian message, intelligent design creationism is a liability to the church. The Dover, PA. intelligent design trial was very revealing. During the trial, proponents did their best to conceal intelligent design's religious roots. In recent years, however, the quality of scholarship in the intelligent design movement has greatly improved.

There are glimmers of hope that a fruitful dialog may be possible between intelligent design and other Christian responses to evolutionary theory, those who support evolution and those who do not.

Natural theology

Many nineteenth-century Christians advocated natural theology, the study of nature from the standpoint of faith. Natural theology proposes that God's nature, as well as his being, can be inferred from the character of his creation.[1] It investigates what Francis Bacon (1561-1626) called "The Book of God's Works."[2] The Rev. Aubrey Moore (1848-1890), curator of the Oxford Botanical Gardens, captured the essence of natural theology when he said, "...the facts of nature are the acts of God."[3] Scriptural support for natural theology is found in Psalm 19, verse 1, which proclaims "...the heavens declare the glory of God; the skies proclaim the work of his hands." (NIV) Also in the Old Testament, God addresses Job using an intelligent design argument.[4] Consider the design-related questions found in Job, chapter 38:4-6. It is interesting to note that God is not forbidding the study of the natural realm here, but actually encouraging it. All these questions that need answers have always motivated what eventually became known as science.

> 4 *"Where were you when I laid the earth's foundation?*
> *Tell me, if you understand.*
> 5 *Who marked off its dimensions? Surely you know!*
> *Who stretched a measuring line across it?*
> 6 *On what were its footings set, or who laid its cornerstone?* (NIV)

In the New Testament, in the book of Romans, chapter 1, verses 18 to 20, the apostle Paul declares that God's invisible qualities are made plain through his creation. Biblical references like these affirm the nonverbal revelation of God in nature.[5] Natural theology is also the primary motivation for scientific concordism (see chapter 9).

Background

The argument from design can be traced back as far as Cicero (106-43 B.C.).[6] Later, in the middle ages, Thomas Aquinas (1225-1274) argued that wherever complex design exists, there must have been a Designer.[7] William Paley (1743-1805) was an English cleric best known for his watchmaker analogy, an argument for the existence of God as described in his book, Natural Theology or Evidences of the Existence and Attributes of the Deity, (1802). Paley maintained that just as a watch discovered in a field implies a watchmaker, so the design apparent in nature suggests a Divine Designer. Paley's Evidences had a powerful, but temporary, effect on the young Charles Darwin during a time in his life when he held an orthodox Christian faith.[8] In an effort to support Paley's natural theology, Francis Henry Egerton (1756-1829), Earl of Bridgewater, commissioned eight Bridgewater Treatises, published between 1833 and 1840, written by leading scientists of the day, to explore "... the Power, Wisdom, and Goodness of God, as manifested in the Creation."[9] Darwin never rejected the idea of design, but did argue that it had to be done secondhand, through natural laws, specifically, by means of natural selection.[10]

Alfred Russel Wallace, (1823-1913) British naturalist and biologist, is best known for independently developing the theory of evolution through natural selection (see chapter 5). Philosopher Michael Ruse is of the opinion that both Wallace and Paley could be considered patron saints of the modern intelligent design movement, Paley for his design argument, and Wallace for his desire to reintroduce the supernatural into mainstream science.[11] Darwin rejected Wallace's suggestion that human origins require special divine intervention.[12] Intelligent design's current proposal that the supernatural be brought back into science is called theistic science by its proponents. Paley's argument from design was soon challenged by evolutionary theories that minimized divine intervention in the creative process or eliminated it altogether. Some contemporary critics argue that intelligent design is little more than Paley's design argument warmed over more than 150 years later.[13] Taking the argument further, contemporary biologist Richard Dawkins insists that evolution is a materialistic process that provides nothing more than an elegant illusion of design.[14]

Darwin on trial

Intelligent design in its current iteration can be traced back to a 1984 publication titled The Mystery of Life's Origin, by Walter L. Bradley and Charles B. Thaxton.[15] Of Pandas and People (1989) was another early expression of intelligent design.[16] The first intelligent design publication with a major impact was Phillip Johnson's Darwin on Trial, published in 1991. Johnson popularized the term intelligent design and has been called the intelligent design movement's intelligent designer.[17] He is a retired law professor at U.C. Berkeley with no formal training in biology. Johnson's critique of evolution is full of technical errors.[18] Johnson, ironically, admitted that a scientist outside the boundaries of their own professional competence is "just another layman."[19] In its early days, intelligent design was called the Wedge Movement which began in 1992. The wedge metaphor represents the forced introduction of the supernatural into science.[20] The goals of the intelligent design movement were originally communicated in what was called the Wedge Document (1999), an in-house, designed-to-be-confidential, five-year plan with the ambitious goal of overcoming scientific materialism, replacing it with a theistic science.[21] The Wedge Document portrays science as hostile to the founding principles of Western society.[22]

Similar to arguments put forth by young earth creationists, the Wedge Document blames evolution for what it perceives as the anti-spiritual materialism destroying modern Western societies today.[23] Phillip Johnson worried that when children learn about evolution they will lose their faith in life having a purpose.[24] A primary goal of the intelligent design movement is the promotion of a theistic agenda as a scientific concept, which, it is believed, will bring about a massive "cultural renewal."[25] Intelligent design therefore seeks nothing less than a fundamental shift in the public perception of science.[26] The Discovery Institute, located in Seattle, Washington, is a non-profit advocacy group for intelligent design, dedicated to challenging what it calls the anti-religious bias in science.[27] Their "Teach the Controversy" campaign is critical of the teaching of evolution in U.S. high schools.[28]

The anthropic principle

Ours is a universe where the conditions that make life possible are built into the fabric of existence.[29] The anthropic principle proposes an answer to the question of why the fundamental physical constants of the universe are just right for life to exist on earth, and not just for life, but for conscious life as well. Whether life exists anywhere else in the universe, of course, is an open question. If life as we know it is to exist, even if it should only exist on earth, a long list of physical constants must have specific values with the precision of many decimal places. The physical constants central to the anthropic principle include the mass of elementary particles, the gravitational constant, and the speed of light.[30] The existence of the vast universe as it is today rests on a knife-edge of improbability.[31] There is no known reason why these constants should have the values they do. For many of these constants, if their value was only slightly different, life would not exist at all. If these fundamental values were only slightly different, for example, the universe would either be a cloud of hydrogen, or nothing but waves of radiation, both inhospitable to life. In 1974, astronomer Brandon Carter formulated the anthropic principle which states that these coincidences are inherent in the universe's structure and that chance has nothing to do with it.[32] Carter proposed two variants of his theory:

- The weak anthropic principle, which implies that the universe we observe must have the conditions to support intelligent life, but that life doesn't necessarily have to arise.
- The strong anthropic principle, which states that the universe is compelled, in some sense, to eventually have conscious and sapient life emerge from within it.[33]

Although the anthropic principle sounds nonscientific, it does have predictive power and so can be tested scientifically.[34] However, science cannot make any statement about why we are here. At this point in time, it is solely a matter of concern to philosophy and religion as to whether God specifically created the universe with the possibility of intelligent life in mind. The anthropic principle is the most recent rendition of the design argument.[35] The strong form of the anthropic principle is a powerful argument for the existence of God, and important to the intelligent design movement, as well as to evolutionary creation / theistic evolution, because it claims, in a teleological sense, that this extraordinary fine-tuning suggests a universe planned beforehand for life and consciousness, obviously pointing to a Designer.[36] An alternative explanation has been proposed, the so-called multiverse hypothesis, which suggests the possibility of a great many universes, not just one. Most of these universes, it is argued, would have physical constants unsuitable for life, but a few would just happen to possess the physical constants that allow conscious beings to exist. We naturally find ourselves in such a universe, because we could not be in a universe unsuitable for life.

Bernard Ramm (1916-1992) anticipated the strong anthropic principle in the 1950's when he said, "Conditions necessary for life are not accidental, but purposed."[37] What is most remarkable, from a Christian and an evolutionary point of view, is that the laws of nature that God himself ordained are so finely tuned as to cause the self-assembly of all these things.[38] Writing one thousand years before the scientific revolution and fifteen hundred years before Darwin, Augustine argued that God had gifted the universe with remarkable capabilities for organizing itself into new structures and forms.[39] Science, it turns out, with its discovery of a universe brimming with evolutionary possibilities, has proven Augustine correct.[40]

Warfare model

Much like its young earth cousin, intelligent design discusses the relationship between science and faith in terms of the familiar warfare model. Phillip Johnson stated that, in his opinion, science is at war with creationism and demands nothing less than unconditional surrender.[41] Intelligent design supporters perceive this conflict as a win-lose scenario; as science advances, religion must retreat, and vice versa.[42] We should not be surprised to find that there are those on the scientific side of the debate who also foster this irreconcilable conflict model. Jerry Coyne, for instance, in a book titled Faith Versus Fact: Why Science and Religion are Incompatible (2015), says that religion and science are "... engaged in a ... war for understanding, a war about whether we should have good reasons for what we accept as true."[43] Coyne's radical views, however, are not held by the majority of scientists (see Appendix).

A recent study by sociologist Elaine Howard Eklund challenges the commonly-held belief that an intractable conflict exists between science and religion.[44] Researchers collected data on scientists from eight different regions around the world – France, Hong Kong, India, Italy, Taiwan, Turkey, the United Kingdom, and the United States. Ecklund found that, in most nations, scientists are indeed more secular in terms of religious belief and practice than the general population. But in four of those regions it was found that scientists did consider themselves to be religious. The study found that most scientists do not think that science is in conflict with religion. The most commonly-held view among scientists is that science and religion operate in separate spheres. Also, most scientists believe that their vocation in science has not made them less religious.

Philosophical underpinnings

In its early days, intelligent design was not necessarily arguing the facts of evolution, but questioning its methods and philosophical underpinnings. For quite some time now, due to health issues, Phillip Johnson has stepped back from a leadership role in the intelligent design movement. But in the early days, his leadership was critical to the success of the movement. Johnson tipped his hand early on when he stated that the debate wasn't really about science but about philosophy.[45] Johnson, by his own admission, described himself as a postmodern deconstructionist. As such, he denied that science can find objective truth.[46] Science, he argued, is really about maintaining cultural power.[47] Like fellow deconstructionists, Johnson claimed that knowledge is not actually discovered but rather fabricated by intellectual capitalists.[48] So scientific knowledge is just another human construct, in this case, a construct that explains life apart from God.[49] Johnson argued that evolutionary theory is the expression of a stifling orthodoxy that has seized control of the scientific community.[50]

Johnson worked diligently to convince his audience that evolution is nothing more than ideology pretending to be science. He argued that science occupies a privileged position as the materialist ideology of the ruling elite.[51] Johnson, ironically, accused evolutionists of conducting a program of indoctrination.[52] A primary concern of intelligent design, therefore, is, and remains, a firm opposition to naturalism as a basic scientific philosophy.[53] Johnson refused to speak of methodological naturalism, preferring "scientific naturalism," which, in his estimation, is a hard-line philosophical naturalism which he believes all scientists advocate.[54] Johnson argued that Darwinism rests on philosophical beliefs that are not subject to scientific test and refutation, (which, of course, turns out to be an accurate description of intelligent design itself.)[55] He refused to acknowledge that scientific methodology must be and remain religiously neutral, claiming repeatedly that scientists want to push God out of reality.[56] Johnson's conflation of methodological and philosophical naturalism is a category mistake, a basic error in classification.[57]

Science and the supernatural

Beginning with Philip Johnson in the early days of intelligent design, right through to prominent contemporary advocates such as Stephen Meyer and Michael Denton, intelligent design has challenged the idea that religious or quasi-religious ideas should not be allowed in science.[58] In place of the current supernatural-free scientific methodology, Johnson proposed a philosophy he called theistic realism, defined as

> *... the idea that God is real, acts in the universe, and is knowable through the senses and reason. Theistic realism holds that the universe can only be comprehensively explained with reference to God. It holds that the design and works of God are manifestly evident in nature, particularly creation, so that evidence and reason lead inevitably to belief in God.*[59]

Intelligent design advocates contend that the distinction between methodological naturalism and philosophical naturalism is a rhetorical move allowing scientists to have their cake and eat it too. Very much like young earth creationists, Johnson argued that Christians are faced with an unenviable choice

– either reject all of nature as young earth creationism does, or all of God, as he believes science does.[60]

Johnson came to the conclusion that an unbending naturalism (understood as ruling out theistic factors, rather than a neutral agnosticism) is how science actually works.[61] Early scientists found it necessary to conduct their investigations as if the material world is all that exists (see chapter 2).[62] It has been argued that breaking free from the supernatural is what cleared the way for many of science's successes. There is no desire, therefore, among the vast majority of scientists, to bring it back. Mainstream science resists the idea of acknowledging the supernatural, because it would "... fundamentally redefine what science is and what it is trying to accomplish."[63]

Like many anti-evolutionists, Johnson conflated the radical atheistic 5 percent of scientists (see Appendix) – the new atheists – with all scientists, arguing that a primary goal of science is to set itself up as a new religion.[64] Johnson did his best to portray the strict scientism of the new atheists as mainstream science, wondering out loud whether Darwinism might be another expression of fundamentalism.[65] Intelligent design proponents are well aware of the fact that new atheist attacks can be turned to their advantage. William Dembski once sent a pointed email to Richard Dawkins thanking him for rallying support for the intelligent design cause.[66] Ironically, both extremes of this debate, either secular (scientism) or religious (scientific creationism in its various iterations) are ideology disguised as science.[67]

As we have seen, Christians have traditionally viewed creation as a teleological (goal or purpose-oriented) process. Debates over teleology and whether it is an appropriate subject for science were common in the nineteenth century. Intelligent design criticizes evolutionary theory (and science in general) for rejecting teleology[68] but again, as we have seen, teleology is scientifically undetectable, a matter best left to faith.[69] Like the supernatural, science must remain agnostic with regard to teleology (see chapter 2). In a generic sense, intelligence in creation is essential in all expressions of the Christian faith. Evolution-friendly approaches such as evolutionary creation (see chapter 8), with their acceptance of mainstream science while respecting traditional Christian teachings, show that is possible to reconcile "intelligence" with mainstream science without calling on science to incorporate the supernatural.[70]

Deep time and common descent

Unlike young earth creationists, most intelligent design proponents are not biblical literalists.[71] Like day-age creationists (and unlike young earth creationists), many in the intelligent design movement acknowledge deep time.[72] This long-established scientific fact, it should be noted, is still problematic for many, especially in the U.S., where one survey found that 36 percent of the general population and 56 percent of evangelicals reject deep time.[73] Eugenie Scott argues that because of its acceptance of deep time, intelligent design could be considered a modern variant of old-earth creationism, specifically, the variant called progressive creationism, but Scott's view has been disputed because intelligent design's big tent is just too broad for such a narrow characterization.[74] For his part, intelligent design spokesman Michael Behe rejects the appearance-of-age Omphalos hypothesis (see chapter 9), arguing that there is no reason to think that God wanted to cover his tracks and create a universe that merely looks old. Because he accepts deep time and the evolutionary concept of common descent,[75] and because he accepts the common ancestry of humans and the great apes, young earth creationists fear that Michael Behe is well on his way toward apostasy.[76] Intelligent design advocate William Dembski, in a book titled, No Free Lunch: Why Specified Complexity Cannot Be Purchased without Intelligence (2001) contends that intelligent design is not a form of anti-evolutionism.[77] In the early days of intelligent design, Phillip Johnson always kept his cards close to his chest, saying only that God might have chosen to work through an evolutionary process.[78] On another occasion, Johnson said that God "... might have created things... through gradual evolution over billions of years."[79]

The cambrian explosion

In the early days of the intelligent design movement, Phillip Johnson claimed that explaining the so-called Cambrian explosion (see chapter 9) was the greatest problem evolutionists face.[80] Johnson and subsequent intelligent design proponents argue that the geologically sudden appearance (estimated to have occurred over a period of 20 to 30 million years) of many different animal forms in the Cambrian is a clear example of God's creative intervention. Stephen Meyer argues that life-forms appeared with no obvious precursors, too quickly for evolution to occur. Meyer proposes the involvement of an intelligent Designer who directly intervened in the story of life on earth. Meyer argues, in God of the gaps fashion, that if a phenomenon cannot be fully explained by today's science, we should assume it is the work of a supreme deity. The genetic machinery of life, he argues, is incapable of dramatic leaps forward in a relatively short period of time. Thus, any dramatic biological innovation can be attributed to the work of an intelligent designer. The scientific literature, however, contains many well-documented counter-examples. In addition, mechanisms by which life's machinery can change quickly have been identified.[81]

Punctuated equilibrium

Punctuated equilibrium, first proposed by Stephen Jay Gould and Niles Eldredge in 1972, is based on the observation that the fossil record shows that species often exist for very long periods, with virtually no changes, a phenomenon called stasis (see chapter 5).[82] And then, when evolutionary change does occur, it happens in fairly rapid bursts, with a subsequent return to stasis. Punctuated equilibrium, therefore, challenges the idea, basic to traditional evolutionary theory, that evolutionary change occurs gradually over very long periods of time. According to punctuated equilibrium, transitional forms must be understood as the exception, not the rule. Intelligent design advocates are attracted to punctuated equilibrium because, in their opinion, it provides indirect support for the idea that an Intelligent Designer occasionally steps into evolutionary history, directing mutations after long periods of stasis. Punctuated equilibrium also requires a saltation-like mechanism capable of producing major evolutionary change quickly. Punctuated equilibrium and saltation are places where intelligent design advocates argue that an Intelligence steps into the process.[83]

Irreducible complexity

Michael Behe came to reject evolution by natural selection after reading Michael Denton's (1985) book, Evolution: A Theory in Crisis.[84] Behe contends that organisms are composed of numerous subsystems far too complex to have developed through natural selection alone.[85] A primary goal of intelligent design, according to Behe, is to seek out aspects of living things which cannot be accounted for by natural processes but could be attributed to God.[86] In Darwin's Black Box (1996), potentially the most influential book in the whole intelligent design movement, Behe explains what he means by irreducible complexity:

> *By irreducibly complex I mean a single system composed of several well-matched, interacting parts that contribute to the basic function, wherein the removal of any one of the parts causes the system to effectively cease functioning. An irreducibly complex system cannot be produced directly (that is, by continuously improving the initial function, which continues to work by*

the same mechanism) by slight, successive modifications of a precursor system, because any precursor to an irreducibly complex system that is missing a part is by definition non-functional. An irreducibly complex biological system, if there is such a thing, would be a powerful challenge to Darwinian evolution.[87]

Similar to progressive creationists, Behe claims that the intelligent designer intervenes at intervals in the creative process. And, at those times, God creates irreducibly complex structures such as the bacterial flagellum.[88] Behe, by the way, believes that irreducible complexity must be ranked as one of the greatest achievements in the history of science.[89] Essentially, Behe, along with other intelligent design advocates, is looking for biological systems that cannot be explained by natural selection alone.

God of the gaps

Numerous writers have criticized concepts like irreducible complexity as a "God of the gaps" argument.[90] "God of the gaps" is a term used to describe situations in which gaps in scientific knowledge are taken to be evidence or proof of God's existence.[91] The history of scientific endeavor, however, has repeatedly shown that proposing God as the answer to scientific mysteries, as intelligent design does, means that when science discovers answers to these questions, God's place in the explanatory system is dramatically reduced. Essentially, a God of the gaps argument confuses the unknown with the unknowable.[92] As Charles Coulson, founding Professor of Theoretical Chemistry at Oxford writes: "When we come to the scientifically unknown, our current policy is not to rejoice because we have found God; it is to become better scientists."[93] Coulson adds, "Either God is in the whole of nature, with no gaps, or he's not there at all."[94]

According to biologist Kenneth Miller, when it comes to the details of evolutionary theory, proponents of intelligent design have not done their homework. They are arguing from a lack of knowledge.[95] In addition to being a God of the gaps argument, irreducible complexity has been described as an argument from incredulity. Daniel Dennett explains: "At every stage in the tumultuous controversies that have accompanied the evolution of Darwin's dangerous idea, there has been a defiance born of fear: '...you'll never explain this!' And the challenge has been taken up: 'Watch me!'"[96] Intelligent design patriarch Philip Johnson once said, with delicious irony, that it is better to admit ignorance than to have confidence in an explanation that is not true.[97]

Divine intervention

As a subset of progressive creationism, then, intelligent design has been criticized for advocating design by installments whereby God occasionally steps into the creative process.[98] Along with the majority of traditional Christianity, both those who advocate an evolutionary point of view and those who do not, intelligent design asserts that a supernatural creator initiated the process of life's development and now supervises it as well.[99] But then, with the young earth creationists and a few others, intelligent design contends that evolution is not up to the task. Intelligent design creationism straddles the fence between young and old-earth creationism.[100] It presents itself as a faith-friendly, common-denominator alternative to godless evolution.[101] Intelligent design wants to be seen as a thinking person's creationism. It is composed of several like-minded groups brought together under a big tent.[102] As might be expected, that big tent brings together some strange ideological bedfellows, including those who accept common descent and those who do not.[103] Not surprisingly, young earth creationists refuse to join, arguing that intelligent design compromises too many substantive issues.

Compatibilism

Phillip Johnson has criticized evolutionary creation (see chapter 8, synonymous with theistic evolution) as compatibilism, which he defines as "the doctrine that science and religion do not conflict because they occupy separate realms."[104] According to Johnson, theistic evolution is a form of "theistic naturalism."[105] Again, Johnson labored mightily to ignore or overlook the fact that mainstream science is agnostic, not antagonistic, towards spirituality and religion. Theistic evolution, as we have seen, maintains that evolution is God's method of creation. It is not surprising, then, that theistic evolution would be specifically excluded from intelligent design's big tent. As an illustration of what he means by compatibilism, Johnson pointed to the American Scientific Affiliation, which, in his view, has concluded that there is no conflict between science and religion because they occupy separate ideological spheres.[106] This seems to be a reference to Stephen Jay Gould's idea of Non-Overlapping Magisteria (NOMA), Gould's paradigm of independence between science and religion.[107] In Rocks of Ages (1999), Gould argues that the magisterium (i.e., the area of expertise) of science covers the empirical realm. Science asks what the universe is made of (fact) and why it works that way (theory). The magisterium of religion, on the other hand, is concerned with questions of ultimate meaning and moral value.

In Gould's opinion, these two magisteria do not overlap.[108]

Bad design

As an apologist for intelligent design, Stephen Meyer avoids the problem of bad design. Well-known examples, drawn from the human body, include the knee, the spine, the appendix, and problems with wisdom teeth.[109] Biologist Kenneth Miller asks why human beings would be designed without a gene that would allow the body to make vitamin C.[110] Other examples of less-than-optimal design in a human context are the backward design of the retina in the eye, the windpipe with its choke-producing crossover of food and air, the means by which waste products and sexual reproduction are handled in the human body, and common problems with childbirth.[111] In addition, if God works to provide desirable genetic variations, why does he not prevent the undesirable ones?[112] Meyer is correct when he says that God's activity is scientifically superfluous or undetectable, scientifically irrelevant.[113] Given the limits of science, it is entirely possible that God might influence His creation in subtle ways that are unrecognizable to scientific observation, that, as it were, fly under the scientific radar.[114] Keith B. Miller, responding to Philip Johnson's claim that science "assumes away" a creator, says that science must remain silent on the existence or action of God.[115] Stephen Jay Gould, an influential scientist himself, was critical of scientists who derived unwarranted philosophical, theological, or ethical conclusions outside the boundaries of science.[116] He said:

> *To say it for all my colleagues and for the umpteenth millionth time: science simply cannot by its legitimate methods adjudicate the issue of God's possible superintendence of nature. We neither confirm nor deny it; we simply can't comment on it as scientists. Science can work only with naturalistic explanations; it can neither affirm nor deny other types of actors – like God.*[117]

Phillip Johnson, incredibly, once dismissed scientific evidence as a "sideshow." Johnson asserted that biologists can certainly tell us about biology, but they lack the philosophical expertise to tell us which philosophical assumptions science should adopt. According to Johnson, arguments about scientific evidence are a distraction from more important philosophical questions. "It's all a matter of priorities," he said.[118] But this is nothing more than an outright refusal to deal with the many substantive scientific issues that impact religious faith.[119] Johnson has also said, appropriately in my opinion, that scientific claims should be determined by scientific evidence rather than philosophical presuppositions.[120] He seems to be confused on the matter. Johnson, however, correctly pointed out, and this is true for scientist and non-scientist alike, that we see what we expect to see unless we very carefully control our biases and expectations, which is what scientific methodology is designed to do.[121] I agree with Johnson when he said that we should do our best to investigate this subject without prejudice.[122]

When scientists are faced with a particularly challenging problem, their inclination is to say "We don't know that yet ..." rather than resorting to metaphysics. As far as scientists are concerned, intelligent design presents non-answers to scientific questions because its claims cannot be falsified. Intelligent design is not a scientific enterprise at the present time. It makes no positive predictions. Going forward, intelligent design must establish a positive research program, rather than relying on a negative one based only on criticism of scientific ideas.[123] When an argument is weak, its proponents spend more time criticizing the views of others than they do in cogently proposing their own views.[124] Meyer, on the other hand, claims that intelligent design is scientifically respectable because, in his opinion, it is testable, it makes predictions and tentative claims. It solves problems.[125] The scientific community, however, is not yet convinced.

Dover, Pennsylvania

A spectacular intelligent design related train-wreck occurred in Dover, Pennsylvania back in 2005. That event rattled the intelligent design movement from top to bottom. On December 14th, 2004, eleven parents filed suit against the Dover Area School District in federal court. They were concerned with what seemed to be an unauthorized introduction of intelligent design-related materials into the local biology curriculum. The controversy began with the local school board's consideration of a new biology textbook. At a June 7th, 2004, board meeting, William Buckingham, chair of the Curriculum Committee, objected to the suggested textbook, saying that it was "laced with Darwinism." His goal as board chair, he indicated, was to secure a textbook that balanced both creationism and evolution.[126] Things got interesting when a group of intelligent design supporters in Dover surreptitiously purchased a set of textbooks written from an intelligent design perspective and made them available to students in the classroom.

That unsolicited and unilateral action led to the parents' objection. And that objection, in turn, eventually led to a court case. When all was said and done, Judge John E. Jones III, (the Republican-appointed judge presiding over the case, appointed by President George W. Bush himself) pointed out the distortions and untruths perpetrated by supporters of intelligent design.[127] The local school board was described by one of the journalists covering the trial as "bullying, mendacious, self-righteous zealots."[128] The judge demonstrated how the advocates of intelligent design had adopted the very postmodern relativistic ethic they themselves railed against.[129] The court added that the Discovery Institute had manufactured a nonexistent controversy in claiming that evolution was a theory in crisis. The court ruled that the Institute was pursuing religious goals and that intelligent design was a form of creationism, not a scientific proposition.[130] When all was said and done, the Dover school board was saddled with one million dollars in court costs. Intelligent design advocate Stephen Meyer characterizes the disastrous Dover Pennsylvania trial as "ill-advised."[131]

Reasonable doubt

Despite major stumbles such as Dover, PA., intelligent design has succeeded in making deep inroads into mainstream culture.[132] Intelligent design proponents are well aware of the fact that if they wore their religious colors openly, they would not be able to gain a foothold in public schools.[133] Intelligent design patriarch Phillip Johnson and the creators of the "Wedge Strategy" succeeded in convincing many in the general public and also in the media that a serious scientific controversy exists about the status of Darwinism.[134] Like any good defense lawyer, Johnson and subsequent intelligent design proponents know they don't have to prove their case. All they have to do is establish a reasonable doubt.[135] Intelligent design denigrates natural selection in the eyes of the general public, with the goal of leaving intelligent design preeminent.[136]

Stephen Meyer

Phillip Johnson suffered a stroke in 2001 and passed along the mantle of leadership in the intelligent design movement to individuals like Stephen Meyer and Michael Denton, among others. Meyer is an influential advocate for intelligent design. Biologist Darrel Falk is impressed with Meyer's technical knowledge and, in addition, appreciates the skill and sincerity of the other intelligent design proponents he has met. Falk's review of Meyer's Darwin's Doubt (2013) is conciliatory.[137] Darwin's Doubt is the book the Discovery Institute hopes will rekindle the intelligent design movement.[138] In Darwin's Doubt, Meyer presents readers with a list of potential processes that, in his opinion, explain the origin of new body plans better than natural selection.[139] As might be expected, intelligent design is given a prominent place in the discussion. According to Robert Bishop of Wheaton College, Meyer presents the strongest argument for intelligent design to be found anywhere.[140] Both Stephen Meyer and fellow intelligent design proponent Michael Denton have the courage to ask difficult questions and pursue the answers single-mindedly.[141] In Darwin's Doubt, Meyer conspicuously displays the trappings of science – the journals, the conferences, and the terminology – which provides credibility in the eyes of his mostly pro-intelligent design audience.[142]

Darwin's Doubt sifts through a mountain of technical data, which puts non-experts at a disadvantage. It's difficult for non-experts to be sure that Meyer is offering an objective and balanced presentation. Robert Bishop says, "A scientifically literate reader gets the impression that Meyer reads the literature hunting for support for his preconceived view rather than in search of insight into what evolutionary and developmental biologists are actually saying."[143] Meyer is critical of both evolutionary creation and young earth creationism. Many evangelicals conflate intelligent design and young earth creationism, but, as we have seen, there are significant differences. Meyer offers a surprisingly strong critique of young earth creationism, which, he says, "... rejects the testimony of science as irrelevant or even dangerous and affirms that just reading the Bible will give all the insight needed to understand how life came to be."[144]

Meyer criticizes evolutionary creation for what he sees as a lack of detail regarding God's involvement in the evolutionary process and also for minimizing the theological challenges raised. Meyer makes it clear that he is not comfortable with evolutionary creation leaving God's intervention an open question. Evolutionary creation, in Meyer's opinion, is an "... uneasy reconciliation of science and faith."[145] As far as he is concerned, intelligent design brings science and faith into real harmony. Theistic evolution, on the other hand, does not.[146] In Darwin's Doubt, Meyer presents the case for intelligent design to a wide cross-section of religious people. Intelligent design, he says, is "faith-affirming." It introduces "significance, wholeness, and hope" into scientific discourse.[147] It brings comfort to people of faith. It introduces a critical sense of purpose into the discussion of origins.

Michael denton

Michael Denton is another well-known spokesman for intelligent design. Denton's Evolution: A Theory in Crisis, (1986) provided the foundation on which later proponents of intelligent design would build. Concerning his newest book, Evolution: Still a Theory in Crisis," (2016) Denton says, "The saltational emergentist strictly non-Darwinian model of origins... that I am defending here and throughout the book implies that the transitions are programmed into nature and arise in particular organisms that were at particular moments in evolutionary history pre-adapted or prefigured for them to occur."[148] Like Meyer, Denton writes primarily for an intelligent design audience. Denton assumes the role of strident polemicist, repeatedly criticizing Darwinian orthodoxy. Denton, however, differs from most other intelligent design proponents in that he is an agnostic,[149] one of only a very few agnostic scientists who oppose evolution on non-religious grounds.[150] As we have already noted, most current advocates of intelligent design like Denton and Meyer accept deep time and common descent. They do, however, reject natural selection as the causative mechanism for evolution.[151]

Structuralism

Denton espouses a structuralist interpretation, which was embraced by Stephen Jay Gould in the final stage of his career.[152] Denton is a disciple of Richard Owen (1804-1892), the nineteenth-century father of British structuralism. Following Owen, Denton argues that "...the basic forms of life are in some sense built into nature."[153] Structuralists claim that due to the fine-tuning of the universe, there is a natural law to nature that results in the lifeforms we see today.[154] Along with other pre-Darwin biologists, Owen envisioned "laws of biological form." Owen believed that these laws limited the structure of organisms to a few basic designs or types.[155] Denton argues that functionalism, by itself, cannot explain all organic order. According to functionalism (which is the currently prevailing mainstream view) the main organizing principle in biology is adaptation to serve various functional ends. In contrast to traditional evolutionary theory, structuralism asserts that causal factors other than cumulative selection play a crucial role in shaping living systems.[156]

For Denton, adaptation is not the primary organizing principle of biology. He argues that modern evolutionary theory, with its functionalist orientation, cannot satisfactorily explain basic animal designs.[157] Evolutionary theory asserts that function comes before and determines structure. In contrast, Denton's structuralism claims that structure is prior to and constrains function.[158] Not all features of living things serve an adaptive purpose.[159] Denton argues that "... the processes which lead to major evolutionary novelties are different from those that cause adaptive modifications."[160] In his book The Runes of Evolution, (2015) Simon Conway-Morris provides numerous examples of evolutionary convergence. For Conway-Morris, convergence suggests an "... underlying framework whereby many outcomes, not least brains and intelligence, are virtually guaranteed on any earthlike planet."[161] Conway-Morris marvels at the "... uncanny ability of evolution to navigate to the appropriate solution..." In an argument that sounds very much like Denton's structuralism, Conway-Morris claims that evolution may be "channeled" in a certain direction.[162]

Orthogenesis

Closely related to structuralism is orthogenesis, popularized by nineteenth century German zoologist Theodore Eimer (1843-1898). Orthogenesis proposes that life has an innate tendency to move in a unilinear fashion toward greater perfection. For Denton and fellow structuralists, the paths of evolution are ordered and directed by causative factors other than natural selection.[163] Denton says, "I believe that the entire pattern of evolution was prefigured into the order of things from the beginning."[164] Structuralism, like orthogenesis, is a kind of biological predestination or determinism.[165] Orthogenesis, however, fell into disrepute when it failed to explain non-linear patterns in the fossil record.[166] Given methodological naturalism's exclusion of the supernatural, scientists could find no naturalistic mechanism which demonstrated a linear progression in mutation events. So, by 1950 orthogenesis was abandoned. A concept closely related to orthogenesis is entelechy, defined as "the vital principle that guides the development and functioning of an organism or other system or organization."[167]

In their review of Denton's Evolution: Still a Theory in Crisis, Sy Garte and Aniko Albert point out that contemporary evolutionary biology, like any mature scientific discipline, is characterized by vigorous in-house debates. Evolutionary models are constantly being refined.[168] Gould and Eldredge's punctuated equilibrium began a dialogue on the pace of evolution, that is, the relative importance of stasis as compared to gradual change. In addition, the long-standing neo-Darwinian gradualist approach is being legitimately challenged by alternatives such as the Extended Evolutionary Synthesis (see chapter 13). Common ancestry is not in doubt. The debate centers around the mechanisms of evolution. Denton's latest book Evolution: Still a Theory in Crisis, (2016) is very different from his original Evolution: A Theory in Crisis (1985). Still a Theory in Crisis raises important issues which the contemporary evolutionary community needs to acknowledge. According to Garte and Albert, Denton defines evolution narrowly as commitment to "...a strict adherence to adaptationist functionalism and an insistence on gradualism."[169]

According to Garte and Albert, Still a Theory in Crisis is oddly out of place in the current intelligent design subculture. The book does not refer to irreducible complexity. It is conversant with the world of contemporary evolutionary biology and extensively quotes its authors. Denton avoids discussing evidence for design. As a matter of fact, he rarely speaks of design. Denton's attack on Darwinism is almost entirely carried out in the context of current evolutionary biology. He agrees that natural selection is the best explanation for microevolution. He points out that macroevolution, on the other hand, requires an entirely different mechanism. Denton agrees that evolution does, in fact, take place and that a proliferation of species has occurred by natural means rather than by special creation or by intelligent design. Denton says, "There is a tree of life. There is no doubt that all extant life forms are related, and descended from a primeval ancestral form at the base of the tree."[170] Garte and Albert are puzzled by the odd title of the book, wondering about the "crisis" Denton refers to. Denton's "crisis," it turns out, is that natural selection is insufficient to explain the entirety of evolution. Here, Denton joins evolutionists the likes of Stephen Jay Gould, Stephen Shapiro, and Simon Conway Morris.

It is important to note that Denton is not critical of all of Darwinism, but only of what Garte and Aniko labels "extreme Darwinism." That important insight is not clarified either in Denton's book or in its title. Denton's actual proposal, sounds very much like the Extended Evolutionary Synthesis which is vying for preeminence in evolutionary biology today. Significantly, according to Garte and Aniko, Denton is not promoting "...the vaguely-crafted, creationist-flavored, non-hypothesis of the original intelligent design movement." Denton departs from intelligent design orthodoxy in not appealing to a creative intelligence. He is not appealing to a creative intelligence in lieu of a biological mechanism, but weighs – as many evolutionary biologists are also doing – the relative importance of natural selection as a driver of evolutionary change. According to Garte and Aniko, Denton is proposing the "... threads of a coherent scientific hypothesis to explain the great question of emergent novelties during evolutionary history." They add:

> *This important book represents an intriguing and fascinating opportunity for real progress in the sometimes bitter debate about evolution among Christians... this book represents a potential for a real breakthrough in dis-*

cussions between evolutionary creation and intelligent design. Denton's new book may very well be a catalyst in the eventual reconciliation of two Christian scientific philosophies on the nature of life.[171]

Biologist Darrel Falk suggests that

Denton's work is highly embedded in the well-established fact of common descent of all living organisms ... hence, if this work does become central to the focus of the intelligent design movement, it would be great if they would focus in on a coherent theory like that which Denton espouses ..."[172]

A childhood fascination

I spent my childhood in Vancouver, British Columbia. As a youngster, I was fascinated with the seeds of the local maple tree. Those seeds bore an amazing resemblance to aircraft propellers. When I picked one up and tossed it in the air, it flew gracefully to the ground in a looping circular motion. As a child, I gave those amazing seeds a lot of thought. I thought about the obvious aerodynamic design, how marvelous it was. To me, those seeds were perfectly designed for flight, perfectly designed to be dispersed from the tree as effectively as possible. So, already as a child, I wondered about the Designer of such a marvel. I certainly did not think that the shape of those seeds happened by chance. Even as a child, I was doing a little natural theology. I have since come to the conclusion that it is a false choice to argue that either modern life-forms evolved or they were designed, because both are true.[173] John Henry Newman (1801-1890), a nineteenth century Roman Catholic cardinal said: "I believe in design because I believe in God; not in God because I see design."[174]

PART THREE

An opportune time

Correctly understanding the Bible's accounts of origins is primarily a hermeneutical task. In other words, in order to correctly understand the Bible accounts of the origins of life, we need to accurately interpret the biblical text. Paradoxically, rather than weakening faith and eroding Biblical authority, evolutionary biology provides the evangelical wing of the Christian church with an opportunity to improve the accuracy of its scriptural interpretation. Science invites believers to view the scriptures in a new light. Scientific discoveries remind Christians that the science in the scriptures is simply the common-sense understanding of an ancient people living in a prescientific world. Rather than inappropriately reading modern notions back into the scriptures, evangelical Christians are learning to let the scriptures speak for themselves, uncovering the message intended by the original authors.

11. RESPECTFUL CONVERSATION

Overview

In the sixteenth century, the Christian church experienced a serious conflict over issues of Biblical interpretation. Martin Luther rejected a system of doctrine that, in his opinion, allowed unscriptural teachings to contradict and obscure the gospel. For Luther and his followers, a new tripartite paradigm was adopted: faith alone, scripture alone, grace alone. Luther's desire that these issues be discussed without fear of retribution were rebuffed. Contemporary evangelicalism is dealing with scientific discoveries that directly impact traditional interpretations of Biblical creation accounts. A growing number of evangelical Christians are willing to acknowledge that, in order to break the current impasse, science and theology must engage in respectful conversation. So far, the results have been less than encouraging.

Around 1514, Nicolaus Copernicus proposed the radically counter-intuitive idea that the earth orbits the sun, not vice versa. After an extended period of time considering the implications of such a controversial idea, which at first seemed to contradict the plain reading of scripture, (and the plain experience of the sun passing across the sky each day) the Church came to acknowledge this cosmological reality and take it into account in its theological deliberations. For the last 150 years, a similar situation has existed with the theory of evolution. In many cases, the findings of evolutionary biology do not align well with a traditional interpretation of the Genesis creation accounts. As we have seen in previous chapters, scientific concordism, the argument that the Bible's statements about the natural realm are always accurate, is being called into question.

As we noted in chapter 8, evolutionary creation endeavors to take science seriously while at the same time upholding historic Christian doctrines such as the incarnation, the substitutionary death of Christ, and his resurrection from the dead. Evolutionary creation asserts that science can make a positive contribution to the understanding of the creation accounts in scripture. A great deal was at stake at the time of the Reformation as the church grappled with the implications of heliocentrism. Similar important issues, also with serious implications, are being discussed today in the context of evolutionary theory.

The power of the paradigm

We all know the joy of being able to perceive some aspect of reality that had previously been hidden to us. All of us have mental filters – often called paradigms – that organize and interpret the constant stream of data that comes our way on a daily basis. To a surprising extent, these mental filters determine what we can or cannot perceive. In his influential book, The Structure of Scientific Revolutions (1962),[1] Thomas Kuhn defines a paradigm as "... universally recognized scientific achievements that, for a time, provide model problems and solutions for a community of practitioners."[2] Paradigms define or suggest problems to investigate; they rule out others, they light the way, simultaneously restricting and enhancing the view."[3] At any given time numerous paradigms compete for dominance in the various scientific disciplines.[4] New paradigms are rarely adopted when they are first proposed.[5]

The human mind is not a blank slate; I liken it to a formatted hard drive. A major paradigm shift or revision in an individual's worldview can be compared to reformatting that hard drive and installing a new operating system. A major paradigm shift takes an individual's understanding from "It can't be so," to "That's the way it is!" Physicist Tom McLeish compares a major intellectual shift to a light being switched on. Everything related to that topic then suddenly makes sense.[6] This is the kind of transformation that happened to Saul of Tarsus as he met Jesus of Nazareth on the road to Damascus and after that fateful day, Saul came to be known as the Apostle Paul. A zealous defender of one faith took on another; amazingly, one that he had previously tried to eliminate.

A change in our basic orientation on a particular subject is often preceded by a period characterized by what Stanford University psychologist Leon Festinger (1919-1989) calls cognitive dissonance.[7] For Festinger, cognitive dissonance is a state of mental discomfort experienced by individuals who hold two or more contradictory beliefs simultaneously, or encounter new information that conflicts with their existing beliefs. Festinger makes the important point that in order to reduce that dissonance, individuals strive to achieve internal mental consistency, which may lead them to reject new information, even though it may turn out to be correct. Most Christians would agree that the theory of evolution speaks at a fundamental level to issues important to both faith and science.[8] Many evangelicals are surprised to discover, as we noted in chapter 8, that the majority of Christians worldwide, including mainline Protestants as well as the Roman Catholic Church, acknowledge that science and faith are indeed compatible.[9] God is not threatened by what science discovers – after all, he made it all possible and granted humankind the cognitive abilities required to make sense of his creation.[10] Ambrose of Milan (337-397 A.D.) once said that all truth, regardless of its source, comes ultimately from the Holy Spirit.[11] Benjamin Warfield (1851-1921), evangelical champion of biblical inerrancy, once said, surprisingly:

> *We must not, then, as Christians, assume an attitude of antagonism toward the truths of reason, or the truths of philosophy, or the truths of science, or the truths of history, or the truths of criticism. As children of light, we must be careful to keep ourselves open to every ray of light. Let us then cultivate an attitude of courage over against the investigations of the day. None should be more zealous in them then we. None should be more quick to discern the truth in every field, or hospitable to receive it, or loyal to follow it, whithersoever it leads.*[12]

Adoption of a new orientation toward science generally and the theory of evolution specifically, is not to be done lightly, however, but deliberately and, for Christians, prayerfully, with the utmost respect for both scripture and science. It can be a disorienting experience for evangelical Christians to realize that scientific discoveries frequently challenge a good number of traditional interpretations of scripture's creation accounts. The majority of Christians who have adopted an evolutionary viewpoint, however, indicate that the change in perspective resulted, not in a loss of faith for them but in a significant enrichment of their faith. It is certainly a worthy goal to protect and defend the authority of scripture, but that need not be accomplished by rejecting science.

A looming crisis?

Calvin College theologian John R. Schneider claims that evangelical Protestantism is on "the brink of crisis" with regard to evolutionary theory.[13] Schneider overstates the case. Science certainly presents evangelical Protestantism with a valuable (and I would argue, God-ordained) opportunity to calmly revisit its teachings with regard to origins. Given the discoveries of the biological sciences, it may be that the church's theology 1.0 needs to be updated to 1.1. But that is for the church, not science, to decide. I have argued that it is time for a new orientation toward science, a re-engagement if you will, on the part of evangelical Christians. Evangelicals are called upon to clarify which aspects of their faith are non-negotiable and which may be appropriately reviewed.[14] The way I see it, even though some Christians would disagree, when seen over the broad sweep of church history, the theological enterprise is a work in progress. The stakes are indeed high. Matters of eternal importance are involved.[15] Zach Hunt:

> *I'm not attempting to cast doubt on the authority of scripture; it is simply a plea to better understand the complexity and richness of the text. The Bible is a complex library of history, law, poetry, wisdom, Gospels, epistles, and apocalyptic literature. But it was written in a time, place, culture, and language that is not ours.*[16]

A key aspect of evangelical theology is the doctrine of inerrancy, the belief that the Bible, in its original autographs, is without error of any kind, regardless of the subject at hand. That foundational doctrine is being revisited. Christian biologist Gary Fugle says, "For most evangelicals, the concept of inerrancy is supported by a modern scientific understanding of the world applied to the scriptures. But in light of modern science, some assertions in the scriptures are inaccurate."[17] John Walton proposes that the traditional definition of inerrancy needs to be revised so as to more accurately reflect the evidence put forward by science.[18] David Dockery offers this revised definition:

The Bible, properly interpreted in the light of the culture and communication developed by the time of its composition, will be shown to be completely true... in all that it affirms, to the degree of precision intended by the author, in all matters pertaining to God and his creation.[19]

According to Thomas Kuhn, a paradigm shift – call it a new ideological orientation, if you will – is required when new facts no longer fit old frameworks.[20] Just before paradigms are abandoned, they approach a tipping point when pesky anomalies accumulate and refuse to be dismissed.[21] Some compare a major paradigm shift to rebuilding a ship while it is still floating on the water.[22] Some paradigms can be updated; others need to be overhauled or even replaced. I believe that the evangelical paradigm which has provided a traditional understanding of the creation accounts does not need to be thrown out. But it does need to be revisited. And, after due consideration, it may need to be revised. That process begins with a serious re-engagement with scientific discovery, particularly in the area of the biological sciences. And that process takes time and requires much discussion along the way.

On the scientific side of the equation, the notion of a paradigm shift is at the heart of the scientific enterprise. It is what scientists win Nobel prizes for.

In the scientific realm, major paradigm shifts have occurred with regularity since the advent of the scientific revolution in the sixteenth century. Copernicus and heliocentrism, Darwin and evolution, Wegener and plate tectonics, Einstein and relativity.[23] A willingness to modify one's views when presented with better data is one of the hallmarks of the scientific method. As we noted in chapter 2, scientific methodology has a built-in accountability system that makes scientists look foolish clinging to a discredited theory.[24] A paradigm shift is often a transformative experience. It can be an intellectual epiphany leading to a cascade of new insights.[25] One writer, using a different metaphor, compared a major paradigm shift to snow slowly melting on a metal roof. All of a sudden, without warning, the snow slides off and hits the ground with a thud.[26] The change I'm advocating is not this radical. It can be accomplished in a series of small steps rather than one giant leap. It can be accomplished with eyes wide open, with theologians taking their time deciding whether making changes to several of the planks on which the church is built is required.

Splendid isolation

In self-referential cultures, everything makes sense as long as individuals remain within those cultural boundaries.[27] Out-of-the-box thinking makes group members nervous.[28] Psychologist John Jost of New York University describes partisans (religious or political), those whose primary motivation is defending the status quo, as system justifiers.[29] In the scientific world, challenges to a conventional view are to be expected, but in evangelicalism, challenges to theological norms are generally viewed with suspicion.[30] Many evangelical denominations, including my own, practice what is known as confessional subscription, which involves a public statement of loyalty to confessional statements typically formulated during or after the Reformation in the sixteenth century. Confessional subscription carries with it the formal expectation that denominational leaders, educational facilities, and clergy will affirm and teach a fixed body of doctrines and articles of faith that officially represent the denomination. Those confessions were designed to protect a precious theological heritage, which is certainly an admirable goal. But those same confessions may have an unintended consequence. They may inadvertently restrict needed changes, changes that could not have been countenanced at the time those confessions were assembled.

Paradoxically, therefore, the same confessional safeguards which admirably protected evangelical faith in years past may inadvertently hinder the enrichment of that same faith today. A number of years ago, a concerned scientist, influential in his field and a member of a young earth creationist denomination, wrote a letter to the editor of his national church publication. In that letter he requested that the church re-engage with science. The fact that his letter was even published was significant. The letter was published, but nothing changed. There is an old Russian proverb that has stayed with me through the years. It states that cloth should be measured seven times before it is cut. Similarly, evangelical Christians must not allow themselves to be pressured into making changes they are not comfortable making.

Evangelicals have been committed to various teachings on the creation accounts in scripture for a very long time. These accounts are found in Genesis, but are an important theme in other parts of the Old Testament, including the Psalms and the prophetic books as well. John Walton puts it this way, "... all our books have been in print for years; our lecture notes are on the internet; the foundations of our fortresses are nearly immovable. But we need to make our best efforts to reconsider the evidence and the possibilities."[31] It's human nature to resist change perceived as leading to the loss of something valuable. It's also human nature to warmly welcome change when it is associated with something positive; in this case, something that will be a real blessing to the church at large.

It's not surprising that administrators and board members of evangelical denominations, as well as educators in evangelical colleges and seminaries, are suspicious of change; it is, as it were, in their theological DNA. They look askance at what they perceive as unnecessary changes to long-standing doctrines and teachings. Confessional subscription may lead church administrators and educators to believe there is no need for any revisiting – let alone revision – of creation-related doctrines. Scientists, on the other hand, are trained to follow the truth wherever it leads. They may have their own pet theories but when the evidence piles up and becomes overwhelming, they know that they must adjust their old model and move on. In the church, however, change is much more problematic. And it is made worse when individuals experience pressure to make changes, seemingly irreversible changes that will adversely affect basic doctrines such as inerrancy and inspiration and, in addition, needlessly cause confusion among the people in the pews. Still more problematic are situations where faithful Christians are ridiculed for their beliefs or have their intelligence impugned.

Evangelicals who adopt a pro-science, pro-evolution perspective often experience pressure as well, but in their case it is pressure to keep their views to themselves. Thankfully, at the end of the day, changed hearts and minds are the Holy Spirit's work. What is needed, as I say, is respectful conversation between scientists and people of faith. What is needed is a removal of the pressure to change. We need safe places where these often-contentious issues can be discussed; an open and collegial atmosphere where dialogue replaces debate. Without these things, a genuine rapprochement is unlikely. It is ironic that the very people who can provide leadership in this area often feel muzzled and sometimes even shunned by their peers. Pro-science individuals in evangelical denominations require much discretion. They must determine what is appropriate to say, to whom, and when. But complete silence is not an option. As we saw in chapter 5, Darwin himself, fearing censure, waited twenty years before bringing his theory to the public. He published his ideas when he could conceal them no longer.[32] And the world has not been the same since.

Groups of all kinds, not just faith-related groups, are vulnerable to a psychological phenomenon called groupthink.[33] In this scenario, a strong desire for group harmony or conformity overrides good decision-making. Group members suppress their real views on the subject at hand so as to support each other and minimize conflict. An artificial consensus is achieved. But alternative viewpoints have not been critically evaluated. Groupthink results in dissenting views being discouraged. In order to foster compliance with the party line, the group may isolate itself from outside influences. A group or an individual with a strong conviction that their views are correct will, as a matter of course, vigorously resist change. Some evangelical leaders respond to scientific discovery by passively opting out of the discussion, preferring not to get involved.[34] An all-too-human failing is to allow ourselves to be lulled to sleep under the comfortable quilt of group conformity rather than courageously facing uncomfortable truths.

Misguided devotion

Christians generally avoid an inappropriate devotion to the Bible as a book, while wholeheartedly acknowledging its life-changing teachings, centered around Jesus of Nazareth. In traditional Christianity, worship is reserved for the Triune God alone.[35] The Bible, important as it is, is not to become an idol. Martin Luther described the scriptures as the cradle of Christ. Christians worship Christ, said Luther, not the cradle.[36] The Holy Scriptures – as commonly understood by evangelicals – possess both human and divine characteristics. I have argued that the common-sense ancient science in the scriptures is evidence of its human component. I have also argued that critical spiritual truths are often embedded in less-than-accurate (in a modern, scientific sense) statements about natural phenomena. It is my contention that a recognition of this aspect of the scriptures can lead to a more accurate interpretation of the creation accounts. So, in the larger scheme of things, much is to be gained, and nothing of value lost by a re-engagement. I distinctly remember the metal ring-puzzles I used to play with as a child. It didn't take long to realize there was only one way to correctly align the rings. But experience also taught, as I experimented a little, that I could cheat. I could force the rings to fit. But my conscience stepped in to remind me that I hadn't found the correct solution should I do that. Christians who steadfastly refuse to allow science to speak in any way to their faith, it seems to me, find themselves forcing scripture's statements about the natural realm to fit with its spiritual truths. In so doing, they are missing an important opportunity to improve the accuracy of their Bible interpretation.

A host of scientific facts, unknown by earlier generations, are now common knowledge. It's important for modern Christians to come to grips with that. I also contend that it's important to imagine what the world and the cosmos looked like to the ancient Israelites, and how they did their best to explain it. In terms of the whole of human history, the vast increase in scientific knowledge that we have experienced in our own lifetimes is a relatively recent phenomenon. My grandparents, for example, were born at a time when scientists thought the entire universe was the Milky Way.[37] Contemporary Christians often overlook the fact that individuals in biblical times did not know about one hundred billion galaxies. They didn't know that the earth is a sphere floating unsupported in space; they didn't know about continents and that they actually move, or that massive extinctions occurred in past ages and that those extinctions may be caused by asteroids colliding with the earth. But we do, and we are responsible for rightly handling that knowledge and letting it speak, as appropriate, to our most holy faith.

Biologist Darrel Falk argues that the scientific evidence consistently points in one direction – that God created through a gradual process, not a sudden one. A critical question in this entire discussion, then, is this: "What does science demand of theology?" Falk asserts that the discoveries of science require some rethinking of the early chapters of Genesis – a willingness to view the text figuratively rather than literalistically. But science, he argues, does not ask any more than that. Should Christians agree to that most fundamental adjustment, science can let the church and its theologians take the time they need to deal with these issues, motivated by an ongoing desire to achieve the most accurate interpretation of scripture possible. As the perceived pressure declines, Christians' willingness to engage with these issues often increases. According to Falk, the clear implication is that science does not require a reformation of Christian theology.[38]

Christians who avoid science, or unfairly criticize it, are missing a great opportunity to build a bridge of understanding to the wider secular society, especially its younger cohort. One Sunday, on the advice of friends, a science major attended worship in a church he had never visited before. In the pastor's sermon that morning, the pastor strongly criticized the theory of evolution, not on the basis of the scientific evidence, but under the presupposition that should science and faith disagree, science must be in the wrong. And, in the opinion of that student, the pastor was clearly uninformed.

An opportunity for dialogue was missed that day. Nothing really changed. And nothing will, unless respectful conversations about these emotionally-laden topics are encouraged and individuals are willing to let down their guard and enter an ongoing process of dialogue. Pro-science evangelicals need to be able to come out of the closet and engage brothers and sisters in the faith in a non-threatening discussion of these issues. Christian leaders are duty-bound to speak the truth and to do that in love (Ephesians 4:15). They are also duty-bound to deal with others with gentleness and respect (1 Peter 3:15). Science is an important part of contemporary daily life. Scientific topics are in the news every day. Christian church members do not live in a vacuum. They want to be able to talk about these issues with their pastors and fellow Christians. Respectful conversation would go a long way towards resolving conflict at the intersection of faith and science.

12. HERMENEUTICS

Overview

At the end of the day, our goal of "Resolving Conflict at the Intersection of Faith and Science" takes us back to square one – to hermeneutics. The anti-evolutionist's insistence that their interpretation of scripture's creation accounts is inviolate – is the logjam holding back progress. My contention is that until this is recognized, and appropriate adjustments made, little, if anything will change. Hermeneutics as you will recall, is a technical term referring to the theory and methodology of textual interpretation. A primary goal of the interpreter is exegesis; extracting the meaning of the text, entering the time period under consideration, thinking the thoughts of the original authors after them. In order to accomplish that goal, interpreters gather details about the original author and audience. They determine the purpose of those documents. They analyze the type of literature. They do their best to avoid reading modern notions back into ancient texts. We have noted that a common characteristic of anti-evolutionism is giving too much credence to the Bible's common-sense ancient statements about nature and too little recognition to the discoveries of modern science.

Common sense alone is not a reliable guide to understanding the natural realm. Anti-evolutionists do not give sufficient attention to the fact that the Israelites were Bronze Age people and that their descriptions of nature were pre-scientific, not anti-scientific. The message-incident principle asserts that the Bible's spiritual truths are often expressed in the context of out-of-date statements about the natural realm. Young earth creationists seek to make their interpretation of scripture's creation accounts normative for all Christians, for all time. The commonly-heard statement, "The Bible says..." is code for "My interpretation of the Bible says..." It is worth noting that most of the church fathers, up to but not including Martin Luther, were not biblical literalists in the modern sense. As we have already noted, St. Augustine emphasized an important hermeneutical principle, one that has stood the test of time; that a "literal" interpretation is one that is faithful to the authors' original intention, not simply a "literal" reading of the words as they stand on the page, without any concern for context or other literary considerations.

It is all about hermeneutics

A central argument put forward in these chapters has been that a critically important component of the science-religion debate is hermeneutics. The scientific genie has been out of the bottle for more than four hundred years. Many scientific discoveries, as we have seen, have implications for basic church teachings on creation. Many of today's evangelical Christians, however, are not convinced that science is trustworthy. As we saw in chapter 8, should Christians adopt an evolutionary point of view, a good number of creation-related doctrines are affected and must be revisited. The way this dispute is presently handled is not working well, either for the church or for science. Maintaining the so-called warfare model results in an uncomfortable impasse where very little, if any, real change occurs. Urgently required is some sort of bridge-building, or trust-building, where the two sides can come together with the goal of at least trying to understand one another.

An important question for Christians is whether fallible human beings can ever hope to interpret the Bible infallibly.[1] Various Christian groups, all claiming the inspiration of the same Holy Spirit, interpret scripture's creation accounts in very different ways. It is not an unreasonable assumption that each group, in its own way, wants to be faithful to the scriptures as a whole, and would generally recognize that it is important to seek, as much as is possible, the original intention of the author, while remaining faithful to their confessional and doctrinal heritage. I am proposing that accurate Bible interpretation will take into account all possible sources of relevant information, and that would include science, in order to understand what God is truly communicating through his word. Theologian N.T. Wright says, "... anti-evolutionists have developed long-standing and subtle interpretive strategies for not listening to what the Bible is in fact saying."[2] At the end of the day, an inaccurate hermeneutics has the potential to cause unnecessary problems for the church, and in the case of young earth creationism, straining the church's credibility in the eyes of scientifically-literate individuals.

I believe it is helpful to distinguish between a literal translation and one that is literalistic. A literalistic interpretation of the Bible simply reads the words as they appear on the page without giving sufficient credence to context and genre. Donald A. Carson has been quoted saying that "Text without context is pretext."[3] Advising interpreters to "just read the words," is not a helpful basis for accurately interpreting biblical texts.[4] As much as possible interpreters must view the text from the author's perspective; specifically, through the author's value system, beliefs and conventions. The interpreter's personal preferences, at the end of the day, only get in the way.[5] Readers with vested interests of all sorts apply their modern understanding of the text to extract from it any number of inaccurate claims.[6] No interpreter, no matter how skilled, can claim complete objectivity. Each interpreter reads the scriptures through their particular "lens," often unconsciously incorporating their theological worldview, their educational background, gender, ethnicity, and political views into their interpretation. Interpreters must be aware of these assumptions and allow them to be identified and tested. Tim Reddish says, "Authentic engagement with the biblical text occurs when we allow the text to challenge and change our starting assumptions. This is one way the Spirit can work." (John 16:13).[7] St. Augustine was first in a long line of theologians who argued that faith would benefit by recognizing the findings of science.[8]

A young earth creationist hermeneutic

It is a commonly-held view among young earth creationists (see chapter 9) that the doctrine of creation supports the gospel message as well as the doctrines of biblical inspiration and inerrancy.[9] Young earth creationists fear that, should Christians adopt an evolutionary point of view, the integrity and authority of the Bible will be lost.[10] Some claim that the slightest movement away from their interpretation of Genesis will result in apostasy and even a loss of salvation.[11] A typical creationist all-or-nothing argument says: "If evolution is true, then the Bible is wrong and we must give up Christ, salvation, and the entire New Testament."[12] For a committed young earth creationist, there are only two alternatives: first, an entirely supernatural, divine creation or second, atheistic evolution in which God plays no part.[13] Bernard Ramm (1916-1992) pointed out that Lutheran young earth creationist Alfred M. Rehwinkel (1887-1979) identified his personal view (i.e., acceptance of George McCready Price's flood geology) with the inspiration of scripture, with the clear (and intentional) implication that disagreement with his point of view would be a denial of the Bible's inspiration and authority.[14]

Locked or unlocked

Anti-evolutionism has been adopted by many different denominations and each denomination supports its position in slightly different ways. My own heritage is confessional Lutheranism and the following describes how young earth creationism is implemented in that context. The gold-standard systematic theology for many confessional Lutherans is Francis Pieper's Christian Dogmatics (published first in German in 1924, subsequently translated into English in 1934).[15] Pieper (1852-1931) clearly advocates the warfare model. He argues that the "scientific spirit" serves only to cause divisions in the church.[16] He predicts that the struggle between theology and science will never cease. Advocates for evolution, in his opinion, are "radicals."[17] Pieper argues that Christian doctrine has been finalized and must not be changed.[18] Quoting scripture which admonishes Christians not to add anything to the faith they once received, and not to remove anything either (Deuteronomy 4:2) the argument is made that Christian doctrine is not to be changed.[19]

Consider a locked cellphone. When a cellphone is locked, it is linked to a single cell carrier. A locked phone therefore cannot be connected to another company's network. Pieper argues that Christians are bound by their hermeneutic; their beliefs are locked into a proprietary system by their interpretation of scripture. As support for his argument, Pieper quotes Romans 16:17 where the apostle Paul says, "I urge you, brothers and sisters, to watch out for those who cause divisions and put obstacles in your way that are contrary to the teaching you have learned. Keep away from them." (NIV)

Pieper's argument about unchanging doctrine, although it may be true in the abstract, is not always matched by the actual practice of the church. A number of church teachings, many dealing with women, have been modified over the years. Examples include allowing church members to buy insurance (which, it was argued in the nineteenth century, showed a lack of trust in God's provision); also the practice, now largely abandoned, of women wearing hats in church, women being allowed to vote at congregational meetings, relaxing the requirement that women be silent in church, and women being allowed to read scripture in worship services. Another example would be a change in the practice of circumcision, which is no longer given the same priority it once was. Similarly, the practice of private confession with the pastor the night before communion is now rarely practiced. Finally, cremation is much more common now than it was in the past.

Church fathers

According to Pieper, the scriptures are entirely trustworthy, from cover to cover and on any subject. Science, on the other hand, is not. As support for his argument, Pieper quotes the apostle Paul who says in 2 Corinthians 10:5, (NIV) "We demolish arguments and every pretension that sets itself up against the knowledge of God, and we take captive every thought to make it obedient to Christ." We have seen that modern science raises a host of questions for Christians. For example, if scientific discoveries about nature do not match scriptural statements, are Christians forced to choose one or the other? Does the doctrine of biblical inerrancy include spiritual truths as well as the Bible's statements about nature? Or should the doctrine of inerrancy be limited to spiritual concepts only?[20] An increasing number of evangelical scholars are calling for a review of inerrancy.[21] Current thinking points to an emphasis on spiritual concepts. The church fathers generally expressed their views on creation tentatively. There is no indication that they sharply debated these issues or took a dogmatic stance one way or the other. Instead they charitably tolerated a diversity of views. Augustine, Origen, and other early church fathers were already interpreting Genesis figuratively in the early centuries A.D.[22] Unlike the church fathers, today's young earth creationists require a literalistic interpretation of scripture. An old evangelical motto I grew up with says, "God said it. I believe it. That settles it!"

Most of the church fathers, up to the time of the Reformation in the sixteenth century, did not look to the Bible for scientific insights.[23] Ironically, in the grand sweep of church history, contemporary young earth creationism has drifted far from the traditional interpretation of the Genesis creation accounts advocated by church fathers such as Philo of Alexandria (approx. 15-50 A.D.), Origen (184-254 A.D.), Augustine of Hippo (354-430 A.D.) and Moses Maimonides (1135-1204 A.D.). These individuals did not consider the first chapters of Genesis to be speaking of six literal twenty-four hour days. The Venerable Bede, (672?-735 A.D.) English monk, one of the most influential Christian scholars in the period between 600 and 800 A.D., understood that his role was to explain nature on its own terms so as to counter superstition and foster amazement at God's creative activity.[24]

Augustine wrestled with the early chapters of Genesis throughout his career. He refused to be pinned down on the meaning of the word "day." In the City of God (426 A.D.), he said, "As for those days it is difficult, perhaps impossible to think, let alone explain in words, what they mean."[25] For Augustine, the days of creation were not understood chronologically, but served to categorize God's creative work.[26]

Human reason

Martin Luther was critical of the use of reason when it came to theological deliberations. Luther once said:

> *But the devil's bride, reason, the lovely whore, then comes in and wants to be wise, and what she says, she thinks, is the Holy Spirit. Who can be of any help then? Neither jurist, nor physician, nor king, nor emperor; for she is the foremost whore the devil has. The other gross sins can be seen, but nobody can control reason.*[27]

Luther's argument is a clear expression of a point of view philosophers call fideism, the argument that faith is either independent of reason, or that reason and faith are incompatible.[28] Fideism claims that faith is superior for arriving at particular, usually spiritual truths. Fideism comes from fides, the Latin word for faith, and literally means "faith-ism."[29] Fideism, as might be expected, can negatively affect the relationship of faith and science. In his day, Luther proposed ideas that eventually set in motion the reformation of a theological system that, up to that point had quite effectively resisted theological dissent. Ironically, Luther and his followers created a system that, in some of its expressions, does much the same thing. As an example of how resistance to change can be built into a theological system, Alister McGrath quotes a Catholic apologist, who said, back in 1688 –

> *The teaching of the church is always the same. The gospel is never different from what it was before. Hence, if at any time someone says that the faith includes something which yesterday was not said to be of the faith, it is always heterodoxy, which is any doctrine different from orthodoxy. There is no difficulty about recognizing it; there is no argument about it. It is recognized at once, whenever it appears, simply because it is new.*[30]

Books published under Catholic auspices were reviewed by official censors, and received an imprimatur, which literally means "let it be printed."[31] This same resistance to change is evident in young earth creationism today. Those who question young earth creationism's standard anti-evolutionary views are considered outliers. These individuals, knowing that their denomination, as well as many of their friends, and others close to them, do not accept evolution, will often accede to social pressure and choose not to rock the boat.[32] A Lutheran layperson with a deep and abiding interest in science and the theory of evolution recently told me that he very much wanted to talk to his pastor about the theory of evolution but never got around to it because he feared a negative response.

Scientific concordism

Scientific concordism, expecting to find modern science in the Bible, has been described as a category mistake.[33] Another example of a category mistake would be reading Shakespeare looking for gardening tips. There is no contradiction between the scriptural creation accounts and modern evolutionary theory if the creation accounts were never intended to convey modern scientific information in the first place. It is my contention that proposing a modern scientific explanation for everything in the Bible is not actually defending biblical authority, but is defending an inaccurate hermeneutic instead. In his Commentary on Genesis, Augustine warned Christians that claiming knowledge where one is in fact ignorant is damaging to the faith. Augustine was concerned that "reckless and incompetent interpreters of scripture would be taken to task by intelligent unbelievers."[34] Scientific concordism sets up anti-evolutionary views for criticism in the face of growing scientific evidence pointing to evolution as God's method of creation over time. Those who value the Bible, as evangelicals certainly do, need not make it "speak science" in order to uphold its truth claims or its credibility.[35] Some individuals are proud to be defenders of the faith (defensor fidei) while others pride themselves on being defenders of the truth (defensor veritas). I am an advocate for both, since they are, or at least should be, two sides of the same coin.

It is claimed that as many as 90 percent of evangelical Christians in the U.S. are scientific concordists.[36] As we have seen repeatedly, scientific concordism claims that all of the Bible's statements are accurate "... whether they pertain to history, science, morals, or fishing and farming."[37] Writing in the 1950's, Baptist theologian Bernard Ramm (1916-1992) claimed that there are no scientific errors in the Bible because God kept the authors from making them.[38] Old-earth creationist and founder of the old-earth advocacy group Reasons to Believe (see chapter 7) Hugh Ross expresses typical concordist views when he says, "The facts of nature and scripture will always agree,"[39] and "The Bible consistently affirmed, and even predicted, scientific advances."[40] Henry Morris (1918-2006) claimed that, since the Bible is inspired and inerrant, it is unthinkable that it should contain scientific errors. Without scientific concordism, says Morris, the Bible would be just another human book.[41]

In mainstream young earth subculture, science is kept on a short leash. On the basis of his evangelical understanding of inerrancy and his concordist views, Morris claimed that he was forced to the conclusion that the earth is young, regardless of what geologists had to say.[42] Should a contradiction arise between science and his interpretation of the creation narratives, Morris was convinced that the problem must lie with science. The anti-evolutionist's preoccupation with scientific concordism makes adoption of the theory of evolution less likely. Scientific concordism fails to differentiate scripture's scientific from its theological content. Scientific concordism is an expression of what amounts to a pre-scientific worldview.[43] Theologian J.I. Packer says, "Scripture was given to reveal God, not to address scientific issues in scientific terms."[44] Evolutionary creationist Denis Lamoureux puts it in black and white, saying it in a way that makes evangelicals uncomfortable, "To say it plainly: the opening chapters of scripture do not align with the facts of modern science and history."[45]

We should not be surprised to hear that the Bible's statements about nature are time-and-culture bound. These statements about the natural realm, I have argued, are an example of the humanity of the scriptures. Young earth creationists assume that the views of scripture's authors regarding nature were correct when they were first adopted, and remain correct for all time. Many church leaders, however, including Luther's contemporary John Calvin (1509-1564) adopted a different point of view. Calvin argued at one point that the Holy Spirit had no intention of teaching astronomy.[46] The Genesis creation accounts are primarily concerned, not with scientific questions, but with how humanity's relationship with God was established. It is claimed that these accounts are not, and were never meant to be, scientific accounts of our origins. Theologian Ian Barbour says:

> *... we must acknowledge the human limitations of [scripture's] authors and the cultural influences on their thought. Their opinions concerning scientific questions reflect the pre-scientific speculations of ancient times. We should read the opening chapters of Genesis as a symbolic portrayal of the basic relation of humanity and the world to God, a message about human creatureliness in the goodness of the natural order. These religious meanings can be separated from the ancient cosmology in which they were expressed.*[47]

If biblical authority (and inerrancy) rests, even partially, on inaccurate statements about nature, then scientific concordism has a problem. Either the scriptures are sprinkled with scientific inaccuracies (a point of view worthy of further study by evangelicals) and have therefore lost their authority (which is not the case), or Christians have misunderstood the true nature of the scriptures. Failure to adequately account for the ancient science in the scriptures, I contend, is a failure to acknowledge scriptures' humanity.[48] Many evangelicals are unaware that these are not new issues for Christians. The pitfalls of scientific concordism were being discussed as early as the seventeenth century. The Rev. Thomas Burnett (1635-1715) said, "… 'tis a dangerous thing to engage the authority of scripture in disputes about the natural world."[49]

ANCIENT SCIENCE IN SCRIPTURE	
STRUCTURES	**SCRIPTURE**
Flat circular earth with ends, foundations & underworld	Prov 3:19; Heb 1:10; Rev 5:13
Flat circumferential sea around earth & bordered by horizon	Is 40:22; Prov 8:22-31; Job 26:7-14
Firmament overhead in heaven & set on foundations	Ps 104:5; Job 26:11; 37:18; 2 Sam 22:8
Sun, moon & stars set in firmament	Gen 1:14-19
Sea of waters above in heaven & held up by firmament	Ps 148:4
Beams of divine dwelling set in sea of waters above	Gen 1:6-8; Ps 104:2-3; Ps 148:4
OPERATIONS	
Earth stationary & immovable	1 Chr 16:30; Pss 93:1, 96:10
Sun moves daily across sky & under horizon	Eccl 1:5; Ps 19:6; 50:1
Sun, moon & stars move through firmament	Gen 1:14-19
Stars occasionally fall to earth	Is 34:4; Mt 24:29; Rev 6:13; 12:4

Figure 12.1 – Ancient Science in Scripture. *The science in the Bible reflects a common-sense, phenomenological interpretation of what the eye could see, unaided by modern technology. This was the reality for the ancient Hebrew people. Reading modern scientific notions back into these ancient texts is characteristic of the hermeneutical error of eisegesis.* Adapted from Denis Lamoureux, I Love Jesus and I Accept Evolution, loc. 1431. Used with permission.

Presuppositionalism

In addition to fideism and scientific concordism, anti-evolutionists typically subscribe to a point of view called presuppositionalism. Presuppositionalism is a branch of Christian apologetics which claims that the Christian faith is the only basis for rational thought. It attempts to expose flaws in other worldviews.[50] Presuppositionalism originated with Cornelius Van Til, (1895-1987) Christian philosopher and Reformed theologian. Hugh Ross explains this point of view by saying: "According to some of its advocates, presuppositionalism says all human reasoning and interpretation of scientific evidence must be subordinate to a Biblical interpretation of reality. Some young earth creationists adopt an extreme form of presuppositionalism, asserting that any scientific interpretation of the record of nature can be discounted in light of their young earth interpretation of the words of the Bible."[51]

In an article titled "Evidentialism vs. Presuppositionalism," Libby Anne says,

> *Answers in Genesis, a young earth creationist group that runs the creationist museum in Kentucky and has recently embraced presuppositionalism apologetics wholeheartedly, is actually completely open about the fact that it simply rejects evidence that contradicts their interpretation of the Biblical account of creation. It is not about the evidence. It is about the presupposition. And no matter what you say, you are not going to change their minds.*[52]

And Ben Holloway, in a blog post titled Young Earthers and Presuppositionalism adds:

> *A presuppositional apologetic assumes a hermeneutic of literalism. Since presuppositionalists typically hold that scripture is the ultimate authority on what is true, and since there is no indication found in the text that the six-day creation account was anything but an account of actual events in twenty-four hour days, there is no reason found in scripture to abandon a young earth, six-day creation position. The only reason for abandoning this view is found outside scripture and entails borrowing from methodological scientific naturalism or other non-biblical methods and worldviews.*[53]

It is fair to say that, for presuppositionalists at least, the starting point for interpreting a biblical text is knowing in advance the results you are looking for. Presuppositionalists tend to be unbending in their arguments because they truly believe they have the infallible word of God backing them up. In an article titled Presuppositional Apologetics Drives Creationism, we read: "They will, by necessity, and without a second thought, reinterpret the data to fit a young earth by looking for any explanation that fits [their] presuppositions no matter how much it may seem to be putting a square peg in a round hole."[54] In a now-famous debate held February 14th, 2014 featuring creationist spokesman Ken Ham and scientist Bill Nye, Ham was asked by a member of the audience what evidence, if any, would convince him that the theory of evolution was in fact true. In his response, Ham dramatically played the presuppositional trump card. His answer: "The Bible says..."[55] It should not be surprising, then, that when evidence is presented that threatens a partisan's idiosyncratic worldview, that evidence can be turned around and serve to strengthen their beliefs.[56]

Interpretive boundaries

As we have seen, many evangelical Christians, whether they mean to or not, give others the impression that their interpretation of scripture is inerrant. This interpretation is a given. It is not negotiable. It is the way things are. A few years ago, an individual wanted to talk to me after two very busy worship services on Easter Sunday. He immediately pressed me for my views about the theory of evolution. I quickly realized that this individual was a committed young earth creationist and was very forceful about his views. I am convinced that, once he got an inkling that I was open to the theory of evolution, he was confused. We sat down in my office to chat. I lent him a copy of Francis Collins' The Language of God. He returned it to me a few weeks later with sticky notes affixed to many of the pages. His comments, which were voluminous, made it quite obvious that he was not open to dialogue. He was right. And I was wrong. End of discussion. Well-known evangelical spokesman James Dobson correctly observes the discussion of the theory of evolution is essentially a matter of scripture interpretation.[57] It is my contention, as I have noted already, that a "plain" or "literal" reading of the Bible is, in and of itself, already a particular interpretive method. Just reading the words off the page as they appear is not the default way to read the Bible so as to preserve its authority. Those words are not just there, they have to be interpreted accurately.[58]

Science shock

Christian professor of medicine, Luke Janssen, says that applying new scientific findings to his unexamined faith was, in his words, "massively disrupting."[59] He says that the insight that kept him from abandoning his faith was the realization that even though scripture is inspired, it must be interpreted correctly.[60] Christians who are exposed to the theory of evolution respond in very different ways. Some, like Dr. Janssen, are left feeling very uncomfortable. Some, unfortunately, abandon their faith. An individual I talked to recently said that his son had left the church over the issue of science. Other individuals are exposed to scientific discovery and are motivated to embark on a journey of discovery. Still others do their best to avoid the topic altogether. One pastor – and remember this is a church leader speaking – says: "Had I not found a way of reconciling belief in the Bible as God's word with acceptance of some form of evolutionary theory, I seriously doubt that I would have ever found my way back into an evangelical version of the Christian faith."[61] My advice to Christians struggling with this issue is to do your homework, read widely, seek out Christians on both sides of this issue and engage in dialogue.

The Biblical interpreter's task is, and will always remain, critically important. When the interpretive task is handled well, believers will have a much better understanding of an ancient world very different from their own. One writer compares accurate biblical interpretation to an "archaeology of human knowledge," which entails digging down through layers of cultural strata to access the original time period. It means stepping into a world very different from our own. And it means letting that very different ancient world tell us what it wants to say rather than us overlaying that world with our own presuppositions.[62] Biblical writers were no less intelligent than ourselves, but, as one writer says, not meaning this as a criticism, they were "not playing with a full deck, scientifically speaking."[63] Scott Buchanan says:

> *The authors and early readers of the Bible had a "science" of their day, a shared understanding of the physical world. God could have corrected this ancient science, but chose not to. God wisely and graciously accommodated his spiritual revelation to the existing physical understanding, in order to facilitate communication of vital spiritual and relational concepts.*[64]

Ancient near eastern influence

Christians generally believe that the first eleven chapters of Genesis contain ancient origins accounts inspired by the Holy Spirit. But how does that inspiration actually work? A major complicating factor is the discovery that several origins motifs, very similar to biblical motifs, were well-established by Israel's neighbors in the ancient near east as early as 1500 BC, many years before similar ideas appeared in Israel (see chapter 3).[65] Evangelical Christians are often surprised to learn that biblical authors, under the inspiration of the Holy Spirit, sometimes borrowed and recycled motifs from neighboring cultures.[66] Significantly, data from outside the scriptures may actually provide information that helps correct faulty interpretations of those same scriptures. Scripture conveys spiritual truths in the context of the dominant ideas (motifs) commonly expressed in those days. The parallels between Genesis 1 and other ancient near eastern origin accounts are striking. The similarities certainly appear to be more than just coincidence. But, and this is critical, the theological differences are also significant. And those theological differences are intentional.[67] Under the inspiration of the Holy Spirit, ideas and motifs that originated in Mesopotamia were cleansed of their pagan theology. Evolutionary creationist Denis Lamoureux says:

> *... this process can be pictured as the inheritance of antique intellectual furniture by a fledgling preliterate Hebrew tribe. Inspired by the Holy Spirit, Israel stripped away pagan cloth from the historical frameworks and then reupholstered them with the fabric of holiness.*[68]

It is true; the Genesis creation and flood accounts closely parallel much older Mesopotamian narratives such as the Epic of Gilgamesh.[69] In Israel, however, unlike Mesopotamia, there was one God, not many gods. In Genesis, unlike Mesopotamia, the heavenly bodies – the sun, moon, and stars – were inanimate entities under God's control, in service to humanity, not divinities. The moon was a god in the rest of the ancient near east, but definitely not in Genesis. It is not an exaggeration to say that all of the ancient near eastern gods were summarily dismissed by the author of Genesis.[70] In Genesis, creation is peaceful and benevolent, not violent and oppressive as it is in the other accounts. In the ancient near east, the gods created human beings to be their slaves. But in the Genesis account, it is God's intention to exalt humans so that they bear his own image. In Genesis 2, God exalts human beings to the level of co-artisans, co-governors, and co-nurturers.[71]

	Sumerian Flood 2000-1700 BC	Epic of Atrahasis 1700 BC	Epic of Gilgamesh 1600 BC	Biblical Flood 1000-500 BC
God/s	37 lines missing			
Number	many gods	many gods	many gods	one Holy God
Reason to destroy humans		noise	overpopulation	sin
Warn/s hero of flood	✔	✔	✔	✔
Flood Hero				
Name	Ziusudra	Atrahasis	Utnapishtim	Noah
Builds ark	✔	✔	✔	✔
Age given	(36,000 years)*	(600+ years)**		600 yrs
Construction of Ark	40 lines missing			
Materials used (e.g., pitch)		✔	✔	✔
Multiple decks		✔	✔	✔
Roof		✔	✔	✔
Dimensions (cubits)			120 X 120 X 120	300 X 50 X 30
Duration		7 days	7 days	
Preservation of Life in Ark	40 lines missing			
Family of hero		✔	✔	✔
Animals		✔	✔	✔
Birds		✔	✔	✔
Wild & domestic		✔	✔	✔
Clean & unclean		✔		✔
Flood				
Ark door closed		✔	✔	✔
Destruction of all life	✔	✔	✔	✔
Duration	7 days	7 days	7 days	40/150 days
God/s frightened by flood		✔	✔	
Retreat of Flood		58 lines missing		
Ark rests on mountain			Mt Nisir	Ararat Mts
Hero opens hatch	✔		✔	✔
Bird reconnaissance			✔	✔
Dove & raven			✔	✔
Duration			7 days	7/7 days
Water removed & earth dried			✔	✔
Duration			7 days	150/40/7/7 days
After Flood	39 lines missing			
Hero sacrifices to God/s	✔	✔	✔	✔
God/s smell/s sacrifice		✔	✔	✔
God/s regret/s flood & quarrel		✔	✔	
God/s offer/s hero	Eternal life	Eternal life?	Eternal life	Covenant

Figure 12.2 – Ancient Near Eastern Flood Accounts. *The flood narrative found in Genesis 6 through 9 contains many elements identical to or similar to other ancient near Eastern flood stories, especially the Babylonian Epic of Gilgamesh, which, most scholars agree, predates the Genesis account.* Credit: Denis Lamoureux, Evolutionary Creation, p. 221. Used with permission.

Accurate interpretation of Old Testament documents requires, among other things, a thorough knowledge of the conventions of Hebrew literature.[72] According to John Walton, traditional interpretations or understandings of English words do not necessarily constitute the best reading of a biblical text.[73] The lure of a simplistic (i.e., "literalistic") reading of the scriptures is always present and can potentially lead to an incorrect interpretation.[74] I propose that the author of the Genesis creation accounts did not understand himself to be writing history as we know it today, but his priority was theological.[75]

In ordinary English, a story is "historical" if the author wants the audience to believe the events really happened. That is, "history" is not really a kind of literature (or genre); it is a way of referring to or talking about events in the real world. This means that a variety of literary types can actually recount "history," and each type uses its own conventions for doing so. Therefore, a poem can be historical.[76] "Historical" is not the same as "prose," and certainly does not imply that an account has no figurative or imaginative elements. "Historical" is not the same as "complete in detail" or "free from ideological bias." "Historical" is not necessarily the same as "told in exact chronological sequence" unless the text claims that for itself.[77]

The Israelites were not asking scientific questions in the modern sense of the word in Genesis. They wanted to know who had created the heavens and the earth. Was it multiple deities who battled in the heavens, as neighboring nations believed? The writer of Genesis wanted to reassure them that their God was indeed creator of all things. Questions about life's purpose are answered in the Genesis creation accounts. For example, in Genesis 1:26, 28, God calls his people to be good stewards of his gifts, an eternally important theme.[78]

Interpretive malpractice

Scriptural interpreters must do their best to avoid what John Walton calls "interpretive malpractice."[79] It is a strange irony that some Christians attempt to honor the Bible by promoting the kind of literalistic interpretation that would most likely have had the Bible's original authors scratching their heads at the obvious disconnect between what they intended to say and what people thousands of years later understood their words to mean.[80] Thomas Aquinas (1225-1274) reminded Christians of his day of two important interpretive principles that originated with Augustine:

> *The first is to hold the truth of scripture without wavering. The second, since Holy Scripture can be explained in a multiplicity of senses, one should adhere to a particular explanation only in such measure as to be ready to abandon it, if it proved with certainty to be false; less Holy Scripture be exposed to the ridicule of unbelievers, and obstacles be placed to their believing."*[81]

Accurate hermeneutics seeks answers to questions like these:

- What language are we dealing with?
- What type of literature is this?
- What was the composition of the original audience?
- What was the purpose of the document?
- What relevant cultural knowledge assists in understanding this text?
- Is the text figurative, symbolic, historical, scientific, or straightforward?[82]

Genres

Most scholars agree that the opening chapters of Genesis are a special type of literature, a unique genre. The literary form or genre of the Genesis creation accounts as, of course, been much debated. Some call it saga, very different from the way history is written today. Saga is generally defined as narrative dealing with heroic achievements, a long, involved story with many details, especially about something dramatic. Many scholars argue that Genesis chapters 1 through 11 is a separate literary unit containing divine theology, ancient science, and ancient poetry.[83] The Holy Spirit used ancient literary techniques in biblical revelation. We should adapt our expectations to the literary forms the sacred writers used.[84]

Accurate interpretation of the Genesis origins accounts involves a recognition that these passages have a distinct character. Scholars generally advocate what is called a literary-cultural analysis, which asks what each passage meant to convey, not to us, but to the original audience.[85] The books of the Bible can be classified according to genre, and there are many different genres evident in the Bible: letters, laws, wisdom literature, apocalyptic, prophetic, parable. Identifying the correct genre is critical in establishing an accurate interpretation of scripture. The best scriptural interpretation occurs when biblical texts are compared with similar writings from the ancient world.[86]

Genealogies

Biblical genealogies present interpreters with a challenging interpretive puzzle. That is because many scholars argue that the primary purpose of biblical genealogies is theological, not historical.[87] The Bible's genealogies often contain gaps, with many individuals missing. And Biblical genealogies are not always strict father-son relationships. For example, the genealogy in the first chapter of Matthew's Gospel omits three names in verse 8. It appears that Matthew is omitting certain individuals so as to maintain his symmetry of fourteen generations, suggesting that there may be a non-historical, stylistic intent at work here.[88]

1st 14 Generations	1 Chr 1:34, 2:1-15	2nd 14 Generations	1 Chr 3:4-5, 3:10-16	3rd 14 Generations	1 Chr 3:17-24
1. Abraham	✔	1. Solomon	✔	1. Shealtiel	Pedaiah
2. Isaac	✔	2. Rehoboam	✔	2. Zerubbabel	✔
3. Jacob	✔	3. Abijah	✔	3. Abiud	Hananiah
4. Judah	✔	4. Asa	✔	4. Eliakim	Shecaniah
5. Perez	✔	5. Jehoshaphat	✔	5. Azor	Neariah
6. Hezron	✔	6. Joram	✔	6. Zadok	Elioenia
7. Ram	✔		Ahaziah	7. Akim	**End of Genealogy**
8. Amminadab	✔		Joash	8. Eliud	
9. Hahshon	✔		Amazriah	9. Eleazar	
10. Salmon	✔	7. Uzziah	✔	10. Matthan	
11. Boaz	✔	8. Jotham	✔	11. Jacob	
12. Obed	✔	9. Ahaz	✔	12. Joseph	
13. Jesse	✔	10. Hezekiah	✔	13. Jesus	
14. David	✔	11. Manasseh	✔	14. Christ	
		12. Amon	✔	**Total: 42**	
		13. Josiah	✔		
			Jehoiahkim		
		14. Jeconiah	✔		

Figure 12.3 – Matthew's Genealogy of Jesus. *(Matthew 1: 1-16). The check marks indicate agreement between Matthew 1 and genealogies found in 1 Chronicles 1–3. Areas of disagreement are also indicated.* Credit: Denis O. Lamoureux, Evolutionary Creation, p. 398. Used with Permission.

Apparently Matthew feels free to compress or stretch generations in order to accommodate the theological point he is making.[89] And, of course, this makes modern evangelicals quite uncomfortable. So what, in fact, is going on here? Are we missing something? Matthew's genealogy goes back to Abraham and portrays Jesus as the king of David's line who will bring an end to Israel's exile. It has been said that the primary purpose of a genealogy in the ancient world was to offer an important, reassuring message about the community or the nation. We moderns focus on historicity; the ancients focused on relationships and a community's place in the world. In biblical genealogies, any ancestor was regarded as the father of all his descendants. For these reasons, it appears that biblical genealogies, unlike their modern equivalents, were not primarily concerned with historical accuracy. This of course has important implications for our definition of biblical inerrancy.[90] Benjamin Warfield is quoted as saying, "These genealogies must be esteemed trustworthy for the purpose for which they are recorded; but they cannot be safely pressed into use for any other purpose for which they were not intended, and for which they are not adapted."[91]

Generations of Sons	Matt 1:1-16		Matt 1:1-16		Gen 5:1-32, 11:10-26
1. Jesus		29. Joshua		57. Terah	✓
2. Joseph	✔	30. Eliezar		58. Nahor	✓
3. Heli		31. Jorim		59. Serug	✓
4. Matthat		32. Matthat		60. Reu	✓
5. Levi		33. Levi		61. Peleg	✓
6. Melki		34. Simeon		62. Eber	✓
7. Jannai		35. Judah		63. Shelah	✓
8. Joseph		36. Joseph		64. Cainan	
9. Mattahias		37. Jonam		65. Arphaxad	✓
10. Amos		38. Eliakim		66. Shem	✓
11. Nahum		39. Melea		67. Noah	✓
12. Esli		40. Menna		68. Lamech	✓
13. Naggi		41. Mattatha		69. Methuselah	✓
14. Maath		42. Nathan		70. Enoch	✓
15. Mattahias		43. David	✔	71. Jared	✓
16. Semein		44. Jesse	✔	72. Mahalaleel	✓
17. Josech		45. Obed	✔	73. Cainan	✓
18. Joda		46. Boaz	✔	74. Enos	✓
19. Joanan		47. Salmon	✔	75. Seth	✓
20. Rhesa		48. Nahshon	✔	76. Adam	✓
21. Zerubbabel	✔	49. Amminadab	✔	77. God	
22. Shealtiel	✔	50. Ram	✔		
23. Neri		51. Hezron	✔	**Total: 77**	
24. Melki		52. Perez	✔		
25. Addi		53. Judah	✔		
26. Cosam		54. Jacob	✔		
27. Elamadam		55. Isaac	✔		
28. Er		56. Abraham	✔		

Figure 12.4 – Luke's Genealogy of Jesus. *(Luke 3: 23–38). The bold checkmarks indicate agreement between Luke 3 and the genealogy of Jesus in Matthew 1. The light checkmarks indicate agreement between Luke 3 and Genesis 5: 1–32 and 11: 10–26.* Credit: Denis O. Lamoureux, Evolutionary Creation, p. 399. Used with permission.

The issue of historicity is one of the most contentious topics in contemporary Christendom. Some believe it is possible to view Genesis as divinely inspired, and find Holy Spirit-inspired motivations in its pages, without the requirement that it be historical in the modern sense.[92] Some have even argued, in the context of the flood narrative, that the basic theological messages and spiritual insights of Genesis 6-8 remain the same, whether the flood event was metaphorical, localized, or global.[93] These sorts of statements, of course, tend to raise alarm bells for evangelicals who are concerned as to where such thinking may lead. They are not at all comfortable with the idea of sitting down and sorting scriptures into two piles, historical and non-historical or literal and metaphorical.

Two creation accounts

Many scholars argue that the early chapters of Genesis contain two independent creation accounts. Evangelicals generally disagree, arguing the writer told the same story from two different perspectives. Those who believe there are two independent accounts here point out that each has a different chronological order. If these two accounts are indeed independent, attempts to harmonize them will be futile.[94]

There are fundamental differences in these two accounts. In Genesis chapter 1, for example, birds are created on the fifth day, prior to humans. But in Genesis chapter 2, birds are created after humanity. Also, in the first account, people are created after the plants and animals; in the second account, humanity appears before the plants and animals.[95] The first Genesis creation account seems to have been structured on the Hebrew work week and Sabbath. To some, this suggests it has a primarily theological, not historical (again, in the modern sense of the word) purpose. Interestingly, these two creation accounts are contradictory only if they are taken literally.[96]

Most Christians are unaware of the fact that contemporary Judaism generally treats the Genesis creation accounts as symbolic or figurative.[97] Deciding whether a text is symbolic or figurative is a critical, and very challenging interpretive task. With some texts, making such a decision is quite straightforward. With others, and the creation accounts would certainly be included here, finding answers is more difficult, especially considering the fact that the interpretation will have serious implications for the very foundations of one's theology. Consider Job 38:22. Are there literal storage bins for snow and hail? Are we literally knit together in our mother's womb as Psalm 139 states?

Many contemporary scholars are of the opinion that the first eleven chapters of Genesis describe a primordial world, a world of rich symbolism, of mystical numbers, of talking snakes, magical trees, and a being named "earthling."[98] The early chapters of Genesis, according to this point of view, are not communicating history as we moderns understand it. Further complicating this debate is the fact that the early chapters of Genesis were considered to be historical fact in Jesus' day. Both Jesus and the apostle Paul, by their comments, indicate that this was in fact the way they viewed the scriptural creation accounts.[99]

As I say, Jesus and Paul referred to the early chapters of Genesis as literal historical accounts. The biblical authors had no reason to believe otherwise and it is my contention that Jesus himself accommodated this information to the knowledge of his contemporaries. Many scholars view the Genesis creation accounts as polemical texts, expressing a theology radically different from neighboring nations. Unlike their ancient near eastern neighbors, Israel's theology vigorously supported monotheism and opposed polytheism.[100] In the Genesis creation account, for example, the sun and the moon are identified as the "greater light" and the "lesser light." They are not given names which would identify them as pagan gods. They serve humanity not vice versa. In Israel's theology, God has given boundaries to the heavenly bodies and turned them over to positive functions.[101] The creation story in Genesis 1 has been described as a confession of faith in God as Creator. Interestingly, it seems that this account is not intended to explain exactly how God created the world, but why.[102]

Framework interpretation

The framework interpretation originated in the latter half of the nineteenth century.[103] According to this perspective, the "days" mentioned in the text are not normal historical time. They are a literary device, employed by God to communicate the creation story in terms ancient readers could understand. The six days of creation are arranged in a "framework" of two groups of three (days 1-3 and days 4–6), with parallel activities occurring in each group. The sun was not made until the fourth day, yet it was given the task of producing the day and the night and the phrase "evening and morning" had been employed by the author since the first day. This, by itself, suggests a non-literal interpretation. In the creation event God is confronted by challenges that must be overcome; darkness, the watery abyss, the formless earth. He deals with them in sequential order over the next six "days."

First, on "days" 1 to 3, God prepares the heavens and the earth as a dwelling place for the great creatures to come. God therefore...

- separates the light from the darkness
- separates the waters above the firmament from the waters below
- causes dry land to "appear" and to "put forth" vegetation

And then, on "days" 4 to 6, God puts these created entities into the places he had prepared for them. Therefore...

- the sun and the moon are placed into the "firmament of heaven"
- the birds take their place in the air, and the fish in the seas
- "the beasts of the earth" and "man" take their place on the land

The framework interpretation, therefore, is not about science. The "days" mentioned in this account are days as people understand them, but are expressed as a literary form that is not to be taken literally.

The cosmic temple

J. Richard Middleton suggests that in Israel and other ancient near eastern cultures (Babylon, Assyria, Egypt, Sumer, etc.) the world was thought of as a building, a habitable space for humans and other creatures. In the Bible, the world is God's "house," a cosmic sanctuary, a temple for God. Having constructed the cosmos as his "house" or temple, the Divine King then takes up residence in the world. God sits on his throne, reigning as Lord of the universe.[104] In The Lost World of Genesis One (2009), Old Testament scholar John Walton proposes a radically different understanding of the Genesis creation accounts, a "functional cosmic temple view." Walton interprets the cosmology of Genesis 1 in light of its ancient near eastern cultural context. He claims that the creation account is best understood as a functional rather than a material account.[105] Viewed from the perspective of ancient Israel, Walton argues that the Genesis creation account would have been seen as a temple inauguration text. The cosmos is God's temple, the place where he takes up his residence, the sacred place from which he sustains the universe and exercises his rule. For Walton, the temple is not a building; it is the entire cosmos. God cannot be contained in the building; heaven (his throne) and earth (his footstool) cannot contain him. Genesis 1 is an ancient description of the creation of the universe for people with a very different worldview from our own.

To understand Genesis 1 properly, says Walton, both the actual words and the accompanying worldview must be understood. When we moderns think of what it means to create, we normally think about bringing material stuff into existence. In the ancient near east, however, entities exist when they have a function in an ordered system. Walton notes that, both in the Bible and in the ancient world, God rests in the temple. When the creation account says that God rested on the seventh day, the ancient Israelites would have understood that to mean that the cosmos was being presented as a temple. At that time, the temple was understood as a miniature version of the cosmos.

The seven-day structure of Genesis 1 would have reinforced the idea that the creation account was a cosmic temple text. In the culture of that day, the seventh day was the most important day of the creation week because, if God had not entered his rest, the temple would not function as it should. Walton believes that his reading of Genesis 1 is the true "literal" reading of the text which would not be possible without an understanding of the Hebrew words and culture, as well as neighboring cultures. If Walton is correct and Genesis 1 is, indeed, a functional not material creation account, then scientific concordism is ruled out. Walton is of the opinion that anti-evolutionists impose modern ways of thinking on ancient texts. The result, he argues, is a fundamental misunderstanding of Genesis 1 and has young earth proponents defending a view of origins that, ironically, may not be supported by the Bible or by science.[106]

The message-incident principle

The message-incident principle states that inerrant spiritual truths are often communicated in the context of out-of-date statements about nature. In other words, the Holy Spirit often used what amounts to ancient science to reveal infallible messages of faith.[107] This principle challenges the scientific concordist hermeneutic frequently encountered in this discussion.

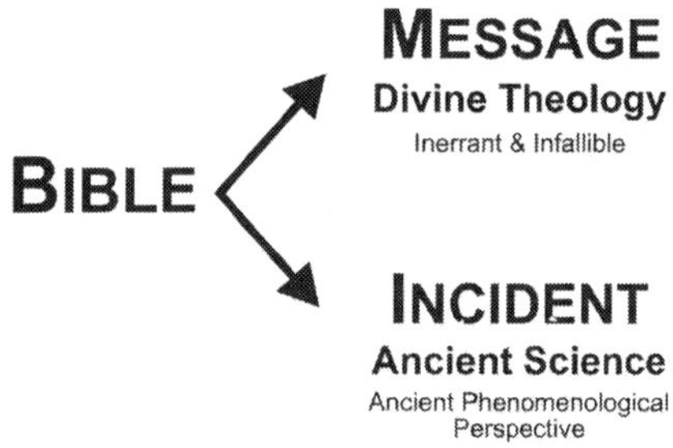

Figure 12.5 – The Message–Incident principle. Credit: Denis O. Lamoureux, Evolutionary Creation, p. 110. Used with permission.

Challenging traditional interpretive practices, of course, is nothing new. Jesus of Nazareth repeatedly challenged the biblical interpretation practiced by the religious leaders of his day. Many of the prophets before him did the same. Jesus' calls for change were ignored. Martin Luther's call for change in the sixteenth century was likewise ignored by the religious authorities. Those who insist on a young earth interpretation of scripture are convinced they are putting their faith in God's word. What they do not realize, or reject, is the idea that their interpretation may not be the most accurate. If it is not, an unnecessary stumbling block to faith has been created.[108]

Young earth creationists, when they encounter a discussion of presuppositionalism, immediately point out that evolutionists, too, have their own presuppositions. And that is absolutely correct. It would be next to impossible to live out our lives without presuppositions of one kind or other. Tim Reddish says, "Yes, of course we have presuppositions. In both our science and our biblical interpretation."[109] It would be fair to ask whether any interpretation of scripture can be accomplished without presuppositions. And, in my opinion, the answer would be "no." At the end of the day, all interpreters bring their own unique presuppositions to the text. What is important is that those presuppositions be identified and open to adjustment should better information appear.

A divine/human document

Christians believe that the Bible contains both human and divine elements. It is a serious challenge to disentangle the two. John Calvin argued that the Bible is primarily concerned with the knowledge of Jesus Christ. He argued that it is not an astronomical, geographical, or biological textbook.[110] I have proposed that should inaccuracies appear in the Bible's descriptions of the natural realm, they are a reflection of its humanity. Ted Davis says, "Just as we do not take biblical astronomy literally, with its three-tiered universe, we should not take biblical biology literally, with its fixed species and separate creations a few thousand years ago."[111] Modern interpreters of the scriptures are faced with a choice: they can either defend what appears to be an outdated interpretive methodology and work diligently to stretch science to make it fit; or they can search for, and rejoice in the truth, no matter where it may be found and no matter how uncomfortable it may make us feel at first.

Both the new atheists and young earth creationists practice, perhaps unconsciously, what may be called the fallacy of the excluded middle.[112] Christians are told by young earth advocates that they must choose either supernatural creation or atheistic evolution. That's it. Stark choices. There is a third way, however, but it is seldom mentioned. This third way is the topic of chapter 8, Evolutionary Creation. Evolutionary creation considers the biblical creation narratives and the scientific narratives to be two distinct but complementary ways of describing the same phenomena.[113] Christians are accountable for what they believe, teach, and confess, and should they be in error, in this case, should their interpretation of scripture be wanting, they are duty-bound to correct it. It has been said that true greatness involves a willingness to adopt a new point of view when that becomes mandatory. True greatness, as I say, has to do with following the truth wherever it may lead, even when it leads into the unknown or uncomfortable places of the excluded middle.[114]

Evangelical theology and evolutionary theory

In his book, Standing on the Shoulders of Giants, Luke Janssen says, "... recent scientific discoveries in genetics threatened to completely shatter the traditional Genesis version of human origins."[115] When evangelical Christians hear statements like this, they wonder what their faith will look like after the shattered pieces are removed. When they hear statements like these, many withdraw even further into their enclaves. There is no denying the fact that scientific discoveries do have an impact on some of the most basic Christian doctrines. And, should Christians adopt a pro-science, pro-evolutionary perspective, they have no choice but to revisit these doctrines. But they also know that the God of the cosmos is also the God of the Holy Scriptures. They believe that God's works, rightly understood, should not contradict his words. Hopefully, they will be able to trust that, at the end of the day, the Holy Spirit will guide His church into a God-pleasing resolution of these currently vexing issues.

Theological issues

Adoption of an evolutionary perspective has the potential to impact multiple doctrines, including, but not limited to:

- original sin
- death before the fall
- the image of God
- the historicity of Adam and Eve
- a global versus a local flood
- biblical genealogies
- inerrancy
- inspiration
- theodicy
- the authority of scripture
- interpretation of scripture's creation accounts

Original sin

The traditional doctrine of original sin is, according to theologian John Haught, one of the most difficult to align with Darwin's theory.[116] Evolutionary theory strongly suggests that there never was, at least not in a physical sense, an original cosmic perfection.[117] Several types of evidence (fossils, genetic evidence, and the like) have led scientists to the conclusion that the human race did not emerge from a single pair of individuals. Anatomically modern humans emerged from primate ancestors approximately 300,000 years ago, long before the Genesis timeframe, and apparently from a population that was never fewer than 10,000 individuals.[118] Scientific data also lead to the conclusion that hominids are not separate from the rest of creation but are descended from a common ancestor. John Walton suggests a compromise position worth considering: Adam and Eve were "... elect individuals drawn out of the human population and given a particular representative role in sacred space."[119]

Death before the fall

Young earth creationism asserts that there was no death, human or animal, before Adam and Eve fell into sin. The argument that suffering and death were present for billions of years before humans appeared is therefore problematic for traditional Christian theology.[120] Evolutionary creation, on the other hand, proposes that Adam and Eve introduced only spiritual death into the world, claiming that the apostle Paul's reference to the "world" in Romans 5:12 (which says, "Therefore, just as sin entered the world through one man, and death through sin, and in this way death came to all people, because all sinned...") (NIV) refers only to humanity, and not to all of creation.[121] This argument has a long history. In the nineteenth century, Edward Hitchcock (1793-1864) made the same point, separating death in the animal kingdom, which had occurred for millions of years before humans arrived on the scene, from human death in a spiritual sense.[122]

Given their interpretation of Romans 5:12, young earth creationists speculate that all animals, including carnivores, were vegetarian before the fall. In the New Testament book of 1 Corinthians, chapter 15, verse 22, the apostle Paul says, "As in Adam all die, so in Christ all will be made alive." (NIV) Again, some scholars argue that the apostle Paul is referring here to spiritual death and resurrection and that this reality only involves human beings. Darrel Falk adds: "... certainly there is nothing in this chapter to build a whole theology around the notion of grass-eating mountain lions, vegetarian hawks and anteaters that did not eat ants; all because there was no death on the earth during the Garden of Eden era."[123] Also, if animals and insects did not die, they would have overwhelmed the environment. And, at a cellular level, death is inevitable.[124] Some Christian scholars have pointed out that vegetarianism is an ancient motif that ends with the loss of the idyllic age.[125] Normal biological processes, including the cessation of life, have occurred from long before Adam and Eve and continue to the present day.

Theodicy

Christians who have adopted an evolutionary point of view will, at one time or another, be faced with the issue of theodicy. Theodicy is defined as the "... answer to the question of why God permits evil,"[126] specifically, why a loving God would allow the suffering and death inherent in natural selection to occur. Creation, understood in evolutionary terms, as Robert John Russell puts it, "... has suffering and death written all over it."[127] Theodicy has challenged the faith of many down through the years. The evolutionary process can appear to be a wasteful, untidy affair.[128] Theodicy points to what appears to be a contradiction between the apparent cruelty of nature and the benevolence of God. It has been claimed that theodicy is "the Achilles' heel" of faith; one of its greatest challenges.[129] Some have gone so far as to claim that the cruelty and suffering so common in nature reflects a God who is "careless, indifferent, almost diabolical."[130] Many claim that it was theodicy that caused them to abandon their faith. Others say that, even though they didn't abandon their faith, theodicy raised serious questions that remain unanswered.

Intelligent design creationism proposes that God intervenes in the creative process from time to time to create "irreducibly complex" structures (see chapter 10). Intelligent design also claims that living things exhibit the kind of exquisite design that strongly implies an Intelligent Designer. One of the challenges for the intelligent design movement, however, is the question which asks why, if God controls mutations, he does not delete those that cause suffering.[131] Theodicy was a major concern for Darwin, characterized as a sensitive soul "whose compassion was assaulted by what he observed in the natural world."[132] He was especially bothered by the behavior of a parasitic wasp species called ichneumonidae. This family of wasps lays its eggs in the body of a caterpillar. The eggs then develop into larvae which feed on their living host from the inside out. Somewhere along the way the host will eventually die, or be kept in a state very near death until, finally, a little wasp makes its appearance. For Darwin this kind of behavior was fundamentally incompatible with the traditional concept of God.[133]

Evolutionary creationists believe that God is responsible for abiogenesis, the first spark of life, still a mystery for scientists. After that, God established an evolutionary system that allowed that first life to flourish, branching out into a myriad of forms, leading eventually to the appearance of human beings. And finally, God is responsible for maintaining that evolutionary system. God, then, is responsible for the development of a huge spectrum of organisms, the whole system of descent with modification. The process is his. Intrinsic to the evolutionary system is intense competition for resources, including competition for food, which, in some cases includes unpleasant realities like predation or parasitism. Suffering and death, then, are built in to the God-ordained natural processes that have enabled life to flourish, and even rebound from serious extinction-level events, over vast expanses of time.[134] To say that these things are cruel is to anthropomorphize nature.[135] Although it may sound counterintuitive, nature is neither kind nor unkind; these terms are appropriate for human societies but not for nature. Suffering and death, as well as competition and even cooperation, are all essential components of God's evolutionary economy.

A common, typically inadvertent, error made in the context of theodicy is known as the naturalistic fallacy, requiring an "ought" from that which simply "is."[136] The naturalistic fallacy sets up a prescription on the basis of what should be thought of as mere description. We human beings tend to view the existence of certain organisms as marked by suffering and distress. The naturalistic fallacy implies that nature ought to match our human standards.

Herbert Spencer, as we saw in chapter 6, committed the naturalistic fallacy. He argued that because evolution involves the "survival of the fittest," human societies ought to be based on the same principle, with the strong dominating the weak. In terms of the naturalistic fallacy, then, because evolution is, therefore society ought to be. So this, in my opinion, is the essence of the challenge to faith posed by theodicy. What evolution ought to be, based on human standards, is beside the point as far as science is concerned. What is important is the way evolution actually works. The way it works is the expression of his will, not ours. Niels Bohr once told Albert Einstein, "Albert, stop telling God what to do.[137] The root of the problem here, I would suggest, is mapping human standards onto the evolutionary process.

The scriptures clearly outline God's role in maintaining the entire evolutionary system:

- Psalm 104: 25–30 "These all look to you to give them their food at the proper time. ... when you open your hand, they are satisfied with good things." (NIV)
- Isaiah 43:20–21 "The wild animals honor me, the jackals and the owls, because I provide water in the desert and streams in the wasteland." (NIV)
- Matthew: 10:29 "Are not two sparrows sold for a penny? And not one of them will fall to the ground apart from your father." (NIV)

Rather than viewing the evolutionary system in an overly negative light, then, it is preferable to see it as an amazing system of mutual dependence.[138] God has created an amazingly robust system that has initiated, produced, and maintained life on earth for several billion years. We need to reframe this issue. In order to counterbalance the concerns raised in the context of theodicy, a key concept here is providence.[139] The evolutionary process is ordained and sustained by God.[140] So the theodicy concern ought to be disentangled from biological evolution. It is significant that in the book of Job, "God does not attempt to justify anything that happens in the world as he has designed it."[141]

One final thought. God is not unaware of suffering; suffering, significantly, is at the heart of the gospel. Christ emptied himself, gave up his privileges, for the sake of humanity. He became poor so that we might become rich. He suffered and died to earn salvation and make it available to all people. Jesus' ministry began with forty days of suffering and temptation in the desert. And it ended with the intense suffering of the cross, including the events that led up to it. Because of Jesus, suffering and death now have a God-glorifying and eternal meaning.[142] Someday, according to the scriptures, suffering and death will end. Someday, sin's pervasive negative influence will end. The lion will indeed lie down with the lamb. (Isaiah 11:6–9) In the meantime, however, according to Romans 8:28, all things work together for the good of those who love the Lord and are called according to his purpose. Even though creation now groans (Romans 8:22) waiting for the consummation of all things, we have God's promise that all things will be made new (Revelation 21). In the meantime, we take comfort in knowing that the God who made the universe cares for us and calls us by name. (Isaiah 43:1) For that, we thank and praise God!

The image of God

Prior to the discoveries of modern biology, Christians believed that humans were separate and distinct from other animals. Because humans were created in God's image, they were thought to be unique.[143] Despite the scientific realities, however, that uniqueness, in a theological sense, is not threatened. God's love for humanity, and his intervention on behalf of humanity, in the person of his Son, remains. Evolutionary theory links humanity with all other living things. We are one small twig on the tree of life. A very special twig, granted, but a twig nonetheless. Bearing the "image of God," humanity is God's representative, God's ambassador.[144] For Martin Luther, the image of God relates to God's gift of righteousness, innocence, and blessedness. In the book of

Ephesians, chapter 4, verse 24, the apostle Paul says "... put on the new nature, created after the likeness of God, in true righteousness and holiness." (RSV) and, referring to the church, the apostle Peter says in 1 Peter 2:9, "But you are a chosen people, a royal priesthood, a holy nation, God's special possession, that you may declare the praises of him who called you out of darkness into his wonderful light." (NIV) Regardless of what science says about the evolutionary history of humanity, Christians can be assured that the image of God is not affected by evolution. We stand in the same relationship to God whether we were created instantaneously or over a long period of time. We still have sins that need to be forgiven and a Savior who accomplished that task for us at the cross. His final cry, "It is finished," affirms that salvation is completed and available to all. (John 19:30, NIV) The original Greek word here carries the meaning of "paid in full." And so it is.

Adam and Eve

Richard Ostling summarizes the kinds of questions that arise related to Adam and Eve in the context of evolutionary theory:

> *... is the Adam and Eve question destined to become a groundbreaking science and scripture dispute, the twenty-first century equivalent of the once-disturbing proof that the earth orbits the sun? The potential is certainly there. The emerging science could be seen to challenge not only what Genesis records about the creation of humanity but the species' unique status in bearing the 'image of God,' Christian doctrine on original sin and the fall, the genealogy of Jesus in the Gospel of Luke, and, perhaps more significantly, Paul's teaching that links the historical Adam with redemption through Christ (Romans 5:12-19; 1 Corinthians 15:20-23, 42-49; and his speech in Acts 17).*[145]

Scott McKnight argues that the Adam of the holy scriptures is "... an adjustable figure who can be used in theology for a variety of presentations and ideas."[146] McKnight contends that seven different characterizations of Adam are to be found in the Old Testament.[147] In addition, some scholars see interesting parallels between Adam's story and that of Israel as a nation.[148] Christians believe that all people are descended from Adam. In today's Christian church, there are competing views as to whether there was an actual historical couple named Adam and Eve. Some, including the Roman Catholic Church, argue that there was, but that they were selected by God as representatives from a larger population. Others claim that Adam and Eve are typological figures.[149] In an article titled Hominids in the Garden? James Hurd outlines three possible scenarios with regard to the historicity of Adam and Eve –

1) Adam and Eve were real historical people who lived a few thousand years ago. This view is challenged by the DNA evidence.
2) Gap-theory creationists (see chapter 7) speculate that a pre-Adamite race existed. Adam and Eve, therefore were not the first humans.
3) The Roman Catholic Church teaches that approximately 40,000 years ago, a human pair were given souls by God.

The Roman Catholic teaching on Adam and Eve is known as monogenism and proposes that humans are descended from a unique couple selected from hominids living approximately 40,000 years ago.[150] Some claim that the scriptural "Adam" is symbolic of humanity.[151] Philosopher Robin Collins proposes what he calls the "Historical–Ideal" view.[152] He argues that the original situation described in the Garden of Eden story represents an ideal state that was never realized, showing what an ideal relation with God would be like. For Collins, Adam and Eve represent every person who has ever lived, but they also represent the first hominids, or group of hominids, who had the capacity for free choice and self-consciousness. Ted Davis adds, "Just as the first hominids made sinful choices, so do we now, and original sin involves the resulting bondage to sin and spiritual darkness that is inherited from our ancestors and generated by our own choices."[153]

Michael Ruse contends that, rather than connecting the concept of original sin to a historical pair of human beings, it could be understood more universally, as a component of the biological package – part of being human.[154] Some scholars speculate that, in the course of human evolution, there must have been a first moment of conscious moral choice.[155] The Bible places Adam and Eve in a Neolithic world, with cities and agriculture, whereas scientific evidence shows that humans existed for a very long time before cities and agriculture became a reality. Davis says, "In my opinion, a clear and convincing picture of an historical Adam and Eve, reconciling the biblical picture with human antiquity, has not yet been produced, and I am doubtful that we will ever have one."[156]

Many Christians are interested in what Jesus and Paul believed about the historicity of Adam and Eve. Some have suggested that the apostle Paul was a first-century individual, steeped in the historical and scientific categories of his day. The only option available to him at the time, therefore, was to take the Genesis accounts literally.[157] The apostle Paul, as we saw in Chapter 3, believed in the same three-part heavens as is found in the Old Testament.[158] Early Christians accepted the Genesis origins account at face value; they had no other choice; nothing else to compare it to.[159] We might never have known which view of the first chapter of Genesis was most accurate were it not for God allowing humans to examine the fossil record and discover the true nature of his creative work in all of its majesty.[160] The Bible's authors, in both the Old and the New Testaments, were aware that there was much they did not know; much that was hidden from them. In 1 Corinthians 13:12–13, for example, the apostle Paul openly admitted that his knowledge was, at best, only partial. Paul's views about the historicity of Adam and Eve are congruent with what was known then. As we have already noted, new knowledge has encouraged some Christians to revisit their teachings about Adam.

For much of traditional Christian theology, "... all roads lead to Adam."[161] Adam is the archetype of humanity's choice between obedience and disobedience. According to the apostle Paul, only a second Adam, Jesus Christ, could restore humanity's broken relationship with God. In Genesis chapters 2 and 3, humanity lives in a state of spiritual death and separation from God after the fall into sin. This separation is overcome by the death and resurrection of Jesus Christ. Evangelicals tend to take an all-or-nothing view of historicity, arguing that without an historical Adam and the traditional fall into sin, there is no need for the gospel of Christ or for salvation history as a whole.[162]

Scott McKnight, however, suggests that even if Adam is not historical in the modern sense of the word, the apostle Paul's theology of Adam is not diminished because sin and death remain a vivid reality. They are, says McKnight, "... irrefutable facts of human existence." We are natural born sinners, "... wired for perversity and prone to do evil."[163] Adam and Eve are indeed key characters in the overarching biblical narrative. The question of whether that narrative would lose its veracity if the elements within it were declared non-historical is a controversial one. Some argue that, regardless of the historicity of Adam, humanity will always need a Savior from sin and death. The final word on these critical issues has not yet been spoken.

13. CONCLUSION

Overview

The modern-day relationship between creationists and evolutionists has many parallels with the relationship between the Renaissance and Enlightenment scholars that we explored in chapter 2. Young earth and intelligent design creationism share some of the characteristics of Renaissance thought, including the belief that everything truly worth knowing had been discovered by the ancients, but was lost in the intervening years. Recovering that lost wisdom, therefore, is of primary importance. Contemporary advocates of an evolutionary point of view, on the other hand, share with Enlightenment scholars a focus on the discovery and application of new knowledge. Among Enlightenment scholars there is respect for ancient wisdom but a desire to move on with an orientation towards the future. There is a hardline rigidity at the edges of the science / faith divide, with the scientism of the New Atheists on the one hand and the presuppositionalism characteristic of many anti-evolutionists on the other. This inflexibility has led to an impasse. Young earth creationists are strongly committed to their particular interpretation of scripture's creation accounts while those who promote scientism are not ready to give up their belief that science is the only source of real knowledge. We have seen repeatedly that a critical issue in this debate is hermeneutics, the process of achieving what is hopefully the most accurate interpretation of ancient scriptural texts.

It has been my contention that anti-evolutionists tend to read modern scientific ideas back into the scriptural creation accounts. I believe that this is done, in most cases, inadvertently. This hermeneutical error, called eisegesis, forces ancient documents to say what their authors never intended them to say. Anti-evolutionists presuppose that, because their interpretation of scripture is, for all intents and purposes, inerrant, no amount of scientific evidence is sufficient to change their minds. Thus, proponents spend a great deal of time and effort defending their proprietary interpretation of scripture's creation accounts. Another important issue in this context is accommodation, whether and to what extent Christians should allow their teachings to be influenced by science. I have argued that the young earth position has an unintended consequence – it causes more problems than it solves. Since the proliferation of young earth creationist ideas in the 1960's, positions have hardened, and the relationship with science is primarily antagonistic. These two groups have become two solitudes. In order to break the impasse, one group or the other must take the first step. Mutually agreeable ground rules have to be established.

The battle of the books

Sixteenth-century British philosopher and scientist Sir Francis Bacon (1561-1626) was an early advocate of the scientific method. In a now famous discussion of various ways of discerning truth, Bacon proposed an analogy involving an ant, a spider, and a bee. Charles H. Hinnant summarizes Bacon's argument:

> *Men of experiment are like the ant; they only collect and use; the reasoners resemble spiders, who make cobwebs out of their own substance. But the bee takes a middle course; it gathers its material from the flowers of the garden and of the field, but transforms and digests it by a power of its own.*[1]

Bacon's analogy is taken from an article titled The Ant, the Spider, and the Bee, part of a larger work, The Novum Organum (The New Science), published in 1620. In 1704, eighty-four years later, Jonathan Swift, (1667-1745) in a document titled The Battle of the Books, focused specifically on the spider and the bee. Swift's Battle of the Books describes a fictional battle that took place in St. James Library, London, between works representing ancient authors on the one hand, and modern writers on the other. The ancients are represented by the bee; the moderns, by the spider.[2] In The Hedgehog, the Fox, and the Magister's Pox (published posthumously in 2003), Stephen Jay Gould (1941-2002) outlines Swift's analysis of Bacon's argument. According to Gould, "Swift introduces the battle with a three-page gem that forms one of the greatest extended metaphors in all Western literature."[3] From the fourteenth through the seventeenth centuries, a shift from Renaissance to Enlightenment thinking was taking place. The Enlightenment put less emphasis on venerating the wisdom of the ancients and more emphasis on extending knowledge by discovering the new.[4]

Renaissance thought

Swift's bee represented the ancients and later, Renaissance thought. "Renaissance" literally means "rebirth." The spider, on the other hand, symbolized the moderns and Enlightenment thinking.[5] Renaissance scholars made respect for ancient knowledge a high priority. That which was worth knowing, they claimed, had already been discovered. Their task was to rediscover and reinstitute what the ancients had achieved and what, in their opinion, had subsequently been lost.[6] They argued that knowledge had deteriorated following the Golden Ages of Greece and Rome, and their primary task was to rediscover it.[7] Swift's bees argued that the old ways must be retained and defended. Foreshadowing today's young earth creationists, Renaissance scholars claimed that textual authority is the only path to genuine knowledge.[8] For them, the literary claims of ancient writers were more important than the direct observations of science.[9] Many ancient Greek philosophers discounted observations and experiments, relying instead on logical deduction from what they consider to be self-evident first principles.[10]

Enlightenment thought

Swift's spider symbolized Enlightenment thought. Enlightenment scholars were not convinced that ancient knowledge is inherently superior.[11] Their goal was to balance past and future knowledge. They were determined to assess new information with an open mind, and they emphasized reason over faith.[12] They sought to apply their new knowledge. For Enlightenment thinkers, personal observation took precedence over ancient testimony.[13] Young earth creationists, for their part, are inclined to consider Enlightenment thought as an assault on traditional Christianity and an attack on its supernatural aspects.[14] So how do Christians then do justice to ancient knowledge while recognizing critical new information? In our contemporary faith communities, we need to be able to look back to the past and also forward to the future. We must be able to retain the best of the past, along with the best of current knowledge, both faith-based and scientific. Does the Bible, as it is variously interpreted by different faith communities, supersede all other knowledge? Surely not! The Bible, as we have been arguing, must be interpreted correctly. And not all interpretations are equally valid. Christians must be free to utilize the best of faith and the best of science.

Stumbling blocks

Both science and religion are vulnerable to idolatry.[15] Scientists, as we have seen, sometimes fall victim to a form of idolatry called scientism. And creationists, if they are not careful, are susceptible to an idolatry of the scriptures (bibliolatry) or of a particular interpretation of the scriptures.[16] Some scientists take science beyond its self-imposed limits while some creationists ask questions of the Bible that it is not prepared to answer. Science, as we have seen, cannot reveal everything that humans believe is worth knowing.[17] Young earth creationists are convinced that the position they have taken on science and evolution is, in the long run, an asset to the Christian church. They believe that young earth creationism defends the integrity of the scriptures and is a bulwark against pro-science, pro-evolutionary views which erode confidence in the historicity and integrity of the scriptures. But a defend-at-all-costs mentality, and a willingness to deny the validity of several scientific disciplines looks very different to those outside the church. One scholar criticizes young earth creationism for its use of what he calls "unprincipled techniques of deliberate distraction..."[18] This practice, it is argued, has done serious damage to Christian integrity and harms Christian outreach. When young people who have left the church are asked why they made that decision, many will say that they perceive the church as being anti-science and overly certain about its conclusions regarding science and the theory of evolution.

It is much easier to be critical of others than it is to be critical of ourselves and our own views. We often magnify the faults of others, while minimizing our own. Some pro-evolution folks have convinced themselves that it is not worth arguing with anti-evolutionists. Such thinking is not helpful. Those on both sides of this equation need to establish lines of communication and work very hard to at least understand each other. No one wants to misrepresent the scriptures. No one wants their beliefs and practices to be an impediment to the faith of others. The apostle Paul says in 2 Corinthians 6:3, "We put no stumbling block in anyone's path, so that our ministry will not be discredited." (NIV) Consider the following scenario. A soon-to-be-married couple participates in a premarital counseling course with a pastor. The young man's vocation is science, at the Ph.D. level. That young man is not a churchgoing kind of person, but his fiancée is. On learning the young man's profession, the pastor launches into a theologically-based argument against evolution. That young man is left with a lasting impression of the church and its clergy, and, suffice it to say, that impression is less than positive.

There are those in the scientific community who are quite harsh in their criticism of young earth creationism and, of course, there are some anti-evolutionists who are more than willing to return the favor. I am convinced that what individuals in each community say about their opponents is, in the long run, actually less important than how they say it. No one wants to be ridiculed. No one wants to be the object of jokes or derision. No one wants their intelligence questioned. A call for tolerance certainly works both ways.

Questions ancients asked

Tolerance for the views of others need not mean acceptance of those views. Tolerance for, rather than an instantaneous rejection of the views of others, is the first step in understanding the nuances of this debate. John Pickering, for example, argues that young earth advocates ask the wrong questions of the creation accounts and focus instead on issues that would not have been a high priority for the ancients. He says:

> *Creationism misrepresents the Bible. When the Hebrews were standing on the banks of the Jordan wondering what would befall them should they cross, they were not asking, "How did God create the world?" Rather, they were wondering if Yahweh, who had led their parents' generation out of Egypt, and seemed to be in charge in the desert, actually knew anything about farming across the Jordan. It seemed to them that the local fertility gods must know something, after all it was a rich land. The two stories of creation we now find in the book of Genesis speak to the fears of the Hebrews then, and in later generations, to fears held when they were in exile. The message is clear; Yahweh is in charge, the so-called gods (e.g., the sun and the moon) are creations of his. Those stories are definitely not scientific accounts. Indeed, science-writing was not to be invented for thousands of more years. They answer "who is in charge" and "what is my purpose" questions, not "how" questions.*[19]

On the creationist side of the fence, Answers in Genesis founder Ken Ham is a staunch critic of science and evolution. His style is polemical which makes him a lightning rod for criticism. In my opinion, Ken Ham is not doing the Christian church a favor by his actions or by his words. He says what his supporters want to hear, but he speaks with what appears to be an attitude of superiority, which alienates many. Joel Edmund Anderson has authored a no-holds-barred book critiquing Ken Ham titled The Heresy of Ham: What

Every Evangelical Needs to Know about the Creation–Evolution Controversy (2016).[20] Anderson goes so far as to say that the kind of young earth creationism advocated by Ken Ham and his Answers in Genesis organization, is heresy plain and simple. Anderson says:

> *The heresy of Ham that is actively "subverting, destabilizing, and destroying" the core of the Christian faith is the claim that a modern, scientific interpretation of Genesis 1–11 as literal history is a fundamental prerequisite for the trustworthiness of the gospel of Christ. It is the claim that if the universe is not six thousand years old, if there was no historical Adam and Eve, and if there was no worldwide flood four thousand years ago, then that would make God a liar, that would mean there is no such thing as sin, and that would mean Christ died for nothing. Such a message is heresy, and that message has subverted, destabilized, and destroyed the Christian faith of many people, has destroyed careers, and unfortunately, has taken root within a significant portion of Evangelical Christianity.*[21]

Contrast Ham's arguments with those put forward by evolutionary creationists. Their argument is that if Scriptures creation accounts are not meant to be taken literalistically, then the findings of science are not faith-destroying but faith-affirming, leading to a more accurate understanding of God's actual method of creation. Ken Ham believes he is mounting a heroic defense of the Bible's integrity and authority, but at the cost of all-or-nothing thinking that alienates people and fosters conflict. Changing our hermeneutic gives us the space to accept what both science and faith have to offer, but it takes considerable courage and vulnerability to be open to understanding familiar biblical texts in unfamiliar ways.

Consider this comment from nineteenth-century Presbyterian T. DeWitt Talmadge (1832-1902) "The moment you begin to explain away the miraculous and supernatural, you surrender the Bible."[22] We are not free, in science or in theology, to pick and choose ideas that fit our worldview and reject the rest. The critical factor here, as we have seen repeatedly, is not evolutionary theory per se, but hermeneutics, with the goal of achieving the most accurate interpretation of scripture possible. Physicist Lawrence M. Krauss says:

> *Ancient religious documents are historical documents reflecting the understanding of nature and divinity by individuals who lived in societies where modern scientific knowledge was not available as a vital part of understand-*

ing and interpreting these documents.[23]

Very few Christians would argue with what young earth creationists want to accomplish, and that is to defend the Bible's authority, inerrancy, and inspiration. Not all Christians agree with their methods, however. Many Christians would argue that their methods are counter-productive and do not portray evangelicalism in a positive light. For evangelicals who view the scriptural text as authoritative, it would be counterproductive to allow the text to be interpreted in such a way as to twist or even obliterate its original meaning.[24] All of this depends on hermeneutics. If the young earth hermeneutic is absolutely correct, if it truly is the gold standard for all Christians for all times, then their arguments are convincing. But if their hermeneutic is not in line with the original intention of scripture's authors, then it would be a liability to the church and to its outreach. In 2 Timothy, chapter 2, verse 15, the apostle Paul counsels young Timothy: "Do your best to present yourself to God as one approved, a worker who does not need to be ashamed and who correctly handles the word of truth." (NIV)

Scientific literacy

A lack of scientific literacy is a problem not only in the wider society, but also in the church. An article by Tanya Lombroso posted on the National Public Radio (NPR) website, reports the results of a 2015 poll by the Pew Research Center. That research indicated that only 6 percent of respondents were able to achieve a perfect score on a 12-question test assessing respondent's knowledge of basic science. An 11-question test developed by John Miller, director of The International Center for the Advancement of Scientific Literacy at the University of Michigan, found that 86 percent of respondents knew that light travels faster than sound. But only 37 percent agreed with the idea of human evolution and 53 percent believe, with young earth creationists, that humans and dinosaurs co-existed.[25] According to Miller, 70 percent of Americans cannot read and understand the science section of the New York Times. Miller estimates that 28 percent of Americans are scientifically literate, an increase from the 10 percent value in the late 1980's and early 1990's. Miller says,

> *Having a basic knowledge of scientific principles is no longer a luxury but, in today's complex world, a necessity. And while Americans are holding their own, they are not even close to where they should be.*[26]

Anti-evolutionists often make statements about science that many in their audience do not have the ability to properly evaluate. Regarding incorrect or misleading claims being propagated by young earth creationists, Francis Collins and Karl Giberson observe that,

> *These [incorrect scientific] claims abound within the anti-evolutionary literature and are repeated so often by so many different and apparently credible people that it is easy to be misled. They are aimed at laypeople unfamiliar with science and the scientific community, which is why it can take root and flourish.*[27]

The truth of evolution cannot and should not be decided by those who are not scientifically literate. It is important that Christian leaders possess a basic scientific literacy if they are to evaluate science and scientists. We have seen that it is not helpful to the church or to its integrity when church leaders make statements about science that are clearly ill-informed.

The internet and social media have made vast amounts of information, of widely varying quality, easily accessible to the majority of the population. It is much easier to network with like-minded people these days, making contact through Twitter or Facebook. But the internet is a mixed blessing. The same technology that brings people together also keeps them apart. In our increasingly polarized and (some have even used the word "tribal") society, many seek refuge in self-referential, self-segregated communities. Anti-evolutionists have created a subculture with its own media, facts, history, and science.[28] Many creationists live out their entire lives at arms length from real science. At the end of the day, having our worldview challenged is very uncomfortable, but, in the long run, that challenge is more valuable than having our views endlessly affirmed.

The power of ideology

We have already seen that, to a surprising degree, our worldview determines what we can or cannot perceive. Walter Oland (1879-1938), the Swedish American actor who played the character Charlie Chan, once said that ideology is "... like mist on eyeglasses, obscure facts."[29] The New Testament Pharisees, with their own proprietary interpretation of the scriptures, once asked Jesus, (who consistently challenged that interpretation), "Are we blind, too?" (John 9:40) Jesus shocked them by answering in the affirmative. It is important to be reminded that ideological blindness is a common human malady, not limited to any particular group or worldview. The Old Testament prophet Isaiah (44:18) said, "They know nothing; they understand nothing; their eyes are plastered over so they cannot see, and their minds are closed so that they cannot understand." (NIV) Well-entrenched beliefs are extremely difficult to change. And that is true of any one of us. Should our worldview be challenged, we tend to dig in and refuse to budge. With some searching on the internet, virtually any view, no matter how odd or idiosyncratic, can be affirmed and strengthened.

Geneticist and evolutionary biologist Theodore Dobzhansky (1900-1975) once said, "No evidence is powerful enough to force acceptance of a conclusion that is theologically distasteful."[30] That is true for all people of faith. We tend to grasp our faith even more tightly when we feel that it might be taken from us. It is important to be able to decide what is critical and what's not. My Lutheran faith tradition distinguishes between essential and optional aspects of faith. The Latin word adiaphora refers to practices in the church that are optional, not required. Of course, deciding what fits into this category is very controversial. But my point remains. If an evangelical Christian is asked to give up what they consider to be an essential element of their faith, they will refuse. If, on the other hand they are being asked to let go of something they consider adiaphora – optional – they will be more amenable. Interestingly, current research (see Appendix) suggests that many evangelical Christians are uncertain when it comes to their beliefs about creation. They know what they "should" believe, which is the anti-evolutionism their church teaches, but they also know that they have not done their homework so as to settle the issue in their minds.

It is been said that those who cannot be trusted are those who are always right.[31] One former creationist said that, once he came to understand the scientific evidence supporting the theory of evolution, he saw the arguments for a young earth in an entirely new way. The arguments that used to convince now seemed very weak indeed.[32] The scientific evidence supporting the theory of evolution, especially discoveries in genomics and DNA, is growing stronger as each year goes by. No one wants to be in the kind of situation described by William James (1842-1910) in a book titled Varieties of Religious Experience (1902). In that book, James describes people "... living on a frozen lake, surrounded by cliffs over which there is no escape, yet knowing that, little by little, the ice is melting, and the inevitable day drawing near when the last film of it will disappear."[33]

A quest for truth

Scientific facts are true whether we approve of them or not, and whether we understand them or not.[34] Objective reality does not disappear because some people choose not to believe it. Truth is not decided by plebiscite. God is not honored by an outright denial of the truths science has worked so hard to discover. A lesson we all learn growing up has been called the "rubber-band effect," that is, the more we stretch the truth, the more "snap" we get coming back.[35] A few years ago, I was given a copy of the movie "Expelled: No Intelligence Allowed." In the movie, Ben Stein poses as a courageous individual who stands up to the scientific establishment. He is defending the open and honest discussion of controversial ideas like intelligent design. Unfortunately, the movie doesn't live up to its own standards. For example, Charles Darwin is quoted in a selective manner in an attempt to connect his ideas to eugenics and the Holocaust. Stein's speech to a crowded auditorium was a setup. Scientists in the film thought they were being interviewed for a different movie. Expelled did not own up to the fact that science (i.e., methodological naturalism) does not reject religious or "design-based" explanations because of dogmatic atheism. The film did not indicate that many evolutionary biologists are people of faith and, on the other hand, many religious people accept evolution.

I believe that science and religion can be partners in a common quest for truth. Religion deals primarily with faith and revelation, science deals with discovery and analysis.[36] John Polkinghorne illustrates the difference between science and religion with a metaphor drawn from the world of music. Science, he says, studies musical notes individually; religion, on the other hand, deals with the symphony.[37] Anti-evolutionists often say, or at least imply, that scientific evidence is just not good enough for them, what some have called the argument from incredulity.[38] Too many people "prefer living in the cool shade of delusion rather than under the hot sun of the truth."[39] But Christianity is all about truth. In John 8:22, Jesus of Nazareth said, "Then you will know the truth, and the truth will set you free." (NIV) Francis Collins, founder of the BioLogos Foundation says, "The God of all truth is not well served by lies, no matter how noble the intentions of those who spread them."[40]

More than twenty years ago, in a marginal note, I had asked myself, "Is all truth God's truth?" My answer at that time was "Yes." My opinion has not changed. I have since discovered that St. Augustine (354-430 A.D.) said, "... let every good and true Christian understand that whatever truth may be found belongs to his Master."[41] Both Albert the Great (1206-1280) and Thomas Aquinas (1225-1274) claimed that the study of nature and the practice of religion are two roads to truth, each reliable in its own realm.[42] British scholar Francis Bacon (1561-1626) is best known for promoting this idea. Historian Ronald Numbers reflects the position held by a growing number of evangelical Christians when he claims that scientific truth, rightly understood, is synonymous with religious truth.[43] It is said that German writer and statesman Johann Goethe's (1749-1832) dying words were "mehr licht." [more light][44]

Thankfully, God has made the cosmos intelligible and has given us minds that can penetrate some of its mysteries. Galileo (1564-1642) said that the God who endowed us with intelligence wants to make sure we use it for our good and for his glory.[45] Imagine, if you will, the smile on the Creator's face, knowing that his creatures are beginning to plumb the depths of his creation.[46] Mark 12:30 says, "Love the Lord your God with all your heart and with all your soul and with all your mind and with all your strength." (NIV) When we use all of our mind, that is, all of our mental faculties, to study these things, we are engaged in an activity pleasing to God. The apostle Paul says, "... prove all things; hold fast to that which is good." (1 Thessalonians 5:21, KJV) Charles Darwin once wrote to some creationist friends indicating that he did not expect to change their minds, but he did hope to "stagger them a bit!"[47]

My goal in this discussion has been to show that there are a variety of responses to Darwin and his theory, and to science in general, by people of faith and by others as well. In the Preface, I indicated that irenics (e.g., calmly seeking reconciliation), is a more effective communication strategy than polemics (engaging in controversial debate or dispute). Those of us who have chosen to travel this journey of discovery need a safe place – a rest stop, if you will – where we may freely discuss these issues. As this book was being prepared, I talked to a wide variety of individuals. I found that coming to terms with science and the theory of evolution is important to a surprising number of people. Some churchgoing folks told me – either directly or indirectly – that they do not accept the theory of evolution, and are not interested in any further discussion of the issue. But most try to keep an open mind and are genuinely interested in learning more. Martin Luther once counseled Christians to put the best construction on things, that is, to see things in the most positive light. I am not sure that he always practiced what he preached, but that was the standard he set for himself and for others. Of course, whenever we communicate the truth as we see it, there will always be naysayers. The apostle Paul experienced that. He said, "Have I now become your enemy by telling you the truth?" (Galatians 4:16, NIV)

Changing our minds

Research suggests that we are more likely to change our views on a controversial topic when information is presented to us in a manner that avoids a defensive, emotional reaction. We are more likely to embrace a new idea if it is communicated by someone we trust.[48] Our social context has a powerful effect on our choices and attitudes (see Appendix). Psychologist Jonathan Haidt points out we do not change our minds because we were out-argued and put in our place. That tends to encourage us to cling to our views even more vigorously.[49] Put us into combat mode and our capacity for change is reduced even further. We nod in agreement when we hear philosopher Daniel Dennett state that "No dogma ever rolled over and died without a fight."[50] What those around us take to be normative and true is easily taken into our worldview as well.[51]

Sometimes a person's identity is so centered around opposition to another point of view that to change their mind would require a complete overhaul of their worldview. It has been said that ideas only persuade when individuals are in a social position that allows them to seriously consider what has been presented.[52] Science writer Chris Mooney advises, "Do not lead with the facts in order to convince; lead with the values to give the facts a fighting chance."[53] Nap Nazworth, writing for The Christian Post, makes the critically important point that "... attitudes about science may be as much about social and relational considerations as they are about information."[54] There is a good chance that addressing creationist social networks, rather than putting more effort into science education, will increase awareness and perhaps even acceptance of evolutionary theory. For many anti-evolutionists, their particular social context, their friends and family, leaders at their church, and people or groups they follow on social media, keep them from considering evolution. The anti-evolutionist's social context provides an effective counter-argument to scientific consensus.[55] This is the reality for many who were raised in an anti-evolutionary environment. If you fear losing your status in your social group if you change your views, (i.e.: "I'll be on the outs with my family when I go home for Christmas if they know I now accept evolution.") there is very strong pressure not to change.

In an article published on the website of Britain's Guardian newspaper.[56] Richard P. Grant discusses methods used by scientists in communicating important scientific findings to the public. Scientists, he says, are strongly motivated by a desire to get to the truth of a matter. But their audience, as we have seen, may not be conversant in science. Grant claims that when people reject science they are not so much rejecting science per se, but the methods used by scientists to try to convince them. People do not like being told what to do by experts, scientific or otherwise. And they certainly do not like being told what to think, especially about controversial subjects like science. People do not want to be pushed. Instead, they want to be heard. They want to know someone is listening. They want to know someone cares. They want to know that what they are being offered will improve their lives. According to Grant, a positive argument is better than a negative one.

Grant says that persuasion is more about who we are and our relationships, in other words, our social context, than it is about what is right and true. When scientists push too hard, they appear, as Grant puts it, "supercilious and judgmental." It is imperative that science communicators listen to and understand their audience. Science communicators must step out of their scientific bubble and reach people where they are. Scientists need to take the time required to clarify issues. When scientists stick to the facts and expose bad science or pseudoscience, that is only part of the story and, unfortunately, misses the point. Grant points out that science skeptics are well aware of the importance of listening to their base; well aware of the importance of reaching people on their own level, and reassuring them.

Defending scriptural authority

In our discussion of various denominational iterations of young earth creationism (see chapter 9) we encountered Lutheran systematic theologian Francis Pieper. In his three-volume Christian Dogmatics, (1934) Pieper denigrates science and criticizes its proponents, calling them "nitwits" and "wiseacres."[57] A true polemicist, Pieper claims that science seeks to destroy faith and to make it impossible for individuals to trust the scriptures. He argues that science wants to sit in judgment on scripture.[58] Science, therefore, is not under any circumstances to be granted equal authority to scripture. As I say, Pieper loves polemics. But, in my opinion, polemics only serves to alienate. It often brings meaningful conversation to a halt. Polemics sets up a defensive posture psychologists call reactance which occurs when a person feels that their choices are being taken away. Reactance, ironically, often causes the one being criticized to strengthen the very view that concerns the polemicist. Reactance increases resistance to persuasion.[59] A helpful strategy is to find common ground, to respect people's motivations and their intelligence. A helpful strategy as I mentioned earlier, is to actually talk to people rather than about them.

I cannot overemphasize the fact that young earth creationists have a very high regard for scriptural authority. That concern is praiseworthy and needs to be recognized and respected. Unfortunately, however, they also believe, as we have already mentioned, that their particular interpretation of the scriptural creation accounts is virtually unassailable. Young earth creationism, to a large degree, is motivated by fear – fear of losing something valuable. The young earth community desperately fears atheism. They fear what they see as liberalism in theology and in the media. They fear the higher critical method of biblical interpretation. They believe that should the Bible's historicity be lost, or redefined, their faith will be lost with it. Add to this the fact that should creationists adopt an evolutionary position, they fully expect serious conflict and loss of connection and belonging with friends, and family, with church members and pastors too. It is not difficult to see why, for many who hold this view, delving into these matters is not worth the trouble.

A universal problem

Across the denominational spectrum, a question church leaders regularly hear is, "Where are our young people?" There is no single answer to this important question. Several interrelated variables seem to be at work. One of them has to do with what the church has to say about science. There's no doubt about it. Passing on ideas to the next generation is one of the most important things anyone can do.[60] When it comes to science, however, questions abound. What, specifically, are evangelical churches teaching their young people about science? Is that teaching accurate? How do the students themselves perceive that content? There's more. Are Christian leaders approachable? Should Christian leaders not adequately prepare their young people for what they will encounter in university, those students are in for a rude awakening, what I call "science shock."

When naïve evangelical students are exposed to genuine scientific evidence for evolution, often for the very first time, they come to the realization that they have not heard the full story from their church leaders or denomination. Albert Szent-Gyorgi (1893-1986) said, "For every complex problem, there is a simple, easy to understand, incorrect answer."[61] Sadly, too many evangelical students are given the impression they must choose either science or religion. Fred Clark is as critical of creationism as many creationists are toward science. He says, in an article titled "Why Are Young People Leaving the Church?"[62]

> *Very often, it is because the church lied to them. Specifically, it is often because the church lied to them about the age of the earth. Many young Christians have been reared to believe that this concept of creation is a virtual*

> *article of faith that represents the biblical teaching. Those young Christians then go off to college, to a museum or another source of knowledge where they may be exposed to legitimate geology and are stunned by the force of geologic evidence for the earth's antiquity. They have been personally confronted with an intellectual and spiritual fixed great gulf that is far wider than the Grand Canyon, between their newfound scientific understanding and the religious views of their youth. Having been poorly equipped to handle the resulting intellectual and spiritual stresses, they all too often conclude, because the geologic evidence is so persuasive, that what they were taught about creation must be incorrect. To them, the Bible now becomes a flawed book. Since they have been misled about creation by the religious authorities of their youth, they lose confidence in the rest of their religious upbringing.*

Clark is correct in the sense that the church's attitude toward science is one of the factors that may lead young people to leave the church. However, it is not the only factor, and not the most important. My experience in ministry has taught me that young people want to be heard. They want to be accepted on their own terms. They want to be taught how to think, not fed a steady diet of predigested information. When a controversial subject like the theory of evolution is presented to them, they want a fair and objective summary of the various ways Christians and others have responded. In our day, what church leaders or pastors say about science is seen by our young people as just one source of information. If they believe they are not getting the full story from their church, a quick internet search will soon reveal that there are many other opinions on the subject.

According to David Kinnaman of the Barna Research Group, one of the reasons why one third of 18 to 30-year-olds leave the church is that they perceive the church to be "anti-science."[63] Many evangelical students enter university heavily armed with anti-evolution arguments. Years ago, in my first year at university, I was one of them. Just recently a friend said, "There is someone I think you should talk to. He has been interested in science and religion for a very long time. I am sure he would love to talk to you." I called this individual and learned that he has been studying the subject for years. And, like myself, he has adopted a position at odds with mainstream evangelicalism. I was concerned to hear that his son had left the church over the issue of science and faith. I would love to talk to this young man, and to others like him, and tell them that they can have the best of faith and the best of science without compromising either one. I would love to tell them that they are not required to choose one or the other. My experience is that young people want to talk about science and its relationship to their faith. They want to be assured that the older generation values their opinion and wants to know why they hold the views they do.

Recently, at a coffee shop, a group of retirees – myself included – were discussing science and the theory of evolution. A young man, most likely a student at the nearby university, was within earshot, assembling an artwork display. He listened in for a while. And then he approached us and said, "I could not help overhearing what you are saying about science." He shared his views and was invited by the group to join the discussion in the future.

A worthy vocation

Science and faith are not two different worlds, but different aspects of one world, God's world.[64] A harmonious relationship between them has the potential to attract many to the Christian church and faith. An all-out culture war, on the other hand, drives many away, and that includes many young people. I have argued that science, rightly understood and rightly appropriated, is not a threat to the Christian church generally, or its evangelical wing, specifically, but is, in fact, a gift from God. I am certainly not advocating a scientific takeover of theology, but I am asking that science be given a fair hearing. For Christians, the practice of science can be a form of worship and a worthy vocation. That, however, is not what scientists who are members of evangelical congregations commonly experience. They are discouraged to see that church teaching programs, communicated through sermons or study courses typically avoid speaking of science. Physicist Tom McLeish says, "... locally within congregations scientists become bewildered at the uncertainty with which their vocations are valued."[65] Francis Collins said this about the stewardship of knowledge:

Nearly five centuries ago, Copernicus argued, 'To know the mighty works of God, to comprehend his wisdom and majesty and power, to appreciate in degree the wonderful working of his laws, surely all this must be a pleasing acceptable mode of worship to the Most High, to whom ignorance cannot be more grateful than knowledge.'[66]

For people of faith, science will never replace scripture, nor is there any desire on the part of mainstream science to do so, but because science studies the natural realm it has the potential to assist Christians in understanding the scriptures when they speak along those lines. Our Christian young people need to be assured the science does not invalidate scripture but complements and enriches it. It is incumbent upon Christian leaders to build bridges between science and religion.

Dialogue not debate

Too often, discussion of these issues takes place in the context of a debate. Dialogue is a preferable option for the following reasons:

- In a debate, the goal is to win, often at all costs.
- In a dialogue, the goal is understanding.
- In a debate, the atmosphere is threatening. Attacks are expected and permitted.
- In a dialogue, the atmosphere is encouraging and there is mutual respect.
- In a debate, individuals stick to the party line.
- In a dialogue, differences of opinion are permitted and even encouraged.
- In a debate, participants listen in order to refute.
- In a dialogue, participants listen to understand and gain insight.
- In a debate, the goal is to win.
- In a dialogue, the goal is to learn and to grow.[67]

Science can be a valid pathway to God. It can be an additional source of grace.[68] Science reveals a universe of great ingenuity and subtlety. A self-assembling world made over billions of years is no less a miracle than one made in six twenty-four hour days.[69] Scientific discoveries have the very real potential to increase a believers' sense of awe and amazement that God's creation. Louis Pasteur once said, "The more I study nature, the more I stand amazed at the work of the creator."[70] Nature may be, as J.B. Haldane famously proclaimed, "... not only queerer than we suppose, but queerer than we can suppose."[71]

Contemporary evolutionary theory

Biologist Theodosius Dobzhansky (1900-1975) once famously said that, "... nothing in biology makes sense except in the light of evolution."[72] Evolutionary theory has been tested for more than 150 years and its core concepts have stood the test of time. The evidence for evolution is stronger than ever.[73] Contrary to intelligent design's contention that it is time to repeal and replace evolutionary theory, biologists are refining their views on the mechanisms of macroevolution. Like all scientific theories, the theory continues to be updated. Evolutionary biologists are evaluating what some have called an Extended Evolutionary

Synthesis, a blending of neo-Darwinian evolution with developmental biology and epigenetics. Among the issues being considered are the possibility that nongenetic [i.e., epigenetic] sources of information may influence the course of evolution. Functional genes, it has been discovered, make up only 5 or 6 percent of the total human genome.[74]

It is good for Christians to keep their options open when it comes to the relationship between science and religion. There is value in questioning and pushing the envelope as long as the arguments proposed are fair and accurate, representing the actual state of affairs. In the future, argues Darrel Falk, evolutionary biologists must focus more on how biological information is generated, changed, and used and less on the natural selection filter.[75]

British theologian N.T. Wright encourages people of faith with these words, "Jesus is Lord of the world, so all truth is his truth. Let us go and explore it with reverence and delight."[76] And Stephen Jay Gould, whose writings encouraged me to embark on this journey almost thirty years ago, recommends assembling the disparate patches of science and religion into a common quilt called wisdom.[77] Gould says:

> *Our greatest intellectual adventures often occur within ourselves, not in the restless search for new facts and new objects on the earth or in the stars, but from a need to expunge old prejudices and build new conceptual structures. No hunt can promise a sweeter reward, a more admirable goal, than the excitement of a thoroughly revised understanding.*[78]

An ongoing journey

When I was in my early 20's, my faith was rekindled. It became clear to me that I ought to investigate the possibility of becoming a pastor. As an evangelical Christian, I was warned about Charles Darwin. His views, I was told, were corrosive to faith. All kinds of negative things were associated with Darwin's theory: Nazism. Social Darwinism. Atheism. Eugenics. Evolution, I was told, tears the heart out of the Bible and destroys its authority. In 1975, in my first semester as an undergraduate at Simon Fraser University, I enrolled in Archaeology 100. At one point, the professor raised the subject of the age of the earth. He quoted Archbishop Ussher who, in the 17th century, as we saw in chapter 4, using Biblical genealogies as his guide, calculated that the creation took place on October 22nd, 4004 B.C. The professor used that information to poke holes in young earth creationism. In a course assignment, I took issue with the professor. I did my best to defend a young earth view. Suffice it to say my arguments received a less-than-positive assessment. I received a "D" for my efforts.

After university came seminary. I was preoccupied with various issues at that stage of my life, but my interest in science continued. Almost thirty years ago, I embarked on an intellectual journey that continues to this day. When I read a book, I usually highlight portions of text, and sometimes make notes in the margin. It's interesting to look back at those notes now. They chronicle my struggles and questions as I encountered scientific discovery. At that time I knew, in a general way at least, what my church believed about the theory of evolution. We were against it. But exactly why was another question. As each year went by, I became more and more convinced that the scientific consensus was correct. I could see it in the ancient vastness of the cosmos and stellar evolution. I could see it in the biological reality of descent with modification and the resulting speciation. I could see it in the geological reality of deep time. The appendix included with this book cites research demonstrating that, although the default perspective for most evangelicals is young earth creationism, a great deal of ambivalence remains. Many evangelicals aren't sure what they believe. That was my own situation at that point in time. I have seen evidence of that ambivalence in my discussions with laypeople and some clergy as well. For many of our young people, evolution is a non-issue. They have no problem with it. What they do have a problem with is the way the church denies it. They have a problem with not being told the whole story.

Christians must learn to trust one another. "Safe zones" are needed – places where we can leave fears and polemics behind and get on with establishing the truth of the matter. Christian leaders must initiate dialogue and tolerate a diversity of opinions on subjects such as evolution. They must encourage people to do their homework – to read widely – to think critically – and to personally reserve judgment until all the facts are in. It's true. Evolution is the E-word. It's a subject that, for many, is too hot to handle. I follow a few science and religion groups on Facebook. What surprises me is how nasty people can be with one another – belittling, impugning the intelligence of others. But it's not about intelligence. It's about ideology. It's about Biblical interpretation, otherwise known as hermeneutics. This is God's world. He created it. And he decided which method he would use. Thankfully, He's left a great deal of evidence behind.

Social media has allowed me to get in touch with international experts in the field – scientists with an incredibly strong and vibrant faith. I value the friendships I have acquired. I now know – and rejoice in the fact – that it's possible to be scientifically literate and, at the same time, a faithful follower of the Lord Jesus Christ. As I said in the preface, "If, at the end of the day, our interpretation of the scriptures is more accurate, our doctrines have been appropriately reviewed, our respect for science has grown, and our personal faith has been enriched, then the excursion described in this book has been worthwhile." As a familiar Christian hymn says:

Take my life and let it be,
consecrated, Lord to thee.
Take my intellect and use,
every power as thou shalt choose.

Francis R. Havergal, 1874. Public domain

APPENDIX

Overview

There is a widely-held perception among evangelicals that scientists are overwhelmingly atheistic. Research, however, indicates otherwise. It is true that scientists are less religious than the general public. But approximately 40 percent of scientists are believers, most of whom are associated with the more liberal mainline churches. The overwhelming majority of believing scientists are proponents of evolutionary creation. A surprising finding is that the radical new atheists (Dawkins, Dennett, Coyne, et. al.) make up only a small percentage of all scientists, approximately 5 percent. Only 15 percent of scientists believe that a fundamental conflict exists between science and religion. And among the general population, just 25 percent hold this view.

Two basic research methodologies have been used to investigate beliefs about evolution. An example of the first would be research conducted by the Gallup and Pew organizations. Over a thirty-two year period, for example, Gallup conducted a dozen polls on the topic of evolution. These surveys are made up of true / false-type questions linked to a limited series of suggested responses. Respondents are asked to select the responses that come closest to their own views. Forced choice, predetermined responses like these, however, do not take into account the possibility that individuals may have beliefs that do not match the suggestions, or that they are uncertain about their answers, or that they are not interested in the subject. This first research methodology does not adequately account for the social context of a person's beliefs.

An example of an alternate methodology is the National Study of Religion and Human Origins (NSRHO) sponsored by the BioLogos Foundation. In addition to assessing beliefs about evolution and creation, the NSRHO also delves into the social context of those beliefs. It sets out to determine, in depth, just what people believe and, in addition, how strongly those beliefs are held. The result? When individuals are pressed about their beliefs, confidence erodes fairly quickly. The NSRHO suggests therefore that the polling numbers published by Gallup and Pew are most likely skewed. Individuals, it seems, are not as sure about their views as traditional surveys indicate.

The National Study of Religion and Human Origins suggests that an individual's social identity and social context often have a powerful impact on their beliefs and behavior. Young earth creationists, for example, typically belong to social networks that share their anti-evolutionary views. Significantly, young earth creationists expect that, should they embrace evolution, they will face negative consequences from their social network. These constraints help explain why creationists find it so difficult to change their minds about evolution. They also explain why learning about evolution in school has so little impact on changing minds. Learning that takes place in school is negated away from school. The NSRHO suggests that a survey methodology which takes both sociological and theological factors into account will more accurately explain why people come to hold and subsequently maintain their young earth beliefs. It also suggests that the most effective way to encourage people to change their minds about origins is to work with, not against, these critical social realities.

Gallup polling

Between January 1982 and May 2014, the Gallup organization conducted a dozen polls on the topic of evolution. The surveys included the following instructions:

> *Which of the following statements comes closest to your views on the origin and development of human beings –*

- human beings have developed over millions of years from less advanced forms of life, but God guided this process;
- human beings have developed over millions of years from less advanced forms of life, but God had no part in this process;
- God created human beings pretty much in their present form at one time within the last 10,000 years or so.[1]

The Gallup organization has posted an article on its website, quoted above, summarizing results from the 12 surveys mentioned above, which were administered over a 32-year period. During that time, support for evolutionary creation declined slightly from 38 percent to 31 percent. Support for atheistic evolution (defined as those who believe God was not involved in the process, not whether the respondents believe in God) rose substantially from 9 percent to 19 percent. Young earth creationism remained around 43 percent. The number of individuals claiming "No Opinion" was around 10 percent. The Gallup website also summarized results from a selection of other surveys conducted between 2001 and 2015.[2]

	VERY INFORMED	SOMEWHAT INFORMED	NOT TOO INFORMED	NOT INFORMED AT ALL	NO OPINION
How informed are you about the theory of evolution?	34%	47%	11%	6%	2%
How informed are you about creationism?	40	40	10	7	3

***Table A1.** – Gallup (2001) – Respondents' Knowledge of the Issues*

Religion among academic scientists

Religion Among Academic Scientists (RAAS) is a survey conducted between 2005 and 2008 by Elaine Howard Ecklund, assistant professor of sociology in the College of Arts and Sciences at the University at Buffalo and principal investigator. The RAAS is based on responses from 1,646 academic scientists at 21 research universities and in-depth interviews with 271 individuals. The survey sample consisted of academics in seven different natural and social science disciplines: physics, chemistry, biology, sociology, economics, political science, psychology and sub-fields like molecular biology, biochemistry, social psychology and neuroscience.[3] The rate of response was nearly 75 percent, which Ecklund says is extremely high for a faculty survey.[4]

Raas – natural vs. social scientists

With only one exception, the RAAS survey found no difference in attitudes about religion between scientists in the natural sciences as opposed to the social sciences. The difference was that biologists scored lower on levels of religiosity than did physicists. Ecklund hypothesized that this may be due to the fact that biologists are on the front lines of the conflict between evolutionists and creationists.[5]

	NATURAL SCIENCES	SOCIAL SCIENCES
Which of the following comes closest to your views about religion?		
"There is very little truth in any religion."	28.6%	22.8%
"There are basic truths in many religions."	68.5	73.5
"There is the most truth in only one religion."	2.9	3.7
Which of the following statements comes closest to expressing what you believe about God?		
"I do not believe in God."	37.6	31.2
"I do not know if there is a God and there is no way to find out."	29.4	31.0
"I believe in a higher power, but it is not God."	8.2	7.2
"I believe in God some-times."	4.2	5.4
"I have some doubts, but I believe in God."	12.9	15.5
"I have no doubts about God's existence."	7.8	9.7
Religious service attendance		
More than once a week	1.2	1.5
Once a week	5.8	7.1
2 to 3 times a month	5.9	5.8
Once a month	3.6	4.3
6 to 11 times a year	5.1	4.5
1 to 5 times a year	23.1	26.5
Not at all in the last year	55.3	50.3

Table A.2 *– Religion Among Academic Scientists (RAAS) Natural versus Social Scientists on their views about religion.*

Raas – gender & age variables

In the general population, women tend to be more religious than men, but this was not the case with the RAAS. Similarly, older individuals tend to have higher levels of religious belief and practice than younger people, but, again, this was not observed.[6]

Pew – by age

As a comparison to the RAAS polling, a Pew Research poll, conducted in 2013, found that younger people are more accepting of evolution than are their parents or grandparents. 68 percent of 18 to 29-year-olds accept evolution. But only 49 percent of those who are 65 or older do the same.[7] There is a complicating factor, however. Older people tend to be more religious than younger people and creationists as a whole are more religious than the general population. Paradoxically, the RAAS found that middle-aged scientists surveyed were less likely to believe in God than 18 to 35 year olds. The older group was also less likely to attend worship services.[8]

Raas – childhood religiosity

The RAAS assessed childhood religiosity among scientists, in other words, the religious tradition in which they were raised, and the importance of religion in their family as they grew up. The survey found that scientists raised as Protestants were more likely to retain their religious beliefs and practices as compared to those raised without a religious affiliation. Similarly, those who said that religion was important when they were growing up were less likely as adults to say that they saw no truth in religion, did not believe in God, or attend religious services.[9] The survey concluded that "scientists who are raised religious often stay relatively religious."[10]

Raas – believing scientists

A sizable minority of scientists are committed religious believers and could be effective evangelists in getting the scientific word out to the general population and to the churches. Believing scientists at Christian colleges and universities were not included in the RAAS.[11] In chapter 8, we noted that many educators at evangelical seminaries have adopted an evolutionary viewpoint.[12] These individuals have found a way to reconcile their faith and their science and, if they would be willing to go public with their experiences, could profitably share this information with the wider church.

Raas – scientists' faith

Nearly 20 percent of scientists are actively involved in a house of worship.[13] Nearly 50 percent are religious in a traditional sense; and an additional 20 percent describe themselves as spiritual.[14] Ecklund found that radical (some critics use the term 'fundamentalist') atheists like Richard Dawkins comprise only 5 percent of scientists.[15] This makes the so-called new atheists a definite minority in the scientific community. This information, however, is not widely known by the general public, or, it seems, by young earth creationists. As for those scientists who are believers, the vast majority, 94 percent, are evolutionary creationists.[16]

Raas – scientists compared to the general public

Scientists surveyed were disproportionately Jewish compared to the general population (15 percent vs. 2 percent).[17] Only 2 percent were evangelical Protestants, compared to 28 percent of the wider U.S. population.[18] To put it another way, there are 14 times more evangelicals in the general population than there are among top scientists.[19] 52 percent of the scientists had no religious affiliation. The corresponding number in the U.S. population is 14 percent. Ecklund found that approximately 64 percent of scientists were either atheists or agnostics compared to only 6 percent of the general population.[20]

It is interesting to compare the RAAS findings with a September 1999 Scientific American study described by Nancy Pearcey. She says,

> *A survey by Edward Larson and Larry Witham (Scientific American, September 1999) reveals that more than 90 percent of N.A.S. (National Academy of Sciences) members reject belief in a personal God – and, furthermore, they think science itself compels that conclusion.*[21]

Because the Scientific American results are so different from those of other studies like the RAAS, further research is required.

	SCIENTISTS	GENERAL PUBLIC
Atheist or Agnostic	64%	6%
New Atheist	5	—
With No Religious Tradition	53	16
Religious Affiliation	52	14
Self-describe As Spiritual	70	—
Some Form of Belief in God	36	94
Religious in a Traditional Sense	50	—
Active in a House of Worship	20	—
Have No Doubt God Exists	9	60
Believe One Religion Holds the Most Truth	3	—
Raised in a Protestant Home	39	—
Evangelical Protestant	2	28
Jewish Heritage	15	2
Inherent Conflict between Science and Religion	15	25
Evolutionary Creationists	94	—

Table A.3 – Religion Among Academic Scientists (RAAS) Scientists' views on religious issues vs. U.S. general public.

Raas – scientists' faith

Fifty-three percent of scientists surveyed in the RAAS have no religious tradition, compared to only 16 percent of the American population.[22] 36 percent of scientists have "some form of belief in God." This is contrasted with 94 percent of the American public who express faith in God.[23] A 2000 Gallup poll found that 82 percent of Americans believe God created the universe.[24] As an interesting comparison with the RAAS findings, a 1997 study found that 39 percent of scientists believe in God; a parallel study, conducted back in 1916, 81 years previously, found the percentage of believing scientists to be around 42 percent. It appears there has been little change in the beliefs of scientists over that time.[25]

Thirty-nine percent of scientists were raised in a Protestant home, but, in their vocation as scientists, most hesitate to use the term evangelical when describing themselves.[26] Most scientists report that they struggled with their faith as young people.[27] 9 percent of scientists have no doubt that God exists, which is true of 60 percent of the general public.[28] Only 3 percent of scientists consider one religion to hold the most truth.[29]

Raas – warfare model

Ecklund's research suggests that the perception that scientists are hostile towards religion does not match reality.[30] Only 25 percent of the American public are of the opinion that scientists are hostile to religion (the warfare model). This means, of course, that three-quarters of the general public, a full 75 percent, do not see a conflict![31] And only 15 percent of scientists surveyed believe there is an inherent conflict between science and religion.[32] Ecklund found that many scientists equate all religious people with fundamentalist Protestants.[33] That may be the case because fundamentalists tend to be vocal and are often mentioned in the media. It is important to correct these stereotypes whenever possible.

Pew research

In December 2013, the Pew Research Center released the results of a survey of American attitudes toward evolution.[34] Conducted in March and April 2013, with a representative sample of 1983 adults ages 18 and older, the survey found that 60 percent of Americans believe in evolution in some form. 33 percent are creationists who reject the idea of evolution and an old earth. 32 percent advocate atheistic evolution, and 24 percent are evolutionary creationists. 64 percent of white evangelical Protestants are creationists, while only 15 percent of white mainline Protestants hold this view (emphasis added). Of mainline Protestants, 78 percent believe in evolution, 36 percent are evolutionary creationists (believing that God used the process of evolution to foster various life-forms) and 36 percent are atheistic evolutionists (while they believe in God, they do not believe he was involved in the evolutionary process). In their political and theological views, as would be expected, mainline Protestants are more liberal than evangelicals. The Catholic Church mirrors the mainline denominations, not in theology, but in its official endorsement of evolution.

Pew – by political party

American conservatives reject evolution at a much higher rate than self-identified liberals.[35] As a matter of fact, anti-evolutionism is virtually an article of faith among Republicans.[36] The 2013 Pew Poll referred to above outlines a growing polarization between Democrats and Republicans over evolution. In just four years, the gap widened from just 10 points to a 24-percentage point margin. In 2009, 54 percent of Republicans and 64 percent of Democrats endorsed evolution. In 2013, just 43 percent of Republicans and 67 percent of Democrats say humans evolved, a 24-point gap.[37] While 98 percent of scientists in the American Association for the Advancement of Science (AAAS) say they believe humans evolved over time, only two thirds (66 percent) of Americans overall perceive that scientists generally agree about evolution. Those in the general public who reject evolution are divided on whether there is a scientific consensus on this topic, with 47 percent saying scientists agree on evolution and 46 percent saying they do not.[38]

By Country

A 2006 survey conducted by Jon Miller of Michigan State University, investigated attitudes about evolution in 32 European countries (including data from the US and Japan). Miller's research showed that only Turkey was less willing than the U.S. to accept evolution.[39] Miller's study, however, did not include Latin America. A 2013 Pew research study found that, compared to the U.S., even larger percentages of people in many other countries reject evolution. In Latin America for example, roughly 40 percent of residents in several countries reject evolution. This is true even though Catholicism, the majority religion in that area, officially endorses evolution. In addition, most Muslims in Afghanistan, Indonesia, and Iraq reject evolution.

	ATHEISTIC EVOLUTION	THEISTIC EVOLUTION	TOTAL EVOLUTION	YOUNG EARTH CREATIONIST
U.S. Population	32%	24%	60%	33%
White Evangelical	8	18	27	64
Republican		43		46
Black Protestant	17	25	44	50
White Mainline Protestant	36	36	78	15
Democrat		67		27
White Catholic	33	33	66	
Age 18–29			68	27
Age 65+			49	36
American Association for the Advancement of Science			98	

***Table A.4 – Pew Research** (2013). Three views on human evolution compared*

National Study of Religion and Human Origins

The National Study of Religion and Human Origins (NSRHO)[40] was released in December 2014. The study was sponsored by the BioLogos Foundation and conducted by Calvin College sociologist Jonathan Hill. The NSRHO is a nationally representative survey of 3,034 U.S. adults.[41] In addition to an in-depth exploration of various positions on human origins, the NSRHO also examined the social context of those beliefs. The NSRHO offers more nuanced polling which supplements, and sometimes challenges, traditional Gallup-type data.[42] A primary goal of the NSRHO was to determine the various positions individuals hold on human origins and, in addition, assess how strongly they hold those views.[43] The study found that the more vigorously individuals were pressed about their beliefs, the less confident they tended to be.[44]

The NSRHO claims to be the first survey to investigate the public's beliefs about human origins in depth. A primary goal was to "... develop a better map of the public's beliefs by disaggregating the components of the most common survey questions on human origins and focusing on each in detail," as well as "... to gauge the influence of social context on these beliefs."[45]

NSRHO – Methodology

Traditional polling has repeatedly shown that the American public is divided over human evolution. Most polls suggest a fairly even split between those who accept human evolution and those who do not. Since the 1980's, several surveys have had some variation on a dichotomous true / false question asking whether humans have evolved from earlier species of animals. Many surveys ask respondents to select from a list of "packaged" views and select the one that comes closest to what they believe. This is the approach the Gallup organization used twelve times between 1982 and 2014.[46] These studies have consistently found that between 40 and 47 percent of the population self-identify as young earth creationist. Theistic evolution is held by between 31 and 40 percent. Atheistic evolution is the least popular option (although increasing in popularity), moving from 9 to 19 percent over that time period.[47]

NSRHO – Old-earth creationism

Survey questions that require respondents to choose predetermined responses discount the possibility that some individuals may have beliefs that do not match the suggested positions, or are uncertain about what they believe, or some simply have no interest in the issue. Choosing old-earth creationism, for example, is not an option on the traditional Gallup surveys.[48] The difference between Gallup and the NSRHO is almost certainly due to Gallup respondents being forced to choose from limited options, even when many are unsure of what they believe or maintain beliefs that do not fit into the options available.[49]

Prepackaged responses can lead to inaccurate conclusions about the views people hold. The crucial social context of those beliefs is not sufficiently acknowledged. All individuals, no matter what their beliefs about evolution, are situated in groups of family and friends, organizations and collections of various social identities which, together, have a powerful impact on beliefs and attitudes.[50] Previous surveys have shown that investigators often fail to take into account the social processes that foster and serve to maintiain these beliefs.[51] If we label the old-earth view as those creationists (using a stricter definition) who –

- do not believe that the days of creation recounted in Genesis were literal days, and
- who do not believe that humans came into existence in the past 10,000 years

– then only 1 percent of the US adult population can be classified as old-earth creationists.[52]

NSRHO – Methodology

Unlike previous surveys, the NSRHO asks multiple questions about human origins. The goal in the survey was to "deconstruct" the various components and "reconstruct" them in ways that more accurately reflect the range of possible beliefs. For each item, respondents were given the opportunity to express their degree of certainty.[53]

NSRHO – Young earth creationism

To clarify, if young earth creationism is defined as –

- denying human evolution and
- affirming that God created humans,

– then 37 percent of the general public can be categorized as creationists and 29 percent are convinced (absolutely or very certain) creationists. But if creationism is defined as further requiring

- that God miraculously created a historical pair of progenitors of the entire human race

– then only 25 percent of the public are creationists and 22 percent are convinced. Amazingly, only 8 percent of the public are young-earth creationists who accept the above three characteristics, and also believe that

- the days of creation were literal twenty-four hour days and that
- humans came into existence within the last 10,000 years.

Many individuals are simply unsure whether the days of creation were literal, and they are especially unsure about when humans first came into existence. Again, this would be unclear using the standard Gallup methodology. Many Americans select a young earth creationist view when presented as a package with other beliefs they are more certain of, but not many are able to clearly affirm the full position when it is deconstructed into its component parts. The remaining 39 percent of the population are unsure or hold "uncommon views such as believing that humans did not evolve from earlier species while simultaneously believing that God had nothing to do with the emergence of humans."[54]

NSRHO – Correct beliefs

Respondents were asked if they consider it important to have correct beliefs about human origins. Forty-two percent indicated that this was very or extremely important, with 63 percent of creationists, 52 percent of atheistic evolutionists, 35 percent of evolutionary creationists, and 23 percent of unsure respondents indicating agreement.[55] When asked specifically which beliefs were most important, the most common response for creationists referred to upholding the authority of the Bible and defending the Christian faith.[56]

Theistic evolutionists were also asked about correct beliefs. Their answers were very different from those of the young earth creationists. Theistic evolutionists indicated their desire to gain a better understanding of themselves through their investigation of this topic and that their knowledge of evolution would assist them in assuring a better future for humanity. A common theme expressed by evolutionary creationists was the importance of knowing the truth about a matter and being intellectually honest about what they had learned.[57] The most frequent evolutionary creationist responses, therefore, were not about faith or religion. Some evolutionary creationists mentioned their belief in the compatibility of science and religion, a topic seldom mentioned by the other two groups. So when it comes to correct beliefs, young earth creationists believe salvation is at stake, while evolutionary creationists do not.[58]

NSRHO – Atheistic evolutionists

The most common response about correct beliefs from atheistic evolutionists was that scientific facts are superior to superstition and irrational belief.[59] Both YEC's and evolutionary creationists said that having true or accurate beliefs is very important to them.[60]

NSRHO – Young earth attitudes regarding science

Surprisingly, young earth creationists do not agree among themselves about evolution or about the scientists who study it. For some young earth advocates, evolution is not scientifically up to par and scientists are biased. Other creationists, however, disagree. This suggests a lack of uniformity in reasons why creationists reject evolution.[61] There is a fairly strong anti-science attitude in American society as a whole. More than 50 percent of the American general public agree with the statement that "we depend too much on science and not enough on faith."[62]

NSRHO – Conflict model

When science and religion conflict, young earth advocates default to religious ways of knowing (what they would call a "literal" reading of scripture, as opposed to Augustine's definition of the word as the original intention of the author) and atheistic evolutionists favor scientific ways of knowing (trusting the mainstream scientific establishment to provide accurate information). The only perspective consistently opposing the conflict model is evolutionary creation.[63]

NSRHO – Theistic evolution

Theistic evolution (or evolutionary creation) is less popular than young earth creationism. Using the broadest definition, theistic evolutionists –

- believe in human evolution and
- believe that God (or an intelligent force) was somehow involved in the creation of humans

Sixteen percent of the population fits into this category. But only 8 percent are very or absolutely certain of both these beliefs. So, although the latest Gallup report shows that 31 percent of Americans are evolutionary creationists, it is clear from the NSRHO that a majority of those individuals are uncertain about their beliefs, and many have chosen this option because they simply do not like the other options. For much of the population, the evolutionary creation position does not come with a high degree of confidence.[64]

NSRHO – Atheistic evolution

Atheistic evolution is the view that humans evolved from simpler life forms and that God had nothing to do with the process. Atheistic evolutionists do not necessarily fit the classic definition of atheists or agnostics (less than half directly identify as such). When the general public is asked separate questions about evolution and God's involvement in the process, approximately 9 percent can be classified as atheistic evolutionists. Like evolutionary creationists, this group is about half the size of the comparable category from the latest Gallup poll. This suggests that a sizable number of Gallup respondents who chose the atheistic evolutionist option were unsure of their beliefs. When the NSRHO included a supplemental measure of certainty, only 6 percent of the population reported that they

- believe in human evolution,
- believe that God had nothing to do with it, and
- that they are very or absolutely certain about both these beliefs.[65]

	YOUNG EARTH CREATION	THEISTIC EVOLUTION	ATHEISTIC EVOLUTION	UNSURE
Historical Adam and Eve	87%	50%	11%	40%
24-hour creation days	60	29	5	23
Recent creation	36	27	23	17
Very certain of beliefe	77	52	71	NA
Correct beliefs important	63	35	52	23
Evangelical Protestant	36	16	4	16
Attend church weekly	45	26	4	18
Faith important daily	76	48	10	34
Pray daily	65	41	7	30
Bible without error	76	47	7	39
Politically conservative	42	34	30	36
Age 50+	46	46	47	46
Bachelors degree	27	38	33	27
Southerner	35	40	38	37
Family shares beliefs	68	47	46	31
Friends share beliefs	57	38	36	24
Changed views, trouble with family	35	15	21	15
Changed views, trouble with friends	28	17	19	12
My Church rejects evolution	62	31	19	26
Evolution reference in worship	63	54	27	49
Members mention evolution	61	54	79	49
Changed views, trouble with church members	44	27	23	23
Changed views cause trouble with church leaders	45	24	10	26
High school taught only evolution correct	20	30	40	20
Public high school taught only evolution correct	21	31	41	21
Kept belief after school teaching	85	71	82	79
College taught only evolution correct	13	13	22	11

	YOUNG EARTH CREATION	THEISTIC EVOLUTION	ATHEISTIC EVOLUTION	UNSURE
Public university taught only evolution correct	19	17	29	19
Kept belief after high school teaching	90	62	77	75
Only evolution in public school	13	13	22	11
Only creationism in public school	34	13	4	6
Teach combination in public school	50	54	22	11
Evolution speculative not factual	50	20	12	19
Scientists disagree on evolution	40	25	13	19
Scientists let personal beliefs interfere	47	30	20	30
Scientists free to do any research	38	25	13	19
Scientists hostile towards religion	40	24	17	21
Sometimes feel science and religion conflict	51	51	69	47
Science and religion are compatible	32	53	19	24
Science, facts; religion, faith. No overlap	28	32	59	30

***Table A.5 – National Study of Religion and Human Origins** (NSRHO). Views on human origins compared.*

NSRHO – Social context

The NSRHO also investigated the social context of respondents' beliefs. Young earth creationists, as we have seen, typically belong to social networks that share their anti-evolutionary views. In addition, young earth creationists expect disagreements with family and friends should they accept evolution. Add to this the fact that these individuals generally belong to congregations that reject evolution. They expect disagreements with religious leaders and fellow church members should they accept evolution. Creationist social networks and institutions, it seems, are critically important in establishing and reinforcing the creationist worldview.[66]

Studies in the sociology of knowledge emphasize that an individual's social location – in other words, their social identity and group memberships – strongly influences what they consider to be "common sense" interpretations of the world around them. What seems natural and normal to one person cannot be assumed to be so for others. All of us belong to communities that influence how we see the world. When those views are threatened, we strive to maintain them because our personal identity and social relationships are linked to them. The NSRHO emphasizes that individual beliefs, practices, and identities are important, but only become a strong lead-in to specific views such as young earth or atheistic evolution when these social factors are added.[67] The bottom line is this: the social context of an individual's beliefs is as important as individual factors, and this is especially true for young earth creationists.[68]

NSRHO – Social pressures

To summarize, a creationists' friends and family have a powerful impact on their views on evolution. Sixty-eight percent of creationists reported that all or most of their family members share their beliefs. And 56 percent said that this is also true of their closest friends. The comparable figure for evolutionary creationists is 38 percent and for atheistic evolutionists the number is 37 percent.[69] The NSRHO included questions about the social consequences of changing beliefs for each of these groups. Creationists are substantially more likely to expect difficulties with family members (35 percent) should they change their minds about evolution when compared to either evolutionary creationists (15 percent) or atheistic evolutionists (20 percent). The same expectation is true for friends as well.[70] In many ways, atheistic evolutionists are the flip-side of the young earth advocates.[71] Atheistic evolutionists feel no social pressure from their family and friends should they change their minds about evolution.[72]

The NSRHO asked the various groups if their congregation had a definite position on human evolution. About half belonged to congregations that reject evolution. For young earthers, however, the percentage rises to two thirds.[73] Creationists, as we have seen, expect disagreements with other church members should they change their minds about evolution. Only about a quarter of theistic and atheistic evolutionists expect the same. And a similar percentage of young earth creationists (47 percent, almost half) anticipate increased disagreements with church leaders as well.[74]

NSRHO – Religious identity

The NSRHO's findings on the influence of social context on an individual's belief system are corroborated by a 2014 Associated Press poll which found that an individual's religious identity is a key factor in their attitude toward science.[75] Chris Mooney, writing for the Washington Post, states that when individuals deny science, they do so on the basis of a perception that it conflicts with their personal identity of which religion is often a critical component.[76]

NSRHO – Science education

There is little indication that educational efforts promoting evolution, in and of themselves, are sufficient in changing people's minds about evolution. The NSRHO says:

> *The science education model assumes that humans are fundamentally rational actors that simply need more and better information. But this does not fit the evidence. Recent studies in cognitive science have emphasized the importance of non-rational mental mechanisms when people come to accept or reject beliefs about evolution.*[77]

As an example of the power of social context on the maintenance of creationist beliefs, the majority of creationists did not change their position on evolution after hearing what was taught at school or college.[78] Those most likely to change their minds are the evolutionary creationists.[79]

NSRHO – Biblical authority

As we have seen throughout this discussion, young earth creationists reject evolution primarily on the basis of their beliefs about the Bible and their personal salvation. Creationists are taught that a rejection of evolution is an affirmation of the evangelical teaching on biblical authority. Other factors, such as as political orientation, age, education, and geographic location are important, but remain secondary to a "literal" interpretation of the Genesis creation accounts.[80] Even though creationists list a number of reasons why their beliefs are important, faith and defending the Bible predominate. The most common creationist response (22 percent) referred to the responsibility of maintaining biblical authority. Some creationists referred to the so-called "slippery slope" argument. One person, for example, said, "If we do not believe God's word and his promises in their entirety, there is no basis for our faith and our salvation." Creationists are convinced that having the wrong beliefs about evolution threatens their relationship with God and even their salvation. In addition, they believe that wrong belief denigrates "the authority of the Bible and the belief that God is the source of all creation."[81]

NSRHO – Public schools

When atheistic evolutionists were asked what should be taught about human origins in public schools, a majority of (77 percent) said only evolution should be taught. Anti-evolutionists also, as one would expect, are strongly against this option (only 3 percent support it). Theistic evolutionists take a middle position with 28 percent. Significantly, most creationists do not want creationism to be the only option in public schools. Only 34 percent are in favor of this option.[82] As a comparison, Pew research done in July 2005 reported that 40 percent of U.S. citizens were in favor of replacing evolution with creationism in the classroom.[83] Less than 10 percent of any group wants intelligent design to be taught exclusively. The most popular option, for both young earth and evolutionary creationists (50 percent and 54 percent respectively), is some combination of evolution, creationism, and intelligent design. Ecklund reports that 65 percent of Americans think that some form of the Old Testament creation story should be taught side-by-side with evolution.[84]

NSRHO – Assumptions about science

Approximately half of the anti-evolutionists surveyed believe that the theory of evolution is actually based on good evidence, but reject it anyway. Thirty-nine percent believe there is controversy in the scientific community over the issue of evolution. But, surprisingly, 61 percent do not.[85] Twenty-three percent of creationists believe that evolution is not a scientific fact, that scientists do not agree on the scientific validity of evolution, and that scientists are biased. But 28 percent do not affirm any of these statements. Clearly, there is a lack of unity over reasons why young earth creationists reject evolution.[86]

NSRHO – Warfare model

Forty percent of young earth creationists believe that scientists are hostile to religion, while only 16 percent of atheistic evolutionists believe the same. Theistic evolutionists come in at 24 percent. It's important to point out, however, that young earthers who believe that scientists are hostile to religion are in the minority.[87] The evidence points to the fact that creationists are not opposed to science in general, but many do question whether evolutionary science is real science, claiming that it is speculative and not factual.[88] Atheistic evolutionists are less likely (21 percent) than creationists to believe that science and religion are compatible.[89]

NSRHO – Creationist certainty

What makes anti-evolutionists so certain about their beliefs? Religious factors are important as we have seen, as is the influence of family, friends, and congregation.[90] The NSRHO found five key pathways that lead to certain creationism and, significantly, all five include beliefs that, "... the Bible should be taken either completely literally, or that it should be taken to be inspired and error-free."[91] Another essential factor is membership in a church that rejects evolution. Statistically, a combination of the Bible beliefs above, and belonging to such a congregation, will produce a certain creationist 81 percent of the time. Secondary factors include belonging to an evangelical Protestant congregation and sensing that changing one's beliefs would result in disagreements with religious leaders and other church members. Social pressure from the congregation to maintain anti-evolutionary beliefs appears in four out of the five pathways to certain creationism, and having family that believes the same thing about origins is in three out of five. Thus, the combination of a particular set of beliefs, in concert with a unique set of social realities, is much more likely to lead to confident creationism.[92]

NSRHO – Church attendance

As we have seen, the NSRHO findings are more specific and focused than previous surveys. Previously, we heard that "...the single most relevant variable indicating young earth creationism is church attendance; 69 percent of young earth creationists are regular church attenders."[93] Given the findings of the NSRHO, we now realize that this is inaccurate, or even misleading. Much relevant detail is missing.

NSRHO – A plausible alternative

When it comes to defending their anti-evolutionary beliefs, creationists are in an interesting position. They are obligated to provide a plausible alternative to the mainstream position. We have seen that family, friends, and congregations play an important role in making that alternative seem feasible.[94] Social support is especially important for creationists because their beliefs run counter to the scientific establishment. Young earth advocates must generate persuasive alternate arguments in the face of strong scientific evidence. The NSRHO suggests that a two-pronged strategy – one that takes into account both sociological and theological factors – best explains why people hold – and maintain – their beliefs about origins.[95] The NSRHO provides important insights into how people come to change their minds about issues as important as the theory of evolution. It seems that in order to convince people to change their minds, persuasion must move beyond purely intellectual arguments. The NSRHO concludes that "... ideas only persuade when individuals are in a social position that allows them to seriously consider what is before them."[96]

NSRHO – Changing minds

As we have seen, the NSRHO provides credible evidence suggesting that creationists resist changing their minds about evolution primarily because they feel constrained by the possible negative response of family, friends, and congregation. Anti-evolutionist subculture provides a possible account of human origins which is then strongly reinforced by important social relationships.[97] The internet and social media have made it easier for people who hold strong views on issues to live in a bubble of like-minded individuals.[98] In chapter 10, we saw that creationists choose their beliefs from a buffet of opinions provided by the creationist subculture. The NSRHO strongly suggests that those who promote an evolutionary point of view are not likely to be successful in changing minds if they ignore or downplay the social context of an individual's beliefs. Strategies that provide a safe environment for the discussion of these issues may be helpful in allowing Christians to entertain new and challenging ideas.

Barna survey of pastors regarding origins issues

In 2012, the BioLogos Foundation commissioned a survey of pastors on origins.[99] The following is a summary of the report's methodology and findings.

Barna pastors' survey – methodology

The Barna Group conducted 743 telephone interviews with pastors from across the U.S., from churches of varying attendance, and from many different Christian denominations. This comprehensive, in–depth survey provides an important analysis of views held by clergy today. Overall, while a slight majority of the pastors surveyed fall under the label of young earth creationist

(54 percent), sizable portions of clergy accept progressive creation (15 percent) and evolutionary creation (18 percent). Pastors of mainline churches were most likely to accept evolutionary creationism, while non–mainline, charismatic, and Southern Baptist pastors were overwhelmingly young earth. Pastors of larger churches were also more likely to accept evolutionary creation.

Barna pastors' survey – science and faith

Most pastors are of the opinion that science and faith questions are important. Regardless of their views, the majority of pastors surveyed feel that the church needs to reconsider how it handles issues of science. Seventy-two percent of pastors with young earth views and 73 percent of pastors with theistic evolution views agree with the statement that "... the Christian community needs to take a serious look at its understanding of science and human origins in order to maintain its witness in the world." Sixty-six percent of young earth oriented pastors and 61 percent of both theistic evolution and progressive creationist pastors agree that "... younger adults today are more concerned than ever about whether faith and science are compatible." A majority of theistic evolution pastors (63 percent) agreed that "The church's posture toward science prevents many non-Christians from accepting Christianity..." while a majority of young earth and progressive creation-leaning pastors disagreed (59 percent).

Barna pastors' survey – science and scripture

The majority of clergy holding all four viewpoints also agreed with the statement

> *"Just as scripture should influence human interpretation of science, science should also inform our understanding of scripture."*

The numbers were highest for theistic evolution pastors and those who are uncertain (81 percent and 72 percent, respectively), though over half of young earth and progressive creation pastors also agreed (52 percent and 65 percent, respectively). However, they are concerned about evolution for biblical reasons. Over half of pastors said they had "major concerns" about the idea that God used evolution. The main reasons for that concern were that the idea "undermines the authority of scripture" (64 percent), "views portions of the Bible as non-literal, like Genesis" (62 percent), "raises doubts about a historical Adam and Eve" (61 percent), and "raises questions about how and when death and sin entered the world" (59 percent). However, 26 percent of pastors saw no concern with the idea that God used evolution.

Pastors' survey – social context

Clergy are concerned that changing their views on origins might compromise their ministry. Over half of pastors (58 percent) who fell under the young earth category agreed that

> *"If you publicly admitted your own doubts about human origins, you feel you would have a lot to lose in your ministry."*

Forty-one percent of pastors in the progressive creation group also agreed with the statement. Pastors who were uncertain or who fell under the evolutionary creation group were less concerned, with only 26 percent and 17 percent respectively agreeing with the statement.

NOTES

Preface

1. Rehwinkel, A. M., *The Flood: In the Light of the Bible*, Geology, and Archaeology. St. Louis, MO: Concordia Publishing House, 1951.
2. Gould, S. J., *Wonderful Life: The Burgess Shale and the Nature of History*, 1st ed. New York: W.W. Norton, 1989.
3. Pieper, F., *Christian Dogmatics. Volume 1*. St. Louis: Concordia Publishing House, 1950. pp. 163, 473.
4. Walton, J. H., "A Historical Adam: An Archetypal View," *Four Views on the Historical Adam*, M. Barrett and A. B. Caneday, Eds., Grand Rapids, MI: Zondervan, 2016, loc. 2359.

Chapter 1 – Introduction

1. Braaten, L. J., May the Glory of the Lord Endure Forever! Biblical Reflections on Creation Care. *In Perspectives on an Evolving Creation*, Miller, K. B., Ed. Wm. B. Eerdmans: Grand Rapids, MI and Cambridge, U. K., 2003; p. 414.
2. Darwin, C., *The Origin of Species*, (1859). W.W. Norton: New York, 1970.
3. Davis, T., Science and the Bible: "Theistic Evolution. Part 5." October 8, 2012. http://biologos.org/blogs/ted–davis-reading-the-book-of-nature/science-and-the-bible-theistic-evolution-part-5
4. Peters, T., Hewlett, M. J., *Evolution From Creation to New Creation : Conflict, Conversation, and Convergence*. Abingdon Press: Nashville, TN, 2003. p. 29.
5. Giberson, K.; Collins, F. S., *The Language of Science and Faith : Straight Answers to Genuine Questions*. Kindle Edition. SPCK: London, 2011; p. 31.
6. Ruse, M., *The Evolution–Creation Struggle*. Harvard University Press: Cambridge, Mass. ; London, 2005; p. 267.
7. Miller, K. R., *Only a Theory : Evolution and The Battle for America's Soul*. Viking Penguin: New York ; London, 2008. p. 193.
8. Venema, D. R., *Adam and the Genome: Reading Scripture after Genetic Science*. Grand Rapids: Brazos Press, 2017. Foreword.
9. Janssen, L. J., *Standing on the Shoulders of Giants: Genesis and Human Origins*. Eugene, OR: Wipf & Stock, 2016. p. 16.
10. Boyd, G. A., "Pastoral Reflections: Whether or Not There Was a Historical Adam, Our Faith Is Secure," *Four Views on the Historical Adam*, M. Barrett and A. B. Caneday, Eds., Grand Rapids, MI: Zondervan, 2016. loc. 4918.
11. Fugle, G. N., *Laying Down Arms to Heal the Creation – Evolution Divide*. Eugene, OR: Wipf & Stock, 2015. p. 11.
12. Janssen, L. J., *Standing on the Shoulders of Giants*. ibid., p. 2.
13. Janssen, L. J., ibid, p. 211.
14. Ramm, B. L., *The Christian View of Science and Scripture*. 1st ed.; Grand Rapids: 1954; p 26.
15. Peters & Hewlett, *Evolution: From Creation to New Creation. Conflict, Conversation, and Convergence*. Nashville, TN: Abingdon Press, 2003. p. 77.
16. Numbers, R. L., *The Creationists : From Scientific Creationism to Intelligent Design*.

Expanded ed., 1st Harvard University Press pbk. ed.; Harvard University Press: Cambridge, Mass. ; London, 2006; p. 152.
17. Numbers, R. L., *The Creationists*: ibid., p. 26.
18. Ruse, M., *The Evolution – Creation Struggle*, ibid., p. 266.
19. Thomson, K., Introduction – The Religion and Science Debate: Why Does It Continue? In *The Religion and Science Debate: Why Does It Continue?* Kindle Edition, Attridge, H. W., Ed. Yale University Press: New Haven, CT. And London, U. K., 2009; p. 224.
20. Numbers, R. L., *The Creationists*. ibid., p. 153.
21. Giberson, K.; Collins, F. S., *The Language of Science and Faith*, p. 113.
22. Barbour, I. G., *When Science Meets Religion : Enemies, Strangers, Or Partners?* 1st ed.; Harper: San Francisco, 2000; p. 8.
23. Fugle, G. N., *Laying Down Arms to Heal the Creation – Evolution Divide*. Eugene, OR: Wipf & Stock, 2015. p. 225.
24. Berry, R. J., Foreword. In *True Scientists, True Faith: Some of the world's leading scientists reveal the harmony between their science and their faith*. Kindle Edition., Berry, R. J., Ed. Oxford, U.K. and Grand Rapids, MI, 2014; p. 10.
25. Krauss, L. M., Religion Vs. Science? In *The Religion and Science Debate: Why Does It Continue?* Kindle Edition., Attridge, H. W., Ed. Yale University Press: New Haven, CT. and London, U.K., 2009; loc. 1932.
26. Harrison, P. R., Introduction. In *The Cambridge Companion to Science and Religion*. Kindle Edition., Harrison, P. R., Ed. Cambridge University Press: Cambridge, U. K., 2010; p. 24.
27. Peters, T.; Hewlett, M., *Evolution: From Creation to New Creation*, ibid., p. 181.
28. Woods, M., "Prof. Brian Cox Condemns 'Toxic' Rows between Science and Religion." http://www.christiantoday.com/article/professor.brian.cox.condemns.toxic.rows.between.science.and.religion/95038.htm
29. Barrett, M. and A. B. Caneday, "Introduction: Adam, to Be or Not to Be," *Four Views on the Historical Adam*, M. Barrett and A. B. Caneday, Eds., Grand Rapids, MI: Zondervan, 2016, loc. 314.
30. Dowd, M., *Thank God for Evolution!* 1st ed.; Publishers Group UK: San Francisco, 2007; p. 32.
31. Conway Morris, S., Evolution and the Inevitability of Intelligent Life. In *The Cambridge Companion to Science and Religion*, Harrison, P., Ed. Cambridge University Press: Cambridge, UK, 2010; p. 148.
32. Wilkinson, L., Does Methodological Naturalism Lead to Metaphysical Naturalism? In *Darwinism Defeated: The Johnson – Lamoureux Debate on Biological Origins*, Johnson, P. E.; Lamoureux, D. O., Eds. Regent College Publishing: Vancouver, B.C., 1999; p. 167. See also McLeish, T., Faith and Wisdom in Science, Oxford University Press, Oxford, UK., 2014. p. 41, 220.
33. Walton, J. H., *The Lost World Of Genesis One : Ancient Cosmology and the Origins Debate*. Kindle Edition. IVP Academic: Downers Grove, Ill., 2009; loc. 1720.
34. Murphy, G. L., Remembering God's people. In *Perspectives on an Evolving Creation*, Miller, K. B., Ed. Wm. B. Eerdmans: Grand Rapids, 2003; p. 524.
35. Haught, J. F., *God After Darwin : A Theology of Evolution*. Westview Press: Boulder, Colo. ; Oxford, 2000; p. 8.
36. Picard, R., Building Technology with Emotion. In *True Scientists, True Faith: Some of the World's Leading Scientists Reveal the Harmony Between their Science and their*

Faith. Kindle Edition., Berry, R. J., Ed. Monarch Books, Kindle Edition: Oxford, U.K. and Grand Rapids, MI., 2014; p. 320.
37. Gould, S. J., *Wonderful Life : The Burgess Shale and the Nature of History*. 1st ed.; W.W. Norton: New York, 1989; p. 142.
38. Eldredge, N., *Reinventing Darwin : The Great Debate at the High Table of Evolutionary Theory*. Wiley: New York ; Chichester, 1995; p. 7.
39. Walton, J. H., *The Lost World of Genesis One*, ibid., p. 165.
40. Janssen, L. J., *Standing on the Shoulders of Giants: Genesis and Human Origins*. Eugene, OR: Wipf & Stock, 2016. p. 171.
41. Walton, J. H., *The Lost World of Scripture : Ancient Literary Culture and Biblical Authority*. Downers Grove, Illinois: IVP Academic, 2013, p. 51.
42. Ross, H., *A Matter of Days: Resolving a Creation Controversy*. Navpress: Colorado Springs, CO., 2004, p. 221
43. Janssen, L. J., *Standing on the Shoulders of Giants*: ibid, p. 42.
44. Dennett, D. C., *Darwin's Dangerous Idea: Evolution and the Meanings of Life*. New York & London: Simon & Schuster, 1995. p. 377.
45. Janssen, L. J., *Standing on the Shoulders of Giants*: ibid, p. 251.
46. Walton, J. H., *The Lost World of Scripture : Ancient Literary Culture and Biblical* Authority. Downers Grove, Illinois: IVP Academic, 2013, p. 58.
47 Lamoureux, D. O., *I Love Jesus & I Accept Evolution*. Kindle Edition., Eugene, OR: Wipf & Stock, 2009. loc. 955.
48. Janssen, ibid., p. 44.
49 Janssen, ibid., p. 43.
50. Briggs, A., And Information Became Physical. In *True Scientists, True Faith: Some of the World's Leading Scientists Reveal the Harmony Between Their Science and Their Faith*. Kindle Edition., Berry, R. J., Ed. Monarch Books: Grand Rapids, Michigan, 2014; p. 40.
51. Gould, S. J., *Wonderful Life*, ibid., p. 206.
52. Ramm, B., *The Christian View of Science and Scripture*, ibid., p. 8.
53. Collins, F. S., *The Language of God: A Scientist Presents Evidence for Belief*. Free Press: New York & London, 2006; p. 146.
54. Gosler, A., Surprise and the Value of Life. In *True Scientists, True Faith: Some of the World's Leading Scientists Reveal the Harmony Between their Science and their Faith*, Berry, R. J., Ed. Monarch Books: Oxford, U.K. and Grand Rapids, MI, 2014; p. 189.
55. Numbers, *The Creationists*, ibid., p. 210.
56. Gould, S. J., *Dinosaur in a Haystack: Reflections in Natural History*. Harmony: New York, 1995; p. 86.
57. Numbers, R. L., Aggressors, Victims, and Peacemakers – Historical Actors in the Drama of Science and Religion. In *The Religion and Science Debate: Why Does It Continue?* Kindle Edition., Attridge, H. W., Ed. Yale University Press: New Haven & London, 2009; p. 613.
58. Brother Consolmagno was interviewed on *CBC Radio Quirks & Quarks*, March 30, 2013.
59. Van Till, H. J., Is the Universe Capable of Evolving? In *Perspectives on an Evolving Creation*, Miller, K. B., Ed. Wm. B. Eerdmans: Grand Rapids, MI and Cambridge, U.K., 2003; p. 330.
60. Draper, J. W., *History of the Conflict Between Religion and Science*. New York, NY, 1903.

61. White, A. D., *A History Of the Warfare Of Science With Theology In Christendom.* MacMillan And. Co Ltd.: [S.l.], 1896.
62. Gould, S. J., *Wonderful Life*, ibid., p. 44.
63. Gould, S. J., ibid., p. 45.
64. Gould, S. J., ibid., p. 46.
65. Numbers, R. L., in Attridge, ibid., p. 453.
66. Gould, S. J., *Dinosaur in a Haystack*, ibid., p. 47.
67. Gould, S. J., ibid., p. 47.
68. Clark, K. J., "The Science-Religion Crisis at Christian Colleges." http://www.huffingtonpost.com/kelly-james-clark/science-religion-christian-colleges_b_5565641.html
69. Miller, K. R., Darwin, God, And Dover: What the Collapse of "Intelligent Design" Means for Science and Faith in America. In *The Religion and Science Debate: Why Does It Continue?* Kindle Edition., Attridge, H. W., Ed. Yale University Press: New Haven and London, 2009; loc. 1060.
70. Dennett, D. C., *Darwin's Dangerous Idea : Evolution and the Meanings of Life.* Simon & Schuster: New York & London, 1995; p. 82.
71. Ruse, M., *Science and Spirituality : Making Room for Faith in the Age of Science.* Cambridge University Press: Cambridge, 2010; p. 233.
72. Berry, R. J., Foreword, in Berry, R. J., Ed. ibid., p. 11.
73. Wiseman, J. J., Inspired by the Heavens. In *True Scientists, True Faith: Some Of The World's Leading Scientists Reveal The Harmony Between Their Science And Their Faith.* Kindle Edition., Berry, R. J., Ed. Monarch Books: Oxford, U.K. and Grand Rapids, MI, 2014; p. 208.
74. McGrath, A. E., Science, Faith And Making Sense of Things. In Berry, Ed., *True Scientists, True Faith*: ibid., p. 26.
75. Houghton, J., A God Big Enough. In Berry, Ed., *True Scientists, True Faith*: ibid., p. 29.
76. Humphreys, S. C. J., Can Science and Christianity Both be True? In Berry, Ed., *True Scientists, True Faith*: ibid., p. 69.
77. Wiseman, J., Inspired by the Heavens, in Berry, Ed., ibid, p.203.
78. Pennock, R. T., *Tower of Babel : The Evidence Against The New Creationism.* MIT Press: Cambridge, Mass. ; London, 1999; p. 304.
79. Ruse, M., *The Philosophy Of Human Evolution.* Kindle Edition. Cambridge University Press: Cambridge ; New York, 2012; p. 172.
80. Mooney, C., "The Science of Why We Don't Believe In Science." 2011. http://www.motherjones.com/politics/2011/03/denial-science-chris-mooney
81. Polkinghorne, J. C., *Belief in God in an Age of Science.* Yale University Press: New Haven, Conn. ; London, 1998; p. 29.
82. Meyer, S. C., *Darwin's Doubt: The Explosive Origin of Animal Life and the Case for Intelligent Design*, 1st ed. New York, NY: HarperOne, 2013. p. 453.

Chapter 2 – The Scientific Revolution

1. Wikipedia, "Scientist." See also McLeish, T., *Faith and Wisdom in Science*, Oxford University Press, Oxford, UK., 2014. p. 25.
2. Harrison, P. R., Introduction. In *The Cambridge Companion to Science and Religion.* Kindle Edition., Harrison, P. R., Ed. Cambridge University Press: Cambridge, U. K., 2010; p. 34.
3. Dowd, M., *Thank God for Evolution!* . 1st ed.; Publishers Group UK: San Francisco,

2007; p. 108.

4. Barbour, I. G., *When Science Meets Religion : Enemies, Strangers, Or Partners?* 1st ed.; Harper: San Francisco, 2000; p. 23.
5. Miller, K. R., *Finding Darwin's God : A Scientist's Search for Common Ground Between God and Evolution.* Cliff Street Books: New York, 1999; p. 196. See also McLeish, T., Faith and Wisdom in Science, ibid., p. 40.
6. Thomson, K., Introduction – The Religion and Science Debate: Why Does It Continue? In *The Religion and Science Debate: Why Does It Continue?* Kindle Edition, Attridge, H. W., Ed. Yale University Press: New Haven, CT. And London, U. K., 2009; p. 89.
7. McGrath, A. E., *Science And Religion : An Introduction.* Kindle Edition. 2nd ed.; Wiley-Blackwell: Chichester, 2010; loc. 757.
8. Giberson, K.; Artigas, M., *Oracles of Science : Celebrity Scientists Versus God and Religion.* Oxford University Press: Oxford ; New York, 2007; p. 156.
9. Hawking, S., *A Brief History of Time : From the Big Bang to Black Holes.* Bantam Books: Toronto ; New York, 1988; p. 179.
10. Gribbin, J., *The Scientists : A History of Science Told Through the Lives of its Greatest Inventors.* 1st U.S. ed.; Random House: New York, 2003; p. 19.
11. Gould, S. J., *Dinosaur in a Haystack : Reflections in Natural History.* Harmony: New York, 1995; p. 153.
12. Gribbin, J., *Scientists*, ibid., p. 242.
13. Gribbin, J., ibid., p. 451.
14. Gould, S. J., *Bully for Brontosaurus : Reflections in Natural History.* Norton: New York, 1991. p. 143.
15. Conway Morris, S., *The Runes Of Evolution: How The Universe Became Self-Aware.* Templeton Press: West Conshohocken, PA, 2015. p. 232. See also McLeish, T., Faith and Wisdom in Science, Oxford University Press, Oxford, UK., 2014. p. 97.
16. Thomson, K., *Introduction, in Attridge,* H.W. (ed.), The Religion and Science Debate, ibid., p. 89.
17. Eldredge, N., *Reinventing Darwin : The Great Debate at the High Table of Evolutionary Theory.* Wiley: New York ; Chichester, 1995; p. 222. See also McLeish, T., Faith and Wisdom in Science, p. 30.
18. Giberson, K., *Saving Darwin: How To Be A Christian And Believe In Evolution.* Harper One: New York, 2008; p. 214.
19. Pennock, R. T., *Tower of Babel : The Evidence Against The New Creationism.* MIT Press: Cambridge, Mass. ; London, 1999; p. 51
20. Wright, N. T., *Surprised by Scripture: Engaging Contemporary Issues.* New York: HarperOne, 2014; p. 142.
21. Barbour, I. G., *When Science Meets Religion: Enemies, Strangers, or Partners?,* 1st ed. San Francisco: Harper, 2000; p. 19.
22. Peters, T. and M. J. Hewlett, *Evolution from Creation to New Creation: Conflict, Conversation, and Convergence.* Nashville, TN: Abingdon Press, 2003; p. 119.
23. Ramm, B. L., *The Christian View of Science and Scripture,* 1st ed. Grand Rapids, 1954; p. 192.
24. Peters, T. and M. J. Hewlett, *Evolution from Creation to New Creation*: ibid., p. 164.
25. Wilkins, J. S., "God and Evolution 2: The Problem of Creation." http://evolvingthoughts.net/2013/04/god-and-evolution-2-the-problem-of-creation/
26. Mooney, C., "The Science of Why We Don't Believe Science." http://www.mother-

jones.com/politics/2011/03/denial-science-chris-mooney
27. Ecklund, E. H., *Science Vs. Religion : What Scientists Really Think*. Kindle Edition. Oxford University Press: New York ; Oxford, 2010; p. 17.
28. Louis, A., "Miracles & Science, Part 2." BioLogos Foundation. http://biologos.org/blogs/archive/miracles-and-science-part-2
29. Rutherford, A., "Why Scientific Truth May Hurt." The Guardian, April 5, 2005. https://www.theguardian.com/science/2015/apr/05/scientific-truth-genetics-darwin-adam-rutherford
30. Gould, S. J., *The Lying Stones of Marrakesh : Penultimate Reflections in Natural History*. Harmony Books: New York, 2000; p. 56.
31. Dawkins, R., *The Greatest Show On Earth : The Evidence For Evolution*. iBook Edition. Black Swan: London, 2009; p. 805.
32. Haidt, J., *The Righteous Mind : Why Good People Are Divided By Politics And Religion*. Kindle Edition. Allen Lane: London, 2012; p. 138.
33. Pennock, R. T., *Tower of Babel*, ibid., p. 354.
34. Plantinga, A., Science and Religion: Why Does the Debate Continue? In *The Religion and Science Debate*: Attridge, H. W., Ed. ibid., loc. 1264.
35. Berra, T. M., Evolution and the Myth of Creationism : A Basic Guide to the Facts In the *Evolution Debate*. Stanford University Press: Stanford, Calif., 1990; p. 3.
36. Personal correspondence.
37. Ferguson, K., *Stephen Hawking : Quest for a Theory of Everything*. Bantam: 1992; p. 17.
38. Dennett, D., *Darwin's Dangerous Idea*, ibid., p. 380.
39. Polkinghorne, J. C., *Belief in God in an Age of Science*. Yale University Press: New Haven, Conn. ; London, 1998; p. 17.
40. Pennock, R. T., *Tower of Babel*, ibid., p. 353.
41. Gould, S. J., *Rocks of Ages : Science and Religion in the Fullness of Life*. Ballantine Books: New York, 1999. p. 16.
42. Suzanne Massie, a writer in Russia, met with President Ronald Reagan many times between 1984 and 1987. She taught him the Russian proverb, "Trust, but verify," advising him that "The Russians like to talk in proverbs. It would be nice of you to know a few." The proverb was adopted as a signature phrase by Reagan, who subsequently used it frequently when discussing U.S. relations with the Soviet Union. Wikipedia. https://en.wikipedia.org/wiki/Trust,_but_verify
43. McGrath, A. E., "Big Picture or Big Gaps? Why Natural Theology Is Better Than Intelligent Design," BioLogos Foundation, 2014. http://biologos.org/blogs/archive/big-picture-or-big-gaps-why-natural-theology-is-better-than-intelligent-design
44. Wright, N. T., *Surprised by Scripture: Engaging Contemporary Issues*. New York: HarperOne, 2014; p. 137.
45. Polkinghorne, J. C., *Belief in God*, ibid., p. 76.
46. Ruse, M., *Defining Darwin : Essays on the History and Philosophy of Evolutionary Biology*. Kindle Edition. Prometheus ; Lancaster : Gazelle [distributor]: Amherst, N.Y., 2009; loc. 926.
47. Giberson, K., *Saving Darwin*, ibid., p. 159.
48. Barbour, I., *When Science Meets Religion*, ibid., p. 70.
49. Harrison, P. R., Introduction, in Harrison, P. R., Ed., *The Cambridge Companion*, ibid., p. 12.
50. Barbour, I., *When Science Meets Religion*, ibid., p. 72.

51. University of Regina physicist Garth Huber says: According to the scientific method, facts are individual measurements made preferably in controlled or repeatable conditions. Scientific laws summarize those facts. And those laws must have predictive power. Science then moves from laws to theories with much larger domains of prediction. Science can only make statements on things which can be measured. Science cannot make any statements about the supernatural or the existence of God until such time as the facts backing up those statements can be measured in a controlled manner. It is important to note that this does not negate the existence of such things; it simply says that science cannot make any statements about them at the present time. It is not possible at present to measure supernatural phenomena and, in addition, supernatural explanations lack predictive power. Science is poorly equipped to answer "why" questions. It is best equipped to make statements along the lines of "if event 'a' happens, then event 'b' will follow." Personal correspondence. The software illustration was received through personal correspondence with Luke Janssen.
52. Gould, S. J., *Eight Little Piggies : Reflections in Natural History*. Norton: 1993; p. 174. See also McLeish, T., *Faith and Wisdom in Science*, Oxford University Press, Oxford, UK., 2014. p. 19.
53. Slack, G., *The Battle over the Meaning of Everything : Evolution, Intelligent Design, and a School Board in Dover, PA*. Jossey-Bass ; Chichester : John Wiley: San Francisco, Calif., 2007. p. 213.
54. Funes, J. G. (S. J.), "Religion, Science and Society." https://thoughteconomics.com/religion-science-and-society/
55. Personal correspondence.
56. Harrison, P. R., Introduction, in Harrison, P. R., Ed., *The Cambridge Companion*, ibid., p. 12.
57. Ruse, M., *The Evolution-Creation Struggle*. Harvard University Press: Cambridge, Mass. ; London, 2005; p. 17.
58. Johnson, P. E., Response to Denis O. Lamoureux. In *Darwinism Defeated? The Johnson - Lamoureux Debate on Biological Origins*, Johnson, P. E.; Lamoureux, D. O., Eds. Regent College Publishing: Vancouver, B.C., 1999; p. 50.
59. Ruse, M., *The Evolution - Creation Struggle*, ibid., p. 283.
60. Slack, G., *The Battle Over the Meaning of Everything*, ibid., p. 120.
61. Miller, K. R., *Only a Theory: Evolution and The Battle for America's Soul*. Viking Penguin: New York ; London, 2008. p. 185.
62. Ecklund, E. H., *Science vs. Religion*, ibid., p. 24.
63. Slack, G., *The Battle Over the Meaning of Everything*, ibid., p. 99.
64. Medawar, P. B., *The Limits of Science*. Oxford University Press, 1985: Oxford, 1984.
65. Berry, R. J., Foreword. In *True Scientists, True Faith: Some Of The World's Leading Scientists Reveal The Harmony Between Their Science And Their Faith*. Kindle Edition., Berry, R. J., Ed. Oxford, U.K. and Grand Rapids, MI, 2014, p. 9.
66. Krauss, L. M., Religion Vs. Science? In *The Religion and Science Debate*: ibid., Attridge, H. W., Ed. loc. 1686.
67. Miller, K. R., Darwin, God, and Dover: What the Collapse of "Intelligent Design" Means for Science and Faith in America. In *The Religion and Science Debate*: ibid., Attridge, H. W., Ed., loc. 1197.
68. Miller, K. B., Design and Purpose within an Evolving Creation. In *Darwinism Defeated?* Johnson, P. E.; Lamoureux, D. O., Eds. ibid., p. 112.

69. Peters, T.; Hewlett, M. J., *Theological and Scientific Commentary on Darwin's Origin of Species*. Abingdon Press: Nashville, 2008; p. 54.
70. Lamoureux, D. O., *I Love Jesus & I Accept Evolution*. Kindle Edition. Wipf and Stock Publishers: Eugene, OR, 2009; p. 160.
71. Peters, T.; Hewlett, M. J., *Evolution: From Creation to New Creation*, ibid., p. 109.
72. Giberson, K., *Saving Darwin*, ibid., p. 210.
73. Giberson, K.; Artigas, M., *Oracles of Science*, ibid., p. 36.
74. Scott, E. C., *Evolution vs. Creationism : An Introduction*. University of California Press: Berkeley, Calif. ; London, 2005; p. 74.
75. Gould, S. J., *Wonderful Life: The Burgess Shale and the Nature of History*. 1st ed.; W.W. Norton: New York, 1989; p. 292.
76. Roughgarden, J., *Evolution and Christian Faith : Reflections of an Evolutionary Biologist*. Island Press: Washington, D.C. ; London, 2006; p. 52.
77. Young, M.; Strode, P. K., *Why Evolution Works (And Creationism Fails)*. Kindle Edition. Rutgers University Press: New Brunswick, N.J. ; London, 2009; p. 13.
78. Pennock, R. T., *Tower of Babel*, ibid., p. 335.
79. Ruse, M., *Can a Darwinian be a Christian? : The Relationship Between Science and Religion*. Cambridge University Press: New York, 2000; p. 112.
80. Roughgarden, J., *Evolution and Christian Faith*, ibid., p. 57.
81. McGrath, A. E., Augustine's Origin of Species: How the Great Theologian Might Weigh in on the Darwin Debate. In *The Origins Debate: Evangelical Perspectives on Creation, Evolution, and Intelligent Design*, The Editors of Christianity Today, Eds. Christianity Today: Carol Stream, IL, 2012; loc. 569.
82. Giberson, K.; Artigas, M., *Oracles of Science*, ibid., p. 10.
83. Pennock, R. T., *Tower of Babel*, ibid., p. 282.
84. Wiseman, J. J., "Why Should Christians Care About Science?" https://www.bigquestionsonline.com/2013/09/24/why-should-christians-care-about-science/
85. Louis, A., Miracles and Science, Part II. ibid., BioLogos Foundation. http://biologos.org/blogs/archive/miracles-and-science-part-2
86. McGrath, A. E., Science, Faith and Making Sense of Things. In *True Scientists, True Faith: Some of the World's Leading Scientists Reveal the Harmony between Their Science and Their Faith*. Kindle Edition., Berry, R. J., Ed. Monarch Books: Oxford, U.K. and Grand Rapids, MI, 2014; p. 16.
87. Woods, M., Prof. Brian Cox Condemns 'Toxic' Rows between Science and Religion. http://www.christiantoday.com/article/professor.brian.cox.condemns.toxic.rows.between.science.and.religion/95038.htm
88. Gould, S. J., *Bully for Brontosaurus*, ibid., p. 317.
89. Numbers, R. L., Aggressors, Victims, and Peacemakers – Historical Actors in the Drama of Science and Religion. In *The Religion and Science Debate: Why Does It Continue?* Kindle Edition., Attridge, H. W., Ed. Yale University Press: New Haven & London, 2009; p. 597.
90. Godfrey, S. J.; Smith, C. R., *Paradigms on Pilgrimage: Creationism, Paleontology, and Biblical Interpretation*. Clements Pub.: Toronto, Ont., 2005; p. 131.
91. Miller, K., *Finding Darwin's God*, ibid., p. 55.
92. A comment from Deborah Haarsma, referring to a statement made by John Polkinghorne. Haarsma was being interviewed by Vikas Shah. "Religion, Science and Society." 2016.

https://thoughteconomics.com/religion-science-and-society/
93. McGrath, A. E., "A Meaningful Conversation." Huffington Post. http://www.huffingtonpost.com/thought-matters/a-meaningful-conversation_b_8638386.html
94. Gould, S. J., *Bully*, ibid., p. 278.
95. Haught, J. F., Science, God and Cosmic Purpose. In *The Cambridge Companion*. Harrison, P., Ed. ibid., p. 263.
96. McGrath, A. E., *Science and Religion*, ibid., p. 294.
97. Walton, J. H., *The Lost World Of Genesis One : Ancient Cosmology and the Origins Debate*. Kindle Edition. IVP Academic: Downers Grove, Ill., 2009; loc. 2266.
98. Burnett, T., "What is Scientism?" BioLogos Foundation. http://biologos.org/blogs/archive/what-is-scientism
99. Ross, H., *A Matter of Days*, ibid., p. 35.
100. Funes, J.G. (S.J.), interviewed by Vikas Shah. One Dimensional View of Reality. ibid. Fr. Funes is the former Director of the Vatican Observatory. https://thoughtecomonics.com/religion-science-and-society
101. Primack, J., Transcendental Theory. In Richardson, W. M.; Slack, G., Eds. *Faith in Science: Scientists Search for Truth*, ibid., p. 159.
102. Miller, K., *Finding Darwin's God*, ibid., p. 311.
103. Ayala, F., Parallel Evolution. In Richardson, W. M.; Slack, G., Eds. *Faith in Science: Scientists Search for Truth*, ibid., p. 7.

Chapter 3 – The Cosmological Revolution

1. Godfrey, S. J.; Smith, C. R., *Paradigms on Pilgrimage: Creationism, Paleontology, and Biblical Interpretation*. Clements Pub.: Toronto, Ont., 2005; p. 14.
2. Godfrey, S. J.; Smith, C. R., ibid., p. 137.
3. Walton, J. H., *The Lost World Of Genesis One: Ancient Cosmology and the Origins Debate*. Kindle Edition. IVP Academic: Downers Grove, Ill., 2009; loc. 168.
4. Lamoureux, D. O., *Evolutionary Creation: A Christian Approach to Evolution*. Lutterworth Press: Cambridge, England, 2008; p. 162.
5. Buchanan, S., "Was the Expanse Overhead in Genesis 1 a Solid Dome?" https://letterstocreationists.wordpress.com/2012/09/03/was-the-expanse-overhead-in-genesis-1-a-solid-dome/
6. McGrath, A. E., *Science And Religion : An Introduction*. Kindle Edition. 2nd ed.; Wiley-Blackwell: Chichester, 2010. loc. 2012.
7. Janssen, L. J., *Standing on the Shoulders of Giants: Genesis and Human Origins*. Eugene, OR: Wipf & Stock, 2016; p. 26.
8. Walton, J. H., *The Lost World*, ibid., loc. 1600.
9. Ramm, B. L., *The Christian View of Science and Scripture*. 1st ed.; Grand Rapids: 1954; p. 51.
10. Godfrey, S. J.; Smith, C. R., *Paradigms*, ibid., p. 196
11. Gribbin, J., *The Scientists : A History of Science Told Through the Lives of its Greatest Inventors*. 1st U.S. ed.; Random House: New York, 2003; p. 41.
12. Godfrey, S. J.; Smith, C. R., *Paradigms*, 2005, p. 135.
13. Gould, S. J., *Dinosaur in a Haystack : Reflections in Natural History*. Harmony: New York, 1995; p. 153.
14. Mayr, E., *What Evolution Is*. Basic Books: New York, 2001. p.4.
15. Oxford Dictionary, "phenomenon." https://en.oxforddictionaries.com/definition/us/

phenomenon
16. Falk, D. R., *Coming To Peace With Science: Bridging The Worlds Between Faith And Biology*. InterVarsity Press: Downers Grove, IL, 2004. p. 296.
17. Haarsma, D., "Seeing God in Everyday Work, Part II." http://biologos.org/blogs/deborah-haarsma-the-presidents-notebook/seeing-god-in-everyday-work-part-2
18. Lamoureux, D. O., *Evolutionary Creation*, ibid., p. 138.
19. Scott, E. C., *Evolution vs. Creationism : An Introduction*. University of California Press: Berkeley, Calif. ; London, 2005; p. 49.
20. Dawkins, R., *The Greatest Show On Earth : The Evidence For Evolution*. iBook Edition. Black Swan: London, 2009. loc. 1058.
21. Collins, F. S., *The Language of God: A Scientist Presents Evidence for Belief*. Free Press: New York & London, 2006; p. 83.
22. Lamoureux, D. O., "The Ancient Science in the Bible." BioLogos Foundation. http://biologos.org/blogs/archive/the-ancient-science-in-the-bible
23. Buchanan, S., Was the Expanse Overhead in Genesis 1 a Solid Dome? ibid. https://letterstocreationists.wordpress.com/2012/09/03/was-the-expanse-overhead-in-genesis-1-a-solid-dome/
24. Gould, S. J., I Have Landed : *The End of a Beginning in Natural History*. 1st ed.; Harmony Books: New York, 2002. p. 272.
25. Scott, E., *Evolution vs. Creationism*, ibid.; p. 58.
26. Godfrey, S. J.; Smith, C. R., *Paradigms*, ibid., p. 190.
27. Scott, E., *Evolution vs. Creationism*, ibid., p. 59.
28. Lamoureux, D. O., *Evolutionary Creation*, ibid., p. 128.
29. Scott, E., *Evolution vs. Creationism*, ibid., p. 59.
30. Walton, J., *The Lost World*, ibid., loc. 937.
31. Walton, J., ibid.
32. Lamoureux, D. O., The Ancient Science in the Bible, ibid. BioLogos Foundation. http://biologos.org/blogs/archive/the-ancient-science-in-the-bible
33. Godfrey, S. J.; Smith, C. R., *Paradigms*, ibid., p. 184.
34. Godfrey, S. J.; Smith, C. R., ibid., p. 182.
35. Luther, M., *Luther's Works. Vol. 1. Lectures on Genesis*, Jaroslav Pelikan, Ed., Concordia Publishing House, St. Louis, Missouri, 1958, pp. 30, 42, 43.
36. Ramm, B., *The Christian View*, ibid., p. 86.
37. Lamoureux, D. O., *I Love Jesus & I Accept Evolution*. Kindle Edition. Wipf and Stock Publishers: Eugene, OR, 2009. loc. 1543.
38. Walton, J., *The Lost World*, ibid., loc. 984.
39. Numbers, R. L., *The Creationists : From Scientific Creationism to Intelligent Design*. Expanded ed., 1st Harvard University Press pbk. ed.; Harvard University Press: Cambridge, Mass. ; London, 2006; p. 37.
40. "The Start of Scientific Cosmology." From The Center for History of Physics website. A division of the American Institute of Physics. https://www.aip.org/history/exhibits/cosmology/ideas/start-of-scientific-cosmology.htm
41. Gribbin, J., ibid., p. 46.
42. Giberson, K., *Saving Darwin: How To Be A Christian And Believe In Evolution*. Harper One: New York, 2008. p. 25.
43. Gribbin, J., ibid., p. 45.
44. Giberson, K., *Seven Glorious Days : A Scientist Retells The Genesis Creation Story*.

Kindle Edition. Paraclete Press: Brewster, Mass., 2012; p. 64.
45. Giberson, K.; Artigas, M., *Oracles of Science : Celebrity Scientists Versus God and Religion*. Oxford University Press: Oxford ; New York, 2007; p. 156.
46. Lamoureux, D. O., *Evolutionary Creation*, ibid., p. 112.
47. Hawking, S., *A Brief History of Time : From the Big Bang to Black Holes*. Bantam Books: Toronto ; New York, 1988; p. 3.
48. Gribbin, J., ibid., p. 17.
49. Hawking, S., ibid., p. 4.
50. Gribbin, J., ibid., p. 81.
51. Hawking, S., ibid., p. 4.
52. Lamoureux, D. O., *Evolutionary Creation*, ibid., p. 125.
53. Gribbin, J., ibid., p. 13.
54. This quote, attributed to Luther, was recounted by Anthony Lauterbach, who was a dinner guest in the Luther household in 1539. Known in Lutheran circles as Luther's "table talk" conversations. https://buythetruth.wordpress.com/2011/05/25/copernicus-and-the-lutherans/
Also quoted by Vanderbilt University College of Arts and Science. Department of Physics and Astronomy. Course notes for students. http://www.vanderbilt.edu/AnS/physics/astrocourses/ast203/Copernicus.htm
55. Vanderbilt University course notes. ibid.
56. Collins, F., *The Language of God*, ibid., p. 154.
57. Janssen, L. J., *Standing on the Shoulders of Giants: Genesis and Human Origins*. Eugene, OR: Wipf & Stock, 2016; p. 30.
58. Pieper, F., *Christian Dogmatics*. 3 Vols.,. Theodore Engelder, Trans., St. Louis: Concordia Publishing House, 1950.
59. Fugle, G. N., *Laying Down Arms to Heal the Creation - Evolution Divide*. Eugene, OR: Wipf & Stock, 2015; p. 227.
60. Fugle, G. N., ibid., p. 58.
61. Venema, D. R., *Adam and the Genome: Reading Scripture after Genetic Science*. Grand Rapids: Brazos Press, 2017, p. 94.
62. Janssen, L. J., *Standing on the Shoulders of Giants*. ibid., p. 34.
63. Janssen, L. J., ibid., p. 35.
64. Janssen, L. J., ibid.
65. Gould, S. J., *Lying Stones*, ibid., p. 35.
66. Gould, S. J., *Hedgehog*, ibid., p. 88.
67. Roughgarden, J., *Evolution and Christian Faith : Reflections of an Evolutionary Biologist*. Island Press: Washington, D.C. ; London, 2006. p. 54.
68. Pennock, R. T., *Tower of Babel*, ibid., p. 155.
69. Giberson, K., *Seven Glorious Days*, ibid., p. 82.
70. Wilkinson, L., Does Methodological Naturalism Lead to Metaphysical Naturalism? In *Darwinism Defeated: The Johnson - Lamoureux Debate on Biological Origins*, Johnson, P. E.; Lamoureux, D. O., Eds. Regent College Publishing: Vancouver, B.C., 1999; p. 167.
71. Gribbin, J., *Scientists*, ibid., p. 52.
72. Davis, E., The Word and the Works: Concordism and American Evangelicals. In Miller, Keith B., (ed). *Perspectives on an Evolving Creation*, Wm. B. Eerdmans: Grand Rapids, MI and Cambridge, U.K., 2003; p. 37.

73. Davis, E., *The Word and the Works*: ibid., p. 36.
74. Giberson, K., *Seven Glorious Days*, ibid., p. 20.
75. Giberson, K.; Artigas, M., *Oracles of Science*, ibid., p. 101.
76. Haarsma, D.; Wiseman, J. J., *An Evolving Cosmos. In Perspectives on an Evolving Creation*, Miller, Keith B., (ed.) Eerdmans: Grand Rapids, MI and Cambridge, UK, 2003; p. 108.
77. Haarsma, D.; Wiseman, J., ibid., p. 107.
78. Barbour, I. G., *When Science Meets Religion : Enemies, Strangers, Or Partners?* 1st ed.; Harper: San Francisco, 2000; p. 62.
79. Van Till, H. J., What Good is Stardust? The Remarkably Equipped Universe. In *The Origins Debate: Evangelical Perspectives*, From the Editors of Christianity Today. ibid., loc. 986.
80. Giberson, *Seven Glorious Days*, ibid., p. 75.
81. MacKay, D. M., Science and Christian Faith Today. In *True Scientists, True Faith: Some of the World's Leading Scientists Reveal the Harmony between Their Science and Their Faith*. Kindle Edition., Berry, R. J., Ed. Monarch Books: Oxford, U.K. and Grand Rapids, MI, 2014; p. 328.
82. Haarsma, D.; Wiseman, J., *An Evolving Cosmos*, in Keith B. Miller, Perspectives on an Evolving Creation, 2003, ibid., p. 102.
83. PBS special, Australia: First Four Billion Years. http://www.pbs.org/wgbh/nova/earth/australia-first-years.html
84. Falk, D., *Coming to Peace with Science*, ibid., loc. 832.

Chapter 4 – The Geological Revolution

1. Ramm, B. L., *The Christian View of Science and Scripture*. 1st ed.; Grand Rapids: 1954; p. 121.
2. Eldredge, N., Darwin : *Discovering the Tree of Life*. 1st ed.; W.W. Norton & Co.: New York ; London, 2005; p. 217.
3. Toal, C., "How Science and Faith Grew Up Together." The Guardian. April 24, 2009. https://www.theguardian.com/commentisfree/belief/2009/apr/24/religion-science-creationism-reiss
4. Larson, E. J., *Evolution : The Remarkable History of a Scientific Theory*. Kindle Edition. Modern Library: New York, 2004; loc. 454.
5. Numbers, R. L., Aggressors, Victims, and Peacemakers – Historical Actors in the Drama of Science and Religion. In *The Religion and Science Debate: Why Does It Continue?* Kindle Edition., Attridge, H. W., Ed. Yale University Press: New Haven & London, 2009; loc. 335.
6. Larson, E. J., *Remarkable* History, ibid., loc. 484.
7. Wikipedia, Stratigraphy.
8. Larson, E. J., *Remarkable History*, ibid., loc. 715.
9. Wikipedia, Uniformitarianism.
10. Ramm, B., *The Christian View*, ibid., p. 135.
11. Pennock, R. T., *Tower of Babel: The Evidence Against The New Creationism*. MIT Press: Cambridge, Mass. ; London, 1999; p. 19.
12. Numbers, R., Aggressors, Victims, and Peacemakers. In Attridge, (ed.), *The Religion and Science Debate*: ibid., loc. 320.
13. Wikipedia, Old Earth Creationism.

14. Numbers, R. L., *The Creationists: From Scientific Creationism to Intelligent Design*. Expanded ed., 1st Harvard University Press pbk. ed.; Harvard University Press: Cambridge, Mass. ; London, 2006; p. 16.
15. McGrath, A. E., *Science And Religion : An Introduction*. Kindle Edition. 2nd ed.; Wiley-Blackwell: Chichester, 2010. loc. 1076.
16. This statement, however, does not match research findings reported in the Appendix (NSRHO, p.9) which determined that the number of old earth creationists in the U.S. is around 1 percent of the population. More study on this issue is required.
17. Kitcher, P., *Abusing Science : The Case Against Creationism*. MIT Press: Cambridge, Mass. ; London, 1982; p. 63.
18. Eldredge, N., *Darwin: Discovering the Tree of Life*, ibid., p. 20.
19. Ruse, M., *The Evolution-Creation Struggle*. Harvard University Press: Cambridge, Mass. ; London, 2005; p. 68.
20. Gould, S. J., *Eight Little Piggies : Reflections in Natural History*. Norton: 1993; p. 25.
21. Conway Morris, S., *The Crucible of Creation : The Burgess Shale and the Rise of Animals*. Oxford University Press: Oxford, 1998; p. 204.
22. Larson, E. J., *Remarkable History*, ibid., loc. 919.
23. Ruse, M., *The Philosophy Of Human Evolution*. Kindle Edition. Cambridge University Press: Cambridge ; New York, 2012; p. 31.
24. Ricciardi, M., "Australian Expedition Discovers 'Lost World'" http://planetsave.com/2013/10/28/australian-expedition-discovers-lost-world-three-never-seen-vertebrates-found-photos/
25. Gould, S. J., *The Lying Stones of Marrakesh : Penultimate Reflections in Natural History*. Harmony Books: New York, 2000; p. 20.
26. Miller, K. R., *Finding Darwin's God : A Scientist's Search for Common Ground Between God and Evolution*. Cliff Street Books: New York, 1999; p. 32.
27. Pennock, R. T., *Tower of Babel*, ibid., p. 72.
28. Kitcher, P., *Abusing Science : The Case Against Creationism*. MIT Press: Cambridge, MA, 1982; p. 127
29. Gribbin, J., *The Scientists : A History of Science Told Through the Lives of its Greatest Inventors*. 1st U.S. ed.; Random House: New York, 2003; p. 155.
30. Wikipedia, Paleontology.
31. Ruse, M., *Philosophy of Human Evolution*, ibid., p. 41.
32. Larson, E. J., *Remarkable History*, ibid., loc. 230.
33. Ross, H., *A Matter of Days: Resolving a Creation Controversy*. Navpress: Colorado Springs, CO, 2004; p. 21.
34. Ross, H., ibid.
35. Gribbin, J., *Scientists*, ibid., p. 226.
36. Gould, S. J., *Lying Stones*, ibid., p. 154.
37. Giberson, K.; Collins, F. S., *The Language of Science and Faith : Straight Answers to Genuine Questions*. Kindle Edition. SPCK: London, 2011; p. 76.
38. Grossman, C. L., "Associated Press Survey on Faith and Science Reveals that Science is Often Trumped by Religious Belief." Huffington Post, May 1, 2014. http://www.huffingtonpost.com/2014/05/01/ap-survey-faith-science_n_5249154.html
39. Gosse, P. H., : *An Attempt to Untie the Geological Knot*. ... With fifty-six illustrations on wood. London: 1857.
40. Wikipedia, Age of the Earth.

41. Ross, H., *A Matter of Days*, ibid., p. 25.
42. Ross, H., ibid., p. 86.
43. Haarsma, D.; Wiseman, J. J., An Evolving Cosmos. In *Perspectives on an Evolving Creation*, Miller, K. B., Ed. Eerdmans: Grand Rapids, MI and Cambridge, UK, 2003; p. 97.
44. Penzias, A., The Elegant Universe. In *Faith in Science: Scientists Search for Truth*, Richardson, W. M.; Slack, G., Eds. Routledge: London and New York, 2001; p. 31.
45. Peters, T.; Hewlett, M. J., *Evolution: From Creation to New Creation : Conflict, Conversation, and Convergence*. Abingdon Press: Nashville, TN, 2003; p. 91.
46. Collins, F. S., "There Is An Uneasiness About Evolution." Huffington Post, January 25, 2014. http://www.huffingtonpost.com/2014/01/25/francis-collins-davos_n_4635338.html
47. Peter Enns offers the following critique of the apparent-age hypothesis. Enns discusses this issue several times on his blog in October 2011 and April 2017. "The apparent-age hypothesis accepts scientific observation but rejects the scientific interpretation. It is committed to biblical literalism. Science studies only what God appears to have done, leaving scientists free to do their work. Scripture, it is argued, tells us what God actually did. The apparent-age hypothesis manipulates facts to fit the theory, assuming that one particular interpretation is not to be questioned. Scientific counter-evidence is either stretched to fit the theory or ignored altogether. The apparent-age hypothesis is a clear example of ideological self-preservation. Abundant evidence (e.g., fossils, geological records, human genome) points to billions of years of evolution. Some advocates of the apparent-age thesis claim that God created with an "apparent evolutionary process" as well. But why would God provide all this evidence and then not want us to draw appropriate conclusions? The apparent-age view arbitrarily chooses which portions of scripture are to be read "plainly" and which are not. The bottom line? The 'apparent age' hypothesis creates many more problems that it solves. https://www.peteenns.com/god-did-not-create-the-cosmos-with-apparent-age-3-reasons/
48. Gould, S. J., *Lying Stones*, ibid., p. 154.
49. Eldredge, N., *Discovering*, ibid., p. 85.
50. Ramm, B., *The Christian View*, ibid., p. 124.
51. Larson, E., *Remarkable History*, ibid., loc. 467.
52. Isaak, M., *The Counter-Creationism Handbook*. Greenwood ; Oxford : Harcourt Education : Westport, Conn., 2005; p. 128.
53. Godfrey, S. J.; Smith, C. R., *Paradigms on Pilgrimage : Creationism, Paleontology, and Biblical Interpretation*. Clements Pub.: Toronto, Ont., 2005; p. 39.
54. Godfrey, S. J.; Smith, C. R., *Paradigms*, ibid., p. 61.
55. Personal correspondence.
56. Personal correspondence.
57. Greenberg, J., Geological Framework of an Evolving Creation. In *Perspectives on an Evolving Creation*, Miller, K. B., Ed. Wm. B. Eerdmans: Grand Rapids, MI and Cambridge, U.K., 2003; p. 142.
58. Wikipedia, Radiometric dating.
59. Numbers, R. L., *The Creationists*, ibid., p. 185.
60. Haarsma, L., Does Science Exclude God? Natural Law, Chance, Miracles, And Scientific Practice. In *Perspectives on an Evolving Creation*, ibid, p. 88.
61. Giberson, K.; Collins, F. S., *The Language of Science and Faith*, ibid., p. 67.
62. Greenberg, J., Geological Framework of An Evolving Creation, in Miller, K. B., (ed.),

Perspectives on an Evolving Creation, ibid., p. 142. A very good non-technical summary of radiometric dating is found in Kitcher Living with Darwin, (2007) p. 39.

63. Brain, M., "How Carbon-14 Dating Works." http://science.howstuffworks.com/environmental/earth/geology/carbon-14.htm
64. Isaak, M., *Counter-Creationism Handbook*, ibid., p. 202.
65. Giberson, K.; Collins, F. S., *Language of Science and Faith*, ibid., p. 61.
66. See this article on the Natural Historian website. "A 60,000 Year Varve Record from Japan Refutes the Young-Earth Interpretation of Earth's History." https://thenaturalhistorian.com/2016/08/16/a-60000-year-varve-record-from-japan-refutes-the-young-earth-interpretation-of-earths-history
67. Ogburn, S. P., "Scientists Close in on Planet's Oldest Ice." Scientific American. https://www.scientificamerican.com/article/scientists-close-in-on-planets-oldest-ice/
68. Voosen, P., Record Shattering 2.7 million-year-old ice core reveals start of the ice ages. AAAS website, August 15, 2017. Science Magazine August 2017. http://www.sciencemag.org/news/2017/08/record-shattering-27-million-year-old-ice-core-reveals-start-ice-ages
69. Eric Weisstein, "Alfred Wegener Biographical Note." http://pangaea.org/wegener.htm
70. Kitcher, P., *Abusing Science*, ibid., p. 170.
71. Gould, S. J., *Wonderful Life : The Burgess Shale and the Nature of History*. 1st ed.; W.W. Norton: New York, 1989; p. 282.
72. Falk, D. R., *Coming To Peace With Science: Bridging The Worlds Between Faith And Biology*. InterVarsity Press: Downers Grove, IL, 2004; p. 152.
73. Gould, S. J., *Wonderful Life*, ibid., p. 282.
74. Gould, S. J., *Dinosaur in a Haystack : Reflections in Natural History*. Harmony: New York, 1995; p. 107.
75. Giberson, K.; Artigas, M., *Oracles of Science : Celebrity Scientists Vs. God and Religion*. Oxford University Press: Oxford ; New York, 2007; p. 218.

Chapter 5 - The Biological Revolution

1. Neve, M.; Messenger, S., *Charles Darwin: Autobiographies*. Penguin Classics: London, 2002. p. 15.
2. Neve, M.; Messenger, S., ibid., p. 34.
3. Neve, M.; Messenger, S., ibid., p. 35.
4. Neve, M.; Messenger, S., ibid.
5. Young, M.; Strode, P. K., *Why Evolution Works (And Creationism Fails)*. Kindle Edition. Rutgers University Press: New Brunswick, N.J. ; London, 2009. p. 81.
6. Neve, M.; Messenger, S., ibid., p. 35
7. Larson, E. J., *Evolution : The Remarkable History of a Scientific Theory*. Kindle Edition. Modern Library: New York, 2004. loc. 845.
8. Peters, T.; Hewlett, M. J., *Evolution From Creation to New Creation : Conflict, Conversation, and Convergence*. Abingdon Press: Nashville, TN, 2003. p. 41.
9. Larson, E.J., ibid., loc. 895.
10. Peters, T.; Hewlett, M., *Evolution: From Creation to New Creation*. p. 41.
11. Mayr, E., *What Evolution Is*. Basic Books: New York, 2001. p. 9.
12. Neve, M.; Messenger, S., ibid., p. 85.
13. Gould, S. J., *Ever Since Darwin : Reflections in Natural History*. 1st ed.; Norton: New York, 1977. p. 32.

14. Neve, M., Messenger, S.. *Darwin: Autobiographies*. Introduction, ibid., xvii
15. Neve, M.; Messenger, S., ibid., p. 49.
16. Gould, S. J., *Bully for Brontosaurus : Reflections in Natural History*. Norton: New York, 1991. p. 25.
17. Pennock, R. T., *Tower of Babel : The Evidence Against The New Creationism*. MIT Press: Cambridge, Mass. ; London, 1999; p. 62.
18. Ruse, M., *The Evolution-Creation Struggle*. Harvard University Press: Cambridge, Mass. ; London, 2005; p. 32.
19. Ramm, B. L., *The Christian View of Science and Scripture*. 1st ed.; Grand Rapids: 1954; p. 79.
20. Ruse, M., *Evolution-Creation Struggle*, ibid., p. 48.
21. Gould, S. J., *Leonardo's Mountain of Clams and The Diet of Worms : Essays on Natural History*. Harmony Books ; London : Random House: New York, 1998. p. 31.
22. Eldredge, N., *Discovering the Tree of Life*, ibid., p. 45. Additional comments on Wallace from Darrel Falk. Personal communication.
23. Larson, E.J., *Remarkable History*, ibid., loc. 1085.
24. Larson, E.J., ibid., loc. 1554.
25. Ruse, M., *The Philosophy of Human Evolution*. Kindle Edition. Cambridge University Press: Cambridge ; New York, 2012; p. 192.
26. Ruse, M., *Defining Darwin : Essays on the History and Philosophy of Evolutionary Biology*. Kindle Edition. Prometheus ; Lancaster : Gazelle [distributor]: Amherst, N.Y., 2009. loc. 839.
27. Ruse, M., *Defining Darwin*, ibid., loc. 909.
28. Larson, E.J., *Remarkable History*, ibid., loc. 1391.
29. Darwin, C., *The Origin of Species*. W.W. Norton: New York, 1970.
30. Neve, M.; Messenger, S., ibid., p. xvi.
31. Eldredge, N., *Darwin : Discovering the Tree of Life*. 1st ed.; W.W. Norton & Co.: New York ; London, 2005. p. 42.
32. Gould, S.J., *Ever Since Darwin*, ibid., p. 25.
33. Gould, S. J., *Eight Little Piggies : Reflections in Natural History*. Norton: 1993. p. 302.
34. Gould, S.J. *Ever Since Darwin*, ibid., p. 25.
35. Eldredge, N., *Darwin: Discovering the Tree of Life*, ibid., p. 10.
36. Giberson, K.; Collins, F. S., *The Language of Science and Faith : Straight Answers to Genuine Questions*. Kindle Edition. SPCK: London, 2011; p. 48.
37. Murphy, G. L., Remembering God's people. In *Perspectives on an Evolving Creation*, Miller, K. B., Ed. Wm. B. Eerdmans: Grand Rapids, 2003; p. 379.
38. Gould, S. J., *Dinosaur in a Haystack : Reflections in Natural History*. Harmony: New York, 1995; p. 327.
39. Darwin, C., *The Descent of Man, and Selection in Relation to Sex*. By Charles Darwin ... In two volumes...With illustrations. London: John Murray: 1871.
40. Eldredge, N., Darwin: *Discovering the Tree of Life*. ibid., p. 40.
41. Neve, M.; Messenger, S., Darwin: Autobiographies, ibid., p. 71.
42. Neve, M.; Messenger, S., ibid., p. 3.
43. Gould, S.J., *Dinosaur in a Haystack*, ibid., p. 149.
44. Gould, S.J., *Ever Since Darwin*, ibid., p. 26.
45. Eldredge, N., *Darwin: Discovering the Tree of Life*, ibid., p. 18.
46. Larson, E.J., *Remarkable History*. loc. 1403.

47. Neve, M.; Messenger, S., ibid., p. 94.
48. Wikipedia, Joseph Hooker. Information on Darwin's home life from Darrel Falk. Personal correspondence.
49. Eldredge, N., *Discovering the Tree of Life*, ibid., p. 114.
50. Eldredge, N., ibid., p. 59.
51. Kitcher, P., *Living with Darwin : Evolution, Design, and the Future of Faith.* Oxford University Press: Oxford ; New York, 2007. p. 44.
52. Collins, F. S., *The Language of God: A Scientist Presents Evidence for Belief.* Free Press: New York & London, 2006; p. 167.
53. Ruse, M., *The Evolution-Creation Struggle*, ibid., p. 90.
54. Huxley was an English biologist, educator, and advocate of agnosticism (he coined the word). The seeds of his later agnosticism were planted early. Huxley's parents were Anglican but, as a boy, Thomas sympathized with the town's nonconformists, individuals who wanted religious equality and an end to Anglican control of public institutions. Huxley was also influenced by Unitarian thinking. Huxley joined the Navy and served for four years (1846-1850) as assistant surgeon on HMS Rattlesnake. Huxley considered it a moral duty to weigh the evidence before believing church teachings. Charles Darwin and his wife Emma were baptismal sponsors for two of Huxley's children. [Wikipedia]
55. Miller, K. R., *Finding Darwin's God : A Scientist's Search for Common Ground Between God and Evolution.* Cliff Street Books: New York, 1999. p. 7.
56. Ruse, M., *The Evolution-Creation Struggle*, ibid., p. 70.
57. Dawkins, R., *The Greatest Show On Earth : The Evidence For Evolution.* iBook Edition. Black Swan: London, 2009. p. 95.
58. Dennett, D., *Darwin's Dangerous Idea : Evolution and the Meanings of Life.* Simon & Schuster: New York & London, 1995; p. 35.
59. Larson, E.J., *Remarkable History*, ibid., loc. 943.
60. Janssen, L. J., *Standing on the Shoulders of Giants: Genesis and Human Origins*. Eugene, OR., Wipf & Stock, 2016; p. 276.
61. Berra, T. M., *Evolution and the Myth of Creationism : A Basic Guide to the Facts In the Evolution Debate.* Stanford University Press: Stanford, Calif., 1990. p. 6.
62. Pennock, R., *Tower of Babel*, ibid., p. 57.
63. Larson, E.J., *Remarkable History*, ibid., loc. 1627.
64. Young, M.; Strode, P., *Why Evolution Works*, ibid., p. 105.
65. Eldredge, N., *Discovering the Tree of Life*, ibid., p. 138.
66. Berra, T., *Evolution and the Myth of Creationism*, ibid., p. 6.
67. Kitcher, P., *Living with Darwin*, ibid., p. 21.
68. Larson, E.J., *Remarkable History*, ibid., loc. 2253.
69. Barbour, I. G., *When Science Meets Religion: Enemies, Strangers, Or Partners?* 1st ed.; Harper: San Francisco, 2000; p. 91.
70. Larson, E.J., *Remarkable History*, ibid., loc. 1236
71. Eldredge, N., *Discovering the Tree of Life*, ibid., p. 66.
72. Peters, T.; Hewlett, M., *Theological and Scientific Commentary on Darwin's Origin of Species.* Abingdon Press: Nashville, 2008; p. 58.
73. Ruse, M., *Philosophy of Human Evolution*, ibid., p. 6.
74. Lamoureux, D. O., *I Love Jesus & I Accept Evolution.* Kindle Edition. Wipf and Stock Publishers: Eugene, OR, 2009. p. 221.
75. Larson, E.J., *Remarkable History*, ibid., loc. 1236.

76. Dawkins, R., *Greatest Show*, ibid., loc. 757.
77. Neve, M., Messenger, S., *Darwin: Autobiographies*, ibid., p. 49.
78. D'Sousa, D., The Evolution of Darwin: The Scientists' Problem with God. In *The Origins Debate: Evangelical Perspectives on Creation, Evolution, and Intelligent Design*, Team, C. T. E., Ed. Christianity Today: Carol Stream, IL, 2012. loc. 1181.
79. Neve, M.; Messenger, S., *Darwin: Autobiographies*, ibid., p. 22.
80. Ruse, M., *The Philosophy of Human Evolution*, ibid., p. 156.
81. Neve, M.; Messenger, S., *Darwin: Autobiographies*, ibid., p. 53.
82. Pennock, R.T., *Tower*, ibid., p. 71.
83. Neve, M.; Messenger, S., *Darwin: Autobiographies*, ibid., p. xxi.
84. Neve, M.; Messenger, S., ibid., p. 50.
85. Giberson, K., *Saving Darwin: How To Be A Christian And Believe In Evolution*. Harper One: New York, 2008. p. 21.
86. Giberson, K., ibid., p. 19.
87. Giberson, K., ibid., p. 21.
88. Moore, J. R., *The Darwin Legend*. Hodder & Stoughton, 1995: London, 1994. p. 23.
89. Davis, T., "The Evolution of Darwin's Religious Faith." BioLogos Foundation. http://biologos.org/blogs/ted-davis-reading-the-book-of-nature/the-evolution-of-darwins-religious-faith
90. Peters, T.; Hewlett, M., *From Creation to New Creation*, ibid., p. 8.
91. Peters, T.; Hewlett, M., *Theological and Scientific Commentary*, ibid., p. 10.
92. Larson, E.J., *Remarkable History*, ibid., loc. 1027.
93. Peters, T.; Hewlett, M., *Theological and Scientific Commentary*, ibid., p. 109.
94. Kitcher, P., *Living with Darwin*, ibid., p. 1.
95. Berry, R. J., Foreword. In *True Scientists, True Faith: Some of the world's leading scientists reveal the harmony between their science and their faith*. Kindle Edition., Berry, R. J., Ed. Oxford, U.K. and Grand Rapids, MI, 2014; p. 221.
96. Wright, N.T., *Suprised by Scripture : Engaging with Contemporary Issues*. SPCK Publishing, 2014; p. 1.
97. Giberson, K., ibid., p. 21.
98. Moore, J. R., *The Darwin Legend*. Hodder & Stoughton, 1995: London, 1994. p. 23.
99. Gould, S.J., *Leonardo's Mountain of Clams and the Diet of Worms*, ibid., p. 149.
100. Berra, T.M., *Evolution and the Myth of Creationism*, ibid., p. 68.
101. Gould, S. J., *Wonderful Life : The Burgess Shale and the Nature of History*. 1st ed.; W.W. Norton: New York, 1989; p. 228.
102. Roughgarden, J., *Evolution and Christian Faith : Reflections of an Evolutionary Biologist*. Island Press: Washington, D.C. ; London, 2006. p. 40.
103. Mayr, E., *What Evolution Is*, ibid., p. 112.
104. Young, M.; Strode, P.K., *Why Evolution Works*, ibid., p. 109.
105. Skybreak, A., *The Science of Evolution*, ibid., p. 301.
106. Scott, E., *Evolution vs. Creationism : An Introduction*. University of California Press: Berkeley, Calif. ; London, 2005. p. 37.
107. Berra, T.M., *Evolution and the Myth of Creationism*, ibid., p. 152.
108. Roughgarden, J., *Evolution and Christian Faith*, ibid., p. 39.
109. Scott, E., *Evolution Vs. Creationism*, ibid., p. 30.
110. Ruse, M., *The Philosophy of Human Evolution*, ibid., p. 186.
111. Scott, E., *Evolution vs. Creationism*, ibid., p. 34.

112. Pennock, R.T., *Tower of Babel*, ibid., p. 97.
113. Roughgarden, J., *Evolution and Christian Faith*, ibid., p. 43.
114. Dennett, D., *Darwin's Dangerous Idea*, ibid., p. 125.
115. Dennett, D., ibid., p. 112.
116. Dowd, M., *Thank God for Evolution!* 1st ed.; Publishers Group UK: San Francisco, 2007; p. 32.
117. Young, M.; Strode, P.K., *Why Evolution Works*, ibid, p. 92.
118. Gould, S. J., *I Have Landed : The End of a Beginning in Natural History*. 1st ed.; Harmony Books: New York, 2002. p. 106.
119. Campbell, D.; Miller, K. B., The "Cambrian Explosion," A Challenge to Evolutionary Theory? In *Perspectives on an Evolving Creation*, Miller, K. B., Ed. Wm. B. Eerdmans: Grand Rapids, MI and Cambridge, U.K., 2003; p. 198.
120. Roughgarden, J., *Evolution and Christian Faith*, ibid., p. 32.
121. Miller, K.R., *Finding Darwin's God*, ibid., p. 104.
122. Pennock, R.T., *Tower*, ibid., p. 88.
123. Ruse, M., *Evolution-Creation Struggle*, ibid, p. 171.
124. Berra, T.M., *Evolution and the Myth of Creationism*, ibid., p. 53.
125. Kitcher, P., *Abusing Science : The Case Against Creationism*. MIT Press: Cambridge, Mass. ; London, 1982. p. 98.
126. Mayr, E., *What Evolution Is*, ibid., p. 114.
127. Miller, K.R., *Finding Darwin's God*, ibid., p. 49.
128. Mayr, E. *What Evolution Is*, ibid., p. 98.
129. Miller, K.R., *Finding Darwin's God*, ibid., p. 104.
130. Miller, K.R., ibid, p. 107.
131. Giberson, K.; Collins, F., *The Language of Science and Faith*, ibid., p. 35.
132. Isaak, M., *The Counter-Creationism Handbook*. Greenwood ; Oxford : Harcourt Education : Westport, Conn., 2005. p. 52.
133. Collins, F., *Language of God*, ibid., p. 131.
134. Bucklin, S. A., "Conductor of Evolution's Subtle Symphony." https://www.quantamagazine.org/20161103-richard-lenski-interview-evolution/
135. Miller, K. R., *Only a Theory: Evolution and The Battle for America's Soul*. Viking Penguin: New York ; London, 2008. p. 143.
136. Gould, S.J., *Wonderful Life*, ibid., p. 14.
137. Gould, S.J., ibid., p. 51.
138. Barbour, I., *When Science Meets Religion*, ibid., p. 112.
139. Haught, J. F., *God After Darwin : A Theology of Evolution*. Westview Press: Boulder, Colo. ; Oxford, 2000; p. 100.
140. Mayr, E., *What Evolution Is*, ibid., p. 221.
141. Gould, S.J., *Bully for Brontosaurus*, ibid., p. 61.
142. Miller, K., *Finding Darwin's God*, ibid., p. 101.
143. Ruse, M., *Science and Spirituality : Making Room for Faith in the Age of Science*. Cambridge University Press: Cambridge, 2010; p. 78.
144. Miller, K.R., *Finding Darwin's God*, ibid., p. 139.
145. Dawkins, R., *Greatest Show on Earth*, ibid., loc. 688.
146. Gray, T. M., Biochemistry and Evolution. In *Perspectives on an Evolving Creation*, Miller, K. B., Ed. Eerdmans: Grand Rapids, MI. Cambridge, UK, 2003; p. 277.
147. Skybreak, A., *The Science of Evolution*, ibid., p. 263.

148. Dennett, D., *Darwin's Dangerous Idea*, ibid., p. 408.
149. Campbell, D.; Miller, K.B., The "Cambrian Explosion": A Challenge to Evolutionary Theory? in Miller, Keith B. Ed., *Perspectives on an Evolving Creation*, ibid, p. 203.
150. Gould, S.J., Leonardo's *Mountain of Clams and the Diet of Worms*, ibid., p. 328.
151. Campbell, M., "Humans and Squid Evolved Same Eyes Using Same Genes." http://theconversation.com/humans-and-squid-evolved-same-eyes-using-same-genes-26265
152. Dennett, D., *Darwin's Dangerous Idea*, ibid., p. 255.
153. Gould, S.J., *Dinosaur in a Haystack*, ibid., p. 117.
154. Ardern, Z., "Book Review: The Runes Of Evolution: How The Universe Became Self-Aware by Simon Conway Morris." BioLogos Foundation. http://biologos.org/blogs/jim-stump-faith-and-science-seeking-understanding/book-review-simon-conway-morris-the-runes-of-evolution-how-the-universe-became-self-aware
155. Giberson, K.; Collins, F., *The Language of Science and Faith*, ibid., p. 203.
156. Conway Morris, S., *The Crucible of Creation : The Burgess Shale and the Rise of Animals*. Oxford University Press: Oxford, 1998. p. 204.
157. Pierce, B. A., *Transmission and Population Genetics : A Conceptual Approach*. 4th ed.; W. H. Freeman & Company: New York, 2012.
158. Skybreak, A., *The Science of Evolution*, ibid., p. 136.
159. Eldridge, N., *Discovering the Tree of Life*, ibid., p 111.
160. Wikipedia, Allopatric Speciation.
161. Gould, S.J., *Ever Since Darwin*, ibid., p. 61.
162. Wikipedia, Sympatric Speciation.
163. Giberson, K., *Seven Glorious Days : A Scientist Retells The Genesis Creation Story*. Kindle Edition. Paraclete Press: Brewster, Mass., 2012; p. 112.
164. McGrath, A. E., *Science And Religion : An Introduction*. Kindle Edition. 2nd ed.; Wiley-Blackwell: Chichester, 2010. loc. 968.
165. Mayr, E., *The Growth of Biological Thought : Diversity, Evolution and Inheritance*. Belknap Press: Cambridge, Mass. ; London, 1982. p. 330.
166. Gould, S.J., *Ever Since Darwin*, ibid., p. 90.
167. Gould, S. J., *The Lying Stones of Marrakesh : Penultimate Reflections in Natural History*. Harmony Books: New York, 2000. p. 168.
168. Skybreak, A., *The Science of Evolution*, ibid., p. 65.
169. Eldridge, N., *Discovering the Tree of Life*, ibid., p. 166.
170. Berra, T.M., *Evolution and the Myth of Creationism*, ibid., p. 48.
171. Gould, S.J. *Eight Little Piggies*, ibid., p. 316.
172. Eldredge, N., *Reinventing Darwin : The Great Debate at the High Table of Evolutionary Theory*. Wiley: New York ; Chichester, 1995; p. 153.
173. Eldredge, N., ibid., p. 157.
174. Larson, E.J., *Remarkable History*, ibid., loc. 679.
175. Gould, S.J., *Eight Little Piggies*, ibid., p. 63.
176. Dawkins, R., *Greatest Show on Earth*, ibid., loc. 555.
177. Ruse, M., *Defining Darwin*, ibid., loc. 1970.
178. Berra, T.M., *Evolution and the Myth of Creationism*, ibid., p. 21.
179. "Fossil," thefreedictionary.com http://www.thefreedictionary.com/fossil
180. Allaby, M., Ed., *The Concise Oxford Dictionary of Botany*. Oxford University Press: Oxford, 1996.
181. Ruse, M., *The Philosophy of Human Evolution*, ibid., p. 10.

182. Eldredge, N., *Discovering the Tree of Life*, ibid., p. 128.
183. Collins, F., *Language of God*, ibid., p. 94.
184. Gould, S.J., *Leonardo's Mountain of Clams and the Diet of Worms*, ibid., p. 186.
185. Fugle, G. N., *Laying Down Arms to Heal the Creation - Evolution Divide*. Eugene, OR, Wipf & Stock, 2015; p. 153.
186. Fugle, G.N., ibid., p. 154.
187. Conway Morris, S., *Crucible of Creation*, ibid., p. 2.
188. Eldredge, N., *Reinventing Darwin*, ibid, p. 2.
189. University of California at Berkeley, Evolution Blog: The Cambrian Explosion. http://www.evolution.berkeley.edu/evosite/evo101/VIIB1cCambrian.shtml
190. Dawkins, R., *The Greatest Show on Earth*, ibid., loc. 332.
191. Dawkins, R., ibid., loc. 249.
192. Isaac, M., *The Counter-Creationism Handbook*, ibid., p. 124.
193. Gould, S.J., *Eight Little Piggies*, ibid., p. 286.
194. Peters, T.; Hewlett, M., *Theological and Scientific Commentary*, ibid., p. 65.
195. University of Chicago website. "Meet Tiktaalik Roseae: An Extraordinary Fossil Fish." http://tiktaalik.uchicago.edu/meetTik.html
196. Dawkins, R., *Greatest Show on Earth*, ibid., p. 245.
197. Janssen, L. J., *Standing on the Shoulders*. ibid., p. 146.
198. Venema, D. R., *Adam & the Genome : Reading Scripture After Genetic Science*. Brazos Press, Ada, MI.; p. 60.
199. Age of Rocks website. "A Soft Spot For Dino Bones." https://ageofrocks.org/2015/01/12/monday-minute-a-soft-spot-for-dino-bones/
200. Gibbons, Ann., "Oldest-Ever Proteins Extracted From 3.8-Million-Year-Old Ostrich Shells." Science Magazine. September 2016. http://www.sciencemag.org/news/2016/09/oldest-ever-proteins-extracted-38-million-year-old-ostrich-shells?utm_source=6&utm_medium=social&utm_campaign=AAAS-Dialogue-on-Science,-Ethics-and-Religion-%28AAAS.DoSER%29&utm_term=DoSER&utm_content=AAAS
201 Abrams, A., "Scientists Have Discovered the First Dinosaur Brain Fossil." http://time.com/4548150/first-dinosaur-brain-fossil/ Compare this with another article, this one found on the Science Magazine website: Grammling, C., "A Dinosaur's Brain Preserved in a Pebble." Science Magazine, October 2016. http://www.sciencemag.org/news/2016/10/dinosaur-s-brain-preserved-pebble
202. Mortillaro, N., "Feathered Dinosaur Tail Found Trapped in Amber." CBC News. http://www.cbc.ca/news/technology/feathered-dinosaur-tail-amber-1.3885813?cmp=rss
203. Dawkins, R., *Greatest Show*, ibid., loc. 635.
204. Gould, S.J., *Leonardo's Mountain of Clams*, ibid., p. 330.
205. Campbell, Malcolm, "Humans and Squid Evolved Same Eyes Using Same Genes." ibid. http://theconversation.com/humans-and-squid-evolved-same-eyes-using-same-genes-26265
206. Campbell, D.; Miller, K.B., The "Cambrian Explosion": A Challenge to Evolutionary Theory? In Miller, K.B., Ed., *Perspectives on an Evolving Creation*, ibid., p. 193.
207. Ruse, M., *Philosophy of Human Evolution*, ibid., p. 37.
208. Long, J., "Life on Earth Still Favors Evolution over Creationism." http://theconversation.com/life-on-earth-still-favours-evolution-over-creationism-23419

209. Chivers, T., "7 Things That Show That Evolution is an Actual Fact." https://www.buzzfeed.com/tomchivers/things-that-show-evolution-is-an-actual-fact?utm_term=.iqY2vMY4Mo -.ineDyz3bzn.
210. Mayr, E., *What Evolution Is*, ibid., p. 93.
211. Meyer, S. C., *Darwin's Doubt : The Explosive Origin of Animal Life and the Case for Intelligent Design*. HarperOne, New York, 2013; p. 100.
212. Goodman CS and Coughlin BS (Eds). (2000). "Special feature: The evolution of evo-devo biology." Proceedings of the National Academy of Sciences. 97 (9): 4424–4456.
213. Conway-Morris, S., *Crucible of Creation*, ibid., p. 8.
214. Lamoureux, D. O., Evangelicals Inheriting the Wind: The Phillip E. Johnson Phenomenon. In *Darwinism Defeated? The Johnson - Lamoureux Debate on Biological Origins*, Johnson, P. E.; Lamoureux, D. O., Eds. Regent College Press: Vancouver, Canada, 1999; p. 32.
215. Conway Morris, S., Evolution and the Inevitability of Intelligent Life. In *The Cambridge Companion to Science and Religion*, Harrison, P., Ed. Cambridge University Press: Cambridge, UK, 2010; p. 157.
216. Fugle, G. N., *Laying Down Arms to Heal the Creation - Evolution Divide*. Eugene, OR, Wipf & Stock, 2015; p. 209.
217. Denton, M. J., *Evolution : Still a Theory in Crisis*. Seattle, WA, Discovery Institute Press. 2016; p. 83.
218. Falk, D. R., Thoughts on Darwin's Doubt - Part 1. BioLogos Foundation, September 9, 2014. http://biologos.org/blogs/guest/thoughts-on-darwins-doubt-reviewing-darwins-doubt-darrel-falk-part-1
219. Meyer, S. C., *Darwin's Doubt*., ibid., p. 447
220. Meyer, S. C., ibid., p. 315.
221. Fugle, G. N., *Laying Down Arms*. ibid., p. 146.
222. Meyer, ibid., p. 447.
223. Venema, D. R., *Adam & the Genome*. ibid., p. 26.
224. Janssen, L. J., *Standing on the Shoulders*. ibid., p. 87.
225. Janssen, ibid., p. 101
226. Janssen, ibid., p. 148.
227. Giberson K.; Collins, F., *The Language of Science and Faith*, ibid., p. 21.
228. Giberson, K., *Saving Darwin*, ibid., p. 194.
229. Ruse, M., *The Evolution-Creation Struggle*, ibid., p. 198.
230. Scott, E., *Evolution vs. Creationism*, ibid., p. 170.
231. Collins, F., *The Language of God*, ibid., p. 129.
232. Dawkins, R., *Greatest Show*, ibid., loc. 545.
233. Gould, S. J., Eldredge, N.; *Punctuated Equilibria: An Alternative to Phyletic Gradualism*. Schopf, T. J. M, Ed., Models in Paleobiology, Freeman Cooper, San Francisco, CA., pp. 82-115.
234. Denton, M. J., *Evolution: Still a Theory in Crisis*, ibid., p. 43.
235. Meyer, S. C., *Darwin's Doubt*, ibid., p. 138.
236. Janssen, L. J., *Standing on the Shouders*, ibid., p. 184.
237. Kitcher, P., *Abusing Science*, ibid., p. 50.
238. Fugle, G. N., *Laying Down Arms*. ibid., p. 27
239. Denton, M. J., *Evolution: Still a Theory in Crisis*, ibid., p. 26
240. Haarsma, D. (2014) Reviewing Darwin's Doubt - Introduction. BioLogos Foundation.

The President's Notebook. http://biologos.org/blogs/deborah-haarsma-the-presidents-notebook/reviewing-darwins-doubt-introduction
241. Gould, S.J., *Wonderful Life*, ibid., p. 58.
242. Laland, K., "Evolution Evolves: Beyond The Selfish Gene." New Scientist. https://www.newscientist.com/article/mg23130920-600-evolution-evolves-beyond-the-selfish-gene/
243. Personal communication.

Chapter 6 - Atheistic Evolution

1. Gribbin, J., *The Scientists : A History of Science Told Through the Lives of its Greatest Inventors*; Random House: New York, 2003; p. 241.
2. Numbers, R. L., Aggressors, Victims, and Peacemakers – Historical Actors in the Drama of Science and Religion. In *The Religion and Science Debate: Why Does It Continue?* Kindle Edition., Attridge, H. W., Ed. Yale University Press: New Haven & London, 2009; p. 402.
3. Ecklund, E. H., *Science Vs. Religion : What Scientists Really Think*. Kindle Edition. Oxford University Press: New York ; Oxford, 2010; p. 16.
4. Ecklund, ibid.
5. Topham, J. R., Natural Theology and the Sciences. In *The Cambridge Companion to Science and Religion*. Kindle Edition., Harrison, P., Ed. Cambridge University Press, Kindle Edition: Cambridge, UK, 2010; p. 75.
6. Numbers, R., *The Creationists : From Scientific Creationism to Intelligent Design*. Expanded ed., 1st Harvard University Press pbk. ed.; Harvard University Press: Cambridge, Mass. ; London, 2006; p. 51
7. Numbers, *The Creationists*, ibid., p. 53.
8. Larson, E. J., *Evolution : The Remarkable History of a Scientific Theory*. Kindle Edition. Modern Library: New York, 2004. loc. 1149.
9. Ruse, M., *Defining Darwin : Essays on the History and Philosophy of Evolutionary Biology*. Kindle Edition. Prometheus, Amherst, N.Y., 2009. loc. 1319.
10. Larson, *Remarkable History*, ibid., loc. 3145.
11. Thomson, K., Introduction – The Religion and Science Debate: Why Does It Continue? In *The Religion and Science Debate: Why Does It Continue?* Kindle Edition, Attridge, H. W., Ed. Yale University Press: New Haven, CT. And London, U. K., 2009; p. 157.
12. Ruse, M., *Can a Darwinian be a Christian? . The Relationship Between Science and Religion*. Cambridge University Press: New York, 2000. p. 157.
13. Dennett, D. C., *Darwin's Dangerous Idea : Evolution and the Meanings of Life*. Simon & Schuster: New York & London, 1995; p. 82.
14. Ruse, M., *The Evolution-Creation Struggle*. Harvard University Press: Cambridge, Mass. ; London, 2005; p. 107.
15. Young, M.; Strode, P. K., *Why Evolution Works (And Creationism Fails)*. Kindle Edition. Rutgers University Press: New Brunswick, N.J. ; London, 2009. p. 213.
16. Dennett, *Dangerous Idea*, ibid, p. 461.
17. Larson, *Remarkable History*, ibid, loc. 2400.
18. Ruse, *Defining Darwin*, ibid., loc. 2522.
19. Giberson, K.; Collins, F. S., *The Language of Science and Faith : Straight Answers to Genuine Questions*. Kindle Edition. SPCK: London, 2011; p. 26.
20. Dennett, *Dangerous Idea*, ibid., p. 393.

21. Kitcher, *Abusing Science*, ibid., p. 196.
22. Gould, S. J., *Dinosaur in a Haystack : Reflections in Natural History*. Harmony: New York, 1995; p. 433.
23. Ruse, *Can a Darwinian Be a Christian?* ibid., p. 202.
24. Wikipedia, Eugenics.
25. Wikipedia, Social Darwinism.
26. Larson, *Remarkable History*, ibid., loc. 3510.
27. Kitcher, P., *Living with Darwin : Evolution, Design, and the Future of Faith*. Oxford University Press: Oxford ; New York, 2007. pp. 154, 161.
28. Ruse, M., Divine Action, Emergence, and Scientific Explanation. In *The Cambridge Companion to Science and Religion*, Harrison, P., Ed. Cambridge University Press: Cambridge, UK, New York, 2010; p. 39.
29. Barbour, I. G., *When Science Meets Religion : Enemies, Strangers, Or Partners?* 1st ed.; Harper: San Francisco, 2000; p. 13.
30. Ruse, *Divine Action*, ibid., p. 239.
31. Hooper, S., "The Rise of the New Atheists." November 9, 2006. CNN. http://www.cnn.com/2006/WORLD/europe/11/08/atheism.feature/index.html?_s=PM:W
32. Haidt, J., *The Righteous Mind : Why Good People Are Divided By Politics And Religion*. Kindle Edition. Allen Lane: London, 2012. p. 452.
33. Conway Morris, S., One Impossible Thing Before Breakfast: Evolution and Christianity. In *True Scientists, True Faith: Some of the World's Leading Scientists Reveal the Harmony between Their Science and Their Faith*. Kindle Edition., Berry, R. J., Ed. Monarch Books: Kindle Edition: Oxford, U.K and Grand Rapids, MI, 2014; p 257.
34. Hunt, Z., "Confessions of an Evolving Baptist." In Zack Hunt blog, 2013. http://zackhunt.net/2013/11/27/confessions-of-an-evolving-baptist-by-nathan-hale/
35. Giberson, K.; Artigas, M., *Oracles of Science : Celebrity Scientists Versus God and Religion*. Oxford University Press: Oxford ; New York, 2007; p. 4.
36. Hutchinson, I., *Monopolizing Knowledge: A Scientist Refutes Religion-Denying, Reason-Destroying Scientism*. Fias Publishing. Belmont, Massachusetts 2011.
37. Dennett, D. C., *Consciousness Explained*. 1st ed.; Little, Brown and Co: Boston, 1991. p. 33.
38. Haught, J. F., *God After Darwin : A Theology of Evolution*. Westview Press: Boulder, Colo. ; Oxford, 2000; p. 197.
39. Miller, K. R., Darwin, God, And Dover: What the Collapse of "Intelligent Design" Means for Science and Faith in America. In Attridge, H. W., Ed. *The Religion and Science Debate*, ibid., loc. 1125.
40. Wuthnow, R., No Contradictions Here: Science, Religion, and the Culture of All Reasonable Possibilities. In Attridge, H. W., Ed. ibid., loc. 2116.
41. Meyer, S.C., *Darwin's Doubt : The Explosive Origin of Animal Life and the Case for Intelligent Design*. HarperOne, New York. 2013; p. 210.
42. Numbers, R., Aggressors, Victims, and Peacemakers, In Attridge, H. W., Ed., ibid., loc. 688.
43. Eklund, *Science Vs. Religion:*, ibid., p. 48.
44. Eklund, ibid., p. 78.
45. Eklund, ibid., p. 4.
46. Orr, H. A., "Gould on God: Can Religion and Science Be Happily Reconciled?" *Boston Review* 1999, 33 – 38.

47. Numbers, R., Aggressors, Victims and Peacemakers, In Attridge, Ed., *The Religion and Science Debate* ibid., loc. 665.
48. Ruse, M., *Science and Spirituality : Making Room for Faith in the Age of Science.* Cambridge University Press: Cambridge, 2010; p. 2.
49. Ruse, *Defining Darwin*, ibid., loc. 2657.
50. Haught, *God after Darwin*, ibid., p. 14.
51. Ruse, *Science and Spirituality*, ibid., p. 3.
52. Numbers, R., Aggressors, Victims, and Peacemakers, In Attridge, Ed., *The Religion and Science Debate* ibid., loc. 629.
53. Slack, G., *The Battle over the Meaning of Everything : Evolution, Intelligent Design, and a School Board in Dover*, PA. Jossey-Bass ; Chichester : John Wiley: San Francisco, Calif., 2007. p. 205.
54. Ruse, *Defining Darwin*, ibid., loc. 2669.
55. McGrath, A. E., Science, Faith And Making Sense of Things In *True Scientists, True Faith:* ibid., Berry, R. J., Ed.. p. 12.
56. Thomson, K., Introduction. In Attridge, H. W., Ed., *The Religion and Science Debate*, ibid., p. 113.
57. Ruse, M., Atheism, Naturalism and Science: Three in One? In Harrison, P., Ed., *The Cambridge Companion*, ibid., loc. 239.
58. Dennett, *Dangerous Idea*, ibid., p. 63.
59. Dennett, ibid.
60. The new atheists include Richard Dawkins, Daniel Dennett, Sam Harris, Peter Atkins, Francis Crick, Stephen Weinberg, Stephen Pinker, Christopher Hitchens, and E.O. Wilson. See Giberson, *Saving Darwin*, 2008. p. 44.
61. Slack, *The Battle over the Meaning of Everything.*, ibid., p. 117.
62. Gould, S. J., *The Hedgehog, The Fox, and The Magister's Pox : Ending the False War Between Science and the Humanities.* 1st ed.; Harmony Books: New York, 2003. p. 150.
63. Giberson & Artigas, *Oracles of Science*, ibid., p. 34.
64. Giberson & Artigas, ibid., p. 11.
65. Gould, S. J., *Eight Little Piggies : Reflections in Natural History.* Norton: 1993. p. 387.
66. Ecklund, *Science Vs. Religion*, ibid., p. 153.
67. Ecklund, ibid., p. 102.
68. Lamoureux, D. O., *I Love Jesus & I Accept Evolution.* Kindle Edition. Wipf and Stock Publishers: Eugene, OR, 2009. p. 160.
69. McCaig, A., Most British Scientists Cited in Study Feel Richard Dawkins' Work Misrepresents Science. October 31, 2016. http://news.rice.edu/2016/10/31/most-british-scientists-cited-in-study-feel-richard-dawkins-work-misrepresents-science-2/

    The study can be found at: http://pus.sagepub.com/content/early/2016/10/06/0963662516673501.abstract

    "Responding to Richard: Celebrity and (Mis)representation of Science" appeared in a recent edition of *Public Understandings of Science* and are part of a larger *Religion Among Scientists in International Context* study. The RASIC study includes 20,000 scientists from eight countries. In the UK, 1,581 randomly sampled scientists participated in the survey. 137 also participated in in-depth interviews.

70. Dobson, J., Duane Gish - Hugh Ross Debate on Young Earth vs Old Earth Creationism. *Focus on the Family Radio Broadcast*, April 18, 1991.
71. Lamoureux, *I Love Jesus and I Accept Evolution*, ibid., loc. 455.
72. Ruse, *Evolution - Creation Struggle*, ibid., p. 287.
73. Ramm, B. L., *The Christian View of Science and Scripture*. 1st ed.; Grand Rapids: 1954; p. 36.
74. McGrath, A. E.; McGrath, J. C., *The Dawkins Delusion? Atheist Fundamentalism and the Denial of the Divine*. SPCK: London, 2007. p. 11.
75. Numbers, *The Creationists*, ibid., p. 158.
76. Roughgarden, J., *Evolution and Christian Faith : Reflections of an Evolutionary Biologist*. Island Press: Washington, D.C. ; London, 2006. p. 81.
77. Collins, F. S., *The Language of God: A Scientist Presents Evidence for Belief*. Free Press: New York & London, 2006; p. 230.
78. Eklund, *Science vs. Religion*, ibid., p. 43.
79. Giberson & Collins, *The Language of Science and Faith*, ibid., p. 143.
80. McGrath & McGrath, *Dawkins Delusion?* ibid, p. 34.
81. Numbers, R., Aggressors, Victims, and Peacemakers, In Attridge, H.W., Ed., *The Religion and Science Debate*, ibid., loc. 695.
82. McGrath & McGrath, *Dawkins Delusion?*, ibid., p. 48.
83. Ruse, M., "Curb your Enthusiasm: High priests, Holy Writ and Excommunications. - how did Humanism end up acting like religion?" https://aeon.co/essays/how-humanism-lost-its-way-in-a-charismatic-crusade
84. Ruse, ibid.
85. Gould, S. J., *Rocks of Ages : Science and Religion in the Fullness of Life*. Ballantine Books: New York, 1999. p. 192.
86. McGrath, A.: Science, Faith, and Making Sense of Things., In Berry, R. J., Ed., *True Scientists, True Faith*, ibid., p. 20.
87. Numbers, *The Creationists*, ibid., p. 175.

Chapter 7 - Old-Earth Creationism

1. McGrath, A. E., *Science and Religion : An Introduction*. Kindle Edition. 2nd ed.; Wiley-Blackwell: Chichester, 2010. loc. 1076. Recent research, (see Appendix) however, seems to cast doubt on the popularity of old-earth creationism among Christians today. It appears that further clarification is required.
2. Pennock, R. T., *Tower of Babel : The Evidence Against The New Creationism*. MIT Press: Cambridge, Mass. ; London, 1999; p. 17.
3. Breshears, J., "How Young Earth Creationism Became a Core Tenet of American Fundamentalism, Part II." http://www.reasons.org/articles/how-young-earth-creationism-became-a-core-tenet-of-american-fundamentalism-part-2
4. Numbers, R. L., *The Creationists : From Scientific Creationism to Intelligent Design*. Expanded ed., 1st Harvard University Press; Harvard University Press: Cambridge, Mass. ; London, 2006; p. 23.
5. Numbers, *The Creationists*, ibid., p. 58.
6. Ramm, B. L., *The Christian View of Science and Scripture*. 1st ed.; Grand Rapids: 1954; p. 134.
7. Numbers, *The Creationists*, ibid., p. 7.
8. Numbers, ibid., p. 368.

9. Early advocates of old-earth creationism include many names well known in the Christian community: Charles Hodge (1797–1878) Presbyterian theologian and principal of Princeton Theological Seminary between 1851 and 1878. Edward Hitchcock, (1793-1864) American geologist and President of Amherst College. Benjamin Warfield (1851–1921) professor of theology at Princeton Seminary from 1887 to 1921 was also an old-earth creationist. See Hugh Ross, *A Matter of Days*, Colorado Springs, NavPress, 2004. p. 135.
10. Recent advocates of old-earth creationism include Gleason Archer (1916–2004) Fuller Theological Seminary in Pasadena, California, well-known biblical inerrantist. Norman Geisler (1932-) co-founder of two non-denominational evangelical seminaries (Veritas Evangelical Seminary and Southern Evangelical Seminary). Walter Kaiser Jr. - (1933-), former President of Gordon-Conwell Theological Seminary.
11. Dobson, J., The Duane Gish - Hugh Ross Debate on Young Earth vs Old Earth Creationism. In *Focus on the Family Radio Broadcast*, April 18, 1991.
12. Dobson, ibid.
13. Dobson, ibid.
14. Dobson, ibid.
15. Ross, *A Matter of Days*, ibid., p. 11.
16. Ramm, *The Christian View of Science and Scripture*, ibid., p. 135.
17. Gould, S. J., *I Have Landed : The End of a Beginning in Natural History*. 1st ed.; Harmony Books: New York, 2002. p. 135.
18. Scott, E. C., *Evolution vs. Creationism : An Introduction*. University of California Press: Berkeley, Calif. ; London, 2005. p. 76.
19. Wikipedia, Gap Creationism.
20. Wikipedia, ibid.
21. Ramm, *The Christian View*, ibid., p. 137.
22. Larson, E. J., *Evolution : The Remarkable History of a Scientific Theory*. Kindle Edition. Modern Library: New York, 2004. loc. 454.
23. Larson, ibid., loc. 554.
24. Larson, ibid., loc. 454.
25. Numbers, *The Creationists*, ibid., p. 87.
26. Larson, ibid., loc. 554.
27. Wikipedia, ibid., Gap Creationism.
28. Lamoureux, D. O., Evangelicals Inheriting the Wind: The Phillip E. Johnson Phenomenon. In *Darwinism Defeated? The Johnson - Lamoureux Debate on Biological Origins*, Johnson, P. E.; Lamoureux, D. O., Eds. Regent College Press: Vancouver, Canada, 1999; p. 13.
29. Numbers, R. L., Scientific Creationism and Intelligent Design. In *The Cambridge Companion to Science and Religion*. Kindle Edition., Harrison, P., Ed. Cambridge University Press: Cambridge, U.K., 2010; p. 128.
30. Larson, *Remarkable History*, ibid., loc. 3219.
31. Wikipedia, ibid., Gap Creationism.
32. Numbers, *The Creationists*, ibid., p. 210.
33. Larson., ibid., loc. 467.
34. Davidson, G.; Wolgemuth, K., "Biblical and Scientific Shortcomings of Flood Geology, Part 1." BioLogos Foundation. http://biologos.org/blogs/archive/biblical-and-scientific-shortcomings-of-flood-geology-part-1

35. Larson, ibid., loc. 3219.
36. Numbers, R. L., Aggressors, Victims, and Peacemakers – Historical Actors in the Drama of Science and Religion. In *The Religion and Science Debate: Why Does It Continue?* Kindle Edition., Attridge, H. W., Ed. Yale University Press: New Haven & London, 2009; p. 322.
37. Ramm, *The Christian View*, ibid., p. 33.
38. Pennock, R., *Tower of Babel: The Evidence Against The New Creationism*. ibid., p. 15.
39. Scott, *Evolution vs. Creationism*, ibid., p. 92.
40. Numbers, R.L., Scientific Creationism and Intelligent Design, in Harrison, Ed., *The Cambridge Companion to Science and Religion*, ibid., p. 128.
41. Numbers, *The Creationists*, ibid., p. 58.
42. Numbers, ibid., p. 26.
43. Dobson, *The Gish - Ross Debate*, ibid.
44. Lamoureux, D. O., *I Love Jesus & I Accept Evolution*. Kindle Edition. Wipf & Stock Publishers: Eugene, OR, 2009. loc. 628.
45. Progressive creationism is explained by its proponents at http://www.oldearth.org/progressive.htm
46. Ramm, *The Christian View*, ibid., p. 77.
47. Gould, S. J., *The Panda's Thumb : More Reflections in Natural History*. New York ; London : Norton, 1980 (1982 [printing]): 1980. p. 182.
48. Ramm, ibid., p. 79.
49. Lamoureux, D. O. *Evolutionary Creation: A Christian Approach to Evolution*. Eugene, OR., Wipf & Stock, 2008. p. 446. Lamoureux is referring to John C. Sutherland's article, "Evangelical Biologists and Evolution," *Science*, 309 (1 July 2005), 51.
50. Ramm, ibid., p. 79.
51. Ramm, ibid., p. 148.
52. Wikipedia, Progressive Creationism.
53. Wikipedia, Bernard Ramm.
54. Numbers, *The Creationists*, ibid., p. 211.
55. Ramm, ibid., p. 126.
56. Numbers, R.L., Scientific Creationism and Intelligent Design, in Harrison, Ed., *The Cambridge Companion to Science and Religion*, ibid., p. 32.
57. Wikipedia, Progressive Creationism. ibid.,
58. Numbers, *The Creationists*, ibid., p. 305.
59. Larson, *Remarkable History*, ibid., loc. 430.
60. Larson, ibid., loc. 467.
61. Larson, ibid., loc. 644.
62. Ruse, M., *The Evolution-Creation Struggle*. Harvard University Press: Cambridge, Mass. ; London, 2005; p. 38.
63. Young, M.; Strode, P. K., *Why Evolution Works (And Creationism Fails)*. Kindle Edition. Rutgers University Press: New Brunswick, N.J. ; London, 2009. p. 23.
64. Dennett, D. C., *Darwin's Dangerous Idea: Evolution and the Meanings of Life*. Simon & Schuster: New York & London, 1995; p. 67.
65. Johnson, P. E., *Darwin on Trial*. Regnery Gateway; Lanham, MD : Distributed to the trade by National Book Network: Washington, D.C., 1991. p. 17.
66. Van Till, H. J., Intelligent Design: the Celebration of Gifts Withheld? In *The Johnson-Lamoureux Debate on Biological Origins*, Lamoureux, D. O.; Johnson, P. E., Eds.

Regent College Publishing: Vancouver, B.C., 1999; p. 83.
67. Wikipedia, ibid., *Progressive Creationism.*
68. Ross, *A Matter of Days*, ibid., p. 18.
69. Ramm, *The Christian View*, ibid., p. 126.
70. Lamoureux, *Evolutionary Creation*, ibid., p. 225.
71. Ramm, ibid., pp. 163 & 169.
72. Ramm, ibid., p. 49.
73. Numbers, *The Creationists*, ibid., p. 34.
74. Wikipedia, Intelligent Design Creationism.
75. Miller, K. R., *Finding Darwin's God : A Scientist's Search for Common Ground Between God and Evolution.* Cliff Street Books: New York, 1999. p. 131.
76. Scott, E. C., Darwin Prosecuted: Review of Johnson's 'Darwin on Trial'. *Creation Evolution Journal of the National Center for Science Education* 1993, 13 (2), 36-47.
77. Lamoureux, D.O., "Evangelicals Inheriting the Wind: The Phillip E. Johnson Phenomenon," in Johnson, P. and Lamoureux, P. Eds. *Darwinism Defeated? The Johnson - Lamoureux Debate on Biological Origins*, ibid., p. 13.
78. Scott, *Evolution vs. Creationism*, ibid., p. 120.
79. Dobson, *The Gish - Ross Debate*, ibid.
80. Dobson, ibid.
81. Ecklund, E. H., *Science Vs. Religion : What Scientists Really Think.* Kindle Edition. Oxford University Press: New York ; Oxford, 2010. p. 24.
82. Dobson, ibid.
83. Dobson, ibid.

Chapter 8 - Evolutionary Creation

1. Davis, T., "Science and the Bible: Theistic Evolution, Part 1." BioLogos Foundation. http://biologos.org/blogs/ted-davis-reading-the-book-of-nature/science-and-the-bible-theistic-evolution-part-1
2. Miller, K. R., *Finding Darwin's God : A Scientist's Search for Common Ground Between God and Evolution.* Cliff Street Books: New York, 1999. p. 258.
3. Miller, ibid., p. 243.
4. MacKay, D. M., Science and Christian Faith Today. In *True Scientists, True Faith: Some of the World's Leading Scientists Reveal the Harmony between Their Science and Their Faith.* Kindle Edition., Berry, R. J., Ed. Monarch Books: Oxford, U.K. and Grand Rapids, MI, 2014; p. 329.
5. Prance, A Talent for Science. In *True Scientists, True Faith*: ibid., Berry, R. J., Ed. p. 139.
6. Alexander, D., "How Are Christianity and Evolution Compatible?" https://www.bigquestionsonline.com/2014/06/02/how-are-christianity-evolution-compatible/
7. McGrath, A. E., *Science and Religion : An Introduction.* Kindle Edition. 2nd ed.; Wiley-Blackwell: Chichester, 2010. loc. 3794.
8. Neve, M.; Messenger, S., *Charles Darwin: Autobiographies.* Penguin Classics: London, 2002. p. 93.
9. Gould, S. J., *Bully for Brontosaurus : Reflections in Natural History.* Norton: New York, 1991. p. 30.
10. Ruse, M., *The Evolution-Creation Struggle.* Harvard University Press: Cambridge, Mass. ; London, 2005; p. 132.
11. Larson, E. J., *Evolution : The Remarkable History of a Scientific Theory.* Kindle Edition.

Modern Library: New York, 2004. loc. 1485.

12. Gould, *Bully for Brontosaurus : Reflections in Natural History*. ibid., p. 400.
13. Ramm, B. L., *The Christian View of Science and Scripture*. 1st ed.; Grand Rapids: 1954; p. 200.
14. Gould, *Bully for Brontosaurus* : ibid., p. 432.
15. Peters, T.; Hewlett, M. J., *Theological and Scientific Commentary on Darwin's Origin of Species*. Abingdon Press: Nashville, 2008; p. 74.
16. Giberson, K.; Collins, F. S., *The Language of Science and Faith : Straight Answers to Genuine Questions*. Kindle Edition. SPCK: London, 2011; p. 158.
17. Peters, T.; Hewlett, M. J., *Evolution From Creation to New Creation : Conflict, Conversation, and Convergence*. Abingdon Press: Nashville, TN, 2003. p. 155.
18. Collins, F. S., *The Language of God: A Scientist Presents Evidence for Belief*. Free Press: New York & London, 2006; p. 166.
19. Peters & Hewlett, *Theological and Scientific Commentary*, ibid., p. 74.
20. Peters & Hewlett, *From Creation to New Creation* : ibid., p. 71.
21. Breshears, J., "How Young Earth Creationism Became a Core Tenet of American Fundamentalism, Part II." http://www.reasons.org/articles/how-young-earth-creationism-became-a-core-tenet-of-american-fundamentalism-part-2 It must be stressed that some essays in *The Fundamentals* were critical of any acceptance of evolution. For example, the article by the Rev. Dyson Hague titled "*The Doctrinal Value of the First Chapters of Genesis*", or the anonymous article titled "*Evolutionism in the Pulpit*." Personal correspondence.
22. Giberson, K., *Saving Darwin: How To Be A Christian And Believe In Evolution*. Harper One: New York, 2008. p. 60.
23. Ramm, *The Christian View*, ibid. p. 200.
24. Lamoureux, D. O., *Evolutionary Creation : A Christian Approach to Evolution*. Lutterworth Press: Cambridge, England, 2008. p. 352.
25. Miller, K. B., An Evolving Creation: Oxymoron or Fruitful Insight? In *Perspectives on an Evolving Creation*, Miller, K. B., Ed. Wm. B. Eerdmans: Grand Rapids, MI and Cambridge U. K., 2003; p. 4.
26. Peters & Hewlett, *From Creation to New Creation* : ibid., p. 74.
27. Young, M.; Strode, P. K., *Why Evolution Works (And Creationism Fails)*. Kindle Edition. Rutgers University Press: New Brunswick, N.J. ; London, 2009. p. 23.
28. Numbers, R. L., *The Creationists : From Scientific Creationism to Intelligent Design*. Expanded ed., 1st Harvard University Press pbk. ed.; Harvard University Press: Cambridge, Mass. ; London, 2006; p. 368.
29. Giberson, *Saving Darwin*, ibid., p. 6.
30. Numbers, *The Creationists* : ibid., p. 53.
31. Lamoureux, D. O., "The Ancient Science in the Bible." BioLogos Foundation. http://biologos.org/blogs/archive/the-ancient-science-in-the-bible
32. McGrath, *Science And Religion*. ibid., loc. 692.
33. Fradd, M., "Evolution vs Genesis." http://mattfradd.com/evolution-vs-genesis/
34. Davis, E. T. B., The Word and the Works: Concordism and American Evangelicals. In *Perspectives on an Evolving Creation*, ibid., Miller, K. B., Ed. p. 36.
35. Barbour, I. G., *When Science Meets Religion : Enemies, Strangers, Or Partners?* 1st ed.; Harper: San Francisco, 2000; p. 8. Galileo famously said, "The Bible teaches us how to go to heaven, not how the heavens go." This phrase was quoted by Galileo in his letter to

the Grand Duchess, Christina.

36. Ruse, *The Evolution-Creation Struggle.* ibid., p. 55.
37. Ruse, M., *Can a Darwinian be a Christian? : The Relationship Between Science and Religion.* Cambridge University Press: New York, 2000. p. 53.
38. Falk, D. R., *Coming To Peace With Science: Bridging The Worlds Between Faith And Biology.* InterVarsity Press: Downers Grove, IL, 2004. p. 292.
39. Davis, E.T.B., "The Word and the Works: Concordism and American Evangelicals," in *Perspectives on an Evolving Creation,* ibid., Miller, K.B. Ed., p. 37.
40. Falk, *Coming To Peace With Science*: ibid., p. 258.
41. Ramm, *The Christian* View, ibid. p. 15.
42. Giberson, *Saving Darwin*: ibid., p. 174.
43. Giberson, K.; Artigas, M., *Oracles of Science : Celebrity Scientists Versus God and Religion.* Oxford University Press: Oxford ; New York, 2007; p. 74.
44. Ruse, *Can a Darwinian be a Christian?* : ibid.
45. McGrath, *Science And Religion.* ibid., loc. 653.
46. Davis, "Science and the Bible: Theistic Evolution, Part 1." ibid.
47. Fugle, G.N., *Laying Down Arms to Heal the Creation - Evolution Divide.* Wipf & Stock, Eugene, OR., 2015; p. 275.
48. Fugle, ibid., p. 280.
49. Giberson & Artigas, *Oracles of Science* : ibid., p. 156.
50. Information about the United Methodists and evolution can be found at http://www.umc.org/what-we-believe/what-is-the-united-methodist-churchs-position-on-evolution
51. The Presbyterian decision regarding evolution is found at https://ncse.com/news/2016/08/presbyterians-add-their-voice-evolution-0018343
52. Gould, S. J., *Eight Little Piggies : Reflections in Natural History.* Norton: 1993. p. 415.
53. Lamoureux, *Evolutionary Creation* : ibid., p. 352.
54. Lamoureux, ibid., p. 97.
55. Lamoureux, ibid., p. 30.
56. Lamoureux, D. O., *I Love Jesus & I Accept Evolution.* Kindle Edition. Wipf and Stock Publishers: Eugene, OR, 2009. loc. 681.
57. Lamoureux, *Evolutionary Creation* : ibid., p. 59.
58. Lamoureux, *I Love Jesus & I Accept Evolution.* ibid., loc. 2745.
59. Miller, *Finding Darwin's God,* ibid., p. 283.
60. Lamoureux, D. O., "Evolutionary Creation: A Christian Approach to Evolution." BioLogos Foundation. http://biologos.org/uploads/projects/Lamoureux_Scholarly_Essay.pdf
61. Saletan, W., "Creativity for Creationists: An evolutionary creationist Evangelizes to Christians About Science." December, 2012. http://www.slate.com/articles/health_and_science/human_nature/2014/12/evolutionary_creationism_jeff_hardin_reconciles_evangelical_christianity.html
62. Trasancos, S., "Why say Theistic Evolution? Is There Any Other Kind?" http://www.ncregister.attcom/blog/trasancos/why-say-theistic-evolution-is-there-any-other-kind
63. Plantinga, Science and Religion: Why Does the Debate Continue? In *The Religion and Science Debate,* ibid., Attridge, H. W., Ed. loc. 1519.
64. Gould, *Eight Little Piggies* : ibid., p. 366.
65. Van Till, Intelligent Design: The Celebration of Gifts Withheld? In *The Johnson-Lamoureux Debate,* ibid., Lamoureux, D. O.; Johnson, P. E., Eds. p. 83.

66. Larson, *Remarkable History*. ibid., loc. 1697.
67. MacKay, D.M., "Science and Christian Faith Today," *True Scientists, True Faith*: ibid., in Berry, R.J. Ed., loc. 328.
68. MacKay, "Science and Christian Faith Today," ibid., in Berry, R.J. Ed., *True Scientists, True Faith*, loc. 330.
69. Peters & Hewlett, *From Creation to New Creation* : ibid., p. 25.
70. Greenberg, Geological Framework of an Evolving Creation. In *Perspectives on an Evolving Creation*, ibid., Miller, K. B., Ed.; p. 417.
71. Miller, K.B., An Evolving Creation: Oxymoron or Fruitful Insight?, in *Perspectives on an Evolving Creation*, ibid., Miller, K.B., Ed., p. 8.
72. Haarsma, L., Does Science Exclude God? Natural Law, Chance, Miracles, And Scientific Practice. In *Perspectives on an Evolving Creation*, ibid., Miller, K. B., Ed. p 73.
73. Gould, S. J., *I Have Landed : The End of a Beginning in Natural History*. 1st ed.; Harmony Books: New York, 2002. p. 229.
74. Haught, J. F., *God After Darwin : A Theology of Evolution*. Westview Press: Boulder, Colo. ; Oxford, 2000; p. 99.
75. Barbour, I.G. *When Science Meets Religion : Enemies, Strangers, or Partners?* Harper, San Francisco, 2000; p. 60.
76. Barbour, ibid., p. 103.
77. Barrett, M.; Caneday, A.B., Introduction: Adam, To Be or not To Be. In Barrett & Caneday, Eds., *Four Views on the Historical Adam*. Zondervan, Grand Rapids, MI. 2016; loc. 227.
78. Peters & Hewlett, *From Creation to New Creation* : ibid., p. 30.
79. Gould, S. J., *Rocks of Ages : Science and Religion in the Fullness of Life*. Ballantine Books: New York, 1999. p. 22.
80. Collins, *Language of God*: ibid., p. 53.
81. Fugle, G.N., *Laying Down Arms to Heal the Creation - Evolution Divide*. Wipf & Stock, Eugene, OR., 2015; p. 122.
82. Collins, ibid.
83. Kramer, B., "Growing Up Evangelical. My Story of Making Peace with Evolution." BioLogos Foundation. http://biologos.org/blogs/brad-kramer-the-evolving-evangelical/growing-up-evangelical-my-story-of-making-peace-with-evolution
84. Wikipedia, The BioLogos Foundation.
85. BioLogos Editorial Team, Introduction and Mission Statement. http://biologos.org/about-us/
86. Ostling, R.N. "The Search for the Historical Adam," in *The Origins Debate*, ibid., The Editors of Christianity Today, Ed., loc. 168.
87. Numbers, *The Creationists* : ibid., p. 54.
88. Stone, R. M., "When Religious (and Political) Identity Trumps Inquiry – and Facts." http://religionnews.com/2014/07/07/religious-political-identity-trumps-inquiry-facts/
89. Ecklund, *Science Vs. Religion* : ibid., loc. 29.
90. Ecklund, ibid., loc. 43.
91. Slack, G., *The Battle over the Meaning of Everything : Evolution, Intelligent Design, and a School Board in Dover*, PA. Jossey-Bass ; Chichester : John Wiley [distributor]: San Francisco, Calif., 2007. p. 205.
92. Collins, *Language of God*, ibid., p. 16.
93. Stenmark, M., Ways of Relating Science and Religion. In *The Cambridge Companion*

to *Science and Religion*. Kindle Edition., Harrison, P., Ed. Cambridge University Press: Cambridge, U.K., 2010; p 278.

94. Ecklund, E. H., *Science Vs. Religion : What Scientists Really Think*. Kindle Edition. Oxford University Press: New York ; Oxford, 2010. p. 45.
95. Kramer, "Growing Up Evangelical", ibid.
96. McGrath, A. E.; McGrath, J. C., *The Dawkins Delusion? Atheist Fundamentalism and the Denial of the Divine*. SPCK: London, 2007. p. 8.
97. McGrath & McGrath, ibid., p.75.
98. Contemporary theistic evolutionists include Os Guinness, Philip Yancey, former creationists Darrell Falk & Stephen Godfrey, Karl Giberson, Denis Lamoureux; Dennis Venema, Joan Roughgarden, Norman T. Wright. Keith Miller. Howard Van till. Keith Ward. See Richard N. Ostling, in Christianity Today, *The Origins Debate*, Chapter. 1 "The Search for the Historical Adam." loc. 174.
99. Scientists who are Christians include Ronald Fischer, Sewall Wright, Theodosius Dobzhansky, Simon Conway Morris, Alister McGrath, C.S. Lewis, Janet Roughgarden, Hugh Ross, Francis Collins, Daryl Falk, Denis Lamoureux, Kenneth Miller, Keith Miller, Karl Giberson, and Stephen Godfrey.
100. Ruse, *The Evolution-Creation Struggle*. ibid., p. 249.
101. Ostling, R.N.,"The Search for the Historical Adam" in Christianity Today, *The Origins Debate*, Chapter 1, ibid., loc. 168.
102. Eugenie Scott's article titled "The Creation - Evolution Continuum" is on the National Center for Science Education website. https://ncse.com/library-resource/creationevolution-continuum
103. Pennock, R. T., *Tower of Babel : The Evidence Against The New Creationism*. MIT Press: Cambridge, Mass. ; London, 1999; p. 16.
104. Wikipedia, American Scientific Affiliation.
105. Ostling, R.N.,"The Search for the Historical Adam" in Christianity Today, *The Origins Debate*, Chapter 1, ibid., loc. 133.
106. Ostling, ibid., loc. 174.
107. Stephen Jay Gould notes that several French priests have been distinguished students of ancient life. Pierre Teilhard de Chardin S.J. (1881–1955) was a French philosopher and Jesuit priest who trained as a paleontologist and geologist and took part in the discovery of Peking Man. Henri Édouard Prosper Breuil (1877-1961) was a French Catholic priest, archaeologist, anthropologist, ethnologist and geologist, noted for his studies of cave art. Francisco Ayala is professor of biology at the University of California. John F. Haught is a Roman Catholic theologian and Senior Research Fellow at the Woodstock Theological Center at Georgetown University. See Gould, S. J., *Leonardo's Mountain of Clams and The Diet of Worms : Essays on Natural History*. Harmony Books ; London : Random House: New York, 1998. p. 165.
108. Wikipedia, Kenneth R. Miller.
109. Giberson & Artigas, *Oracles of Science* : ibid., p. 75.
110. Giberson, K., *Seven Glorious Days : A Scientist Retells The Genesis Creation Story*. Kindle Edition. Paraclete Press: Brewster, Mass., 2012; p. 20.
111. Giberson & Artigas, ibid., p. 97.
112. John Paul II, "Message to the Pontifical Academy of Sciences: On Evolution." 1996. p. 1. https://www.ewtn.com/library/PAPALDOC/JP961022.HTM
113. Berra, T. M., *Evolution and the Myth of Creationism: A Basic Guide to the Facts In the*

Evolution Debate. Stanford University Press: Stanford, Calif., 1990. p. 124.

114. Boslough, J., *Stephen Hawking's Universe*. Quill: New York, 1985. p. 109.
115. John Paul II, "Message to the Pontifical Academy," ibid., p. 2.
116. Fradd, "Evolution vs Genesis." ibid.
117. John Paul II, ibid., p. 1.
118. Roughgarden, J., *Evolution and Christian Faith : Reflections of an Evolutionary Biologist*. Island Press: Washington, D.C. ; London, 2006. p. 54.
119. Elliott, Josh, news report, ctvnews.ca Oct 29, 2014. http://www.ctvnews.ca/world/pope-francis-evolution-is-real-god-did-not-wave-a-magic-wand-1.2076772
120. Larson, *Remarkable History*, ibid., loc. 2623.
121. Russell, R. J., Special Providence and Genetic Mutation: A New Defense of Theistic Evolution. In *Perspectives on an Evolving Creation*, ibid., Miller, K. B., Ed. p. 337.
122. Peters & Hewlett, *Theological and Scientific Commentary*, ibid., p. 10.
123. Roughgarden, *Evolution and Christian Faith* : ibid., p. 35.
124. Lamoureux, *Evolutionary Creation* : ibid., p. 365.
125. Haught, *God After Darwin*, ibid., p. 52.
126. Haidt, J., *The Righteous Mind : Why Good People Are Divided By Politics And Religion*. Kindle Edition. Allen Lane: London, 2012. p. 263.
127. Lamoureux, D. O., *I Love Jesus & I Accept Evolution*. Kindle Edition. Wipf and Stock Publishers: Eugene, OR, 2009. loc. 130.
128. Lamoureux, D. O., *Evolutionary Creation : A Christian Approach to Evolution*. Lutterworth Press: Cambridge, England, 2008. Frontispiece.
129. Lamoureux, D. O., "Evolutionary Creation: A Christian Approach to Evolution." (website summary) 2010. http://biologos.org/uploads/projects/Lamoureux_Scholarly_Essay.pdf
130. Fugle, G.N., *Laying Down Arms to Heal the Creation - Evolution Divide*. Wipf & Stock, Eugene, OR., 2015; p. 279.
131. See the four-part blog series by Robert C. Bishop beginning June 24, 2017 at http://biologos.org/blogs/archive/the-extended-synthesis-reviewing-darwins-doubt-robert-bishop-part-1
132. Lamoureux, essay on Evolutionary Creation, ibid.
133. Haught, J. F., *God After Darwin : A Theology of Evolution*. Westview Press: Boulder, Colo. ; Oxford, 2000; p. 37.
134. Miller, K. R., *Finding Darwin's God : A Scientist's Search for Common Ground Between God and Evolution*. Cliff Street Books: New York, 1999. p. 258.
135. In outlining the differences between theistic evolution and evolutionary creation, Denis Lamoureux says: "The term '*evolutionary creation*' seems like a contradiction in terms. However, the most important word in this category is the noun 'creation.' Evolutionary creationists are first and foremost creationists. They believe in a Creator and that the world is His creation. The qualifying term is the adjective "evolutionary," which simply indicates the method that the Lord used to make the universe and life. This view of origins is often called 'theistic evolution.' But that word arrangement places the process of evolution as the primary term and makes our Creator secondary and merely a qualifying adjective. I find such an inversion in priority completely unacceptable. Another reason for employing the category of evolutionary creation is that it distinguishes evangelical Christians who love Jesus and accept evolution from the evolutionary interpretations of

deists (who believe in an impersonal, never-present god-of-the-philosophers) and liberal Christians (who believe that Jesus was merely an enlightened human who never rose physically from the dead)." See also Chapter 1, "No Historical Adam: Evolutionary Creation View," in Barrett and Caneday, Eds., *Four Views on the Historical Adam*," Zondervan, Grand Rapids, MI, 2013; loc. 670.

136. Scott, E. C., *Evolution vs. Creationism : An Introduction*. University of California Press: Berkeley, Calif. ; London, 2005. p. 63.
137. Peters, T.; Hewlett, M. J., *Evolution From Creation to New Creation : Conflict, Conversation, and Convergence*. Abingdon Press: Nashville, TN, 2003. p. 30.
138. Gould, S. J., *Leonardo's Mountain of Clams and The Diet of Worms : Essays on Natural History*. Harmony Books ; London : Random House: New York, 1998. p. 289.
139. Braaten, L. J., May the Glory of the Lord Endure Forever! Biblical Reflections on Creation Care. In *Perspectives on an Evolving Creation*, Miller, K. B., Ed. Wm. B. Eerdmans: Grand Rapids, MI and Cambridge, U. K., 2003; p. 417.
140. Van Till, H. J., Intelligent Design: the Celebration of Gifts Withheld? In *The Johnson-Lamoureux Debate on Biological Origins*, Lamoureux, D. O.; Johnson, P. E., Eds. Regent College Publishing: Vancouver, B.C., 1999; p. 85.
141. Giberson, K.; Collins, F. S., *The Language of Science and Faith : Straight Answers to Genuine Questions*. Kindle Edition. SPCK: London, 2011; p. 156.
142. Haught, *God After Darwin* : ibid., p. 98.
143. Giberson, K., *Seven Glorious Days : A Scientist Retells The Genesis Creation Story*. Kindle Edition. Paraclete Press: Brewster, Mass., 2012; p. 172.
144. Haarsma, L., Does Science Exclude God? Natural Law, Chance, Miracles, And Scientific Practice. In *Perspectives on an Evolving Creation*, ibid., Miller, K. B., Ed. p. 77.
145. Ayala, F., Parallel Evolution. In *Faith in Science: Scientists Search for Truth*, Richardson, W. M.; Slack, G., Eds. Routledge: London and New York, 2001; p. 13.
146. Barbour, I. G., *When Science Meets Religion : Enemies, Strangers, Or Partners?* 1st ed.; Harper: San Francisco, 2000; p. 112.
147. Peters, T.; Hewlett, M. J., *Theological and Scientific Commentary on Darwin's Origin of Species*. Abingdon Press: Nashville, 2008; p. 82.
148. Ruse, M., *Science and Spirituality : Making Room for Faith in the Age of Science*. Cambridge University Press: Cambridge, 2010; p. 7.
149. Ruse, *Science and Spirituality* : ibid., p. 205.
150. Humphreys, S. C. J., Can Science and Christianity Both be True? In *True Scientists, True Faith: Some of the World's Leading Scientists Reveal the Harmony Between their Science and their Faith*. Kindle Edition., Berry, R. J., Ed. Monarch Books: Oxford, U.K. and Grand Rapids, MI, 2014; p. 77.
151. Conway Morris, S., "Is there room in evolutionary creation to believe in miracles?" BioLogos Foundation. http://biologos.org/common-questions/gods-relationship-to-creation/biologos-and-miracles
152. Ostling, R. N., The Search for the Historical Adam. In *The Origins Debate: Evangelical Perspectives on Creation, Evolution, and Intelligent Design*. Kindle Edition., The Editors of Christianity Today, Ed. Christianity Today: Carol Stream, IL, 2012; p loc. 280.
153. Gould, S. J., *Dinosaur in a Haystack : Reflections in Natural History*. Harmony: New York, 1995; p. 85.
154. Ecklund, E. H., *Science Vs. Religion : What Scientists Really Think*. Kindle Edition. Oxford University Press: New York ; Oxford, 2010. p. 107.

155. Brown, W. S., Evolution, Cognitive Neuroscience, and the Soul. In *Perspectives on an Evolving Creation*, Miller, K. B., Ed. ibid., p. 521.
156. Ecklund, *Science Vs. Religion* : ibid., loc. 3652.
157. Ecklund, ibid., loc. 10.
158. Ecklund, ibid., loc. 19.
159. Haarsma, D. Reviewing Darwin's Doubt: Conclusion. January 19, 2015. BioLogos Foundation, The President's Notebook. http://biologos.org/blogs/deborah-haarsma-the-presidents-notebook/reviewing-darwins-doubt-conclusion
160. Janssen, L.J., *Standing on the Shoulders of Giants: Genesis and Human Origins*. Wipf & Stock, Eugene, OR, 2016; p. 229.
161. Fugle, G.N., *Laying Down Arms to Heal the Creation - Evolution Divide*. Wipf & Stock, Eugene, OR., 2015; p. 1111.
162. Venema, D.R., *Adam and the Genome: Reading Scripture after Genetic Science*. Brazos, Grand Rapids, MI., 2017; p. 194.
163. Giberson, K., *Saving Darwin: How To Be A Christian And Believe In Evolution*. Harper One: New York, 2008. p. 1. Karl Giberson began his academic career as a young earth creationist and after doing a thorough review of the evidence, took on an evolutionary viewpoint. Others in this group are Godfrey and Lamoureux, along with many others.
164. Lamoureux, *I Love Jesus & I Accept Evolution*. ibid., loc. 2722.
165. Godfrey, S. J.; Smith, C. R., *Paradigms on Pilgrimage : Creationism, Paleontology, and Biblical Interpretation*. Clements Pub.: Toronto, Ont., 2005; p. 82. With respect to C.S. Lewis, see the following article which appeared on the BioLogos website in May 2011. http://biologos.org/blogs/archive/c-s-lewis-on-evolution-and-intelligent-design-part-5
166. Picard, R., Building Technology with Emotion. In *True Scientists, True Faith*: ibid., Berry, R. J., Ed. p. 320.
167. Roughgarden, J., *Evolution and Christian Faith : Reflections of an Evolutionary Biologist*. Island Press: Washington, D.C. ; London, 2006. p. 21.
168. Gould, S. J., *Eight Little Piggies : Reflections in Natural History*. Norton: 1993. p. 40.
169. Haught, *God After Darwin* : ibid., p. 160.
170. Dennett, D. C., *Darwin's Dangerous Idea : Evolution and the Meanings of Life*. Simon & Schuster: New York & London, 1995; p. 511. See also McLeish, T., *Faith and Wisdom in Science*, Oxford University Press, Oxford, UK., 2014. p. 155.
171. Falk, D. R., *Coming To Peace With Science: Bridging The Worlds Between Faith And Biology*. InterVarsity Press: Downers Grove, IL, 2004. p. 310.
172. Davis, T., "Science and the Bible: Theistic Evolution, Part II." BioLogos Foundation. http://biologos.org/blogs/ted-davis-reading-the-book-of-nature/science-and-the-bible-theistic-evolution-part-2
173. Kramer, B., "Growing Up Evangelical. My Story of Making Peace with Evolution." BioLogos Foundation. http://biologos.org/blogs/brad-kramer-the-evolving-evangelical/growing-up-evangelical-my-story-of-making-peace-with-evolution
174. Collins, F. S., *The Language of God: A Scientist Presents Evidence for Belief*. Free Press: New York & London, 2006; p. 88.
175. Larson, *Remarkable History*. ibid., loc. 3172.
176. Lurie, A., "Is Religion a Science Stopper?" Huffington Post. http://www.huffingtonpost.com/rabbi-alan-lurie/is-religion-a-science-stopper_b_3283004.html
177. Catechism of the Catholic Faith - Part One - The Profession of Faith. http://www.vatican.va/archive/ccc_css/archive/catechism/p1s2c1p4.htm

178. Pope, C., "Polygenism is Problematic." http://blog.adw.org/2013/10/polygenism-is-problematic-a-catholic-caution-on-another-aspect-of-evolutionary-theory/
179. Deborah Haarsma, interviewed by Vikas Shah. The interview is found on the blog, Religion, Science and Society. May 18, 2016. https://thoughteconomics.com/religion-science-and-society/
180. Dowd, M., *Thank God for Evolution!*. 1st ed.; Publishers Group UK: San Francisco, 2007; p. 112.
181. Collins, *The Language of God*, ibid., p. 6.
182. Godfrey, S. J.; Smith, C. R., *Paradigms on Pilgrimage : Creationism, Paleontology, and Biblical Interpretation*. Clements Pub.: Toronto, Ont., 2005; p. 12.
183. Lamoureux, *Evolutionary Creation* : ibid., p. 1.
184. Dowd, *Thank God for Evolution!*, ibid., p. 11.
185. Scott, E. C., *Evolution vs. Creationism : An Introduction*. University of California Press: Berkeley, Calif. ; London, 2005. p. 198.
186. Giberson, *Saving Darwin*, ibid., p. 6.
187. Numbers, *The Creationists* : ibid., p. 24.
188. Ruse, *Can a Darwinian be a Christian?* : ibid., p. 106.

Chapter 9 - Young Earth Creationism

1. Peters, T.; Hewlett, M. J., *Evolution From Creation to New Creation : Conflict, Conversation, and Convergence*. Abingdon Press: Nashville, TN, 2003; p. 75.
2. Pennock, R.T., *Tower of Babel : The Evidence Against the New Creationism*. MIT Press : Cambridge, Mass. ; London, 1999; p. 19.
3. Lamoureux, D.O., *I Love Jesus & I Accept Evolution*, Wipf & Stock, Eugene, OR, 2009; loc. 548.
4. Reeves, J., "Should Christians Trust Scientific Experts?" BioLogos Foundation. http://biologos.org/blogs/archive/should-christians-trust-scientific-experts
5. Buchanan, S., "Was the Expanse Overhead in Genesis 1 a Solid Dome?" https://letterstocreationists.wordpress.com/2012/09/03/was-the-expanse-overhead-in-genesis-1-a-solid-dome/
6. Giberson, K., "Adventist Origins of Young Earth Creationism." BioLogos Foundation. https://biologos.org/uploads/static-content/Giberson-scholarly-essay-1.pdf
7. Numbers, R. L., *The Creationists : From Scientific Creationism to Intelligent Design*. Expanded ed., 1st Harvard University Press pbk. ed.; Harvard University Press: Cambridge, Mass. ; London, 2006; p. 90.
8. Numbers, R.L., *The Creationists* : ibid.; p. 321.
9. Numbers, R.L., ibid.; p. 90.
10. Giberson, K., Adventist Origins of Young Earth Creationism, ibid.; BioLogos Foundation. https://biologos.org/uploads/static-content/Giberson-scholarly-essay-1.pdf
11. Numbers, ibid., p. 91
12. Numbers, p. 107.
13. Numbers, p. 98.
14. Numbers, p. 115.
15. Numbers, p.101.
16. Ramm, B. L., *The Christian View of Science and Scripture*. 1st ed.; Grand Rapids: 1954; p. 126.
17. Numbers, *The Creationists* : ibid., p. 93.

18. Numbers, p. 96.
19. Numbers, p. 99.
20. Numbers, p. 226.
21. Giberson, K.; Collins, F. S., *The Language of Science and Faith : Straight Answers to Genuine Questions*. Kindle Edition. SPCK: London, 2011; p. 159.
22. Numbers, *The Creationists* : ibid., p. 370.
23. MacMillan, D., "Understanding Creationism, VIII: An Insider's Guide By a Former Young Earth Creationist." http://pandasthumb.org/archives/2014/07/understanding-c-7.html
24. Giberson, K.; Collins, F.S., *The Language of Science and Faith* : ibid.; p. 76.
25. Ross, H., *A Matter of Days: Resolving a Creation Controversy*. Colorado Springs, CO., NavPress, 2004. p. 241. The 1982 decision of the International Council on Biblical Inerrancy is discussed in detail here. The decision is also mentioned in the debate between Hugh Ross and Duane Gish on the *Focus on the Family* radio broadcast in April 18, 1991.
26. Dobson, J., "Duane Gish - Hugh Ross Debate on Young Earth vs Old Earth Creationism." *Focus on the Family* Radio Broadcast, ibid.
27. Moore, R. A., "The Impossible Voyage of Noah's Ark." National Center for Science Education. https://ncse.com/cej/4/1/impossible-voyage-noahs-ark
28. Morris, H. M., *The Beginning of the World*. Master Books: El Cajon, CA, 1991; p. 14
29. Morris, H. M., *Biblical Cosmology and Modern Science*. : Baker Book House, 1970, (1973). p. 33.
30. MacMillan, D., "Understanding Creationism II - Variation and Adaptation. https://pandasthumb.org/archives/2014/06/understanding-c-1.html
31. Fugle, G. N., *Laying Down Arms to Heal the Creation - Evolution Divide*. Eugene, OR: Wipf & Stock, 2015; p. 267.
32. Fugle, p. 181.
33. MacMillan, D., "Understanding Creationism VIII: An Insider's Guide by a Former Young Earth Creationist." http://pandasthumb.org/archives/2014/07/understanding-c-7.html
34. Janssen, L. J., *Standing on the Shoulders of Giants: Genesis and Human Origins*. Eugene, OR: Wipf & Stock, 2016; p. 263.
35. Ramm, B. L., *The Christian View of Science and Scripture*. 1st ed.; Grand Rapids; 1954.
36. Morris & Whitcomb, *The Genesis Flood*; ibid.
37. Graham, B., *Billy Graham: Personal Thoughts of a Public Man*. English Language edition ed.; Chariot Victor Publishing: 1997; p. 72.
38. Giberson, K., *Saving Darwin: How To Be A Christian And Believe In Evolution*. Harper One: New York, 2008; p. 132.
39. Numbers, R.L., *Creationists* : ibid.; p. 222.
40. Numbers, R. L., Scientific Creationism and Intelligent Design. In *The Cambridge Companion to Science and Religion*. Kindle Edition., Harrison, P., Ed. Cambridge University Press: Cambridge, U.K., 2010; p. 133.
41. Giberson, K., *Saving Darwin*: ibid.; p. 131.
42. Numbers, R.L., "Scientific Creationism and Intelligent Design," ibid.; p. 133.
43. Numbers, *The Creationists* : ibid.; p. 223.
44. Numbers, p. 232.
45. Scott, E. C., *Evolution vs. Creationism : An Introduction*. University of California Press:

Berkeley, Calif. ; London, 2005; p. 60.
46. Giberson, K., *Saving Darwin*: ibid., p. 137.
47. Giberson, p. 5.
48. Kitcher, P., *Living with Darwin : Evolution, Design, and the Future of Faith*. Oxford University Press: Oxford ; New York, 2007; p. 150.
49. Washington Post: "Truth or Denial – from Climate Change to the Anti-Vaccine Movement. Is Denial on the Rise in America?" Washington Post. http://www.washingtonpost.com/sf/brand-connect/bleecker-street/denial/
50. Milburn, M. A.; Conrad, S. D., *The Politics of Denial*. MIT Press: Cambridge, Mass., 1996. Quoted in Washington Post web article, ibid., "Truth or Denial - From Climate Change to the Anti-Vaccine Movement is Denial on the Rise in America?"
51. Pennock, R. T., *Tower of Babel : The Evidence Against The New Creationism*. MIT Press: Cambridge, Mass. ; London, 1999; p. 38.
52. "Truth or Denial – from Climate Change to the Anti-Vaccine Movement Is Denial on the Rise in America?" Washington Post. November 15, 2016; ibid.
53. Fugle, G. N., *Laying Down Arms to Heal the Creation - Evolution Divide*. Eugene, OR: Wipf & Stock, 2015; p. 227.
54. Numbers, R.L., *The Creationists* : ibid.; p. 124.
55. Pieper, F., *Christian Dogmatics*. 3 Vols; St. Louis: Concordia Publishing House, 1950. Volume 1, pp. 470, 473, 474.
56. Pieper, ibid., Vol. 1, p. 474. See also Vol. 1, p. 473, footnote 11.
57. Numbers, R.L., *The Creationists*, ibid., p. 331.
58. Peters, T.; Hewlett, M.J., *From Creation to New Creation* : ibid.; p. 75.
59. Numbers, R.L., "Scientific Creationism and Intelligent Design," in *The Cambridge Companion to Science and Religion*, ibid., Harrison, P., Ed.; p. 133.
60. Peters, T.; Hewlett, M.J., *From Creation to New Creation* : ibid.; p. 75.
61. Ramm, B.L., *The Christian View*, ibid.; p. 178.
62. Numbers, R.L., *The Creationists* : ibid.; p. 135.
63. Numbers, p. 240.
64. Numbers, p. 335.
65. Numbers, p. 333.
66. Breshears, J., "How Young Earth Creationism Became a Core Tenet of American Fundamentalism, Part II." A good article on George MacReady Price. Found at http://www.reasons.org/articles/how-young-earth-creationism-became-a-core-tenet-of-american-fundamentalism-part-2
67. Lamoureux, D.O., No Historical Adam, in Barrett, Matthew, and Ardel B. Caneday, eds. *Four Views on the Historical Adam*. Ch. 1., Edited by Stanley N. Gundry, Counterpoints: Bible and Theology. Grand Rapids: Zondervan, 2013; loc. 700.
68. Ruse, M., *Science and Spirituality : Making Room for Faith in the Age of Science*. Cambridge University Press: Cambridge, 2010; p. 8
69. The following resolution was adopted by the 2004 convention of the Lutheran Church - Missouri Synod:

RESOLUTION 2-08A: To Commend Preaching and Teaching Creation

Overtures 2-24-25, 5-43-45 (CW, pp. 151–152, 237)

WHEREAS the Scriptures teach that God is the creator of all that exists and is therefore the Author and Giver of Life; and
WHEREAS the hypotheses of macro-, organic, and Darwinian evolution, including theistic evolution or any other model denying special, immediate, and miraculous creation, undercut this support for the honoring of life as a gift of God; and
WHEREAS any teaching that advocates the transition from one species to another, as opposed to maintaining the distinction of species "*according to their kinds*" (Genesis, Chapter 1), rejects the clear teaching of scripture; and
WHEREAS it is the church's duty to produce followers of Christ who not only know the fundamentals of the Christian faith, but also are "*prepared to give an answer . . . for the hope that you have*" (1 Pet. 3:15); therefore be it
RESOLVED that all educational agencies and institutions of The Lutheran Church-Missouri Synod including early childhood programs, elementary schools, high schools, colleges, universities, and seminaries continue to teach creation from the biblical perspective; and be it further
RESOLVED that no educational agency or institution of The Lutheran Church-Missouri Synod tolerate any teaching that contradicts the special, immediate, and miraculous creation by God, Father, Son, and Holy Spirit, as an explanation for the origin of the universe; and be it further
RESOLVED that the Synod's educational agencies and institutions properly distinguish between micro and macro evolution and affirm the scriptural revelation that God has created all species "*according to their kinds*"; and be it finally
RESOLVED that The Lutheran Church-Missouri Synod, in convention, remind its pastors and teachers to increase emphasis to the doctrine of God as the Creator and Author of Life in their preaching and teaching.

70. Numbers, *The Creationists* : ibid., p. 312.
71. Numbers, p. 319.
72. Numbers, p. 330.
73. Ross, H., *A Matter of Days: Resolving a Creation Controversy*. Navpress: Colorado Springs, CO, 2004; p. 33.
74. Wikipedia, Young Earth Creationism.
75. Ross, H., *A Matter of Days*: ibid.; p. 35.
76. Walton, J. H., *The Lost World Of Genesis One : Ancient Cosmology and the Origins Debate*. Kindle Edition. IVP Academic: Downers Grove, Ill., 2009; loc. 1633.
77. Numbers, *The Creationists* : ibid., p. 283.
78. Numbers, p. 219.
79. Collins, F. S., *The Language of God: A Scientist Presents Evidence for Belief*. Free Press: New York & London, 2006; p. 5.
80. Godfrey, S. J.; Smith, C. R., *Paradigms on Pilgrimage: Creationism, Paleontology, and Biblical Interpretation*. Clements Pub.: Toronto, Ont., 2005; p. 151.
81. Gould, S. J., *I Have Landed : The End of a Beginning in Natural History*. 1st ed.; Harmony Books: New York, 2002; p. 107.
82. Miller, K.R., "Darwin, God, And Dover," in *The Religion and Science Debate*, ibid., Attridge, H.W., Ed.; loc. 1060.
83. Gottschall, J., *The Storytelling Animal : How Stories Make Us Human*. iBook Edition. Houghton Mifflin Harcourt: Boston, 2012; p. 228.
84. Wright, N. T., *Surprised by Scripture: Engaging Contemporary Issues*. New York: Harp-

erOne, 2014; p. 18.
85. Fugle, G. N., *Laying Down Arms to Heal the Creation - Evolution Divide*. Eugene, OR: Wipf & Stock, 2015; p. 61.
86. Giberson, K., *Saving Darwin*: ibid.; p. 128.
87. Giberson, p. 122.
88. Ross, *A Matter of Days*: ibid.,; p. 119.
89. Giberson, *Saving Darwin*: ibid.; p. 166.
90. Ramm, *The Christian View*, ibid.; p. 184.
91. Ecklund, E. H., *Science Vs. Religion : What Scientists Really Think*. Kindle Edition. Oxford University Press: New York ; Oxford, 2010; p. 127.
92. Dawkins, R., *The Greatest Show On Earth : The Evidence For Evolution*. iBook Edition. Black Swan: London, 2009; p. 124.
93. Falk, D. R., *Coming To Peace With Science: Bridging The Worlds Between Faith And Biology*. InterVarsity Press: Downers Grove, IL, 2004; p. 208.
94. Ramm, *The Christian View*, p. 22.
95. Giberson, K.; Artigas, M., *Oracles of Science : Celebrity Scientists Versus God and Religion*. Oxford University Press: Oxford ; New York, 2007; p. 50.
96. Carter, N., "Will Evangelicals Ever Learn to Embrace Evolution?" March 13, 2015. http://www.patheos.com/blogs/godlessindixie/2015/03/13/will-evangelicals-ever-learn-to-embrace-evolution/
97. Numbers, *The Creationists* : ibid.; p. 229.
98. For a comprehensive survey, see Mark Isaak's *The Counter-Creationism Handbook*. Greenwood ; Oxford : Harcourt Education : Westport, Conn.; 2005.
99. Pennock, R.T., *Tower of Babel* : ibid., p. 154.
100. Hyers, C., Comparing Biblical and Scientific Maps of Origins. In *Perspectives on an Evolving Creation*, Miller, K. B., Ed. Wm. B. Eerdmans: Grand Rapids, MI and Cambridge U.K., 2003; p. 27.
101. Wikipedia, Baraminology.
102. Hodge, B.; Purdom, G., "What Are "Kinds" in Genesis?" Answers in Genesis. https://answersingenesis.org/creation-science/baraminology/what-are-kinds-in-genesis
103. Hodge, B., "Are Mutations Part of the 'Engine' of Evolution?" Answers in Genesis. https://answersingenesis.org/genetics/mutations/are-mutations-part-of-the-engine-of-evolution
104. Mayr, E., *What Evolution Is*. Basic Books: New York, 2001; p. 114.
105. Ruse, M., *The Evolution-Creation Struggle*. Harvard University Press: Cambridge, Mass. ; London, 2005; p. 171.
106. RationalWiki. Cambrian Explosion.
107. Conway Morris, S., *The Crucible of Creation : The Burgess Shale and the Rise of Animals*. Oxford University Press: Oxford, 1998. p. 140.
108. Meyer, S. C., *Darwin's Doubt : The Explosive Origin of Animal Life and the Case for Intelligent Design*. 1st ed.; HarperOne: New York, NY, 2013; p. 304.
109. Mitchell, E., "Cambrian Explosion was the Culmination of Cascading Causes Evolutionists Claim." Answers in Genesis. https://answersingenesis.org/theory-of-evolution/evolution-timeline/cambrian-explosion-was-the-culmination-of-cascading-causes-evolutionists-claim/
110. Carl Wieland's article titled "Exploding Evolution" argues that creatures found as fossils in Cambrian rocks have no evolutionary ancestors. And no new basic body plans have

appeared since. Creation Ministries International. http://creation.com/exploding-evolution

111. Public Broadcasting System. Cambrian Explosion. 2001. http://www.pbs.org/wgbh/evolution/library/03/4/l_034_02.html
112. The rest of the PBS website article points out that recent research suggests that the period prior to the explosion saw the gradual evolution of a "genetic tool kit" of genes that govern developmental processes. Once assembled, this genetic tool kit enabled an unprecedented period of evolutionary experimentation and competition. Many forms seen in the fossil record disappeared without a trace. Once the body plans that proved most successful came to dominate the biosphere, evolution never had such a free hand again, and evolutionary change was limited to relatively minor tinkering with the body plans that already existed.
113. Miller, K.R., *Finding Darwin's God* : ibid.; p. 173.
114. Gould, S. J., *Dinosaur in a Haystack : Reflections in Natural History*. Harmony: New York, 1995; p. 409.
115. Pennock, R.T., *Tower of Babel* : ibid.; p. 177.
116. Numbers, R.L., *Creationists* : ibid.; p. 316.
117. Isaak, M., *Counter-Creationism Handbook*, ibid.; p. 23.
118. Miller, K.R., *Finding Darwin's God* : ibid.; p. 111.
119. Isaak, M., *Counter-Creationism Handbook*, ibid., p. 29.
120. Shermer, M., "Then a Miracle Occurs." From The work of Michael Shermer. May 2004. http://www.michaelshermer.com/2004/05/then-a-miracle-occurs/
121. Slack, G., *The Battle over the Meaning of Everything : Evolution, Intelligent Design, and a School Board in Dover*, PA. Jossey-Bass ; Chichester : John Wiley: San Francisco, Calif., 2007; p. 10.
122. Giberson, K., *Saving Darwin*: ibid., p. 138.
123. Giberson, K., ibid., p. 171.
124. Ecklund, E. H., *Science Vs. Religion*, ibid., p. 43.
125. Ecklund, E. H., ibid., p. 47.
126. Collins, F. S., *The Language of God*: ibid., p. 141.
127. Paraphrased, based on material from http://notjustatheory.com/ See also Kenneth R. Miller, *Only a Theory: Evolution & the Battle for America's Soul*. (2008).
128. Young, M.; Strode, P. K., *Why Evolution Works (And Creationism Fails)*. Kindle Edition. Rutgers University Press: New Brunswick, N.J. ; London, 2009. p. 97.
129. Denton, M., *Evolution : A Theory in Crisis*. Burnett: [London], 1985.
130. MacMillan, D., "Understanding Creationism, VIII."
An Insider's Guide By a Former Young Earth Creationist. ibid., http://pandasthumb.org/archives/2014/07/understanding-c-7.html
131. Giberson, K., *Saving Darwin*: ibid., p. 146.
132. Bates, G., "That Quote!—About The Missing Fossils." Creation Ministries International. http://creation.com/that-quote-about-the-missing--fossils
133. Conservation biologist David Bodenham has a clear explanation of whale evolution, along with several helpful graphics, on his blog "The Conservation Biologist." It's titled "A Re-examination of Whale Evolution."
http://theconservationbiologist.tumblr.com/post/41713472456/a-re-examination-of-whale-evolution
134. Dawkins, R., *Greatest Show* : ibid., loc. 330.

135. Source: Reuters News, "Tiktaalik Roseae Shows Signs of Rear-Leg Development." http://www.cbc.ca/news/technology/tiktaalik-roseae-shows-signs-of-rear-leg-development-1.2496547
136. Isaak, M., *Counter-Creationism Handbook*, ibid., p. 124.
137. Mayr, E., *What Evolution Is*. ibid., p. 250.
138. Isaak, M., *Counter-Creationism Handbook*, ibid., p. 113.
139. Young M.; Strode, P. K., *Why Evolution Works*, ibid., p. 91.
140. Peters, T.; Hewlett, M. J., *Theological and Scientific Commentary*, ibid., p. 118.
141. Barrett is quoted by C. John Collins, in his article "Response from the Old-Earth View" found in Barrett, Matthew, and Ardel B. Caneday, eds. *Four Views on the Historical Adam*. Ch. 4., Edited by Stanley N. Gundry, Counterpoints: Bible and Theology. Grand Rapids: Zondervan, 2013; loc. 4478.
142. Young, M., "Understanding Creationism: An Insider's Guide by a Former Young Earth Creationist." http://pandasthumb.org/archives/2014/05/understanding-c.html
143. Kramer, B., Growing Up Evangelical. My Story of Making Peace with Evolution. BioLogos Foundation. http://biologos.org/blogs/brad-kramer-the-evolving-evangelical/growing-up-evangelical-my-story-of-making-peace-with-evolution
144. Van Till, H. J., Is the Universe Capable of Evolving? In *Perspectives on an Evolving Creation*, Miller, K. B., Ed. Wm. B. Eerdmans: Grand Rapids, MI and Cambridge, U.K., 2003; p. 314.
145. Johnson, P. E., *Darwin on Trial*. Regnery Gateway ; Lanham, MD : National Book Network: Washington, D.C., 1991. p. 7.
146. McGrath, A. E.; McGrath, J. C., *The Dawkins Delusion? Atheist Fundamentalism and the Denial of the Divine*. SPCK; London, 2007, p. 21.
147. Giberson, K., *Saving Darwin*: ibid., p. 194.
148. Miller, K.R., *Finding Darwin's God* : ibid., p. 62.
149. Fugle, G. N., *Laying Down Arms to Heal the Creation - Evolution Divide*. Eugene, OR: Wipf & Stock, 2015; p. 42.
150. Breshears, J., "How Young Earth Creationism Became a Core Tenet of American Fundamentalism, Part II." ibid., http://www.reasons.org/articles/how-young-earth-creationism-became-a-core-tenet-of-american-fundamentalism-part-2
151. Skybreak, A., *The Science of Evolution and the Myth of Creationism* : ibid., p. 35.
152. Dawkins, R., *Greatest Show* : ibid., loc. 867.
153. Young, M., "Understanding Creationism: An Insider's Guide by a Former Young Earth Creationist," ibid. http://pandasthumb.org/archives/2014/05/understanding-c.html
154. Numbers, R.L., *The Creationists* : ibid., p. 233.
155. Patterson, R., "What is Science?" Answers in Genesis. https://answersingenesis.org/what-is-science/what-is-science/
156. RationalWiki. Historical and Operational Science. http://rationalwiki.org/wiki/Historical_and_operational_science
157. Patterson, R., *What is Science?* ibid.
158. RationalWiki. *Historical and Operational Science*. ibid.
159. Pennock, R.T., *Tower of Babel* : ibid., p. 147.
160. Pennock, R.T., ibid., p. 73.
161. Ross, H., *A Matter of Days*: ibid., p. 172.
162. Isaak, M., *The Counter-Creationism Handbook*, ibid., p. 22.
163. Isaak, M., ibid., p. 23.

164. Dennett, D., *Darwin's Dangerous Idea*, ibid., p. 315. Darrel Falk argues that evolutionary biology does, in fact, also deal with matters that can be studied in the present, so it is not entirely an historical science. Personal communication.
165. Haarsma, L., Does Science Exclude God? Natural Law, Chance, Miracles, and Scientific Practice. In *Perspectives on an Evolving Creation*, Miller, K. B., Ed. Wm. B. Eerdmans: Grand Rapids, MI and Cambridge, U. K., 2003; p. 93.
166. Gould, S.J., *Eight Little Piggies*, ibid., p. 200.
167. Gould, S.J., *Bully for Brontosaurus*, ibid., p. 289.
168. Gould, S.J., ibid., p. 498.
169. Miller, K.R., *Finding Darwin's God*, ibid., p. 31.
170. Gould, S.J., *Dinosaur in a Haystack*, ibid., p. 35.
171. Gould, S.J., *Leonardo's Mountain of Clams and the Diet Of Worms*, ibid., p. 376.
172. Miller, K.R., *Finding Darwin's God*, ibid., p. 23.
173. Gould, S.J., *Dinosaur in a Haystack*, ibid., p. 156.
174. Gould, S.J., *Eight Little Piggies*, ibid., p. 200.
175. Gould, S.J., ibid., p. 201.
176. Isaac, M., *Counter - Creationism Handbook*, ibid., p. 89.
177. Miller, K.R., *Finding Darwin's God*, ibid., p. 28.
178. Miller, K.R., ibid., p. 26.
179. Skybreak, A., *The Science of Evolution*, ibid., p. 69.
180. Meyer, S. C., *Darwin's Doubt : The Explosive Origin of Animal Life and the Case for Intelligent Design*. 1st ed.; HarperOne: New York, NY, 2013; p. 343.
181. Janssen, L. J., *Standing on the Shoulders of Giants: Genesis and Human Origins*. Eugene, OR: Wipf & Stock, 2016; p. 81.
182. McGrath, A. E.; McGrath, J. C., *The Dawkins Delusion? Atheist Fundamentalism and the Denial of the Divine*. SPCK: London, 2007. p. 35.
183. Dennett, D., *Darwin's Dangerous Idea*, ibid., p. 319.
184. Ruse, M., *The Evolution-Creation Struggle*, ibid., p. 82.
185. Dennett, D. C., *Darwin's Dangerous Idea : Evolution and the Meanings of Life*. Simon & Schuster: New York & London, 1995; p. 239.
186. Numbers, R.L., *Creationists* : ibid., p. 89.
187. Numbers, R.L., ibid., p. 112.
188. Numbers, R.L., ibid., p. 342.
189. Gould, S. J., *Bully for Brontosaurus* : ibid., p. 288.
190. Dawkins, R., *Greatest Show* : ibid., loc. 753.
191. Pennock, R.T., *Tower of Babel* : ibid., p. 271.
192. Haidt, J., *The Righteous Mind : Why Good People Are Divided By Politics And Religion*. Kindle Edition. Allen Lane: London, 2012. p. 151.
193. Isaak, M., *Counter-Creationism Handbook*, ibid., p. 27.
194. Dawkins, R., *Greatest Show* : ibid., loc. 395.
195. Gould, S. J., *Leonardo's Mountain of Clams and The Diet of Worms : Essays on Natural History*. Harmony Books ; London : Random House: New York, 1998. p. 311.
196. Wiseman, J. J., "Why Should Christians Care About Science?" https://www.bigquestionsonline.com/2013/09/24/why-should-christians-care-about-science/
197. Pennock, R.T., *Tower of Babel* : ibid., p. 196.
198. Scott, E. C., *Evolution vs. Creationism*. ibid., p. 157.

199. Isaak, M., *Counter-Creationism Handbook*, ibid., p. 23.
200. Ingersoll, S. "I've Evolved, Too." http://biologos.org/blogs/archive/i've-evolved-too
201. Guiderdoni, B., Reading God's Signs. In *Faith in Science: Scientists Search for Truth*, Richardson, W. M.; Slack, G., Eds. Routledge: London and New York, 2001; p 70.
202. Ross, H., *A Matter of Days*: ibid., p. 206.
203. Saletan, W., "God's Work: A New Poll Suggests Americans Aren't so Confident in Their Creationism." http://www.slate.com/articles/health_and_science/human_nature/2014/12/creationism_poll_how_many_americans_believe_the_bible_is_literal_inerrant.html

Chapter 10 - Intelligent Design Creationism

1. Gould, S. J., *Eight Little Piggies : Reflections in Natural History*. Norton: 1993; p. 140.
2. Hyers, C., Comparing Biblical and Scientific Maps of Origins. In *Perspectives on an Evolving Creation*, Miller, K. B., Ed. Wm. B. Eerdmans: Grand Rapids, MI and Cambridge U.K., 2003; p. 27.
3. Alexander, D., How Are Christianity and Evolution Compatible? https://www.bigquestionsonline.com/2014/06/02/how-are-christianity-evolution-compatible/
4. Lamoureux, D. O., *Evolutionary Creation : A Christian Approach to Evolution*. Lutterworth Press: Cambridge, England, 2008; p. 101.
5. Lamoureux, ibid., p. 75.
6. Collins, F. S., *The Language of God: A Scientist Presents Evidence for Belief*. Free Press: New York & London, 2006; p. 86,
7. Miller, K. R., *Only a Theory : Evolution and The Battle for America's Soul*. Viking Penguin: New York ; London, 2008; p. 21.
8. Neve, M.; Messenger, S., *Charles Darwin: Autobiographies*. Penguin Classics: London, 2002; p. 31.
9. Topham, J. R., Natural Theology and the Sciences. In *The Cambridge Companion to Science and Religion*. Kindle Edition., Harrison, P., Ed. Cambridge University Press, Kindle Edition: Cambridge, UK, 2010; p. 70,
10. Ruse, M., *The Evolution-Creation Struggle*. Harvard University Press: Cambridge, Mass. ; London, 2005; p. 70.
11. Ruse, M., *Defining Darwin : Essays on the History and Philosophy of Evolutionary Biology*. Kindle Edition. Prometheus ; Lancaster : Gazelle: Amherst, N.Y., 2009; loc. 909.
12. Ruse, M., *The Philosophy of Human Evolution*. Kindle Edition. Cambridge University Press: Cambridge ; New York, 2012; p. 44.
13. Giberson, K., *Saving Darwin: How To Be a Christian and Believe in Evolution*. Harper One: New York, 2008; p. 30.
14. Dawkins, R., *The Greatest Show On Earth : The Evidence For Evolution*. iBook Edition. Black Swan: London, 2009; loc 698.
15. Scott, E. C., *Evolution vs. Creationism : An Introduction*. University of California Press: Berkeley, Calif. ; London, 2005; p. 116.
16. Young, M.; Strode, P. K., *Why Evolution Works (And Creationism Fails)*. Kindle Edition. Rutgers University Press: New Brunswick, N.J. ; London, 2009; p. 29.
17. Slack, G., *The Battle over the Meaning of Everything : Evolution, Intelligent Design, and a School Board in Dover*, PA. Jossey-Bass ; Chichester : John Wiley : San Francisco,

Calif., 2007; p. 209.
18. Van Till, H. J., Intelligent Design: The Celebration of Gifts Withheld? In *The Johnson-Lamoureux Debate*, ibid., Lamoureux, D. O.; Johnson, P. E., Eds.; p. 81.
19. Johnson, P. E., *Darwin on Trial*. Regnery Gateway ; Lanham, MD : National Book Network: Washington, D.C., 1991; p. 13.
20. Pennock, R. T., *Tower of Babel : The Evidence Against The New Creationism*. MIT Press: Cambridge, Mass. ; London, 1999; p. 69. Pennock's list of intelligent design advocates includes Phillip Johnson, Michael Behe, Dean Kenyon, Alvin Plantinga, William Dembski, Paul Nelson, Stephen C. Meyer, and Jonathan Wells. (p. 29).
21. Young, M.; Strode, P. K., *Why Evolution Works (And Creationism Fails)*, ibid.; p. 216.
22. Miller, K. R., *Only a Theory* : ibid.; p. 173.
23. Miller, K. R., *Finding Darwin's God: A Scientist's Search for Common Ground Between God and Evolution*. Cliff Street Books: New York, 1999; p. 90.
24. Scott, E. C., "Darwin Prosecuted: Review of Johnson's Darwin on Trial." *Creation Evolution Journal of the National Center for Science Education* 1993, 13 (2), 36-47.
25. Scott, E. C., *Evolution vs. Creationism* : ibid.; p. 124.
26. Miller, K. R., *Only a Theory* : ibid.; p. 217.
27. Peters, T.; Hewlett, M. J., *Evolution From Creation to New Creation : Conflict, Conversation, and Convergence*. Abingdon Press: Nashville, TN, 2003; p. 107.
28. Phillip Johnson adopted the Christian faith following a divorce, and later became an elder in the Presbyterian Church. Johnson says, "Something about the Darwinists' rhetorical style, made me think they had something to hide." [Dembski, William A. (2006). *Darwin's Nemesis: Phillip Johnson and the Intelligent Design Movement* (forward: Rick Santorum). IVP Academic.] Despite having no formal background in biology, he felt that he could add insight into the premises and arguments: "I approach the creation-evolution dispute not as a scientist but as a professor of law, which means among other things that I know something about the ways that words are used in arguments." Since the publication of the first edition of *Darwin on Trial* in 1991, he has become a prominent critic of evolutionary theory. Since 2001, Johnson has suffered a series of minor right brain strokes. His rehabilitations have limited his public activities and participation in the debate on intelligent design. From Wikipedia: "Phillip Johnson." https://en.wikipedia.org/wiki/Phillip_E._Johnson
29. Miller, K. R., *Only a Theory* : ibid., p. 122.
30. Janssen, L. J., *Standing on the Shoulders of Giants: Genesis and Human Origins*. Eugene, OR: Wipf & Stock, 2016; p. 276
31. Collins, F. S., *The Language of God*: ibid., p. 73.
32. Carter, B., Large Number Coincidences and the Anthropic Principle in Cosmology, in M. S. Longair, ed., *Confrontation of Cosmological Theory with Astronomical Data*, Reidel, Dordrecht, 1974; pp. 291-298.
33. Shanker, A. K., "What is the Anthropic Principle?" https://www.quora.com/What-is-the-anthropic-principle
34. Physicist Garth Huber, University of Regina, Saskatchewan, Canada. Personal communication.
35. Barbour, I. G., *When Science Meets Religion : Enemies, Strangers, Or Partners?* 1st ed.; Harper: San Francisco, 2000; p. 29.
36. Giberson, K.; Collins, F. S., *The Language of Science and Faith : Straight Answers to Genuine Questions*. Kindle Edition. SPCK: London, 2011; p. 177.

37. Ramm, B. L., *The Christian View of Science and Scripture.* 1st ed.; Grand Rapids: 1954; p. 56.
38. Haarsma, L.; Grey, T. M., Complexity, Self Organization and Design. In *Perspectives on Any Evolving Creation*, ibid., Miller, K. B., Ed. p. 297.
39. Van Till, H. J., What Good is Stardust? The Remarkably Equipped Universe. In *The Origins Debate: Evangelical Perspectives*, Christianity Today Carol Stream, IL, 2012; pp loc. 1015.
40. Miller, K. R., *Only a Theory* : ibid., p. 134.
41. Johnson, P. E., *Darwin on Trial*, ibid., p. 127.
42. Brooke, J. H., Science and Secularization. In *The Cambridge Companion to Science and Religion*, ibid., Harrison, P., Ed.; p. 104.
43. Coyne, J. A., *Faith Versus Fact: Why Science And Religion Are Incompatible.* Viking: New York, 2015.
44. Ritchie, S. L., "Five Surprising Facts About the Religious Beliefs of Scientists Around the World." BioLogos Foundation.
http://biologos.org/blogs/guest/five-surprising-facts-about-the-religious-beliefs-of-scientists-around-the-world
The study can be found in the journal "Socius." *Religion among Scientists in International Context*: A New Study of Scientists in Eight Regions. Elaine Howard Ecklund, David R. Johnson, Christopher P. Scheitle, Kirstin R. W. Matthews, Steven W. Lewis.
http://journals.sagepub.com/doi/abs/10.1177/2378023116664353
45. Scott, *Evolution vs. Creationism* : ibid., p. 217.
46. Skybreak, A., *The Science of Evolution and the Myth of Creationism : Knowing What's Real and Why it Matters.* 1st ed.; Insight Press: Chicago, 2006; p. 218.
47. Pearcey, N., We're Not in Kansas Anymore: the Furor over Intelligent Design. In *The Origins Debate: Evangelical Perspectives on Creation, Evolution, and Intelligent Design* - Kindle Edition, ibid., The Editors of Christianity Today, loc. 820.
48. Pennock, R. T., *Tower of Babel* : ibid., p. 211.
49. Louis, A., "Miracles & Science, Part 2." BioLogos Foundation.
http://biologos.org/blogs/archive/miracles-and-science-part-2
50. Miller, *Only a Theory* : ibid., p. 198.
51. Miller, : ibid., p. 182.
52. Johnson, *Darwin on Trial*, ibid., p. 132.
53. Ruse, *The Evolution-Creation Struggle*, ibid., p. 257.
54. Johnson, ibid., p. 121.
55. Ibid., p. 144.
56. Giberson, *Saving Darwin*: ibid., p. 21.
57. Slack, *The Battle over the Meaning of Everything* : ibid., p. 119.
58. Ruse, *Defining Darwin* : ibid., p. 236.
59. Slack, ibid., p. 121. The definition of theistic realism is from
http:/zcreationwiki.org/Theistic_realism
60. Isaak, M., *The Counter-Creationism Handbook.* Greenwood ; Oxford : Harcourt Education: Westport, Conn., 2005; p. 36.
61. Numbers, R. L., *The Creationists : From Scientific Creationism to Intelligent Design.* Expanded ed., 1st Harvard University Press pbk. ed.; Harvard University Press: Cambridge, Mass. ; London, 2006; p. 376.
62. Slack, ibid., p. 213.

63. Fugle, G. N., *Laying Down Arms to Heal the Creation - Evolution Divide*. Eugene, OR: Wipf & Stock, 2015; p. 107.
64. Johnson, *Darwin on Trial*, ibid., p. 151.
65. Ibid., p. 14.
66. McGrath, A. E.; McGrath, J. C., *The Dawkins Delusion? Atheist Fundamentalism and the Denial of the Divine*. SPCK: London, 2007; p. 49.
67. Giberson, K.; Artigas, M., *Oracles of Science : Celebrity Scientists Versus God and Religion*. Oxford University Press: Oxford ; New York, 2007; p. 40.
68. Scott, *Evolution vs. Creationism* : ibid., p. 74.
69. Lamoureux, *Evolutionary Creation* : ibid., p. 8.
70. Meyer, S. C., *Darwin's Doubt: The Explosive Origin of Animal Life and the Case for Intelligent Design*, 1st ed. New York, NY: HarperOne, 2013; p. 379.
71. Miller, K. R., *Finding Darwin's God* : ibid., p. 255.
72. Ruse, M., *The Evolution-Creation Struggle*, ibid., p. 256.
73. Grossman, C. L., "Associated Press Survey on Faith and Science Reveals that Science is Often Trumped by Religious Belief." Huffington Post, May 1, 2014. http://www.huffingtonpost.com/2014/05/01/ap-survey-faith-science_n_5249154.html
74. Scott, *Evolution vs. Creationism* : ibid., p. 120. Scott's view is challenged by Darrel Falk, who argues that intelligent design's tent is much wider than what Scott implies. Personal communication.
75. Behe, M. J., Comments on Denis Lamoureux's Essays. In *Darwinism Defeated: The Johnson - Lamoureux Debate on Biological Origins*, ibid., Johnson, P. E.; Lamoureux, D. O., Eds.; p. 106.
76. Miller, *Finding Darwin's God* : ibid., p. 164.
77. Peters, T.; Hewlett, M. J., *Evolution From Creation to New Creation* : ibid., p. 103.
78. Johnson, *Darwin on Trial*, ibid., p. 14.
79. Johnson, ibid., p. 113.
80. Johnson, P. E., *Darwin on Trial*, ibid., p. 54. For a scientific explanation of the Cambrian explosion, see chapter 10.
81. Cook, G., "Doubting 'Darwin's Doubt.'" New Yorker. http://www.newyorker.com/tech/elements/doubting-darwins-doubt
82. Gould, S.J., Eldredge, N. "Punctuated Equilibria: An Alternative to Phyletic Gradualism", *Models in Paleobiology*, T.J.M. Schopf, Ed., San Francisco, Freeman Cooper, 1972; pp. 82-115.
83. Meyer, S. C., *Darwin's Doubt* : ibid., p. 146.
84. Slack, G., *The Battle over the Meaning of Everything*, ibid., p. 129.
85. Eldredge, N., *Darwin : Discovering the Tree of Life*. 1st ed.; W.W. Norton & Co.: New York ; London, 2005. p. 231.
86. Miller, K. B., An Evolving Creation: Oxymoron or Fruitful Insight? In *Perspectives on an Evolving Creation*, ibid., Miller, K. B., Ed. p. 12.
87. Behe, M. J., *Darwin's Black Box : The Biochemical Challenge to Evolution*. Touchstone: New York, 1998. p. 39.
88. Scott, *Evolution vs. Creationism* : ibid., p.120.
89. Ruse, M., *Can a Darwinian be a Christian? : The Relationship Between Science and Religion*. Cambridge University Press: New York, 2000.
90. Collins, F. S., *The Language of God*: ibid., p.192.
91. Walton, J. H., *The Lost World Of Genesis One : Ancient Cosmology and the Origins*

Debate. Kindle Edition. IVP Academic: Downers Grove, Ill., 2009; p. loc. 1713.

92. Collins, F. S., *The Language of God*: ibid., p. 188.
93. Briggs, A., And Information Became Physical. In *True Scientists, True Faith: Some of the World's Leading Scientists Reveal the Harmony Between Their Science and Their Faith.* Kindle Edition., Berry, R. J., Ed. Monarch Books: Grand Rapids, Michigan, 2014; p. 49.
94. McGrath, A. E., Science, Faith And Making Sense of Things. In *True Scientists, True Faith*: ibid., Berry, R. J., Ed. p. 12.
95. Miller, K. R., Darwin, God, And Dover: What the Collapse of "Intelligent Design" Means for Science and Faith in America. In *The Religion and Science Debate: Why Does It Continue?* Kindle Edition., Attridge, H. W., Ed. Yale University Press: New Haven and London, 2009; loc. 930.
96. Dennett, D. C., *Darwin's Dangerous Idea: Evolution and the Meanings of Life.* Simon & Schuster: New York & London, 1995; p. 521.
97. Giberson, *Saving Darwin*: ibid., p. 181.
98. Dennett, *Darwin's Dangerous Idea* : ibid., p. 67.
99. Scott, *Evolution vs. Creationism* : ibid., p. 128.
100. Pennock, *Tower of Babel* : ibid., p. 84.
101. Kitcher, P., *Living with Darwin : Evolution, Design, and the Future of Faith.* Oxford University Press: Oxford ; New York, 2007. p. 116.
102. Pennock, *Tower of Babel* : ibid., p. 25.
103. Miller, *Finding Darwin's God* : ibid., p.164.
104. Johnson, *Darwin on Trial*, ibid., p. 126.
105. Johnson, P. E., Response to Denis O. Lamoureux. In *Darwinism Defeated? The Johnson - Lamoureux Debate on Biological Origins*, ibid., Johnson, P. E.; Lamoureux, D. O., Eds.; p. 50.
106. Johnson, P. E., *Darwin on Trial*, ibid., p. 126.
107. Barbour, *When Science Meets Religion* : ibid., p. 98.
108. Gould, S. J., *Rocks of Ages : Science and Religion in the Fullness of Life.* Ballantine Books: New York, 1999; p. 6.
109. Giberson, *Saving Darwin*: ibid., p. 162.
110. Miller, K, *Only a Theory* : ibid., p. 97.
111. Janssen, L. J., *Standing on the Shoulders of Giants: Genesis and Human Origins*. Eugene, OR: Wipf & Stock, 2016; p. 166.
112. Ruse, M., *Science and Spirituality : Making Room for Faith in the Age of Science.* Cambridge University Press: Cambridge, 2010; p. 221.
113. Meyer, S. C., Teleological Evolution: the Difference It Doesn't Make. In *Darwinism Defeated? The Johnson – Lamoreaux Debate on Biological Origins*, ibid., Johnson, P. E.; Lamoureux, D. O., Eds.; p. 102.
114. Giberson, K.; Collins, F. S., *The Language of Science and Faith* : ibid., p. 119.
115. Miller, K. B., Design and Purpose within an Evolving Creation. In *Darwinism Defeated? The Johnson – Lamoureux Debate on Biological Origins*, ibid., Johnson, P. E.; Lamoureux, D. O., Eds. p. 112.
116. Barbour, *When Science Meets Religion* : ibid., p. 100.
117. Collins, *The Language of God*: ibid., p.165.
118. Johnson, P. E., "Response to Denis O. Lamoureux," in *Darwinism Defeated? The Johnson - Lamoureux Debate on Biological Origins*, P. E. Johnson and D. O. Lamoureux, Eds. ibid., p. 53.

119. Lamoureux, D. O., Evangelicals Inheriting the Wind: The Phillip E. Johnson Phenomenon. In *Darwinism Defeated? The Johnson - Lamoureux Debate on Biological Origins*, ibid., Johnson, P. E.; Lamoureux, D. O., Eds. p. 57.
120. Johnson, *Darwin on Trial*, ibid., p. 31.
121. Johnson, ibid., p. 81.
122. Johnson, ibid., p. 153.
123. Falk, D.L., Thoughts on Darwin's Doubt, Part 1 and Further Thoughts on Darwin's Doubt, Part II, from the BioLogos weblog, September 9, 2014. http://biologos.org/blogs/archive/thoughts-on-darwins-doubt-reviewing-darwins-doubt-darrel-falk-part-2
124. Barrick, W.D., A Historical Adam: Young Earth Creationist View, in Barrett, M., Caneday, A.B., Eds., *Four Views on the Historical Adam*, Ch. 4, Grand Rapids, MI, Zondervan; loc. 4235.
125. Meyer, *Darwin's Doubt*: ibid.; p. 389.
126. Paraphrased from the National Center for Science Education website. Nicholas J. Matzke, September 2004. National Center for Science Education. https://ncse.com/library-resource/design-trial-dover-pennsylvania
127. Slack, G., The Battle over the Meaning of Everything, ibid., p. 194. Kitzmiller v. Dover. See also the PBS Nova documentary on the Dover, Pennsylvania intelligent design trial, titled Judgment Day: Intelligent Design on Trial. A video can be found on YouTube at https://youtu.be/7HZzGXnYL5I More information is available at the National Center for Science Education website. https://ncse.com/library-resource/kitzmiller-v-dover-intelligent-design-trial
128. Slack, ibid., p. 206.
129. Slack, ibid., p. 203.
130. Young, M.; Strode, P. K., *Why Evolution Works (And Creationism Fails)*, ibid., p. 32.
131. Meyer, S. C., *Darwin's Doubt*: ibid.; p. 211.
132. Pearcey, N., "We're Not in Kansas Anymore: the Furor over Intelligent Design," *The Origins Debate: Evangelical Perspectives on Creation, Evolution, and Intelligent Design*, ibid., The Editors of Christianity Today, Ed.; loc. 642.
133. Pennock, *Tower of Babel* : ibid., p. 276.
134. Numbers, *The Creationists* : ibid., p. 396.
135. Miller, *Finding Darwin's God* : ibid., p. 91.
136. Slack, *The Battle over the Meaning of Everything*, ibid., p. 120.
137. Falk, D.L., Thoughts on Darwin's Doubt, Part 1 and Further Thoughts on Darwin's Doubt, Part II, from the BioLogos weblog, September 9, 2014. http://biologos.org/blogs/archive/thoughts-on-darwins-doubt-reviewing-darwins-doubt-darrel-falk-part-2
138. Cook, G., "Doubting Darwin's Doubt," The Newyorker. July 1, 2013. https://www.newyorker.com/tech/elements/doubting-darwins-doubt
139. Meyer, S. C., *Darwin's Doubt* : ibid.; p. 336.
140. In a four-part series published on the BioLogos Foundation website, Robert C. Bishop discussed Darwin's Doubt. June 24, 2017. This comment is from Part 1. http://biologos.org/blogs/archive/the-extended-synthesis-reviewing-darwins-doubt-robert-bishop-part-1
141. Vuletic, M., Book Review: Michael J. Denton, Nature's Destiny (1998). http://www.vuletic.com/hume/sc/nd.html
142. Cook, G., "Doubting Darwin's Doubt," ibid.

https://www.newyorker.com/tech/elements/doubting-darwins-doubt
143. Robert C. Bishop discusses Darwin's Doubt in the June 24, 2017 BioLogos blog, Part 4. http://biologos.org/blogs/archive/final-assessments-reviewing-darwins-doubt-robert-bishop-part-4
144. Meyer, *Darwin's Doubt* : ibid., p. 409.
145. Meyer, ibid., p. 410.
146. Meyer, ibid., p. 412.
147. Meyer, ibid., p. 412.
148. Denton, M.J., *Evolution: Still a Theory in Crisis*. Seattle, WA., Discovery Institute Press, 2016; p. 323.
149. Denton, ibid., p. 281
150. Vuletic, M., ibid., http://www.vuletic.com/hume/sc/nd.html
151. Denton, ibid., p. 111.
152. Nigh, G., Greg Nigh's Reviews: Evolution: Still a Theory in Crisis. July 19, 2016. Found at https://www.goodreads.com/review/show/1703571492
153. Denton, ibid., p. 28
154. Hosier, M., "An Evolutionary Crisis?" January 19, 2017. Found at http://thinktheology.co.uk/blog/article/an_evolutionary_crisis
155. Denton, ibid., p. 14
156. Denton, ibid., p. 12
157. Denton, ibid., p. 68
158. Denton, ibid., p. 19
159. Denton, ibid., p. 12
160. Denton, ibid., p. 25
161. Publisher's description of Simon Conway Morris' "Runes of Evolution." Found at https://www.templetonpress.org/books/runes-evolution
162. Meyer, ibid., p. 357.
163. Denton, ibid., p. 39.
164. Denton, ibid., p. 59.
165. Denton, ibid., p. 171.
166. See the discussion of non-Darwinian evolution at https://rationalwiki.org/wiki/Non-Darwinian_evolution
167. A quick Google search on 'structuralism' reveals the following: "Closely related to structuralism and orthogenesis is vitalism, the theory that the origin and phenomena of life are dependent on a force or principle distinct from purely chemical or physical forces. Living organisms are different from nonliving because they contain some nonphysical element and are governed by different principles than nonliving things."
168. Keim, B., "Something Other than Adaptation Could be Driving Evolution." https://www.wired.com/2013/03/neutral-biodiversity/
169. Sy Garte & Aniko Albert, Evolution is Still Not a Theory in Crisis, but Neo Darwinism Might Be. Stump, J.B. Ed. Weblog "Faith and Science Seeking Understanding." BioLogos Foundation. February 9th, 2016. http://biologos.org/blogs/jim-stump-faith-and-science-seeking-understanding/evolution-is-still-not-a-theory-in-crisis-but-neo-darwinism-might-be
170. Denton, ibid., p. 112
171. Garte & Albert, ibid.
172. Darrel L. Falk. "Further Thoughts on 'Darwin's Doubt" : Part 2. BioLogos Foundation

weblog. September 11, 2014. http://biologos.org/blogs/archive/thoughts-on-darwins-doubt-reviewing-darwins-doubt-darrel-falk-part-2

173. Haarsma, L.; Grey, T. M., "Complexity, Self Organization and Design," in *Perspectives on An Evolving Creation*, ibid., K. B. Miller, Ed., p. 289.
174. McGrath, A. E., *Science And Religion : An Introduction*. Kindle Edition. 2nd ed.; Wiley-Blackwell: Chichester, 2010. loc. 3794

Chapter 11 - Respectful Conversation

1. Kuhn, T. S., *The Structure of Scientific Revolutions*. University of Chicago Press: Chicago ; London, 1962.
2. Wikipedia, Paradigm.
3. Ruse, M., *Science and Spirituality : Making Room for Faith in the Age of Science*. Cambridge University Press: Cambridge, 2010; p. 119.
4. Slack, G., *The Battle over the Meaning of Everything : Evolution, Intelligent Design, and a School Board in Dover*, PA. Jossey-Bass ; Chichester : John Wiley : San Francisco, Calif., 2007. p. 200.
5. Boslough, J., *Stephen Hawking's Universe*. Quill: New York, 1985. p. 71.
6. McLeish, T., *Faith and Wisdom in Science*, Oxford University Press, Oxford, UK., 2014. p. 204.
7. Wikipedia, Cognitive Dissonance.
8. Collins, F. S., *The Language of God: A Scientist Presents Evidence for Belief.* Free Press: New York & London, 2006; p. 158.
9. Caruso, G., Ed., *Science and Religion: 5 Questions*. London: Automatic Press / VIP, 2014.
10. Falk, D. R., *Coming To Peace With Science: Bridging The Worlds Between Faith And Biology*. InterVarsity Press: Downers Grove, IL, 2004. p. 39.
11. Peters, T.; Hewlett, M. J., *Evolution From Creation to New Creation : Conflict, Conversation, and Convergence*. Abingdon Press: Nashville, TN, 2003. p. 121.
12. Fugle, G. N., *Laying Down Arms to Heal the Creation - Evolution Divide*. Eugene, OR: Wipf & Stock, 2015; p. 62.
13. Ostling, R. N., The Search for the Historical Adam. In *The Origins Debate: Evangelical Perspectives on Creation, Evolution, and Intelligent Design*. Kindle Edition., From the Editors of Christianity Today : Carol Stream, IL, 2012; p loc. 245.
14. Eldredge, N., *Reinventing Darwin : The Great Debate at the High Table of Evolutionary Theory*. Wiley: New York ; Chichester, 1995; p. 224.
15. Godfrey, S. J.; Smith, C. R., *Paradigms on Pilgrimage: Creationism, Paleontology, and Biblical Interpretation*. Clements Pub.: Toronto, Ont., 2005; p. 46.
16. Hunt, Z., "Confessions of an Evolving Baptist." In Zack Hunt blog, 2013. http://zackhunt.net/2013/11/27/confessions-of-an-evolving-baptist-by-nathan-hale/
17. Fugle, G. N., *Laying Down Arms to Heal the Creation - Evolution Divide*. Eugene, OR: Wipf & Stock, 2015; p. 233.
18. Walton, J. H., *The Lost World of Scripture : Ancient Literary Culture and Biblical Authority*. Downers Grove, Illinois: IVP Academic, 2013, p. 320 pages.
19. Walton, *Lost World of Scripture*. ibid.
20. Scott, E. C., *Evolution vs. Creationism : An Introduction*. University of California Press: Berkeley, Calif. ; London, 2005. p. 76.
21. Gould, S. J., *Bully for Brontosaurus : Reflections in Natural History*. Norton: New York,

1991. p. 315.
22. Dennett, D. C., *Darwin's Dangerous Idea : Evolution and the Meanings of Life*. Simon & Schuster: New York & London, 1995; p. 15.
23. Siegfried, T., "Top 10 Revolutionary Scientific Theories." Science News https://www.sciencenews.org/blog/context/ddtop-10-revolutionary-scientific-theories
24. Haidt, J., *The Righteous Mind : Why Good People Are Divided By Politics And Religion*. Kindle Edition. Allen Lane: London, 2012. p. 168.
25. Gould, S. J., *The Lying Stones of Marrakesh : Penultimate Reflections in Natural History*. Harmony Books: New York, 2000. p. 151.
26. Godfrey, S. J.; Smith, C.R., *Paradigms on Pilgrimage* : ibid., p. 119.
27. Dahlstrom, R., "Four Necessities for Christian Witness - Part 2." BioLogos Foundation. http://biologos.org/blogs/archive/two-books-two-eyes-four-necessities-for-christian-witness-part-2
28. Siegfried, T., Replacing Paradigms Requires Open Minds. Science News. https://www.sciencenews.org/blog/context/replacing-paradigms-requires-open-minds
29. Mooney, C., The Science of Why We Don't Believe In Science. Motherjones. ibid., http://www.motherjones.com/politics/2011/03/denial-science-chris-mooney
30. Gould, S. J., *Wonderful Life : The Burgess Shale and the Nature of History*. 1st ed.; W.W. Norton: New York, 1989; p. 234.
31. Walton, J. H., *The Lost World of Scripture : Ancient Literary Culture and Biblical Authority*. Downers Grove, Illinois: IVP Academic, 2013, p. 235.
32. Eldredge, N., *Darwin: Discovering the Tree of Life*. 1st ed.; W.W. Norton & Co.: New York; London, 2005, p. 59.
33. Wikipedia, Groupthink
34. Eldredge, N., *Darwin : Discovering the Tree of Life*, ibid., p. 3.
35. Wikipedia, Bibliolatry
36. Luther, M., Preface to the Old Testament. In *Luther's Works, American Edition*, Vol. 35., Pelikan, J., Lehmann, H. T., Eds. Fortress Press: Philadelphia, 1965; p. 236.
37. Dowd, M., *Thank God for Evolution!* 1st ed.; Publishers Group UK: San Francisco, 2007; p. 87.
38. Dowd, M., ibid., p. 142. Also, Darrel Falk, private correspondence.

Chapter 12 - Hermeneutics

1. Fugle, G. N., *Laying Down Arms to Heal the Creation - Evolution Divide*. Eugene, OR: Wipf & Stock, 2015; p. 40.
2. Wright, N. T., *Surprised by Scripture: Engaging Contemporary Issues*. HarperOne, New York, 2014; p. 26.
3. Carson, Donald A., A Text Without a Context is a Pretext. 2007. http://theoblogoumena.blogspot.ca/2007/09/text-without-context-is-pretext.html
4. Walton, J. H., *The Lost World of Scripture : Ancient Literary Culture and Biblical Authority*. Downers Grove, Illinois: IVP Academic, 2013, p. 163.
5. Walton, J. H., *The Lost World of Scripture* : ibid., p. 204.
6. Walton, J. H., *The Lost World of Scripture* : ibid., p. 285.
7. Reddish, J., "In Science and Scriptural Interpretation, Communities Matter." BioLogos Foundation. http://biologos.org/blogs/jim-stump-faith-and-science-seeking-understanding/in-science-and-scriptural-interpretation-communities-matter
8. Ruse, M., Atheism, Naturalism, and Science: Three in One? In *The Cambridge Com-*

panion to Science and Religion. Kindle Edition., Harrison, P., Ed. Cambridge University Press: Cambridge, U.K., 2010; p. 230.

9. Peters, T.; Hewlett, M. J., *Evolution From Creation to New Creation : Conflict, Conversation, and Convergence*. Abingdon Press: Nashville, TN, 2003; p. 77.
10. Falk, D. R., *Coming To Peace With Science: Bridging The Worlds Between Faith And Biology*. InterVarsity Press: Downers Grove, IL, 2004; p. 81.
11. Kitcher, P., *Abusing Science : The Case Against Creationism*. MIT Press: Cambridge, Mass. ; London, 1982; p. 188.
12. Ramm, B. L., *The Christian View of Science and Scripture*. 1st ed.; Grand Rapids: 1954; p. 180.
13. Ramm, *The Christian* View, ibid., p. 76.
14. Ramm, ibid., p. 177.
15. Pieper, F., *Christian Dogmatics*. (3 volumes) Trans. by Theodore Engelder, St. Louis: Concordia Publishing House, 1950. This resource was published in the period between 1917-1924. Translated into English 1950-1953.
16. Pieper, *Dogmatics*, ibid., vol. 1, p. 33.
17. Pieper, ibid., vol. 1, p. 129.
18. Pieper, ibid., vol. 1, p. 37.
19. Pieper, ibid., vol. 1, p. 467.
20. Lamoureux, D. O., *I Love Jesus & I Accept Evolution*. Kindle Edition. Wipf and Stock Publishers: Eugene, OR, 2009. loc. 442.
21. Lamoureux, D. O., *I Love Jesus & I Accept Evolution*, ibid., p. 442.
22. White, R., Earthquakes, Volcanoes and Other Catastrophies. In *True Scientists, True Faith*, Berry, R. J., Ed. Monarch Books: Oxford, UK & Grand Rapids, MI, 2014. p. 249. Hugh Ross (A Matter of Days, 2004, p. 49) also discusses the views of the church fathers with regard to the creation accounts.
23. Larson, E. J., *Evolution : The Remarkable History of a Scientific Theory*. Kindle Edition. Modern Library: New York, 2004. p. 278.
24. MacMillan, D., "Understanding Creationism, VIII: An Insider's Guide By a Former Young Earth Creationist." July 2014. http://pandasthumb.org/archives/2014/07/understanding-c-7.html See also McLeish, T., *Faith and Wisdom in Science*, Oxford University Press, Oxford, UK., 2014. p. 49.
25. Ross, H., *A Matter of Days: Resolving a Creation Controversy*. Navpress: Colorado Springs, CO., 2004. p. 45.
26. McGrath, A. E., "Augustine's Origin of Species: How the Great Theologian Might Weigh in on the Darwin Debate," in *The Origins Debate*: ibid., loc. 534.
27. Luther, M., Luther's Last Sermon in Wittenberg. *Luther's Works - American Edition*. Vol. 53: Pelikan, J. and Lehmann, Helmut T., Eds. Fortress Press: Philadelphia 1965; pp. 373-374.
28. Ruse, M., *Science and Spirituality : Making Room for Faith in the Age of Science*. Cambridge University Press: Cambridge, 2010; p. 186.
29. Wikipedia, Fideism. See also Amesbury, R., "Fideism." In Stanford Encyclopedia of Philosophy, 2016.
30. McGrath, A. E., *Science And Religion : An Introduction*. Kindle Edition. 2nd ed.; Wiley-Blackwell: Chichester, 2010; loc. 721.
31. Gould, S. J., *The Hedgehog, The Fox, and The Magister's Pox : Ending the False War Between Science and the Humanities*. 1st ed.; Harmony Books: New York, 2003; p. 23.

32. See the National Study of Religion and Human Origins for more information on the importance of recognizing the social context of creationist beliefs and practices. BioLogos Foundation. https://biologos.org/uploads/projects/nsrho-report.pdf
33. Janssen, L. J., *Standing on the Shoulders of Giants: Genesis and Human Origins*. Eugene, OR: Wipf & Stock, 2016; p. 277.
34. Miller, K.R., *Finding Darwin's God : A Scientist's Search for Common Ground Between God and Evolution*. Cliff Street Books: New York, 1999, p. 256.
35. Walton, John H. *The Lost World of Genesis One : Ancient Cosmology and the Origins Debate*. Kindle Edition. Downers Grove, Ill.: IVP Academic, 2009; loc. 1600.
36. Lamoureux, D. O., *I Love Jesus & I Accept Evolution*, ibid., loc. 414.
37. Giberson, K., *Saving Darwin: How To Be A Christian And Believe In Evolution*. HarperOne, New York. 2008, p. 130.
38. Ramm, B. L., *The Christian View of Science and Scripture*, ibid., p. 55.
39. Ross, H., *A Matter of Days: Resolving a Creation Controversy*. Navpress: Colorado Springs, CO., 2004. p. 90.
40. Ross, H., ibid., p. 228.
41. Numbers, R. L., *The Creationists : From Scientific Creationism to Intelligent Design*. Expanded ed., 1st Harvard University Press pbk. ed.; Harvard University Press: Cambridge, Mass. ; London, 2006; p. 219.
42. Kitcher, P., *Abusing Science* : ibid., p. 188.
43. McGrath, A. E., "Augustine's Origin of Species: in *The Origins Debate*, ibid., The Editors of Christianity Today, Ed. loc. 545.
44. Quoted in Falk, D. R., *Coming To Peace With Science*: ibid., p. 169.
45. Lamoureux, D. O., *Evolutionary Creation : A Christian Approach to Evolution*. Lutterworth Press: Cambridge, England, 2008. p. 381.
46. Hyers, C., Comparing Biblical and Scientific Maps of Origins. In *Perspectives on an Evolving Creation*, Miller, K. B., Ed. ibid., p. 24.
47. Barbour, I. G., *When Science Meets Religion : Enemies, Strangers, or Partners?* 1st ed.; Harper: San Francisco, 2000; p. 18.
48. Lamoureux, D. O., *I Love Jesus*, ibid., loc. 2842.
49. Gould, S. J., *I Have Landed : The End of a Beginning in Natural History*. 1st ed.; Harmony Books: New York, 2002. p. 221.
50. Wikipedia, Presuppositional Apologetics
51. Ross, H., *A Matter of Days*: ibid., p. 35.
52. Anne, L., "Evidentialism vs Presuppositionalism." Patheos. September 2011. http://www.patheos.com/blogs/lovejoyfeminism/2011/09/evidentialism-v-presuppositionalism.html
53. Holloway, B., "Young-Earthers and Presuppositionalism. December 2013. http://www.hollowayquarterly.com/2013/12/young-earthers-and-presuppositionalism.html
54. Natural Historian. "Reflections On A Creationist Approach To Scientific Apologetics." June 15, 2015. https://thenaturalhistorian.com/2015/06/15/reflections-on-a-creationist-approach-to-scientific-apologetics/
55. The Bill Nye - Ken Ham debate on YouTube can be found at: https://youtu.be/z6kgvhG3AkI
56. Cook, J., "Inoculating Against Science Denial." http://theconversation.com/inoculating-against-science-denial-40465
57. Dobson, J., Duane Gish - Hugh Ross Debate on Young Earth vs Old Earth Creationism.

Focus on the Family Radio Broadcast, April 18, 1991.

58. Enns, P., "Eleven Recurring Mistakes In The Debate Over The Historical Adam," Patheos., ibid., May 11, 2015. *http://www.patheos.com/blogs/peterenns/2015/05/11-recurring-mistakes-in-the-debate-over-the-historical-adam/*
59. Janssen, L. J., *Standing on the Shoulders of Giants*: ibid.; p. 243.
60. Janssen, L. J., *Standing on the Shoulders of Giants*: ibid.; p. 242.
61. Boyd, G.O., A Pastoral Reflection: Whether or Not There was a Historical Adam, Our Faith is Secure. In Barrett & Caneday, eds. *Four Views on the Historical Adam.* Ch. 3. Book Series - Counterpoints: Bible and Theology Edited by Stanley N. Gundry, Grand Rapids: Zondervan, 2013; loc. 4881
62. Anne, L., "Evidentialism vs Presuppositionalism." Patheos. September 2011.http://www.patheos.com/blogs/lovejoyfeminism/2011/09/evidentialism-v-presuppositionalism.html
63. Ruse, M., *Science and Spirituality* : ibid., p. 65.
64. Buchanan, S., "Was the Expanse Overhead in Genesis 1 a Solid Dome?" https://letterstocreationists.wordpress.com/2012/09/03/was-the-expanse-overhead-in-genesis-1-a-solid-dome/
65. Lamoureux, D. O., *Evolutionary Creation* : ibid., p. 187.
66. Lamoureux, D. O., *Evolutionary Creation* : ibid., p. 411.
67. Lamoureux, D. O., *Evolutionary Creation* : ibid., p. 194.
68. Lamoureux, D. O., *Evolutionary Creation* : ibid., p. 254.
69. Janssen, L. J., *Standing on the Shoulders*, ibid., p. 61.
70. Venema, D. R., *Adam and the Genome: Reading Scripture after Genetic Science.* Grand Rapids: Brazos Press, 2017; p. 119.
71. Venema, D. R., *Adam and the Genome*: ibid., p. 141.
72. Godfrey,S. J.; Smith, C. R., *Paradigms on Pilgrimage* : ibid., p. 107.
73. Walton, J. H., *The Lost World of Genesis One* : ibid., loc. 2432.
74. Miller, K. R., *Finding Darwin's God* : ibid., p. 270.
75. Godfrey,S. J.; Smith, C. R., *Paradigms on Pilgrimage* : ibid., p. 122.
76. Collins, C. J., A Historical Adam: Old-Earth Creation View. In Barrett & Caneday, eds. *Four Views on the Historical Adam.* Ch. 3. Book Series - Counterpoints: Bible and Theology Edited by Stanley N. Gundry, Grand Rapids: Zondervan, 2013; loc. 2637.
77. Collins, C. J., A Historical Adam: Old-Earth Creation View. In Barrett & Caneday, eds. *Four Views on the Historical Adam.* Ch. 3. ibid.; loc. 265
78. Gustavsen, D., "I Have a Friend Who Believes Science Disproves Faith. Part 2." BioLogos Foundation. http://biologos.org/blogs/archive/i-have-a-friend-who-believes-science-disproves-faith-part-2
79. Walton, J. H., *The Lost World of Scripture* :ibid., p.121 .
80. Fugle, G. N., *Laying Down Arms to Heal the Creation - Evolution Divide.* Eugene, OR: Wipf & Stock, 2015; p. 234.
81. From Aquinas, Summa, First Part, Question 68. See Fugle, *Laying Down Arms*, ibid., p. 39.
82. Giberson, K.; Collins, F. S., *The Language of Science and Faith : Straight Answers to Genuine Questions.* Kindle Edition. SPCK: London, 2011; p. 91.
83. Lamoureux, D. O., "Evolutionary Creation: A Christian Approach to Evolution (Summary). BioLogos Foundation. http://biologos.org/uploads/projects/Lamoureux_Scholarly_Essay.pdf

84. Collins, C. J., A Historical Adam: Old-Earth Creation View. In Barrett & Caneday, eds. *Four Views on the Historical Adam.* Ch. 3. Book Series - Counterpoints: Bible and Theology Edited by Stanley N. Gundry, Grand Rapids: Zondervan, 2013; loc. 3038.
85. Saletan, W., "Creativity for Creationists: An Evolutionary Creationist Evangelizes to Christians About Science." Slate. December 2014, ibid., http://www.slate.com/articles/health_and_science/human_nature/2014/12/evolutionary_creationism_jeff_hardin_reconciles_evangelical_christianity.html
86. Enns, P., For those of you wondering why I interpret the Bible the way I do - which I assume means the entire internet. http://www.peteenns.com/for-those-of-you-wondering-why-i-interpret-the-bible-the-way-i-do-which-i-assume-means-the-entire-internet/
87. Lamoureux, D. O., *Evolutionary Creation* : ibid., p. 399.
88. Lamoureux, D. O., *Evolutionary Creation* : ibid., p. 398.
89. Godfrey,S. J.; Smith, C. R., *Paradigms* : ibid., p. 122.
90. Godfrey,S. J.; Smith, C. R., ibid., p. 113.
91. Collins, C. J., A Historical Adam: Response from the Old-Earth Creation View. In Barrett & Caneday, eds. *Four Views on the Historical Adam.* Ch. 3. Book Series - Counterpoints: Bible and Theology Edited by Stanley N. Gundry, Grand Rapids: Zondervan, 2013; loc. 4396
92. Janssen, L. J., *Standing on the Shoulders*, ibid., p. 204.
93. Fugle, G. N., *Laying Down Arms*, ibid., p. 262.
94. Miller, K. R., *Finding Darwin's God* : ibid., p. 256.
95. Lehmann, M., "Ten Things I Wish Everyone Knew About The Creation / Evolution Debate." https://www.onfaith.co/discussion/10-things-i-wish-everyone-knew-about-the-creation-vs-evolution-debate
96. Hyers, C., Comparing Biblical and Scientific Maps of Origins. In *Perspectives on an Evolving Creation*, Miller, K. B., Ed. Wm. B. Eerdmans: Grand Rapids, MI and Cambridge U.K., 2003; p. 23.
97. Peters, T.; Hewlett, M. J., *Theological and Scientific Commentary on Darwin's Origin of Species.* Abingdon Press: Nashville, 2008; p. 71.
98 Lamoureux, D. O., *Evolutionary Creation* : ibid., p. 263.
99. Lamoureux, D. O., *I Love Jesus & I Accept Evolution*, ibid., loc. 743.
100. Giberson, K.; Collins, F. S., *The Language of Science and Faith* : ibid., p. 97.
101. Hyers, C., "Comparing Biblical and Scientific Maps of Origins," in *Perspectives on an Evolving Creation*, ibid., p. 26.
102. Davis, T.. Science and the Bible: Theistic Evolution. Part 1. BioLogos Foundation. http://biologos.org/blogs/ted-davis-reading-the-book-of-nature/science-and-the-bible-theistic-evolution-part-1
103. Davis, T., "Science and the Bible: The Framework View." BioLogos Foundation. http://biologos.org/blogs/ted-davis-reading-the-book-of-nature/science-and-the-bible-the-framework-view
104. Middleton, J. R., "The Ancient Universe and the Cosmic Temple." BioLogos Foundation. http://biologos.org/blogs/jim-stump-faith-and-science-seeking-understanding/the-ancient-universe-and-the-cosmic-temple
105. Turner, K., "If Walton Is Right on His Function Only View: Some Implications. BioLogos Foundation. http://biologos.org/blogs/archive/if-walton-is-right-on-his-function-only-view-some-implications
106. Johnson, D. J., "Book Review: The Lost World of Genesis One." http://davidjohnstone.

net/blog/2009/12/notes-lost-world-genesis-one-john-walton

107. Ostling, R. N., "The Search for the Historical Adam," ibid., loc. 221.
108. Davidson, G.; Wolgemuth, K., "Biblical and Scientific Shortcomings of Flood Geology. Part 1." BioLogos Foundation. http://biologos.org/blogs/archive/biblical-and-scientific-shortcomings-of-flood-geology-part-1
109. Reddish, J., "In Science and Scriptural Interpretation, Communities Matter." BioLogos Foundation. ibid. http://biologos.org/blogs/jim-stump-faith-and-science-seeking-understanding/in-science-and-scriptural-interpretation-communities-matter
110. A. E. McGrath, *Science and Religion : An Introduction*. ibid., loc. 653.
111. Davis, T., "Science and the Bible: Theistic Evolution, Part 2." BioLogos Foundation. http://biologos.org/blogs/ted-davis-reading-the-book-of-nature/science-and-the-bible-theistic-evolution-part-2
112. Tinker, M., "No conflict." http://www.bethinking.org/does-evolution-disprove-creation/no-conflict
113. Tinker, M., ibid.
114. Gould, S. J., *Leonardo's Mountain of Clams and The Diet of Worms : Essays on Natural History*. Harmony Books ; London : Random House: New York, 1998. p. 154.
115. Janssen, L. J., *Standing on the Shoulders of Giants*, ibid., p. ix.
116. Haught, J. F., *God After Darwin : A Theology of Evolution*. Westview Press: Boulder, Colo. ; Oxford, 2000; p. 137.
117. Haught, J. F., *God After Darwin*, ibid., p. 141.
118. Gibbons, Ann. 2017. World's Oldest Homo Sapiens Fossils Found in Morocco. Archaelogy, Human Evolution - American Association for the Advancement of Science, June 7, 2017. http://www.sciencemag.org/news/2017/06/world-s-oldest-homo-sapiens-fossils-found-morocco
119. Walton, J., A Historical Adam: Archetypal Creation View. In Barrett & Caneday, eds. *Four Views on the Historical Adam*. Ch. 2., Book Series Counterpoints: Bible and Theology Edited by Stanley N. Gundry, Grand Rapids: Zondervan, 2013; loc. 1882
120. Giberson, K.; Collins, F. S., *The Language of Science and Faith* : ibid., p. 131.
121. Ramm, B. L., *The Christian View*, ibid., p. 143.
122. Numbers, R. L., *The Creationists* : ibid., p. 187.
123. Falk, D. R., *Coming To Peace With Science*: ibid., p. 200.
124. Walton, J. H., *The Lost World Of Genesis One* : ibid., loc. 1534.
125. Lamoureux, D. O., *Evolutionary Creation* : ibid., p. 196.
126. Wikipedia. Theodicy
127. Peters, T.; Hewlett, M. J., *Evolution: From Creation to New Creation* : ibid., p. 157.
128. Giberson, K., *Saving Darwin: How To Be A Christian And Believe In Evolution*. HarperOne, New York. 2008, p. 214.
129. Thomson, K., Introduction – The Religion and Science Debate: Why Does it Continue?, pp. in *The Religion and Science Debate: Why Does It Continue?* Kindle Edition, edited by H. W. Attridge. Yale University Press, New Haven, CT. And London, U. K. 2009, p. 208.
130. Haught, J. F., *God After Darwin: A Theology of Evolution*. Westview Press, Boulder, Colo.; Oxford, 2000, p. 6.
131. Ruse, M., *The Philosophy of Human Evolution*. Kindle Edition., pp. Cambridge University Press, Cambridge ; New York. 2012, p. 114.
132. Peters, T., Hewlett, M. J., *Evolution: From Creation to New Creation*: ibid., p. 23.

133. Gould, S. J., *Rocks of Ages: Science and Religion in the Fullness of Life*. Ballantine Books, New York. 1999, p. 183.
134. Ruse, M., *Science and Spirituality: Making Room for Faith in the Age of Science*. Cambridge University Press, Cambridge2010. p. 202.
135. Peters, T., and M. J. Hewlett, *Evolution From Creation to New Creation*: ibid., p. 142.
136. Ruse, M., *Science and Spirituality*: ibid., p. 198.
137. Ruse, M., *Can a Darwinian be a Christian? The Relationship Between Science and Religion*. Cambridge University Press, New York. 2000, p. 202. See also McLeish, T., Faith and Wisdom in Science, Oxford University Press, Oxford, UK., 2014. p. 180.
138. Giberson, K., *Seven Glorious Days : A Scientist Retells The Genesis Creation Story*. Kindle Edition., pp. Paraclete Press, Brewster, Mass. 2012, p. 126.
139. Godfrey, S. J., Smith, C. R., *Paradigms on Pilgrimage: Creationism, Paleontology, and Biblical Interpretation*. Clements Publishing, Toronto, Ont. 2005, p. 156.
140. Lamoureux, D. O., *Evolutionary Creation : A Christian Approach to Evolution*. Lutterworth Press, Cambridge, England. 2008, p. 303.
141. Falk, D., personal communication, March 2018. See also McLeish, T., *Faith and Wisdom in Science*, Oxford University Press, Oxford, UK., 2014. p. 108.
142. Lamoureux, D. O., ibid., p. 301.
143. Janssen, L. J., *Standing on the Shoulders of Giants*: ibid.; p. 104.
144. Janssen, L. J., ibid., p. 206. See also Venema, D. R., *Adam and the Genome: Reading Scripture after Genetic Science*. Grand Rapids: Brazos Press, 2017; p. 129.
145. Ostling, R. N., "The Search for the Historical Adam," *The Origins Debate: Evangelical Perspectives on Creation, Evolution, and Intelligent Design*, ibid., The Editors of Christianity Today, Ed., loc. 151
146. Venema, D. R., *Adam and the Genome*: ibid.; p. 183.
147. Venema, D. R., *Adam and the Genome*: ibid.; p. 150.
148. Wright, N. T., *Surprised by Scripture: Engaging Contemporary Issues*. HarperOne, New York.; ibid; p. 37.
149. Venema, D.; Evans, R. H., "Ask an Evolutionary Creationist: A Q&A with Dennis Venema." BioLogos Foundation. http://biologos.org/blogs/dennis-venema-letters-to-the-duchess/ask-an-evolutionary-creationist-a-qa-with-dennis-venema
150. Hurd, J. P. "Hominids in the Garden," in *Perspectives on an Evolving Creation*, ibid., Miller, K. B., Ed., p. 225. Monogenism is discussed by Michael Ruse, Can a Darwinian be a Christian? (2000). p. 75.
151. Collins, R., Evolution and Original Sin. In *Perspectives on an Evolving Creation*, edited by K. B. Miller. Wm. B. Eerdmans, Grand Rapids, MI and Cambridge, U.K., p. 481.
152. Collins, R., *Evolution and Original Sin*, ibid., pp. 469-501.
153. Davis, T., "Science and the Bible: Theistic Evolution, Part 4." BioLogos Foundation. http://biologos.org/blogs/ted-davis-reading-the-book-of-nature/science-and-the-bible-theistic-evolution-part-4
154 Ruse, M., *Can a Darwinian be a Christian?* : ibid., p. 210.
155. Ruse, M., *Can a Darwinian*, ibid., p. 205.
156. Davis, T., Science and the Bible: Theistic Evolution, Part 4, ibid.
157. Lamoureux, D. O., *Evolutionary Creation* : ibid., p. 324.
158. Lamoureux, D. O., *I Love Jesus & I Accept Evolution*, ibid., loc. 2537.
159. Ruse, M., *The Evolution-Creation Struggle*. Harvard University Press: Cambridge, Mass. ; London, 2005; p. 10.

160. Falk, D. R., *Coming To Peace With Science*: ibid., loc. 902.
161. Venema, D. R., *Adam and the Genome*: ibid.; p. 147.
162. Venema, D. R., ibid.; p. 147.
163. Venema, D. R., ibid.; p. 195.

Chapter 13 - Conclusion

1. Hinnant, C. H., "The Fable of the Spider and the Bee and Swift's Poetics of Inspiration." Colby Library Quarterly 1984, 20 (no. 3), 129-136. http://digitalcommons.colby.edu/cgi/viewcontent.cgi?article=2556&context=cq
2. Michalska, K.; Michalski, S., *Spider*. Reaktion Books: London, 2010. p. 79.
3. Gould, S. J., *Dinosaur in a Haystack : Reflections in Natural History*. Harmony: New York, 1995; p. 82.
4. Gould, S. J., *The Hedgehog, The Fox, and The Magister's Pox : Ending the False War Between Science and the Humanities*. 1st ed.; Harmony Books: New York, 2003. p. 39.
5. Gould, S. J., *Dinosaur in a Haystack* : ibid., p. 82.
6. Gould, S. J., *The Lying Stones of Marrakesh : Penultimate Reflections in Natural History*. Harmony Books: New York, 2000. p. 53.
7. Gould, S. J., *I Have Landed : The End of a Beginning in Natural History*. 1st ed.; Harmony Books: New York, 2002. p. 180.
8. Gould, S. J., *The Hedgehog, The Fox, and The Magister's Pox* : ibid., p. 109.
9. Gould, S. J., ibid., p. 41.
10. Haarsma, L., Does Science Exclude God? Natural Law, Chance, Miracles, And Scientific Practice. In *Perspectives on an Evolving Creation*, Miller, K. B., Ed. Wm. B. Eerdmans: Grand Rapids, MI and Cambridge, U. K., 2003; p. 79.
11. Gould, S. J., Hedgehog, : ibid., p. 70.
12. Ecklund, E. H., *Science Vs. Religion : What Scientists Really Think*. Kindle Edition. Oxford University Press: New York ; Oxford, 2010. p. 56.
13. Gould, S. J., *Hedgehog* : ibid., p. 43.
14. Kitcher, P., *Living with Darwin: Evolution, Design, and the Future of Faith*. Oxford University Press: Oxford ; New York, 2007. p. 133.
15. Primack, J., Transcendental Theory. In *Faith in Science: Scientists Search for Truth*, Richardson, W. M.; Slack, G., Eds. Routledge: London and New York, 2001; p. 159.
16. Wuthnow, R., No Contradictions Here: Science, Religion, and the Culture of All Reasonable Possibilities. In *The Religion and Science Debate: Why Does It Continue?* Kindle Edition., Attridge, H. W., Ed. Yale University Press: New Haven and London, 2009; loc. 2116.
17. Krauss, L. M., *Religion Vs. Science? In The Religion and Science Debate: Why Does It Continue?* Kindle Edition., ibid., Attridge, H. W., Ed. loc. 1944.
18. Dawkins, R., *The Greatest Show On Earth : The Evidence for Evolution*. iBook edition ; Black Swan, London. 2009. loc. 301.
19. Pickering, J., "Teach Creationism, Undermine Theology." In Science and Society, 2013. http://sciblogs.co.nz/kidney-punch/2013/09/24/teach-creationism-undermine-theology/
20. Anderson, J. E., *The Heresy of Ham: What Every Evangelical Needs to Know About the Creation-Evolution Controversy*. Archdeacon Books: 2016.
21. Kidder, J., "Joel Edmund Anderson: The Heresy of Ham." This article is from blog titled Science and Religion: A View from an evolutionary creationist written by Jim Kidder.

It summarizes Anderson's arguments. http://scienceandcreation.blogspot.ca/2016/10/joel-edmund-anderson-heresy-of-ham.html

22. Numbers, R. L., *The Creationists : From Scientific Creationism to Intelligent Design.* Expanded ed., 1st Harvard University Press pbk. ed.; Harvard University Press: Cambridge, Mass. ; London, 2006; p. 26.
23. Krauss, L. M., "Religion Vs. Science?," in Attridge, H.W., Ed., *The Religion and Science Debate: Why Does It Continue?* ibid., loc. 1926.
24. Walton, J. H., *The Lost World Of Genesis One : Ancient Cosmology and the Origins Debate.* Kindle Edition. IVP Academic: Downers Grove, Ill., 2009; p. loc. 176.
25. Lombrozo, T., "Scientific Literacy: It's Not (Just) About The Facts." National Public Radio. September 14h, 2015. http://www.npr.org/sections/13.7/2015/09/14/440213603/scientific-literacy-it-s-not-just-about-the-facts
26. "Scientific Literacy: How do Americans Stack Up?" A research study done under the auspices of Michigan State University. Science Daily. February 2007. https://www.sciencedaily.com/releases/2007/02/070218134322.htm
27. Giberson, K.; Collins, F. S., *The Language of Science and Faith : Straight Answers to Genuine Questions.* Kindle Edition. SPCK: London, 2011; p. 31.
28. Mooney, C., "The Science of Why We Don't Believe Science." Mother Jones, March, 2011. http://www.motherjones.com/politics/2011/03/denial-science-chris-mooney
29. Gould, S. J., *Bully for Brontosaurus : Reflections in Natural History.* Norton: New York, 1991. p. 293.
30. Pennock, R. T., *Tower of Babel* : ibid., p. 146.
31. Isaak, M., *The Counter-Creationism Handbook* Greenwood ; Oxford : Harcourt Education : Westport, Conn., 2005; p. 25.
32. MacMillan, D., "Understanding Creationism, VIII: An Insider's Guide By a Former Young Earth Creationist." http://pandasthumb.org/archives/2014/07/understanding-c-7.html
33. Kitcher, P., *Living with Darwin : Evolution, Design, and the Future of Faith.* Oxford University Press: Oxford ; New York, 2007; p. 122.
34. Young, M.; Strode, P. K., *Why Evolution Works (And Creationism Fails)*, ibid., p. 194.
35. I tried to track down the source of this concept, but had no success.
36. Thomson, K., Introduction – The Religion and Science Debate: Why Does It Continue? In *The Religion and Science Debate*: ibid., Attridge, H. W., Ed. p. 139.
37. Collins, F. S., *The Language of God*: ibid., p. 229.
38. Miller, K. R., *Only a Theory : Evolution and The Battle for America's Soul.* Viking Penguin: New York ; London, 2008. p. 74. See also Miller, K.R. Finding *Darwin's God*, Harper Collins, New York, 1999, p. 111.
39. Slack, G., *The Battle over the Meaning of Everything : Evolution, Intelligent Design, and a School Board in Dover*, PA. Jossey-Bass ; Chichester : John Wiley : San Francisco, Calif., 2007. p. 110.
40. Giberson, K., *Saving Darwin*: ibid., p. 7.
41. Augustine, Bishop of Hippo, *On Christian Doctrine*, Book 2, ch. 18. In The Library of Liberal Arts, D W Robertson Jr, Ed. Bobbs-Merrill Educational Publications: Indianapolis, [1977, ©1958]; Vol. 80.
42. Lindberg, D. C., The Fate of Science in Patristic and Medieval Christendom. In *The Cambridge Companion to Science and Religion*, Harrison, P., Ed. Cambridge University

Press: Cambridge, UK., 2010; p. 33.

43. Numbers, R. L., Aggressors, Victims, and Peacemakers – Historical Actors in the Drama of Science and Religion. In *The Religion and Science Debate*: ibid., Attridge, H. W., Ed. loc. 301.
44. Gould, S. J., *Eight Little Piggies* : ibid., p. 165.
45. Collins, F. S., *Language of God*: ibid., p. 158.
46. Miller, K. R., *Finding Darwin's God : A Scientist's Search for Common Ground Between God and Evolution*. Cliff Street Books: New York, 1999. p. 56.
47. Gould, S. J., *Leonardo's Mountain of Clams and The Diet of Worms : Essays on Natural History*. Harmony Books ; London : Random House: New York, 1998. p. 11.
48. Mooney, C., "The Science of Why We Don't Believe Science." ibid. http://www.motherjones.com/politics/2011/03/denial-science-chris-mooney
49. Haidt, J., *The Righteous Mind* : ibid., p. 104.
50. Dennett, D. C., *Darwin's Dangerous Idea* : ibid., p. 141.
51. Wilkins, J. S., "Are Creationists Rational?" In Science blogs, 2009. Evolving Thoughts. Science Blogs. April, 2008. http://scienceblogs.com/evolvingthoughts/2009/04/28/are-creationists-rational/
52. Greene, E., "You Can't Educate People into Believing in Evolution." November 2014. The Atlantic. November 2014. http://www.theatlantic.com/national/archive/2014/11/you-cant-educate-people-into-believing-in-evolution/382983/
53. Mooney, C., "The Science of Why We Don't Believe Science." ibid.
54. Nazworth, N., "Forget Evolution Vs. Creation, There are (At Least) 6 Different Views, Evangelical Biophysicist Explains." Christian Post. 2015. http://www.christianpost.com/news/forget-evolution-vs-creation-there-are-at-least-6-different-views-evangelical-biophysicist-explains-132178/
55. Arel, D., "Fewer Than 10% Of Americans Are Convinced Young Earth Creationists, New Study Shows." Patheos, 2014. http://www.patheos.com/blogs/danthropology/2014/12/guest-post-loving-jesus-and-accepting-evolution-is-more-common-than-you-think/
56. Grant, R. P., "Why Scientists are Losing the Fight to Communicate Science to the Public." August 2016. The Guardian. August 23, 2016. Science. Occam's Corner. https://www.theguardian.com/science/occams-corner/2016/aug/23/scientists-losing-science-communication-skeptic-cox
57. Pieper, F., *Christian Dogmatics*. (3 Vols.) Trans. by Theodore Engelder, St. Louis: Concordia Publishing House, 1950; vol. 1, p. 467.
58. Pieper, F., ibid., vol. 1, p. 162. See also vol. 2, p. vii.
59. Wikipedia, Reactance
60. Ruse, M., *Defining Darwin : Essays on the History and Philosophy of Evolutionary Biology*. Kindle Edition. Prometheus ; Lancaster : Amherst, N.Y., 2009. p. 35.
61. Pennock, R. T., *Tower of Babel : The Evidence Against The New Creationism*. MIT Press: Cambridge, Mass. ; London, 1999; p. 367.
62. Clark, F., "Why Millennials are Leaving The Church." Slacktivist Blog, August 4, 2013. http://www.patheos.com/blogs/slacktivist/2013/08/04/why-millennials-are-leaving-the-church/ Another interesting article is authored by Rachel Held Evans and is featured in the religion section of the CNN website. http://religion.blogs.cnn.com/2013/07/27/why-millennials-are-leaving-the-church/
63. "Science, Faith, and Emerging Adults: A New Initiative at Fuller Theological Semi-

nary." BioLogos Editorial Team. April 2016. The President's Notebook. http://biologos.org/blogs/deborah-haarsma-the-presidents-notebook/science-faith-and-emerging-adults-an-interview-with-greg-cootsona-on-a-new-initiative-by-fuller-seminary

64. Alexander, D., A Different Drum Beat. In *True Scientists, True Faith: Some of the World's Leading Scientists Revealed the Harmony between Their Science and Their Faith.* Kindle Edition, Berry, R. J., Ed. Monarch Books: Oxford, U. K. and Grand Rapids, MI, 2014; p. 307.
65. McLeish, T., *Faith and Wisdom in Science,* Oxford University Press, Oxford, UK., 2014. p. 238.
66. Collins, F. S., What Do You Believe, Doctor? In *True Scientists, True Faith*: ibid., Berry, R. J., Ed. p. 133.
67. Sension, R., "Moving from Debate to Dialogue." In *Musings On Science,* 2016. The author on the article is listed as "rjs" which, upon some checking, turned out to be Roseanne Sension, professor of chemistry at the University of Michigan. September 1, 2016. https://musingsonscience.wordpress.com/2016/09/01/moving-from-debate-to-dialogue/ - more-5087
68. Miller, K. R., *Finding Darwin's God* : ibid., p. 280.
69. Ramm, B. L., *The Christian View of Science and Scripture.* 1st ed.; Grand Rapids: 1954; p. 153.
70. Wiseman, J. J., "Why Should Christians Care About Science?" September 24, 2013. https://www.bigquestionsonline.com/2013/09/24/why-should-christians-care-about-science/
71. Denton, M.J., *Evolution: Still a Theory in Crisis.* Seattle, WA, Discovery Institute Press, 2016, p. 282.
72. Berra, T.M., *Evolution and the Myth of Creationism : A Basic Guide to the Facts in the Evolution Debate.* Stanford, CA. Stanford University Press. 1990; p. 141.
73. Venema, D. R., *Adam and the Genome: Reading Scripture after Genetic Science.* Grand Rapids: Brazos Press, 2017, p. 11.
74. Venema, D. R., *Adam and the Genome: Reading Scripture after Genetic Science.* Grand Rapids: Brazos Press, 2017, p. 27.s
75. Falk, D.R., Reviewing "Darwin's Doubt": Part 2, ibid. BioLogos Foundation. http://biologos.org/blogs/archive/thoughts-on-darwins-doubt-reviewing-darwins-doubt-darrel-falk-part-2
76. Wright, N. T., *Surprised by Scripture: Engaging Contemporary Issues.* HarperOne, New York.: , 2014. p. 185
77. Gould, S. J., *Rocks of Ages* : ibid., p. 178.
78. Gould, S. J., *I Have Landed* : ibid., p. 355.

Notes – Appendix

1. Gallup, Inc., "Evolution, Creationism, Intelligent Design: Historical Trends." http://www.gallup.com/poll/21814/evolution-creationism-intelligent-design.aspx
2. Gallup, Inc., ibid.
3. Ecklund, E. H.; Scheitle, C. P., Religion Among Academic Scientists: Distinctions, Disciplines, and Demographics. Social Problems 2007, 54, pp. 289–307. Available online at http://www.owlnet.rice.edu/~ehe/doc/Ecklund_SocialProblems_54_2.pdf
4. Ecklund, E. H., *Science Vs. Religion : What Scientists Really Think.* Kindle Edition. Oxford University Press: New York ; Oxford, 2010. p. 5.

5. Ecklund, E. H.; Scheitle, C. P., "Religion Among Academic Scientists," ibid.
6. Ecklund, E. H.; Scheitle, C. P., ibid., p. 300.
7. Pew Research Center. Religion and Public Life. "Public's Views on Human Evolution." http://www.pewforum.org/2013/12/30/publics-views-on-human-evolution/ A more comprehensive summary of Pew research on this subject can be found at http://www.pewinternet.org/2015/07/01/chapter-4-evolution-and-perceptions-of-scientific-consensus/
8. Ecklund, E. H.; Scheitle, C. P., "Religion Among Academic Scientists," ibid., p. 301.
9. Ecklund, E. H.; Scheitle, C. P., ibid. p. 301.
10. Ecklund, E. H.; Scheitle, C. P., ibid. p. 303.
11. Ecklund, E. H.; Scheitle, C. P., ibid. p. 304.
12. Ostling, R. N., The Search for the Historical Adam. In *The Origins Debate: Evangelical Perspectives on Creation, Evolution, and Intelligent Design*. Kindle Edition., The Editors of Christianity Today: loc. 168.
13. Ecklund, E. H., *Science Vs. Religion : What Scientists Really Think.*, ibid., p. 151.
14. Ecklund, E. H., ibid., p. 6.
15. Ecklund, E. H., ibid., p. 78.
16. Ecklund, E. H., ibid., p. 29.
17. Ecklund, E. H., ibid., p. 15.
18. Ecklund, E. H., ibid., p. 15.
19. Ecklund, E. H., ibid., p. 152.
20. Ecklund, E. H., ibid., p. 16.
21. Pearcey, N., We're Not in Kansas Anymore: the Furor over Intelligent Design. In *The Origins Debate*: ibid., The Editors of Christianity Today. loc. 797.
22. Ecklund, E. H., ibid., p. 16.
23. Ecklund, E. H., ibid., p. 35.
24. Washington Times. "Americans Still Hold Faith in Divine Creation." 2006. http://www.washingtontimes.com/news/2006/jun/8/20060608-111826-4947r/
25. Larson, E. J.; Witham, L., *Scientists Are Still Keeping the Faith.* Nature 1997, 386, 435 – 436.
26. Ecklund, E. H., ibid., p. 20.
27. Ecklund, E. H., ibid., p. 29.
28. Ecklund, E. H., ibid., p. 16.
29. Ecklund, E. H., ibid., p. 35.
30. Ecklund, E. H., ibid., p. 5.
31. Ecklund, E. H., ibid., p. 10.
32. Ecklund, E. H., ibid., p. 19.
33. Ecklund, E. H., ibid., p. 18.
34. Pew Research Center. (2013). Religion and Public Life. "Public's Views on Human Evolution." ibid. http://www.pewforum.org/2013/12/30/publics-views-on-human-evolution/
35. Miller, K. R., *Only a Theory : Evolution and The Battle for America's Soul.* Viking Penguin: New York ; London, 2008. p. 202.
36. Larson, E. J., *Evolution : The Remarkable History of a Scientific Theory*. Kindle Edition. Modern Library: New York, 2004. loc. 2804.
37. Carroll, S. B., "Is America Evolving on Evolution?" 2014. https://www.scientificamerican.com/article/is-america-evolving-on-evolution/

38. Masci, D., "On Darwin Day, 5 Facts about the Evolution Debate." http://www.pewresearch.org/fact-tank/2016/02/12/darwin-day/
39. Hecht, J., "Why Doesn't America Believe in Evolution?" 2006. https://www.newscientist.com/article/dn9786-why-doesnt-america-believe-in-evolution/
40. Hill, J., National Study of Religion and Human Origins (NSRHO); 2014. Jonathan P. Hill, Ph.D. is Assistant Professor of Sociology at Calvin College in Grand Rapids, Michigan.
https://biologos.org/uploads/projects/nsrho-report.pdf
41. Hill, J., ibid., p. 4.
42. Arel, D., "Fewer Than 10% Of Americans Are Convinced Young Earth Creationists, New Study Shows." http://www.patheos.com/blogs/danthropology/2014/12/guest-post-loving-jesus-and-accepting-evolution-is-more-common-than-you-think/
43. Alexander, D., "How Are Christianity and Evolution Compatible?" https://www.bigquestionsonline.com/2014/06/02/how-are-christianity-evolution-compatible/
44. Saletan, W., "God's Work: A New Poll Suggests Americans Aren't so Confident in Their Creationism." http://www.slate.com/articles/health_and_science/human_nature/2014/12/creationism_poll_how_many_americans_believe_the_bible_is_literal_inerrant.html
45. Hill, J., "National Study of Religion and Human Origins (NSRHO)." p. 1.
46. Hill, J., ibid., p. 6.
47. Hill, J., ibid., p. 7.
48. Hill, J., ibid., p. 8
49. Hill, J., ibid., p. 1.
50. Hill, J., ibid., p. 4.
51. Hill, J., ibid., p. 7.
52. Hill, J., ibid., p. 9.
53. Hill, J., ibid., p. 5.
54. Hill, J., ibid., p. 8.
55. Hill, J., ibid., p. 12.
56. Hill, J., ibid., p. 2.
57. Hill, J., ibid., p. 14.
58. Hill, J., ibid., p. 15.
59. Hill, J., ibid., p. 15.
60. Hill, J., ibid., p. 16.
61. Hill, J., ibid., p. 2.
62. Ecklund, E. H., *Science Vs. Religion : What Scientists Really Think*, ibid., p. 152.
63. Hill, J., "National Study of Religion and Human Origins (NSRHO)." ibid., p. 2.
64. Hill, J., ibid., p. 10.
65. Hill, J., ibid., p. 10.
66. Hill, J., ibid., p. 2.
67. Hill, J., ibid., p. 18.
68. Hill, J., ibid., p. 40.
69. Hill, J., ibid., p. 22.
70. Hill, J., ibid., p. 23.
71. Hill, J., ibid., p. 37.
72. Hill, J., ibid., p. 38.

73. Hill, J., ibid., p. 24.
74. Hill, J., ibid., p. 25.
75. Grossman, C. L., "Associated Press Survey on Faith and Science Reveals that Science is Often Trumped by Religious Belief." http://www.huffingtonpost.com/2014/05/01/ap-survey-faith-science_n_5249154.html
76. Mooney, C. These Charts Finally Explain Where Science Denial Comes From. 2014. https://www.washingtonpost.com/news/wonk/wp/2014/11/11/whats-a-bigger-driver-of-science-denial-politics-or-religion/
77. Hill, J., "National Study of Religion and Human Origins (NSRHO)." ibid., p. 18.
78. Hill, J., ibid., p. 26.
79. Hill, J., ibid., p. 28.
80. Hill, J., ibid., p. 21.
81. Hill, J., ibid., p. 13.
82. Hill, J., ibid., p. 28.
83. Roughgarden, J., *Evolution and Christian Faith : Reflections of an Evolutionary Biologist.* Island Press: Washington, D.C. ; London, 2006. p. 7.
84. Ecklund, E. H., *Science Vs. Religion : What Scientists Really Think*, ibid., p. 8.
85. Hill, J., "National Study of Religion and Human Origins (NSRHO)." ibid., p. 29.
86. Hill, J., ibid., p. 30.
87. Hill, J., ibid., p. 30.
88. Hill, J., ibid., p. 32.
89. Hill, J., ibid., p. 31.
90. Hill, J., ibid., p. 33.
91. Hill, J., ibid., p. 34.
92. Hill, J., ibid., p. 35.
93. Clark, K. J., "The Science-Religion Crisis at Christian Colleges." http://www.huffingtonpost.com/kelly-james-clark/science-religion-christian-colleges_b_5565641.html
94. Hill, J., "National Study of Religion and Human Origins (NSRHO)." ibid., p. 38.
95. Hill, J., ibid., p. 40.
96. Hill, J., ibid., p. 40.
97. Hill, J., ibid., p. 40.
98. Mooney, C., "The Science of Why We Don't Believe Science." ibid. http://www.motherjones.com/politics/2011/03/denial-science-chris-mooney
99. BioLogos Editorial Team. "A Survey of Clergy and their Views on Origins." 2013. http://biologos.org/blogs/archive/a-survey-of-clergy-and-their-views-on-origins

BIBLIOGRAPHY

Abrams, A. *Scientists Have Discovered the First Dinosaur Brain Fossil.* November 15, 2016. http://time.com/4548150/first-dinosaur-brain-fossil/

Alexander, D., "How Are Christianity and Evolution Compatible?" June 2, 2014. https://www.bigquestionsonline.com/2014/06/02/how-are-christianity-evolution-compatible/

"A Different Drum Beat," *True Scientists, True Faith: Some of the World's Leading Scientists Reveal the Harmony between Their Science and Their Faith.* Kindle Edition, R. J. Berry, Ed., Oxford, U. K. and Grand Rapids, MI: Monarch Books, 2014.

Allaby, M., "The Concise Oxford Dictionary of Botany," Oxford, UK: Oxford University Press, 1996.

Americans Still Hold Faith in Divine Creation. Washington Times. June 8, 2006. http://www.washingtontimes.com/news/2006/jun/8/20060608-111826-4947r/

Amesbury, R., "Fideism." Stanford Encyclopedia of Philosophy, 2016.

Anderson, J. E., *The Heresy of Ham: What Every Evangelical Needs to Know About the Creation-Evolution Controversy.* Archdeacon Books, 2016.

Anne, L., "Evidentialism Vs Presuppositionalism," ed: patheos.com, September 23, 2011. http://www.patheos.com/blogs/lovejoyfeminism/2011/09/evidentialism-v-presuppositionalism.html

Applegate, K. and J. B. Stump, "How I Changed My Mind About Evolution: Evangelicals Reflect on Faith and Science." Kindle Edition. Downers Grove, Illinois: IVP Academic, 2016.

Arand, C. P., "The Five Hundredth Anniversary of the Reformation - Lutherans and Science," *Concordia Journal,* Vol. 43 No. 3, Summer 2017, pp. 7-10.

"The Scientist as a Theologian of the Cross," *Concordia Journal,* Vol. 43 No. 3, Summer 2017, pp. 17-35.

Arand, C. P. and J. Okamoto, "Concordia Seminary and the Science for Seminaries Grant," *Concordia Journal,* Vol. 43 No. 3, Summer 2017, pp. 75-81.

Ardern, Z., "Book Review: The Runes of Evolution: How the Universe Became Self-Aware by Simon Conway Morris," in Faith and Science Seeking Understanding, BioLogos Foundation, December 10, 2015. http://biologos.org/blogs/jim-stump-faith-and-science-seeking-understanding/book-review-simon-conway-morris-the-runes-of-evolution-how-the-universe-became-self-aware

Arel, D., "Fewer Than 10% of Americans Are Convinced Young Earth Creationists, New Study Shows ." patheos.com, December 7, 2014. http://www.patheos.com/blogs/danthropology/2014/12/guest-post-loving-jesus-and-accepting-evolution-is-more-common-than-you-think/

Attridge, H. W., "The Religion and Science Debate : Why Does It Continue? Kindle Edition." New Haven, Conn.; London: Yale University Press, 2009

Augustine, Bishop of Hippo, "On Christian Doctrine, Book 2, Ch. 18," in *The Library of Liberal Arts* vol. 80, D. W. Robertson Jr, Ed., ed. Indianapolis: Bobbs-Merrill Educational Publications, 1977.

"Saint Augustine on Genesis," ed. Washington, D.C.: Catholic University of America Press, 1991.

"Australia: First Four Billion Years," *PBS Special,* Public Broadcasting System. July 2014. http://www.pbs.org/wgbh/nova/earth/australia-first-years.html

Ayala, F., Parallel Evolution," in *Faith in Science: Scientists Search for Truth,* W. M. Richardson and G. Slack, Eds. London and New York: Routledge, 2001.

Baker, J., "Monday Minute: A Soft Spot for Dino Bones," ageofrocks.org, January 12, 2015. https://ageofrocks.org/2015/01/12/monday-minute-a-soft-spot-for-dino-bones/

Barbour, I. G., *When Science Meets Religion: Enemies, Strangers, or Partners?,* 1st ed. San Francisco: Harper, 2000.

Barrett, M. and A. B. Caneday, "*Four Views on the Historical Adam,*" Counterpoints: Bible and Theology. Grand Rapids, MI: Zondervan, 2013.

Barrett, M. and A. B. Caneday, "Introduction: Adam, to Be or Not to Be," *Four Views on the Historical Adam,* M. Barrett and A. B. Caneday, Eds., Grand Rapids, MI: Zondervan, 2016, loc. 314, 333.

Barrick, W.D., A Historical Adam: Young Earth Creationist View. In Barrett, M. and A.B. Caneday, Eds., *Four Views on the Historical Adam.* Ch. 4., Grand Rapids, MI, Zondervan, 2016.

Bates, G. That Quote!—About the Missing Transitional Fossils. February 18, 2008. http://creation.com/that-quote-about-the-missing-transitional-fossils

Becker, M., "The Scandal of the LCMS Mind," in *The Daystar Journal - Gospel Voices in and for thean Church–Missouri Synod,* R. Schmidt, Ed: November 10th, 2013. http://thedaystarjournal.com/the-scandal-of-the-lcms-mind/

Behe, M. J., *Darwin's Black Box : The Biochemical Challenge to Evolution.* New York: Touchstone, 1998.

"Comments on Denis Lamoureux's Essays," in *Darwinism Defeated: The Johnson - Lamoureux Debate on Biological Origins,* P. E. Johnson and D. O. Lamoureux, Eds. Vancouver, B.C.: Regent College Publishing, 1999.

Berra, T. M., *Evolution and the Myth of Creationism: A Basic Guide to the Facts in the Evolution Debate.* Stanford, Calif.: Stanford University Press, 1990.

Berry, R. J., "*True Scientists, True Faith: Some of the World's Leading Scientists Reveal the Harmony between Their Science and Their Faith.*" Kindle Edition. Oxford, U.K & Grand Rapids, Michigan, USA: Monarch Books, 2014.

"Foreword," In True Scientists, True Faith: Some of the World's Leading Scientists Reveal The Harmony Between Their Science And Their Faith. Kindle Edition., R. J. Berry, Ed., Oxford, U.K. and Grand Rapids, MI: Monarch Books, 2014.

"Bill Nye - Ken Ham Debate," in *Countering the Culture* vol. 2016, Answers in Genesis, February 4, 2014. See the YouTube video at https://www.youtube.com/watch?v=z6kgvhG3AkI

BioLogos Foundation, "Introduction and Mission Statement," 2014. http://biologos.org/about-us

Bishop, R. C., "The Extended Synthesis (Reviewing "Darwins Doubt": Part 1)," BioLogos Foundation, September 1, 2014. http://biologos.org/blogs/guest/the-extended-synthesis-reviewing-darwins-doubt-robert-bishop-part-1

"Two Rhetorical Strategies (Reviewing "Darwin's Doubt": Part 2)," vol. 2017, ed: BioLogos Foundation, September 1, 2014. http://biologos.org/blogs/archive/two-rhetorical-strategies-reviewing-darwins-doubt-robert-bishop-part-2

"Meyers' Influence to Intelligent Design as the Best Explanation (Reviewing "Darwins Doubt": Part 3)," BioLogos Foundation, September 8, 2014. http://biologos.org/blogs/archive/meyers-inference-to-intelligent-design-as-the-best-explanation-reviewing-da

"Final Assessments (Reviewing "Darwins Doubt": Part 4)," vol. 2017, ed: BioLogos Foundation, September 9, 2014. http://biologos.org/blogs/archive/final-assessments-reviewing-darwins-doubt-robert-bishop-part-4

Bodenham, D., "A Re-Examination of Whale Evolution," in David Bodenham blog. 2013. http://theconservationbiologist.tumblr.com/post/41713472456/a-re-examination-of-whale-evolution

Boslough, J., *Stephen Hawking's Universe*. New York: Quill, 1985.

Boyd, G. A., "Pastoral Reflections: Whether or Not There Was a Historical Adam, Our Faith Is Secure," *Four Views on the Historical Adam*, M. Barrett and A. B. Caneday, Eds., Grand Rapids, MI: Zondervan, 2016.

Braaten, L. J., "May the Glory of the Lord Endure Forever! Biblical Reflections on Creation Care," in *Perspectives on an Evolving Creation*, K. B. Miller, Ed. Grand Rapids, MI and Cambridge, U. K.: Wm. B. Eerdmans, 2003.

Brain, M., How Carbon-14 Dating Works. June 11, 2016 http://science.howstuffworks.com/environmental/earth/geology/carbon-14.htm

Branch, G. Presbyterians Add Their Voice for Evolution. National Center for Science Education. August 15, 2016. https://ncse.com/news/2016/08/presbyterians-add-their-voice-evolution-0018343

Breshears, J. (2014). How Young Earth Creationism Became a Core Tenet of American Fundamentalism, Part II. http://www.reasons.org/explore/blogs/todays-new-reason-to-believe/read/tnrtb/2014/01/03/how-young-earth-creationism-became-a-core-tenet-of-american-fundamentalism-part-2

Briggs, A., "And Information Became Physical," *True Scientists, True Faith: Some of the World's Leading Scientists Reveal The Harmony Between Their Science And Their Faith*. Kindle Edition., R. J. Berry, Ed., Grand Rapids, Michigan: Monarch Books, 2014.

Brooke, J. H., "Science and Secularization," *The Cambridge Companion to Science and Religion*, P. Harrison, Ed., Cambridge, UK, and New York, NY: Cambridge University Press, 2010.

Brown, W. S., "Evolution, Cognitive Neuroscience, and the Soul," in *Perspectives on an Evolving Creation*, K. B. Miller, Ed. Grand Rapids, MI. and Cambridge, U.K.: Wm. B. Eerdmans, 2003.

Buchanan, S., "Was the Expanse Overhead in Genesis 1 a Solid Dome?" September 3, 2012. https://letterstocreationists.wordpress.com/2012/09/03/was-the-expanse-overhead-in-genesis-1-a-solid-dome/

Bucklin, S., A Conductor of Evolution's Subtle Symphony. November 9, 2016. https://www.quantamagazine.org/20161103-richard-lenski-interview-evolution/

Budd, S., *Varieties of Unbelief : Atheists and Agnostics in English Society*, 1850-1960. London: Heinemann, 1977.

Burnett, T., "What Is Scientism?" in *Common Questions*, BioLogos Foundation weblog, June 11, 2012. http://biologos.org/blogs/archive/what-is-scientism

Cambrian Explosion. Public Broadcasting System. June 25, 2017. http://www.pbs.org/wgbh/evolution/library/03/4/l_034_02.html

The Cambrian Explosion. University of California at Berkeley Evolution blog. April 22, 2016. http://www.ucmp.berkeley.edu/cambrian/cambrian.php

Cambrian Explosion. (2016). http://rationalwiki.org/wiki/Cambrian_explosion

Historical and Operational Science, RationalWiki, 2016

Campbell, D. and K. B. Miller, "*The "Cambrian Explosion": A Challenge to Evolutionary Theory?," in Perspectives on an Evolving Creation*, K. B. Miller, Ed. Grand Rapids, MI and Cambridge, U.K.: Wm. B. Eerdmans, 2003.

Campbell, M., "Humans and Squid Evolved Same Eyes Using Same Genes." May 6, 2014. https://theconversation.com/humans-and-squid-evolved-same-eyes-using-same-genes-26265

Carroll, S. B., Is America Evolving on Evolution? February 11, 2014. https://www.scientificamerican.com/article/is-america-evolving-on-evolution/

Carson, D. A., "A Text without a Context Is a Pretext." September 9, 2007. http://theoblogoumena.blogspot.ca/2007/09/text-without-context-is-pretext.html

Carter, B., "Large Number Coincidences and the Anthropic Principle in Cosmology," in *Confrontation of Cosmological Theory with Astronomical Data*, M. S. Longair, Ed. Dordrecht: Reidel 1974.

Carter, N., "Will Evangelicals Ever Learn to Embrace Evolution," patheos.com, March 13, 2015. http://www.patheos.com/blogs/godlessindixie/2015/03/13/will-evangelicals-ever-learn-to-embrace-evolution/

Caruso, G., Science and Religion: 5 Questions (5 Questions Series). March 24, 2014. Automatic Press. Reviewed by John Shook. http://researcherslinks.com/current-issues/Science-and-Religion-5-Questions-by-Gregg-Caruso/9/7/22/html

Catechism of the Catholic Church – English Translation (U.S.A., 2nd Edition). Section 283. http://www.vatican.va/archive/ccc_css/archive/catechism/p1s2c1p4.htm

Chivers, T., "7 Things That Show That Evolution Is an Actual Fact," February 26, 2015. https://www.buzzfeed.com/tomchivers/things-that-show-evolution-is-an-actual-fact?utm_term=.teMneV2Pa - .vv9ZezwE6

Clark, F., "Why Millennials Are Leaving the Church," patheos.com, August 4, 2013. http://www.patheos.com/blogs/slacktivist/2013/08/04/why-millennials-are-leaving-the-church/

Clark, K. J., The Science-Religion Crisis at Christian Colleges. September 13, 2016. http://www.huffingtonpost.com/kelly-james-clark/science-religion-christian-colleges_b_5565641.html

Collins, C. J., "A Historical Adam: Old Earth Creation View," *Four Views on the Historical Adam*, M. Barrett and A. B. Caneday, Eds., Grand Rapids, MI: Zondervan, 2016.

"A Historical Adam: A Young Earth View: Rejoinder from an Old Earth View," *Four Views on the Historical Adam*, M. Barrett and A. B. Caneday, Eds., Grand Rapids, MI: Zondervan, 2016.

Collins, F. S., *The Language of God: A Scientist Presents Evidence for Belief*. New York & London: Free Press, 2006.

"What Do You Believe, Doctor?," *True Scientists, True Faith: Some of the World's Leading Scientists Reveal the Harmony between Their Science and Their Faith*. Kindle Edition, R. J. Berry, Ed.: Monarch Books, 2014.

There Is an Uneasiness About Evolution. April 11, 2015 http://www.huffingtonpost.com/2014/01/25/francis-collins-davos_n_4635338.html

"Learning the Language of God," How I Changed My Mind about Evolution: Evangelicals Reflect on Faith and Science. Kindle Edition, K. Applegate and J. B. Stump, Eds., Downers Grove, Illinois: IVP Academic, 2016.

Collins, R., "Evolution and Original Sin," in *Perspectives on an Evolving Creation*, K. B. Miller, Ed. Grand Rapids, MI and Cambridge, U.K.: Wm. B. Eerdmans, 2003.

Concordia Journal, Vol. 43, No. 3, Summer 2017. Concordia Publishing House, St. Louis, MO.

Consolmagno, Brother Guy, "CBC Radio Quirks and Quarks," Toronto, Canada. March 30, 2013.

Conway Morris, S., *The Crucible of Creation: The Burgess Shale and the Rise of Animals*. Oxford, UK.: Oxford University Press, 1998.

"Is There Room in Evolutionary Creation to Believe in Miracles?," in *God's Relationship To Creation*. BioLogos Foundation, 2006. http://biologos.org/common-questions/gods-relationship-to-creation/biologos-and-miracles

"Evolution and the Inevitability of Intelligent Life," *The Cambridge Companion to Science and Religion*, P. Harrison, Ed., Cambridge, UK: Cambridge University Press, 2010.

"One Impossible Things before Breakfast: Evolution and Christianity," *True Scientists,*

True Faith: Some of the World's Leading Scientists Reveal the Harmony Between Their Science and Their Faith. Kindle Edition., R. J. Berry, Ed., Oxford, U.K and Grand Rapids, MI: Monarch Books: Kindle Edition, 2014.

The Runes of Evolution: How the Universe Became Self-Aware. West Conshohocken, PA: Templeton Press, 2015.

"The Runes of Evolution." Publisher's description of the book is found at https://www.templetonpress.org/books/runes-evolution

Cook, G., Doubting "Darwin's Doubt," July 2, 2013. http://www.newyorker.com/tech/elements/doubting-darwins-doubt

Cook, J., "Inoculating against Science Denial," in Science & Technology, April 26, 2015. https://theconversation.com/inoculating-against-science-denial-40465

Cootsona, G., "Science, Faith, and Emerging Adults: A New Initiative at Fuller Theological Seminary," in *The President's Notebook* : BioLogos Foundation, April 8, 2016. http://biologos.org/blogs/deborah-haarsma-the-presidents-notebook/science-faith-and-emerging-adults-an-interview-with-greg-cootsona-on-a-new-initiative-by-fuller-seminary

Coyne, J. A., *Faith Versus Fact: Why Science and Religion Are Incompatible.* New York: Viking, 2015.

The Creation / Evolution Continuum. June 25, 2017. National Center for Science Education. https://ncse.com/library-resource/creationevolution-continuum

Crisp, O. D., *"Faith, Truth and Mystery," How I Changed My Mind about Evolution: Evangelicals Reflect on Faith and Science.* Kindle Edition., K. Applegate and J. B. Stump, Eds., Downers Grove, Illinois: IVP Academic, 2016.

D'Sousa, D., "The Evolution of Darwin: The Scientists' Problem with God", *The Origins Debate: Evangelical Perspectives on Creation, Evolution, and Intelligent Design*, From the Editors of Christianity Today, Carol Stream, IL: 2012.

Darwin, C., *The Origin of Species.* (1859) Published at New York by W.W. Norton, 1970.

Darwin, C., *The Descent of Man, and Selection in Relation to Sex.* By Charles Darwin ... In Two Volumes...With Illustrations. London: John Murray, 1871.

"Darwin's Doubt - a Review," in Smilodon's Retreat. Skeptic Ink Network. A review of Stephen Meyer's book, Darwin's Doubt. July 9, 2013. https://www.skepticink.com/smilodonsretreat/2013/07/09/darwins-doubt-a-review/

Davidson, G. and K. Wolgemuth, "Biblical and Scientific Shortcomings of Flood Geology, Part 1 " in *Common Questions*, BioLogos Foundation, September 7, 2012. http://biologos.org/blogs/archive/biblical-and-scientific-shortcomings-of-flood-geology-part-1

Davis, E. T. B., "The Word and the Works: Concordism and American Evangelicals," in *Perspectives on an Evolving Creation*, K. B. Miller, Ed. Grand Rapids, MI and Cambridge, U.K.: Wm. B. Eerdmans, 2003.

Davis, T., "Science and the Bible: The Framework View," ed: BioLogos Foundation, July 31, 2012. http://biologos.org/blogs/ted-davis-reading-the-book-of-nature/science-and-the-bible-the-framework-view

"Science and the Bible: Theistic Evolution, Part 1," in *Reading the Book of Nature*, BioLogos Foundation, August 15, 2012. http://biologos.org/blogs/ted-davis-reading-the-book-of-nature/science-and-the-bible-theistic-evolution-part-1

"Science and the Bible: Theistic Evolution, Part 2," in *Reading the Book of Nature*, BioLogos Foundation, August 29, 2012. http://biologos.org/blogs/ted-davis-reading-the-book-of-nature/science-and-the-bible-theistic-evolution-part-2

"Science and the Bible: Theistic Evolution, Part 4," in *Reading the Book of Nature*, BioLogos Foundation, September 25, 2012. http://biologos.org/blogs/ted-davis-reading-the-book-of-nature/science-and-the-bible-theistic-evolution-part-4

"Science and the Bible: Theistic Evolution, Part 5," in *Reading the Book of Nature*,

BioLogos Foundation, October 8, 2012. http://biologos.org/blogs/ted-davis-reading-the-book-of-nature/science-and-the-bible-theistic-evolution-part-5

Davis, T., "The Evolution of Darwin's Religious Faith," in *Reading the Book of Nature*, BioLogos Foundation, October 20, 2016. http://biologos.org/blogs/ted-davis-reading-the-book-of-nature/the-evolution-of-darwins-religious-faith

Dawkins, R., *The Greatest Show on Earth: The Evidence for Evolution*. Ibook Edition., London: Black Swan, 2009.

Dennett, D. C., *Consciousness Explained*, 1st ed. Boston: Little, Brown and Co, 1991.

Dennett, D. C., *Darwin's Dangerous Idea: Evolution and the Meanings of Life*. New York & London: Simon & Schuster, 1995.

Denton, M. J., *Evolution: A Theory in Crisis*. London: Burnett, 1985.

Denton, M. J., *Nature's Destiny: How the Laws of Biology Reveal Purpose in the Universe*. New York: Free Press, 1998.

Denton, M. J., *Evolution: Still a Theory in Crisis*, Revised edition ed. Seattle, WA: Discovery Institute Press, 2016.

Dobson, J., "Young Earth vs Old Earth Creationism": A Debate by Duane Gish and Hugh Ross." *Focus on the Family* Radio Broadcast, April 18, 1991.

Dowd, M., *Thank God for Evolution! How the Marriage of Science and Religion Will Transform Your Life and Our World*, 1st ed. San Francisco: Publishers Group UK, 2007.

Downard, J., "Review of Michael Denton's Evolution: Still a Theory in Crisis," May 20, 2017. https://www.goodreads.com/topic/show/18618119-source-check-failures-of-denton-s-2016-book - comment_id_166547607

Draper, J. W., *History of the Conflict between Religion and Science*. New York, NY, 1903.

Duff, J., " A 60,000 Year Varve Record from Japan Refutes the Young-Earth Interpretation of Earth's history," Natural Historian. August 16, 2006. https://thenaturalhistorian.com/2016/08/16/a-60000-year-varve-record-from-japan-refutes-the-young-earth-interpretation-of-earths-history/

Ecklund, E. H., *Science Vs. Religion : What Scientists Really Think*. Kindle Edition., New York ; Oxford: Oxford University Press, 2010.

Ecklund, E. H. and C. P. Scheitle, "Religion among Academic Scientists: Distinctions, Disciplines, and Demographics," *Social Problems*, vol. 54, no. 2, pp. 289–307, April 26 2007. http://www.owlnet.rice.edu/~ehe/doc/Ecklund_SocialProblems_54_2.pdf

Ecklund, E. H., Johnson, D. R., Scheitle, C. P., Matthews, K. R. W., Lewis, S. W.: "*Religion among Scientists in International Context: A New Study of Scientists in Eight Regions* " Socius, January - December 2016, Volume 2, September 1, 2016. http://journals.sagepub.com/doi/abs/10.1177/2378023116664353

Eldredge, N., *Reinventing Darwin: The Great Debate at the High Table of Evolutionary Theory*. New York ; Chichester: Wiley, 1995.

Darwin: Discovering the Tree of Life, 1st ed. New York ; London: W.W. Norton, 2005.

Elliott, J. (2014). Pope Francis: Evolution Is Real, God Did Not Wave a 'Magic Wand'. http://www.ctvnews.ca/world/pope-francis-evolution-is-real-god-did-not-wave-a-magic-wand-1.2076772

Enns, P., "Eleven Recurring Mistakes in the Debate over the Historical Adam," ed: patheos.com, May 11, 2015. http://www.patheos.com/blogs/peterenns/2015/05/11-recurring-mistakes-in-the-debate-over-the-historical-adam/

"For Those of You Wondering Why I Interpret the Bible the Way I Do - Which I Assume Means the Entire Internet," September 16, 2016. https://peteenns.com/for-those-of-you-wondering-why-i-interpret-the-bible-the-way-i-do-which-i-assume-means-the-entire-internet/

"A Quick Word About How Genealogies in the Bible aren't History." April 6, 2017. https://peteenns.com/a-quick-word-about-how-genealogies-in-the-bible-arent-history/
"God Did Not Create the Cosmos with "Apparent Age"—3 Reasons," in *The Bible for Normal People*, April 14, 2017, https://peteenns.com/god-did-not-create-the-cosmos-with-apparent-age-3-reasons/

Evans, R. H., "Why Millennials Are Leaving the Church," CNN.com, July 27, 2013. http://religion.blogs.cnn.com/2013/07/27/why-millennials-are-leaving-the-church/

Evolution, Creationism, Intelligent Design: Historical Trends. (2016). http://www.gallup.com/poll/21814/evolution-creationism-intelligent-design.aspx

Falk, D. R., *Coming to Peace with Science: Bridging the Worlds between Faith and Biology*, Downers Grove, IL: InterVarsity Press, 2004.

"Thoughts on "Darwin's Doubt" : Part 1," vol. 2017, BioLogos Foundation, 2014. http://biologos.org/blogs/archive/thoughts-on-darwins-doubt-reviewing-darwins-doubt-darrel-falk-part-1
"Further Thoughts on "Darwin's Doubt": Part 2", BioLogos Foundation, September 11, 2014. http://biologos.org/blogs/archive/thoughts-on-darwins-doubt-reviewing-darwins-doubt-darrel-falk-part-2

Ferguson, K., *Stephen Hawking: Quest for a Theory of Everything*. Bantam Books, 1992.

Fradd, M., "Evolution Vs Genesis," August 22, 2012. http://mattfradd.com/evolution-vs-genesis/comment-page-1/

Fugle, G. N., *Laying Down Arms to Heal the Creation - Evolution Divide*. Eugene, OR: Wipf & Stock, 2015.

Funes, J. G., (S.J.), Interviewed by V. Shah. "Religion, Science and Society," in Thought Economics. May 18, 2016. https://thoughteconomics.com/religion-science-and-society/

Funk, C. and L. Rainie. (July 1, 2015, November 16, 2016). Chapter 4: Evolution and Perceptions of Scientific Consensus (Internet, Science and Tech ed.). http://www.pewinternet.org/2015/07/01/chapter-4-evolution-and-perceptions-of-scientific-consensus/

Garte, S. and A. Albert, "Evolution Is Still Not a Theory in Crisis, but Neo-Darwinism Might Be," in *Faith and Science Seeking Understanding*. J. B. Stump, Ed., BioLogos Foundation, February 9, 2016. http://biologos.org/blogs/jim-stump-faith-and-science-seeking-understanding/evolution-is-still-not-a-theory-in-crisis-but-neo-darwinism-might-be

Gibbons, A. Oldest-Ever Proteins Extracted from 3.8-Million-Year-Old Ostrich Shells. October 8, 2016. http://www.sciencemag.org/news/2016/09/oldest-ever-proteins-extracted-38-million-year-old-ostrich-shells?utm_source=6&utm_medium=social&utm_campaign=AAAS-Dialogue-on-Science,-Ethics-and-Religion-%28AAAS.DoSER%29&utm_term=DoSER&utm_content=AAAS

"World's Oldest Homo Sapiens Fossils Found in Morocco," in Archaeology, Human Evolution. American Association for the Advancement of Science (AAAS), June 7, 2017. http://www.sciencemag.org/news/2017/06/world-s-oldest-homo-sapiens-fossils-found-morocco

Giberson, K., Saving *Darwin: How to Be a Christian and Believe in Evolution*. New York: HarperOne, 2008.

"Adventist Origins of Young Earth Creationism." BioLogos Foundation, 2009. https://biologos.org/uploads/static-content/Giberson-scholarly-essay-1.pdf
Seven Glorious Days : A Scientist Retells the Genesis Creation Story. Kindle Edition., Brewster, Mass.: Paraclete Press, 2012.
The Christian Reformed Church Still Won't Stand up for Science. June 29, 2014. http://www.thedailybeast.com/articles/2014/06/29/the-christian-reformed-church-still-won-t-stand-up-for-science.html

Giberson, K. and M. Artigas, *Oracles of Science: Celebrity Scientists Versus God and Religion.*

Oxford ; New York: Oxford University Press, 2007.

Giberson, K. and F. S. Collins, *The Language of Science and Faith : Straight Answers to Genuine Questions*. Kindle Edition., London: SPCK, 2011.

Godfrey, S. J. and C. R. Smith, *Paradigms on Pilgrimage: Creationism, Paleontology, and Biblical Interpretation*. Toronto, Ont.: Clements Publishing, 2005.

"God's Relationship to Creation: Is There Room in Evolutionary Creation to Believe in Miracles?" in Common Questions. BioLogos Foundation, 2016. http://biologos.org/common-questions/gods-relationship-to-creation/biologos-and-miracles

Goodman, C. S. and B. S. Coughlin, "Special Feature: The Evolution of Evo-Devo Biology," *Proceedings of the National Academy of Sciences*, vol. 97, no. 9, pp. 4424-4456, 2000.

Gosler, A., "Surprise and the Value of Life," *True Scientists, True Faith: Some of the World's Leading Scientists Reveal The Harmony Between Their Science And Their Faith*, R. J. Berry, Ed., Oxford, U.K. and Grand Rapids, MI: Monarch Books, 2014.

Gosse, P. H., Omphalos: *An Attempt to Untie the Geological Knot. ...* With Fifty-Six Illustrations on Wood. London, 1857.

Gottschall, J., *The Storytelling Animal: How Stories Make Us Human*. Ibook Edition., Boston: Houghton Mifflin Harcourt, 2012.

Gould, S. J., *Ever since Darwin: Reflections in Natural History*, 1st ed. New York: Norton, 1977.

The Panda's Thumb: More Reflections in Natural History. New York; London: Norton, 1980.

Wonderful Life: The Burgess Shale and the Nature of History, 1st ed. New York: W.W. Norton, 1989.

Bully for Brontosaurus: Reflections in Natural History. New York: Norton, 1991.

Eight Little Piggies: Reflections in Natural History. Norton, 1993.

Dinosaur in a Haystack: Reflections in Natural History. New York: Harmony, 1995.

Leonardo's Mountain of Clams and the Diet of Worms: Essays on Natural History. New York: Harmony Books ; London : Random House, 1998.

Rocks of Ages: Science and Religion in the Fullness of Life. New York: Ballantine Books, 1999.

The Lying Stones of Marrakesh: Penultimate Reflections in Natural History. New York: Harmony Books, 2000.

I Have Landed: The End of a Beginning in Natural History, 1st ed. New York: Harmony Books, 2002.

The Structure of Evolutionary Theory. Cambridge, MA; London, UK.: The Belknap Press of Harvard University Press, 2002.

The Hedgehog, the Fox, and the Magister's Pox: Ending the False War between Science and the Humanities, 1st ed. New York: Harmony Books, 2003.

Gould, S. J. and N. Eldredge, "Punctuated Equilibria: An Alternative to Phyletic Gradualism," in *Models in Paleobiology*, T. J. M. Schopf, Ed. San Francisco: Freeman Cooper, 1972, pp. 82-115.

Graham, B., *Billy Graham: Personal Thoughts of a Public Man*, English Language edition ed. Chariot Victor Publishing, 1997.

Grammling, C., A Dinosaur's Brain Preserved in a Pebble. January 8, 2017. http://www.sciencemag.org/news/2016/10/dinosaur-s-brain-preserved-pebble

Grant, R. P. Why Scientists Are Losing the Fight to Communicate Science to the Public. The Guardian, August 23, 2016. https://www.theguardian.com/science/occams-corner/2016/aug/23/scientists-losing-science-communication-skeptic-cox

Gray, T. M., "Biochemistry and Evolution," in *Perspectives on an Evolving Creation*, K. B. Miller, Ed. Grand Rapids, MI. Cambridge, UK: Wm. B. Eerdmans, 2003.

Greenberg, J., "Geological Framework of an Evolving Creation," in *Perspectives on an Evolving Creation*, K. B. Miller, Ed. Grand Rapids, MI and Cambridge, U.K.: Wm. B. Eerdmans, 2003.

Greene, E., You Can't Educate People into Believing in Evolution. The Atlantic. November 23, 2014. http://www.theatlantic.com/national/archive/2014/11/you-cant-educate-people-into-believing-in-evolution/382983/

Gribbin, J., *The Scientists: A History of Science Told through the Lives of Its Greatest Inventors*, 1st U.S. ed. New York: Random House, 2003.

Grossman, C. L., A.P. Survey on Faith and Science Reveals That Science Is Often Trumped by Religious Belief. Huffington Post, May 1, 2014. http://www.huffingtonpost.com/2014/05/01/ap-survey-faith-science_n_5249154.html

Guiderdoni, B., "Reading God's Signs," in *Faith in Science: Scientists Search for Truth*, W. M. Richardson and G. Slack, Eds. London and New York: Routledge, 2001.

Gustavsen, D., "I Have a Friend Who Believes Science Disproves Faith, Part 2." BioLogos Foundation, February 27, 2015. http://biologos.org/blogs/archive/i-have-a-friend-who-believes-science-disproves-faith-part-2

Haarsma, D., "Seeing God in Everyday Work, Part II," in The President's Notebook, BioLogos Foundation, May 24, 2014. http://biologos.org/blogs/deborah-haarsma-the-presidents-notebook/seeing-god-in-everyday-work-part-2

Haarsma, D., "Reviewing "Darwin's Doubt": Introduction," in The President's Notebook, BioLogos Foundation, August 25, 2014. http://biologos.org/blogs/deborah-haarsma-the-presidents-notebook/reviewing-darwins-doubt-introduction

Haarsma, D., "Reviewing Darwin's Doubt: Conclusion," in The President's Notebook, BioLogos Foundation, January 19, 2015. http://biologos.org/blogs/deborah-haarsma-the-presidents-notebook/reviewing-darwins-doubt-conclusion

Haarsma, D., *"Learning to Praise God for His Work in Evolution," How I Changed My Mind about Evolution: Evangelicals Reflect on Faith and Science*. Kindle Edition., K. Applegate and J. B. Stump, Eds., Downers Grove, Illinois: IVP Academic, 2016.

"Religion, Science and Society," in *Thought Economics*. May 18, 2016. Interviewed by V. Shah. https://thoughteconomics.com/religion-science-and-society/

Haarsma, D. and J. J. Wiseman, "An Evolving Cosmos," in *Perspectives on an Evolving Creation*, K. B. Miller, Ed. Grand Rapids, MI and Cambridge, UK: Wm. B. Eerdmans, 2003.

Haarsma, L., "Does Science Exclude God? Natural Law, Chance, Miracles, and Scientific Practice," in *Perspectives on an Evolving Creation*, K. B. Miller, Ed. Grand Rapids, MI and Cambridge, U. K.: Wm. B. Eerdmans, 2003.

Haarsma, L. and T. M. Grey, "Complexity, Self Organization and Design," in *Perspectives on an Evolving Creation*, K. B. Miller, Ed. Grand Rapids, MI and Cambridge, U. K.: Wm. B. Eerdmans, 2003.

Haidt, J., *The Righteous Mind: Why Good People Are Divided by Politics and Religion*. Kindle Edition., London: Allen Lane, 2012.

Harrison, P. R., "*The Cambridge Companion to Science and Religion*. Kindle Edition.." Cambridge: Cambridge University Press, 2010.

"Introduction," *The Cambridge Companion to Science and Religion*. Kindle Edition., P. R. Harrison, Ed., Cambridge, U. K.: Cambridge University Press, 2010.

Haught, J. F., *God after Darwin: A Theology of Evolution*. Boulder, Colo. ; Oxford: Westview Press, 2000.

"Science, God and Cosmic Purpose," The Cambridge Companion to Science and Religion, P. Harrison, Ed., Cambridge, UK and New York: Cambridge University Press, 2010.

Hawking, S., *A Brief History of Time: From the Big Bang to Black Holes*. Toronto ; New York: Bantam Books, 1988.

Hecht, J. Why Doesn't America Believe in Evolution? New Scientist. August 20, 2006. https://www.newscientist.com/article/dn9786-why-doesnt-america-believe-in-evolution/ - .UnziL5TF28P

Hemphill, C., G. Davidson, and T. Davis, "*From the Mailbag: Why Would God Allow Scientific Errors in the Bible?*," ed: BioLogos Foundation, 2016.

Hill, J. (2014). Rethinking the Origins Debate. Available: http://www.christianitytoday.com/ct/2014/february-web-only/rethinking-origins-debate.html

Hill, J., "National Study of Religion and Human Origins (NSRHO)." BioLogos Foundation, 2014. https://biologos.org/uploads/projects/nsrho-report.pdf

Hinnant, C. H., "The "Fable of the Spider and the Bee" and Swift's Poetics of Inspiration," Colby Library Quarterly, vol. 20, no. 3, pp. 129-136, September 1984.

Hodge, B. Are Mutations Part of the 'Engine' of Evolution? Answers in Genesis. February 18, 2010. https://answersingenesis.org/genetics/mutations/are-mutations-part-of-the-engine-of-evolution

Hodge, B. and G. Purdom. (2013). What Are "Kinds" in Genesis? Available: https://answersingenesis.org/creation-science/baraminology/what-are-kinds-in-genesis

Hoezee, S., "The "One Thing" Behind the Genesis Debate." BioLogos Foundation, November 12, 2014. http://biologos.org/blogs/guest/the-one-thing-behind-the-genesis-debate

Holloway, B., "Young-Earthers and Presuppositionalism." December 11, 2013. http://www.hollowayquarterly.com/2013/12/young-earthers-and-presuppositionalism.html

Hooper, S. The Rise of the New Atheists. CNN, November 9, 2006. http://www.cnn.com/2006/WORLD/europe/11/08/atheism.feature/index.html?_s=PM:W

Hosier, M., "An Evolutionary Crisis?" January 19, 2017. http://thinktheology.co.uk/blog/article/an_evolutionary_crisis

Houghton, J., "A God Big Enough," *True Scientists, True Faith: Some Of The World's Leading Scientists Reveal The Harmony Between Their Science And Their Faith.* Kindle Edition., R. J. Berry, Ed., Oxford, U.K. and Grand Rapids, MI: Monarch Books, 2014.

Humphreys, S. C. J., "Can Science and Christianity Both Be True?," *True Scientists, True Faith: Some of the World's Leading Scientists Reveal the Harmony Between their Science and their Faith.* Kindle Edition., R. J. Berry, Ed., Oxford, U.K. and Grand Rapids, MI: Monarch Books, 2014.

Hunt, Z., "Confessions of an Evolving Baptist," Zack Hunt blog, November 27, 2013. http://zackhunt.net/2013/11/27/confessions-of-an-evolving-baptist-by-nathan-hale/

Hurd, J. P., "Hominids in the Garden?," in *Perspectives on an Evolving Creation*, K. B. Miller, Ed. Grand Rapids, MI and Cambridge, U. K.: Wm. B. Eerdmans, 2003.

Hutchinson, I., *Monopolizing Knowledge: A Scientist Refutes Religion-Denying, Reason-Destroying Scientism*. Belmont, Massachusetts: Fias Publishing, 2011.

Hyers, C., "Comparing Biblical and Scientific Maps of Origins," in *Perspectives on an Evolving Creation*, K. B. Miller, Ed. Grand Rapids, MI and Cambridge U.K.: Wm. B. Eerdmans, 2003.

Ingersoll, S., "I've Evolved, Too." BioLogos Foundation, January 7, 2014. http://biologos.org/blogs/archive/i've-evolved-too

Isaak, M., *The Counter-Creationism Handbook*. Westport, Conn.: Greenwood ; Oxford : Harcourt Education, 2005.

Janssen, L. J., *Standing on the Shoulders of Giants: Genesis and Human Origins*. Eugene, OR: Wipf & Stock, 2016.

John Paul II, "Message to the Pontifical Academy of Sciences: On Evolution," October 22, 1996. https://www.ewtn.com/library/PAPALDOC/JP961022.HTM

Johnstone, David. J., "Book Review: The Lost World of Genesis One," December 22, 2009. http://davidjohnstone.net/blog/page/4

Johnson, P. E., *Darwin on Trial*. Washington, D.C.: Regnery Gateway ; Lanham, MD, 1991.

"Response to Denis O. Lamoureux," in *Darwinism Defeated? The Johnson - Lamoureux Debate on Biological Origins*, P. E. Johnson and D. O. Lamoureux, Eds. Vancouver, B.C.: Regent College Publishing, 1999.

Johnson, P. E. and D. O. Lamoureux, "*Darwinism Defeated? The Johnson-Lamoureux Debate on Biological Origins*." Vancouver: Regent College Publishing, 1999.

Jones, W., "Evolution: Still a Theory in Crisis. A Review by Will Jones," in ISCAST (Christians in Science and Technology) Online Journal, August 2016. http://www.iscast.org/journal/Jones_W_2016_07_Denton_Review

Judgment Day: Intelligent Design on Trial. PBS Special. October 11, 2007. YouTube video at https://www.youtube.com/watch?v=8_sw60C66jY

Jurchen, J., "The Age of the Earth and Confessional Lutheranism: Speaking the Truth in Love," *Concordia Journal*, Vol. 43 No. 3, Summer 2017, pp. 64-74.

Keim, B., "Something Other Than Adaptation Could Be Driving Evolution." March 28, 2013. https://www.wired.com/2013/03/neutral-biodiversity/

Kidder, J., "Joel Edmund Anderson: The Heresy of Ham," in Science and Religion: A View from an Evolutionary Creationist. October 18, 2016. http://scienceandcreation.blogspot.ca/2016/10/joel-edmund-anderson-heresy-of-ham.html

Kitcher, P., *Abusing Science: The Case against Creationism*. Cambridge, Mass. ; London: MIT Press, 1982.

Living with Darwin: Evolution, Design, and the Future of Faith. Oxford ; New York: Oxford University Press, 2007.

Kitzmiller V. Dover: Intelligent Design on Trial. National Center for Science Education. June 25, 2017. https://ncse.com/library-resource/kitzmiller-v-dover-intelligent-design-trial

Kramer, B., "Growing up Evangelical. My Story of Making Peace with Evolution," in The Evolving Evangelical, BioLogos Foundation, October 20, 2014. http://biologos.org/blogs/brad-kramer-the-evolving-evangelical/growing-up-evangelical-my-story-of-making-peace-with-evolution

Krauss, L. M., "Religion Vs. Science?," In *The Religion and Science Debate: Why Does It Continue?* Kindle Edition., H. W. Attridge, Ed., New Haven, CT. and London, U.K.: Yale University Press, 2009.

Kuhn, T. S., *The Structure of Scientific Revolutions*. Chicago ; London: University of Chicago Press, 1962.

Laland, K. Evolution Evolves: Beyond the Selfish Gene. September 21, 2016. https://www.newscientist.com/article/mg23130920-600-evolution-evolves-beyond-the-selfish-gene/

Lamoureux, D. O., "Evangelicals Inheriting the Wind: The Phillip E. Johnson Phenomenon," in *Darwinism Defeated? The Johnson - Lamoureux Debate on Biological Origins*, P. E. Johnson and D. O. Lamoureux, Eds. Vancouver, Canada: Regent College Publishing, 1999.

Evolutionary Creation : A Christian Approach to Evolution. Cambridge, England: Lutterworth Press, 2008.

I Love Jesus & I Accept Evolution. Kindle Edition., Eugene, OR: Wipf & Stock, 2009.

"The Ancient Science in the Bible," BioLogos Foundation, August 21, 2009. http://biologs.org/blogs/archive/the-ancient-science-in-the-bible

"Evolutionary Creation: A Christian Approach to Evolution." (Summary), BioLogos

Foundation, August 21, 2009. https://biologos.org/uploads/projects/Lamoureux_Scholarly_Essay.pdf
"No Historical Adam: Evolutionary Creation View," *Four Views on the Historical Adam*, M. Barrett and A. B. Caneday, Eds., Grand Rapids, MI: Zondervan, 2016.
"A Historical Adam: Archetypal Creation View. A Rejoinder from an Evolutionary Creation View," *Four Views on the Historical Adam*, M. Barrett and A. B. Caneday, Eds., Grand Rapids, MI: Zondervan, 2016.

Larson, E. J., Evolution: *The Remarkable History of a Scientific Theory*. Kindle Edition., New York: Modern Library, 2004.

Larson, E. J. and L. Witham, "Scientists Are Still Keeping the Faith," *Nature*, vol. 386, pp. 435-436, April 3, 1997.

Lehman, M., "Ten Things I Wish Everyone Knew About the Creation / Evolution Debate." September 24, 2016. https://www.onfaith.co/discussion/10-things-i-wish-everyone-knew-about-the-creation-vs-evolution-debate

Lindberg, D. C., "The Fate of Science in Patristic and Medieval Christendom," *The Cambridge Companion to Science and Religion*, P. Harrison, Ed., Cambridge, UK.: Cambridge University Press, 2010.

Lombrozo, T. (2015). Scientific Literacy: It's Not (Just) About the Facts. National Public Radio. September 14, 2015. http://www.npr.org/sections/13.7/2015/09/14/440213603/scientific-literacy-it-s-not-just-about-the-facts

Long, J., "Life on Earth Still Favors Evolution over Creationism " in Science & technology, September 10, 2014. https://theconversation.com/life-on-earth-still-favours-evolution-over-creationism-23419

Louis, A., "Miracles & Science, Part 2," BioLogos Foundation, July 3, 2010. http://biologos.org/blogs/archive/miracles-and-science-part-2

Lurie, A., "Is Religion a Science Stopper?," in Voices. The Blog. Huffington Post, May 22, 2013. https://www.huffingtonpost.com/rabbi-alan-lurie/is-religion-a-science-stopper_b_3283004.html

Luther, M., Preface to the Old Testament. In *Luther's Works, American* Edition. Vol. 35. Pelikan, J & Lehmann, H.T. Eds., Fortresss Press, Philadelphia. 1965.
Luther's Last Sermon in Wittenberg. In *Luther's Works, American Edition*, Vol. 53. Pelikan, J. & Lehmann H.T. Eds., Philadelphia, Fortress Press, 1965.
Lectures on Genesis Chapters 1-5," In *Luther's Works, American Edition*. Vol. 1: Pelikan, J., Trans., St. Louis, Missouri: Concordia Publishing House, 1958.
Liturgy and Hymns, *Luther's Works, American Edition*. Vol. 53: Pelikan, J. and H. T. Lehmann, Trans., Philadelphia: Fortress Press, 1965.
Word and Sacrament I, *Luther's Works, American Edition*, Vol. 35: Pelikan, J. and H. T. Lehmann, Trans., Philadelphia: Fortress Press, 1965.

MacKay, D. M., "Science and Christian Faith Today," *True Scientists, True Faith: Some of the World's Leading Scientists Reveal the Harmony between Their Science and Their Faith*. Kindle Edition., R. J. Berry, Ed., Oxford, U.K. and Grand Rapids, MI: Monarch Books, 2014.

MacMillan, D., "Understanding Creationism II: Variation and Adaptation." June 4, 2014. https://pandasthumb.org/archives/2014/06/understanding-c-1.html
"Understanding Creationism VIII: An Insider's Guide by a Former Young Earth Creationist," July 16, 2014. https://pandasthumb.org/archives/2014/07/understanding-c-7.html

Malthus, T. R., *An Essay on the Principle of Population*. (1798) Mineola, N.Y.: Dover ; Newton Abbot, 2007.

Masci, D. On Darwin Day, 6 Facts About the Evolution Debate. Pew Research. February 12,

2016. http://www.pewresearch.org/fact-tank/2016/02/12/darwin-day/

Matzke, Nicholas, Design on Trial in Dover, Pennsylvania. National Center for Science Education. September - October, 2004. https://ncse.com/library-resource/design-trial-dover-pennsylvania

Mayr, E., *The Growth of Biological Thought: Diversity, Evolution and Inheritance*. Cambridge, Mass. ; London: Belknap Press, 1982.

What Evolution Is. New York: Basic Books, 2001.

McCaig, A., "Most British Scientists Cited in Study Feel Richard Dawkins' Work Misrepresents Science," in Current News vol. 2016, ed: Rice University News and Media, 2016. http://news.rice.edu/2016/10/31/most-british-scientists-cited-in-study-feel-richard-dawkins-work-misrepresents-science-2/ See also http://journals.sagepub.com/doi/pdf/10.1177/0963662516673501

McGrath, A. E., *Science and Religion: An Introduction*. Kindle Edition., 2nd ed. Chichester: Wiley-Blackwell, 2010.

"Augustine's Origin of Species: How the Great Theologian Might Weigh in on the Darwin Debate," *The Origins Debate: Evangelical Perspectives on Creation, Evolution, and Intelligent Design*, The Editors of Christianity Today, Carol Stream, IL: Christianity Today, 2012.

"Science, Faith and Making Sense of Things," *True Scientists, True Faith: Some of the World's Leading Scientists Reveal the Harmony Between Their Science and Their Faith*. Kindle Edition., R. J. Berry, Ed., Oxford, U.K. and Grand Rapids, MI: Monarch Books, 2014.

"Big Picture or Big Gaps? Why Natural Theology Is Better Than Intelligent Design," BioLogos Foundation, September 15. 2014. http://biologos.org/blogs/archive/big-picture-or-big-gaps-why-natural-theology-is-better-than-intelligent-design

"A Meaningful Conversation," November 25, 2015. https://www.huffingtonpost.com/thought-matters/a-meaningful-conversation_b_8638386.html

McGrath, A. E. and J. C. McGrath, *The Dawkins Delusion? Atheist Fundamentalism and the Denial of the Divine*. London: SPCK, 2007.

McLeish, T., *Faith and Wisdom in Science*, Oxford: Oxford University Press, 2014.

Medawar, P. B., *The Limits of Science*. Oxford: Oxford University Press, 1984.

Meet Tiktaalik Roseae: An Extraordinary Fossil Fish. University of Chicago. May 5, 2016. http://tiktaalik.uchicago.edu/meetTik.html

Meyer, S. C., "Teleological Evolution: The Difference It Doesn't Make," in *Darwinism Defeated? The Johnson – Lamoreaux Debate on Biological Origins*, P. E. Johnson and D. O. Lamoureux, Eds. Vancouver BC: Regent College Publishing, 1999.

Darwin's Doubt: The Explosive Origin of Animal Life and the Case for Intelligent Design, 1st ed. New York, NY: HarperOne, 2013.

Michalska, K. and S. Michalski, Spider (Animal). London: Reaktion Books, 2010.

Middleton, J. R., "The Ancient Universe and the Cosmic Temple," in Faith and Science Seeking Understanding, BioLogos foundation, July 19, 2016. http://biologos.org/blogs/jim-stump-faith-and-science-seeking-understanding/the-ancient-universe-and-the-cosmic-temple

Milburn, M. A. and S. D. Conrad, *The Politics of Denial*. Cambridge, Mass.: MIT Press, 1996.

Miller, K. B., "Design and Purpose within an Evolving Creation," in *Darwinism Defeated? The Johnson – Lamoureux Debate on Biological Origins*, P. E. Johnson and D. O. Lamoureux, Eds. Vancouver, BC: Regent College Publishing, 1999.

Ed., "*Perspectives on an Evolving Creation*." Grand Rapids, Mich. ; Cambridge, U.K.: Eerdmans, 2003.

"An Evolving Creation: Oxymoron or Fruitful Insight?," in *Perspectives on an Evolving*

Creation, K. B. Miller, Ed. Grand Rapids, MI and Cambridge U. K.: Wm. B. Eerdmans, 2003.

Miller, K. R., *Finding Darwin's God: A Scientist's Search for Common Ground between God and Evolution*. New York: Cliff Street Books, 1999.

Only a Theory: Evolution and the Battle for America's Soul. New York ; London: Viking Penguin, 2008.

"Darwin, God, and Dover: What the Collapse of "Intelligent Design" Means for Science and Faith in America," *The Religion and Science Debate: Why Does It Continue?* Kindle Edition., H. W. Attridge, Ed., New Haven and London: Yale University Press, 2009.

Mitchell, E. Cambrian Explosion Was the Culmination of Cascading Causes Evolutionists Claim. Answers in Genesis. October 12, 2013. https://answersingenesis.org/theory-of-evolution/evolution-timeline/cambrian-explosion-was-the-culmination-of-cascading-causes-evolutionists-claim/

Mooney, C., "The Science of Why We Don't Believe in Science," MotherJones. May-June, 2011. http://www.motherjones.com/politics/2011/04/denial-science-chris-mooney/

These Charts Finally Explain Where Science Denial Comes From. Washington Post. November 11, 2014. https://www.washingtonpost.com/news/wonk/wp/2014/11/11/whats-a-bigger-driver-of-science-denial-politics-or-religion/

Moore, J. R., *The Darwin Legend*. London: Hodder & Stoughton, 1994.

Moore, R. A. The Impossible Voyage of Noah's Ark. National Center for Science Education. Winter, 1983. https://ncse.com/cej/4/1/impossible-voyage-noahs-ark

Morris, H. M., *Biblical Cosmology and Modern Science*. Baker Book House, 1970.

The Beginning of the World. El Cajon, CA: Master Books, 1991.

Morris, H. M. and J. Whitcomb, *The Genesis Flood; the Biblical Record and Its Scientific Implications*. Philadelphia,: Presbyterian and Reformed Pub. Co., 1961.

Mortillaro, N. Feathered Dinosaur Tail Found Trapped in Amber. CBC News. January 8, 2017. http://www.cbc.ca/news/technology/feathered-dinosaur-tail-amber-1.3885813?cmp=rss

Moulds, R., "Science, Religion, and God's Two Kingdoms: A Lutheran Framework for Instruction," *Concordia Journal*, Vol. 43 No. 3, Summer 2017, pp. 36-44.

Mouw, R. J., "Safe Spaces," *How I Changed My Mind About Evolution: Evangelicals Reflect on Faith and Science*, K. Applegate and J. B. Stump, Eds., Downer's Grove, IL: IVP Academic, 2016.

Murphy, G. L., "Remembering God's People," in *Perspectives on an Evolving Creation*, K. B. Miller, Ed. Grand Rapids: Wm. B. Eerdmans, 2003.

Murphy, N., "Divine Action, Emergence, and Scientific Explanation," *The Cambridge Companion to Science and Religion*, P. Harrison, Ed., Cambridge, UK, New York. : Cambridge University Press, 2010.

Nazworth, N. Forget Evolution Vs. Creation, There Are (at Least) 6 Different Views, Evangelical Biophysicist Explains. January 6, 2015. http://www.christianpost.com/news/forget-evolution-vs-creation-there-are-at-least-6-different-views-evangelical-biophysicist-explains-132178/

Neve, M. and S. Messenger, "*Charles Darwin: Autobiographies*," Penguin Classics. London: Penguin Books, 2002.

Neyman, G. (2015). Progressive Creationism. http://www.oldearth.org/progressive.htm

Nigh, G., "Greg Nigh's Reviews. Evolution: Still a Theory in Crisis," July 19, 2016. https://www.goodreads.com/review/show/1703571492?book_show_action=true

Non-Darwinian Evolution. RationalWiki. https://rationalwiki.org/wiki/Non-Darwinian_evolution

Numbers, R. L., *The Creationists: From Scientific Creationism to Intelligent Design*, Expanded ed., 1st Harvard University Press pbk. ed. Cambridge, MA.; London, UK.: Harvard University Press, 2006.

"Aggressors, Victims, and Peacemakers – Historical Actors in the Drama of Science and Religion," *The Religion and Science Debate: Why Does It Continue?* Kindle Edition., H. W. Attridge, Ed., New Haven & London: Yale University Press, 2009.

"Scientific Creationism and Intelligent Design," *The Cambridge Companion to Science and Religion*. Kindle Edition., P. Harrison, Ed., Cambridge, U.K.: Cambridge University Press, 2010.

Ogburn, S. P. (2013). Scientists Close in on Planet's Oldest Ice. Scientific American. November 6, 2013. https://www.scientificamerican.com/article/scientists-close-in-on-planets-oldest-ice/

Okamoto, J., "Modern Science, Contemporary Culture, and Christian Theology," *Concordia Journal*, Vol. 43 No. 3, Summer 2017, pp. 45-63.

Orr, H. A. (1999). Gould on God: Can Religion and Science Be Happily Reconciled? http://bostonreview.net/archives/BR24.5/orr.html

The Origins Debate: Evangelical Perspectives on Creation, Evolution, and Intelligent Design. Kindle Edition., The Editors of Christianity Today, Carol Stream, IL: Christianity Today, 2012..

Ostling, R. N., "The Search for the Historical Adam," *The Origins Debate: Evangelical Perspectives on Creation, Evolution, and Intelligent Design*. Kindle Edition., The Editors of Christianity Today, Ed., Carol Stream, IL: Christianity Today, 2012.

Patterson, R. What Is Science? Answers in Genesis. February 22, 2007. https://answersingenesis.org/what-is-science/what-is-science/

Pearcey, N., "We're Not in Kansas Anymore: The Furor over Intelligent Design," *The Origins Debate: Evangelical Perspectives on Creation, Evolution, and Intelligent Design*. Kindle Edition, From the editors of Christianity Today, Carol Stream, IL, 2012.

Pennock, R. T., *Tower of Babel: The Evidence against the New Creationism*. Cambridge, MA.; London, UK.: MIT Press, 1999.

Penzias, A., "The Elegant Universe," in *Faith in Science: Scientists Search for Truth*, W. M. Richardson and G. Slack, Eds. London and New York: Routledge, 2001.

Pesce, M., "Virtually Sacred," in *Faith in Science: Scientists Search for Truth*, W. M. Richardson and G. Slack, Eds. London and New York: Routledge, 2001.

Peters, T. and M. J. Hewlett, *Evolution: From Creation to New Creation: Conflict, Conversation, and Convergence*. Nashville, TN: Abingdon Press, 2003.

Peters, T. and M. J. Hewlett, *Theological and Scientific Commentary on Darwin's Origin of Species*. Nashville: Abingdon Press, 2008.

Picard, R., "Building Technology with Emotion," *True Scientists, True Faith: Some of the World's Leading Scientists Reveal the Harmony Between their Science and their Faith*. Kindle Edition., R. J. Berry, Ed., Oxford, U.K and Grand Rapids, MI.: Monarch Books, Kindle Edition, 2014.

Pickering, J., "Teach Creationism, Undermine Theology," in Science and Society. September 24, 2013. https://sciblogs.co.nz/kidney-punch/2013/09/24/teach-creationism-undermine-theology/

Pieper, F., *Christian Dogmatics*. (3 vols.) T. Engelder, Trans., St. Louis: Concordia Publishing House, 1950.

Pierce, B. A., *Transmission and Population Genetics: A Conceptual Approach*, 4th ed. New York: W. H. Freeman, 2012.

Plantinga, A., "Science and Religion: Why Does the Debate Continue?," *The Religion and Sci-*

ence Debate: Why Does it Continue? Kindle Edition., H. W. Attridge, Ed., New Haven, CT and London, U.K.: Yale University Press, 2009.

Polkinghorne, J. C., *Belief in God in an Age of Science*. New Haven, Conn. ; London: Yale University Press, 1998.

Pope, C., "Polygenism Is Problematic," Archdiocese of Washington, October 23, 2013. http://blog.adw.org/2013/10/polygenism-is-problematic-a-catholic-caution-on-another-aspect-of-evolutionary-theory/

Prance, G. T., "A Talent for Science," *True Scientists, True Faith: Some of the World's Leading Scientists Reveal the Harmony between Their Science and Their Faith*. Kindle Edition., R. J. Berry, Ed., Oxford, U.K. and Grand Rapids, MI: Monarch Books, 2014.

"Preface to the Small Catechism," in *Luther's Small Catechism with Explanation* (ESV) St. Louis: Concordia Publishing House, 2008.

Primack, J., "Transcendental Theory," in *Faith in Science: Scientists Search for Truth*, W. M. Richardson and G. Slack, Eds. London and New York: Routledge, 2001.

Prothero, D., "Stephen Meyer's Fumbling Bumbling Amateur Cambrian Follies," August 28, 2013. http://www.skepticblog.org/2013/08/28/stephen-meyers-fumbling-bumbling-amateur-cambrian-follies/

Ramm, B. L., *The Christian View of Science and Scripture*, 1st ed. Grand Rapids, 1954.

Reddish, J., "In Science and Scriptural Interpretation, Communities Matter," in Faith and Science Seeking Understanding. BioLogos Foundation, October 12, 2016. http://biologos.org/blogs/jim-stump-faith-and-science-seeking-understanding/in-science-and-scriptural-interpretation-communities-matter

Reeves, J., "Should Christians Trust Scientific Experts?" : BioLogos Foundation, December 16, 2014. http://biologos.org/blogs/archive/should-christians-trust-scientific-experts

Rehwinkel, A. M., *The Flood: In the Light of the Bible, Geology, and Archaeology*. St. Louis, MO: Concordia Publishing House, 1951.

Religion and Public Life. Public's Views on Human Evolution. Pew Research Center. December 30, 2013. http://www.pewforum.org/2013/12/30/publics-views-on-human-evolution/

Ricciardi, M., Australian Expedition Discovers 'Lost World' October 28, 2013. http://planetsave.com/2013/10/28/australian-expedition-discovers-lost-world-three-never-seen-vertebrates-found-photos/

Richardson, W. M., "Introduction," in *Faith in Science: Scientists Search for Truth*, W. M. Richardson and G. Slack, Eds. London and New York: Routledge, 2001, pp. 2-5.

Richardson, W. M. and G. Slack, "*Faith in Science: Scientists Search for Truth*." London; New York: Routledge, 2001.

Ritchie, S. L., "Five Surprising Facts About the Religious Beliefs of Scientists around the World." November 1, 2016. BioLogos Foundation. http://biologos.org/blogs/guest/five-surprising-facts-about-the-religious-beliefs-of-scientists-around-the-world

Ross, H., *A Matter of Days: Resolving a Creation Controversy*. Colorado Springs, CO: Navpress, 2004.

Roughgarden, J., *Evolution and Christian Faith: Reflections of an Evolutionary Biologist*. Washington, D.C. ; London: Island Press, 2006.

Ruppel, E., "An Impossible World," in Science and Belief, April 24, 2014. https://scienceandbelief.org/2014/04/24/an-impossible-world/

Ruse, M., *Can a Darwinian Be a Christian? The Relationship between Science and Religion*. New York: Cambridge University Press, 2000.

The Evolution-Creation Struggle. Cambridge, Mass. ; London: Harvard University

Press, 2005.
Defining Darwin: Essays on the History and Philosophy of Evolutionary Biology. Kindle Edition., Amherst, N.Y.: Prometheus ; Lancaster : Gazelle, 2009.
Science and Spirituality: Making Room for Faith in the Age of Science. Cambridge: Cambridge University Press, 2010.
"Atheism, Naturalism, and Science: Three in One?," *The Cambridge Companion to Science and Religion*. Kindle Edition., P. Harrison, Ed., Cambridge, U.K.: Cambridge University Press, 2010.
The Philosophy of Human Evolution. Kindle Edition., Cambridge ; New York: Cambridge University Press, 2012.
Curb Your Enthusiasm: High Priests, Holy Writ and Excommunications. ," B. Hains, Ed., October 1, 2012. https://aeon.co/essays/how-humanism-lost-its-way-in-a-charismatic-crusade

Russell, R. J., "Special Providence and Genetic Mutation: A New Defense of Theistic Evolution," in *Perspectives on an Evolving Creation*, K. B. Miller, Ed. Grand Rapids, MI; Cambridge, UK.: Wm. B. Eerdmans, 2003.

Rutherford, A., Why Scientific Truth May Hurt. The Guardian. April 5, 2015. https://www.theguardian.com/science/2015/apr/05/scientific-truth-genetics-darwin-adam-rutherford

Saletan, W., "Creativity for Creationists: An Evolutionary Creationist Evangelizes to Christians About Science," December 24, 2014. http://www.slate.com/articles/health_and_science/human_nature/2014/12/evolutionary_creationism_jeff_hardin_reconciles_evangelical_christianity.html
Saletan, W. God's Work: A New Poll Suggests Americans Aren't So Confident in Their Creationism. December 4, 2014. http://www.slate.com/articles/health_and_science/human_nature/2014/12/creationism_poll_how_many_americans_believe_the_bible_is_literal_inerrant.html

Scanlan, J., "A Most Human Heresy," in Philosophy & History. September 8, 2016. http://www.lateralmag.com/articles/issue-14/a-most-human-heresy

Scientific Literacy: How Do Americans Stack Up? Science Daily. February 27, 2007. https://www.sciencedaily.com/releases/2007/02/070218134322.htm

Scott, E. C., "Darwin Prosecuted: Review of Johnson's Darwin on Trial," *Creation Evolution Journal of the National Center for Science Education*, vol. 13, no. 2, pp. 36-47, Winter Quarter 1993.

Scott, E. C., "Intelligent Design Creationism: The New Kid on the Block," presented at the American Physical Society, Annual March Meeting, Minneapolis, MN, March 20-24, 2000, 2000. Available: http://adsabs.harvard.edu/abs/2000APS..MAR.M8004S
Scott, E. C., *Evolution vs. Creationism: An Introduction*. Berkeley, Calif. ; London: University of California Press, 2005.

Sension, R., "Moving from Debate to Dialogue," in Musings on Science, September 1, 2016. https://musingsonscience.wordpress.com/2016/09/01/

Shanker, A. K., "What Is the Anthropic Principle?" June 20, 2016. https://www.quora.com/What-is-the-final-anthropic-principle-in-simple-terms

Shermer, M., "Then a Miracle Occurs," in The Work of Michael Shermer, ed, May, 2004. https://michaelshermer.com/2004/05/then-a-miracle-occurs/

Skybreak, A., *The Science of Evolution and the Myth of Creationism: Knowing What's Real and Why It Matters*, 1st ed. Chicago: Insight Press, 2006.

Slack, G., *The Battle over the Meaning of Everything: Evolution, Intelligent Design, and a School Board in Dover*, Pa. San Francisco, Calif.: Jossey-Bass ; Chichester : John Wiley, 2007.

The Start of Scientific Cosmology. American Institute of Physics. May 20, 2016. https://www.aip.org/history/exhibits/cosmology/ideas/start-of-scientific-cosmology.htm

Stearley, R., "Reviewing "Darwin's Doubt," BioLogos Foundation, August 26, 2014. http://biologos.org/blogs/archive/reviewing-darwins-doubt-ralph-stearley

Stenmark, M., "Ways of Relating Science and Religion," *The Cambridge Companion to Science and Religion*. Kindle Edition., P. Harrison, Ed., Cambridge, U.K.: Cambridge University Press, 2010.

Stone, R. M. (2014). When Religious (and Political) Identity Trumps Inquiry – and Facts. http://religionnews.com/2014/07/07/religious-political-identity-trumps-inquiry-facts/

"A Survey of Clergy and Their Views on Origins," BioLogos Foundation, May 8, 2013. http://biologos.org/blogs/archive/a-survey-of-clergy-and-their-views-on-origins

Swamidass, S. J., "A Lutheran Voice in Science," *Concordia Journal*, Vol. 43 No. 3, Summer 2017, pp. 82-90.

Thomson, K., "Introduction – the Religion and Science Debate: Why Does It Continue?," *The Religion and Science Debate: Why Does It Continue?* Kindle Edition, H. W. Attridge, Ed., New Haven, CT. And London, U. K.: Yale University Press, 2009.

Tiktaalik Roseae Shows Signs of Rear-Leg Development. CBC News. January 14, 2014. http://www.cbc.ca/news/technology/tiktaalik-roseae-shows-signs-of-rear-leg-development-1.2496547

Tinker, M., "No Conflict," February, 2009. https://www.bethinking.org/does-evolution-disprove-creation/no-conflict

Toal, C.. How Science and Faith Grew up Together. The Guardian. April 24, 2009. https://www.theguardian.com/commentisfree/belief/2009/apr/24/religion-science-creationism-reiss

Topham, J. R., "Natural Theology and the Sciences," *The Cambridge Companion to Science and Religion*. Kindle Edition., P. Harrison, Ed., Cambridge, UK: Cambridge University Press, Kindle Edition, 2010.

Trasancos, S., "Why Say Theistic Evolution? Is There Any Other Kind?," National Catholic Register, September 1, 2016. http://www.ncregister.com/blog/trasancos/why-say-theistic-evolution-is-there-any-other-kind

Truth or Denial – from Climate Change to the Anti-Vaccine Movement. Is Denial on the Rise in America? Washington Post, November 15, 2016. http://www.washingtonpost.com/sf/brand-connect/bleecker-street/denial/

Turner, K., "If Walton Is Right on His Function Only View: Some Implications," BioLogos Foundation, March 19, 2015. http://biologos.org/blogs/archive/if-walton-is-right-on-his-function-only-view-some-implications

Vanderbilt University ASTR (Astrophysics) 2130 (formerly Astrophysics 203), course Notes. Course title: "The Trial of Galileo and its Background." https://as.vanderbilt.edu/astronomy/classes/

Van Till, H. J., "Intelligent Design: The Celebration of Gifts Withheld?," in *The Johnson-Lamoureux Debate on Biological Origins*, D. O. Lamoureux and P. E. Johnson, Eds. Vancouver, B.C.: Regent College Publishing, 1999.

"Is the Universe Capable of Evolving?," in *Perspectives on an Evolving Creation*, K. B. Miller, Ed. Grand Rapids, MI and Cambridge, U.K.: Wm. B. Eerdmans, 2003.

"What Good Is Stardust? The Remarkably Equipped Universe," *The Origins Debate: Evangelical Perspectives*. From the Editors of Christianity Today, Carol Stream, IL: Christianity Today 2012.

Venema, D. and R. H. Evans, "Ask an Evolutionary Creationist: A Q&a with Dennis Venema," BioLogos Foundation, September 7, 2011. http://biologos.org/blogs/dennis-venema-letters-to-the-duchess/ask-an-evolutionary-creationist-a-qa-with-dennis-venema

Venema, D. R., *Adam and the Genome: Reading Scripture after Genetic Science*. Grand Rapids: Brazos Press, 2017.

Voosen, P., "Record Shattering 2.7 Million-Year-Old Ice Core Reveals Start of the Ice Ages," in ChemistryClimateEarth : American Association for the Advancement of Science, August 15, 2017. http://www.sciencemag.org/news/2017/08/record-shattering-27-million-year-old-ice-core-reveals-start-ice-ages

Vosburg, D., "The Personal Journey of a Faith-Filled Scientist." BioLogos Foundation, September 24, 2013. http://biologos.org/blogs/archive/the-personal-journey-of-a-faith-filled-scientist

Vulctic, M., Book Review: Michael J Denton. (1998). "Nature's Destiny" http://www.talkorigins.org/faqs/denton.html

Walton, J. H., *The Lost World of Genesis One: Ancient Cosmology and the Origins Debate*. Kindle Edition., Downers Grove, Ill.: IVP Academic, 2009.

"Reading Genesis 1 through Ancient (Not Modern) Eyes," BioLogos Foundation, September 18, 2009. http://biologos.org/blogs/archive/reconciling-science-with-scripture
The Lost World of Scripture : Ancient Literary Culture and Biblical Authority. Downers Grove, Illinois: IVP Academic, 2013.
"A Historical Adam: An Archetypal View," *Four Views on the Historical Adam*, M. Barrett and A. B. Caneday, Eds., Grand Rapids, MI: Zondervan, 2016.
"A Historical Adam: Young Earth Creationist View - Rejoinder from an Archetypal View," *Four Views on the Historical Adam*, M. Barrett and A. B. Caneday, Eds., Grand Rapids, MI: Zondervan, 2016.

Webster, B. L. Review: The Lost World of Genesis One: Ancient Cosmology and the Origins Debate. Dallas Theological Seminary. May 22, 2009. http://www.dts.edu/reviews/john-walton-the-lost-world-of-genesis-one

Weisstein, E. W., "Alfred Wegener Biographical Note," March 11, 1996. http://pangaea.org/wegener.htm

What Is the United Methodist Church's Position on Evolution? March 15, 2016. http://www.umc.org/what-we-believe/what-is-the-united-methodist-churchs-position-on-evolution

White, A. D., *A History of the Warfare of Science with Theology in Christendom*. MacMillan And. Co Ltd., 1896.

White, R., "Earthquakes, Volcanoes and Other Catastrophies," *True Scientists, True Faith: Some of the World's Leading Scientists Reveal the Harmony Between their Science and their Faith*, R. J. Berry, Ed., Oxford, UK & Grand Rapids, MI: Monarch Books, 2014.

Wieland, C. (1994). Exploding Evolution. http://creation.com/exploding-evolution

Wilkins, J. S., "Are Creationists Rational?," in Science blogs. April 28, 2009. http://scienceblogs.com/evolvingthoughts/2009/04/28/are-creationists-rational/

"God and Evolution 2: The Problem of Creation." April 4, 2013. http://evolvingthoughts.net/2013/04/04/god-and-evolution-2-the-problem-of-creation/

Wilkinson, L., "Does Methodological Naturalism Lead to Metaphysical Naturalism?," in *Darwinism Defeated: The Johnson - Lamoureux Debate on Biological Origins*, P. E. Johnson and D. O. Lamoureux, Eds. Vancouver, B.C.: Regent College Publishing, 1999.

Wiseman, J. J., "Why Should Christians Care About Science?" September 24, 2013. https://www.bigquestionsonline.com/2013/09/24/why-should-christians-care-about-science/

"Inspired by the Heavens," True Scientists, True Faith: Some Of The World's Leading Scientists Reveal The Harmony Between Their Science And Their Faith. Kindle Edition., R. J. Berry, Ed., Oxford, U.K. and Grand Rapids, MI: Monarch Books, 2014.
"Inspired by an Amazing Universe," How I Changed My Mind about Evolution: Evan-

gelicals Reflect on Faith and Science. Kindle Edition., K. Applegate and J. B. Stump, Eds., Downers Grove, Illinois: IVP Academic, 2016.

Woods, M., Prof. Brian Cox Condemns 'Toxic' Rows between Science and Religion. October 22, 2016. http://www.christiantoday.com/article/professor.brian.cox.condemns.toxic.rows.between.science.and.religion/95038.htm

Wright, N. T., *Surprised by Scripture: Engaging Contemporary* Issues. New York: HarperOne, 2014.

Wuthnow, R., "No Contradictions Here: Science, Religion, and the Culture of All Reasonable Possibilities," *The Religion and Science Debate: Why Does It Continue*? Kindle Edition., H. W. Attridge, Ed., New Haven and London: Yale University Press, 2009.

Young, M. and P. K. Strode, *Why Evolution Works* (*and Creationism Fails*). Kindle Edition., New Brunswick, N.J. ; London: Rutgers University Press, 2009.

SUBJECT INDEX

NAME INDEX

SCRIPTURE INDEX

82726359R00197

Made in the USA
Middletown, DE
05 August 2018